SIR JOHN VANBRUGH

AND LANDSCAPE ARCHITECTURE IN BAROQUE ENGLAND

EDITED BY
CHRISTOPHER RIDGWAY
& ROBERT WILLIAMS

SUTTON PUBLISHING
IN ASSOCIATION WITH THE NATIONAL TRUST

For Laurence Whistler, a great Vanbrugh scholar

First published in the United Kingdom in 2000 by
Sutton Publishing Limited · Phoenix Mill
Thrupp · Stroud · Gloucestershire · GL5 2BU

Paperback edition first published in 2004

Copyright © The Contributors, 2000

British Library Cataloguing in Publication Data
A catalogue record for this book is available from the British Library

ISBN 0 7509 3466 2

Typeset in 11/12pt Ehrhardt.
Typesetting and origination by
Sutton Publishing Limited
Printed and bound in Great Britain by
J.H. Haynes & Co. Ltd, Sparkford.

Contents

List of Illustrations

Preface and Acknowledgements

John Vanbrugh (1664–1726) was a man who collected many titles: he was a London trader, a merchant in India, a soldier, a herald, a civil servant (as Comptroller of Works), a theatre impresario, a knight of the realm, and a devoted husband and father. Today he is known principally as a playwright and as an architect – in his latter capacity he was the designer of some of the most important country houses and landscapes that survive in England. His works include Castle Howard, Blenheim Palace and Seaton Delaval, which today are still privately owned, and Claremont and Stowe, whose gardens are now in the care of the National Trust. These and other commissions were undertaken during a period when a hitherto insular England was transforming itself into Europe's most innovative region for both architecture and landscape design. Among Vanbrugh's contemporaries were the architects Sir Christopher Wren, Nicholas Hawksmoor and William Talman, and the garden designers George London, Henry Wise, Charles Bridgeman and Stephen Switzer, with some of whom he collaborated. This was a formidable constellation of talent, wherein Vanbrugh's star, it is felt by many today, shone the brightest.

While Vanbrugh is famously remembered for his great houses, it should not be forgotten that on many occasions he turned his attention to smaller buildings, sited within planned landscapes that he had also fashioned to some degree. The essays in this volume seek to address these twin aspects of Vanbrugh's working career and the work of leading contemporaries. *Sir John Vanbrugh and Landscape Architecture* therefore marks a novel investigation into the period 1690–1730, and into the direction and spirit of landscape architecture during the reigns of William & Mary, Queen Anne, and George I. Too often these complementary aspects of designed landscape and architecture have been explored in isolation from one another, with the unfortunate result that our appreciation of individual houses and the importance of their garden and estate settings is limited.

With this in mind we invited experts in the worlds of architectural history and landscape design to collaborate on a book of essays that would eschew myopic divisions. Despite the example of Christopher Hussey, Gervase Jackson-Stops and John Harris, too few historians have grasped the fact that architecture and situation constitute a twin experience; buildings, most especially country mansions, do not exist in isolation from their surroundings; their location is often determined by specific topographical considerations – contour, elevation, adjacent water, woodland and approaches. Vanbrugh's written pronouncements on landscape and on garden buildings are few, but there is sufficient evidence in his surviving temples, belvederes, arches, obelisks and fortifications to show just how acutely interested he was in raising structures within the wider landscape, as well as in fashioning the gardens around some of his great houses. There can be little doubt that these fundamental considerations preoccupied Vanbrugh, and many of his contemporaries too, especially when we consider his two greatest commissions – Castle Howard and Blenheim Palace.

Estate management is among the topics tackled in these essays, and Tom Williamson demonstrates just how essential it is to understand the economic base of country properties, as this often provided the income owners needed to pay for improvements. It is important to try to discern the motivations for these improvements. They may have been aesthetic, economic, or a combination of the two. Vanbrugh visited many estates in England, and there is no doubt that he was aware of the status and political affiliations of their owners. Moreover, he would surely have noted many other points of local significance, including the topography and management of those estates. Garden fashions in this period, as David Jacques explains, were various, and defy any simplistic chronology that claims a linear development from the formal to the 'natural'. Vanbrugh would have noted gardens fashioned in different manners: he would have seen examples of French-style and Dutch-style gardens in England (as well as in France, the Low Countries and northern Germany), and their deployment of such stock features as parterres, basins, fountains, gates, sculptures, railings and ornamental planting schemes. Importantly, he would have observed how these features connected with adjacent buildings.

Among the aspects of garden design that have never before been considered in relation to Vanbrugh, or in relation to many of his contemporaries, is the question of horticulture. Because we largely associate Vanbrugh with extensive landscapes, the minutiae of flowers and plants have been forgotten. But, as Mark Laird reveals, Vanbrugh cannot have remained unaware of the pleasures and curiosities of the vegetable world. For instance, he may have chosen to 'plant up' his parterre at Castle Howard with obelisks, vases and lead statues, but he would have recognized that flowers, shrubs, topiary and ornamental trees were also vital materials for good garden design.

At Blenheim, Stowe and Seaton Delaval in particular, Vanbrugh showed a penchant for defensible gardens, which boasted formidable bastions, hahas and palisades. These were more than just the indulgences of a former soldier. Military, or fortified, gardens, as explained by Robert Williams, were a visible reminder of unsettled times, when the security of a moat or a bastion was far more valuable than any number of dressed lawns, clipped hedges or ornamental basins. Water, whether trickling, cascading or steady, was also an essential component in garden design. Judith Roberts shows how designers like Stephen Switzer were able to harness new technologies and exploit water for a variety of decorative and practical purposes, fashioning basins, cascades, fountains and canals.

Nor should we forget the intellectual materials that might have furnished a mind as lively and curious as Vanbrugh's was. Timothy Mowl insists that late-seventeenth-century drama and the burgeoning state of antiquarian studies stimulated Vanbrugh with images and ideas about the past, which undoubtedly influenced his architecture, and the effects he was seeking to achieve. Christopher Ridgway reminds us that Vanbrugh was an intrepid traveller, frequently journeying throughout England, noting the evidence of a rich and intriguing national history that surrounded him; ancient buildings and ruins, plus a wealth of antiquarian researches, both in published or manuscript form, would also have alerted him to the pleasures of the past. His awareness of styles and phases of architecture, whether classical or Gothic, and his knowledge of buildings, both indigenous and foreign, would have been stimulated by contemporary engravings and drawings, if not by first-hand experience. Thus Giles Worsley probes a stylistic continuity between the work of Vanbrugh and that of the generation of Palladian architects and garden designers who succeeded him. The similarities between the work of Vanbrugh and William Kent challenge our assumptions about those useful but complicated terms 'Baroque' and 'Palladian'.

Vanbrugh's reputation suffered in the early eighteenth century, but, as Derek Linstrum sets out in detail, it began to be rehabilitated later in that century by the Adam brothers and Sir Joshua Reynolds, and in our own time Vanbrugh's status as a major architect is no longer questioned. Celebrated as a genius, responsible for some of the grandest buildings and landscapes in England, today's architects, artists and even would-be country house owners turn to his work for inspiration. Kerry Downes, after a lifetime devoted to the study of English architecture in this period, reviews the current state of Vanbrugh studies, which have been boosted by Robert Williams's discovery that Vanbrugh spent time as an East India Company trader in Surat on the west coast of India. Kerry Downes also establishes that 1699 is the correct date for the conception of Vanbrugh's first masterpiece, Castle Howard, and that therefore the last year of the twentieth century marked a significant moment of celebration. Appropriately, he also reminds us that although our academic understanding of Vanbrugh and his work, as well as that of his contemporaries, is more advanced than ever, it is still not possible, nor perhaps even desirable, to disentangle the mysteries of that richest and most enduring of architectural collaborations in the British Isles, namely the relationship between Hawksmoor and Vanbrugh.

The making of this book began as a conference on Vanbrugh, held in July 1999 to celebrate the tercentenary of the building of Castle Howard. It was organized jointly by Castle Howard and the University of York. We would like to express our deep gratitude to The Paul Mellon Centre for Studies in British Art, The British Academy, The Yorkshire Gardens Trust and The British Council, Paris, for generous financial assistance in supporting the conference. Our thanks also extend to Castle Howard, and in particular to the Hon. Simon Howard and the Hon. Nicholas Howard; and at the University of York, to Dr Allen Warren, Professor Harold Mytum, Louise Dewhurst and the staff of I.F.A.B. Communications, for all their support and encouragement, and Peter Goodchild. Many individuals have assisted the editors and contributors for *Sir John Vanbrugh and Landscape Architecture*, generously offering advice and the benefit of their expert knowledge, and we are especially indebted to Dr Brian Allen, Professor Malcolm Andrews, Professor John Dixon Hunt, and Patrick and Bridget Nuttgens, and to Professor Michel Baridon for his input. Additionally, we are grateful to the following for their material and practical assistance: The National Trust; The Historic Houses Association; The Garden History Society; The Georgian Group; The Society of Architectural Historians of Great Britain; The Folly Fellowship; Michael Hall of *Country Life*; Clive Boursnell; David Whiteley;

Gordon Smith; Philip Lewis; Gordon Lee; Deirdre Mortimer; Rosie Wade; Cristiano Ratti; Alison Brisby; Janette Ray Books; Ken Spelman Booksellers; Peter Smith Photography, Malton; Rossmann Haigh; and Fulprint, York. We are also indebted to the many owners of works of art, as well as to the staff of country houses, museums, galleries and libraries for making available to us illustrations of works in their collections, and for other kindnesses. In particular we would like to thank His Grace the Duke of Beaufort, His Grace the Duke of Buccleuch, His Grace the Duke of Devonshire, The Lord Hastings, His Grace the Duke of Marlborough; Elizabeth Heaps and Dr David Griffiths of the J.B. Morrell Library at the University of York; and John Harris. We are also grateful to the Marc Fitch Fund for supporting this publication.

Finally, we would like to thank the authors for their contributions, and for their willingness to identify and explore important but under-researched subjects that are crucial to a richer understanding of landscape architecture in the period 1690–1730. Of course, estate management, theatre, horticulture, hydraulics, garden design, travel, antiquarianism, architectural styles and Vanbrugh's afterlife hardly exhaust the range of enquiry for this period and this subject. Lead sculptures, architectural drawing, topographical art and mapmaking, as well as a badly-needed treatment of the contributions to garden design made by Wren, Hawksmoor and Thomas Archer, await investigation. None the less, we hope that this collection of interdisciplinary essays will advance our understanding of the landscape architecture of Vanbrugh and his contemporaries.

Christopher Ridgway and Robert Williams
Castle Howard

ONE

Vanbrugh over Fifty Years

Kerry Downes

Fifty years ago, in 1949, the late George Howard returned to his family home, Castle Howard, and moved into the Pyramid Gatehouse; a good deal of the south range of the great house was roofless and windowless, and the dome had gone in the fire of 1940. The move was symbolic of his intention, happily realized, to save Castle Howard and return it to something like its original splendour.

This essay was drafted within days of the twenty-ninth anniversary of the death of Geoffrey Webb, a fine and gentle scholar to whom all Vanbrughians owe an enormous debt. In 1949 his edition of Vanbrugh's letters was two decades old,[1] as was Christopher Hussey's account of the buildings – the first ever – in *English Homes*.[2] Laurence Whistler's biography of Vanbrugh was a decade old.[3]

The year 1949 passed without any public celebration of the quarter-millennium of Castle Howard's inception. As an undergraduate I was studying the European Baroque, with Sacheverell Sitwell's *British Architects and Craftsmen* (1945) fresh in my memory as an introduction to the idea of an English variety.[4] Two years later a couple of shelves from Hawksmoor's plan-chest came up at Sotheby's in the Bute Collection. I remember seeing them before the sale in the photographer's studio. I knew enough to grasp the significance of lots 17 and 19 in the sale – early drawings for Castle Howard, which the Victoria and Albert Museum acquired. Until then, apart from those by Hawksmoor for the Mausoleum, there were virtually no known drawings. Suddenly drawings became the main evidence for studying the genesis of the house. Whistler, already working on his second book on Vanbrugh, published the most significant ones in the winter of 1952/3 in advance of his book.[5] The effect on early eighteenth-century studies was galvanic.

There may be some who will wonder whether 1999 was the correct year in which to hold tercentennial celebrations, especially as the tablet on the great obelisk says 'began in 1702'. For better or for worse, the date, like the millennium, was decided upon, but I hope to show that 1699 *was* the crucial year.

It may not be inappropriate, in an opening essay, to say something about landscape architecture and about labels, in addition to my remarks on Vanbrugh. Of *landscaping* I am qualified to say rather little; I shall go no further than to recall that in the long and rather tedious poem composed by Anne, Lady Irwin, Lord Carlisle's daughter, entitled 'Castle Howard', there is not a word about architects.[6] We should not be too surprised at the implication that it was all Carlisle's own work: it has always been the prerogative of the great and the good to do things by delegation, and no doubt His Lordship would excuse, if not welcome, our interest in what was delegated, and to whom.

Labels are dangerous. Fifty years ago it was still customary to offer explanations as to why there was no English Baroque; I remember having done so myself in a school examination. Nowadays, when we have Baroque orchestras, Baroque oboes and Baroque players, the ambiguities between *Baroque* as a style-label and as a date-bracket are more numerous and more confused than ever. After I had abandoned custom and written an exploratory book on, and titled, *English Baroque Architecture*,[7] people said to me of some building or other – 'It must be Baroque: it's in your book!' Personally, it would only be after an exceptionally good dinner that I might put forward Lord Burlington's villa at Chiswick (built in the same years as Vanbrugh's Temple of the Four Winds) as the last masterpiece of the English Baroque, but I quote from a text also written fifty years ago: 'In spite of his academic conviction, Burlington, the artist, deviated from Palladio's models, both when he was more Baroque – as in the exceptional features of the stairs and the lofty dome of Chiswick – and when he was less Baroque.'[8]

Chiswick remains difficult to label, but that attempt shows why labels are dangerous. Writing history, like playing the violin, is not a faculty with which we are born; it is a cultural application and adaptation of some of our natural gifts. One of those gifts is the ability to categorize, to give mental – not necessarily verbal – labels to things. There is a very good reason for this: it saves us from chronic sensory overload. The amount of information constantly coming into our senses is enormous – gigabytes every second. Our brains cannot cope with most of it, so we learn in infancy to ignore most of what is familiar. We begin doing this before we can speak, but language enables us to name things. Two-year-olds are obsessed with the names of things: at twenty-one months of age, Vanbrugh's son knew 'Pillars, & Arches and Round Windows & Square Windows already, whether he finds them in a Book or in the Streets'.[9]

But as we mature it is the things we *cannot quite* see or identify that give us most trouble in daily life, and most enjoyment in picture puzzles. When you have identified, categorized, labelled anything, you can ignore it. In a strange town you have to look at everything – which is both tiring and exhilarating; at home you know the landmarks so well that you can walk past the postbox and forget that you have a letter to put in it. There has to be a good deal of label-making in history, but the danger is that when you have made the labels you stop looking.

And so to 'Sir John Vanbrugh': something about Vanbrugh the man and something about the events of 1699, and also something about Hawksmoor's and Lord Carlisle's part in them. Vanbrugh, it seems to me, was a very private person. It may be fortuitous (in the proper sense of the word) that his most revealing letter is unheaded and unsigned, which is why Webb missed it: it is the letter to an unknown third party (probably one of Carlisle's daughters) about his feelings for Henrietta Yarburgh of Heslington, the young lady who became his wife.[10] One thinks of him as such an easy correspondent because he wrote so naturally, whether for himself in letters or for the characters in his plays, and because his interests were as varied as his acquaintance. But just as his stage dialogue conceals its artifice, his letters do not reveal the degree or depth of thought that preceded the introduction of the pen into the inkwell. And this may also apply to drawing, even though we depend on the accidents of survival. Vanbrugh often drew sketchily, but we have very few *sketches*. Hawksmoor on the other hand, although his letters are mostly about architecture, employment and his health, seems always to have been ready to put pen to paper – and this applies also to drawing. Hawksmoor was not afraid to make on occasion quite lamentable designs; they qualified as what he called 'tryalls, so that we are assured of the good effect'.[11] We *can* say that second thoughts mattered to Hawksmoor because we have seen some of the first ones.

Three hundred surviving Vanbrugh letters tell us nothing of Vanbrugh's parents, his uncles or aunts, their activities or connections, and almost nothing about his early life. There is a solitary joking reference to his inside knowledge of French prisons; no word that he was in them for four and a half years. Nothing about his education, his adventures in the London wine trade, the army, or the marines, where his competence and bravery in the battle at Camaret Bay, near Brest, in 1694 during King William's War only came to light recently because of an obscure pamphlet published by his superior officer.[12] We know of his years as a hostage only from partial French documents and from a few letters relating to his efforts to extricate himself; he must have counted himself lucky that the Jacobite pose he adopted during this process did not rebound on him in later life.

And then there are the missing years, 1682–5. Robert Williams's brilliant discovery now establishes that Vanbrugh sought then his fortune in the East India Company, but that his expectations were not met. Three thoughts strike me here. First, the adolescent tone of his earliest letter – he was nearly twenty-two – seeking a job from his kinsman the Earl of Huntingdon after his return from India, must be seen to reflect not inexperience but the deference to nobility that he never lost.[13] Second, the life of an East India Company merchant was not to his taste. Was the whole venture a desperate attempt by his father and uncle to settle this aimless, star-struck, dreamy elder son in a sound business? If so, it was bound to fail; finding out what was not for him was but a necessary hurdle on the path to his true *métier*. Third, as an official Company passenger *en route* to and from India, he would have been at sea for six months in 1683, and as much again in 1685. Some sixty years later, another future architect, William Chambers, travelling for the Swedish India Company, used his time on board to continue his self-education, and Vanbrugh surely did the same. Maybe that is when he learned shorthand (Shelton's, the system used by Pepys).[14]

Probably his contemporaries knew little more about him than we do. Peter Le Neve, his fellow in the College of Heralds, noted down a page of particulars of the Vanbrugh family.[15] It has more blanks than facts, and some of the facts are wrong; he cannot have obtained them from Sir John. I must confess to forgetting this document when I wrote that there was no contemporary evidence that Vanbrugh's father, Giles, had been a sugar-baker. There is no *other* evidence, for a century, but as the page is in a Harleian manuscript in the British Library it may be the source, and that is what it does say. I still believe it has nothing to do with elegant confectionery, and that Giles had not caramel fingers but shares in the Chester sugar refinery run by a friend of his named Henthorne. That accords with everything else we know of Giles, as someone who dealt wholesale in cloth, European or oriental, and perhaps Irish linen; in real estate, in bulk grain, and in lead mining. Vanbrugh's privacy probably came from his home: the wills of his parents are remarkably uninformative documents. It can only have increased after his experiences with the French judiciary taught him to trust no man. The French prison in which he 'began my days' as a mature adult turned the dreamer into an achiever; with the key that freed him came the key that would at last unlock his fertile, intuitive, creative genius. All he wanted was occasion, and in the course of the 1690s occasion began to bring success. If he had managed to keep quiet his earlier failures, he was no more inclined to publicize the labour that led to his successes. This is the background to the first letter in Webb's edition, dated Christmas Day 1699:

> I have been this Summer at my Ld Carlisle's, and Seen most of the great houses in the North, as Ld Nottings: Duke of Leeds Chattesworth &c. I stay'd at Chattesworth four or five days the Duke being there. I shew'd him all my Ld Carlisle's designs, which he said was quite another thing, than what he imagin'd from the Character yr Ldship gave him on't; He absolutely approv'd the whole design, perticularly the low Wings, which he said wou'd have an admirable effect without doors as well as within, being adorn'd with those Ornaments of Pillasters and Urns, wch he never thought of, but concluded 'twas to be a plain low building like an orange house. There has been a great many Criticks consulted upon it since, and no one objection being made to't, the Stone is raising, and the Foundations will be laid in the Spring. The Modell is preparing in wood, wch when done, is to travel to Kensington where the Kings thoughts upon't are to be had.[16]

Perhaps he had written likewise to his mother after – not before – the success of his first play, *The Relapse*, three years earlier. After a long catalogue of West End gossip (for the addressee was in Paris) he presents a *fait accompli*. Clearly, and by implication, a great deal of quiet desk-work had gone on over the preceding year. Now the designs are made, and universally approved of, especially by the Duke of Devonshire; the stone is raising in the quarry, even a wooden model is being made which will be sent for King William's opinion. This last, which took another six months, was surely quite gratuitous; it was none of the King's business what Lord Carlisle built in Yorkshire, or how – but it does add to the atmosphere of joy. If it was an advertisement, it was for Carlisle rather than for Vanbrugh.

I have published five accounts of Castle Howard, longer or shorter, and I am not going to rehearse them here. But it has been suggested, because they are all different, that I don't know my own mind – which is not true; moreover, there are a couple of pieces of evidence – a memorandum and some little drawings – that were not available then. I do know my own mind, but in the light of this evidence I have changed it somewhat, in respect not of who did what, but of when. The summary I now offer is thus different in some respects, which is my justification for offering it.

Lord Carlisle arrived in Yorkshire in late July 1698 and stayed until November.[17] On 20 August Vanbrugh received a warrant for half-pay as Captain of Marines; effectively he retired from the service and was a free man. On 31 October 1698 Carlisle signed a lease with his grandmother on Henderskelfe Castle – gutted by fire five years earlier – and its estate; the lease was to take effect from March 1699. Because other events preclude it, William Talman's visit to Henderskelfe can have been no later than the autumn of 1698. George London, his associate garden designer, is known to have been there the following year, in July 1699, but Talman must have been involved earlier since Hawksmoor's plan-chest contained layouts with both Talman's and Vanbrugh's house plans. By the end of 1698 Carlisle must have tired of Talman, who (as we know from the subsequent lawsuit) disagreed with both Carlisle and Vanbrugh about the financial value of small and large drawings.[18] It would also have been known about town by then that the Duke of Devonshire, at Chatsworth, had sacked Talman, upset by his extravagant lifestyle as well as by the fact that he, the Duke, had been paying London prices, which were more than twice the local ones.

Carlisle made a short visit to Henderskelfe in March 1699; the estate was now effectively his, and he was back there by 21 June. The key to what had been happening in the previous six months is a memorandum from his neighbouring landowner, Thomas Worsley of Hovingham, dated 26 June. This was mentioned to me forty years ago by George Howard, but its significance was curiously ignored by Charles Saumarez Smith.[19] It includes the following:

In the two first of the Base & Window caseing
att 1^s p foot I think may be wrought ⅓ pte cheaper
than Propos'd, wch will save   61. 0. 0

As For the Higer Prices, As 1^s.6^d. 3. & 5^s p Foot, I know
nothing of, Being Rates Above wt is ever given hear . . .

Norway Oake wth Workmans^p att 6^s p yard. will be sav'd   153. 12. 6
For Deale wth Workmans^p 3^s. 6^d. p Yard
Two Stair Cases with Norway Oak Raile Balister & Wansscott.   70£ . . .

Sash Windows I know Nothing of

Lead for Covering . . .
The Body of the House in Feet – Long – 106. Broad – 75 . . .
The Two Wings in Feet – Long – 142. Broad – 35[20]

Evidently Carlisle was thinking of using direct labour – something one could not do if Talman was in charge, but which Vanbrugh recommended, and Carlisle, under the guidance of Hawksmoor, managed to do and found very satisfactory.[21] Worsley had done so; it is interesting not just that the new high-tech sash-windows were unknown to him but that he assumed Carlisle's staircases were to be of wood, not stone.

More importantly, Carlisle had given Worsley the dimensions of his proposed house – or at least of the main block and the southern wings that had reminded Devonshire of a long, low orangery. It is reasonable to suppose, therefore, that drawings with a main block less than 106 feet long – like, for example, those known ever since Whistler's articles as the 'first' Vanbrugh design – were earlier, and those of about 106 feet, the same as built, were later. The question is, how much later?

It is here that the most remarkable feature of Vanbrugh's house comes in: the great dome that is too big for it but that *makes* the building from a distance. We

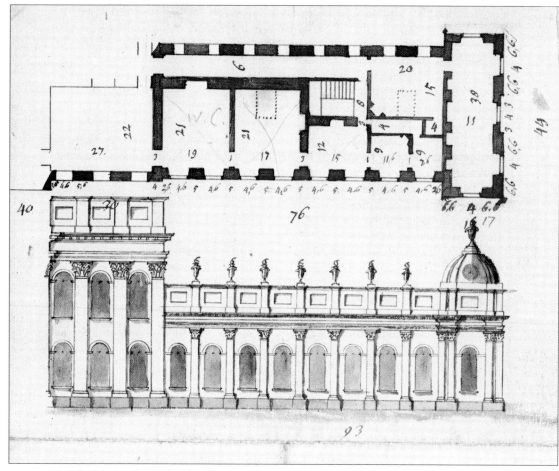

1. John Vanbrugh, Design for South Front, Castle Howard with Inset Plan, *1699.*

know this was an afterthought, because in the 'first' plan there is no support for it and in the 'second' plan it was added at a late stage. Again, how late?

About five years ago, after the death of the 6th Marquess of Bute, Francis Russell of Christie's found a folder containing some more material from Hawksmoor's plan-chest, including three little drawings in Vanbrugh's own hand: drawings 'as big as your hand' – the kind he testified at the lawsuit that you did not pay for – which are now also in the Victoria and Albert Museum. There is a plan with a main block marked only 100 feet long (30+40+30; fig. 1), and an elevation which by calculation is only 96 feet long (fig. 2). Unless the design process went backwards, this means that Vanbrugh drew a domed house in the early part of 1699; therefore, the dome, although an afterthought, was an early one. It was always to be, objectively, too big, although in this little drawing it is by no means as big as it would come to be.

This means that the design – apart from the towered stable- and kitchen-courts – was virtually settled when Vanbrugh showed it to Devonshire at Chatsworth in the late summer of 1699. (Devonshire arrived there in August.) We have all been misled by the fact that Hawksmoor's fine elevations – the sort you certainly did pay for – do not show a dome. But they do not show other things either, and the discussion recorded in Vanbrugh's Christmas letter can – and I now believe should – be read as concerning the south wings, rather than the house as a whole. So when Vanbrugh wrote that it was all going forward, he meant it. Even today a building work may take months before anything is visible: you need not only drains but surfaced tracks for heavy carts to reach the site. Hawksmoor wrote on 26 May 1701:

> I find the work at Henderscelf to go on with vigour and grt industry altho there is not soe much done as I expected by this time but the impediment has been the backward season which has much obstructed us. I am come time enough to regulate some errours and difficultys the workmen were going into, and in generall the worke is firme and strongly performed; the situation yr Lp has chose is under the covert of the Wood but it runs us into some hardships about levelling & makeing our access to the great façade and principall courts, I am takeing all the declivitys and disposition of the ground that they might not Loose time . . .
>
> I have severall instructions and memorandums to draw up for the workemen and I can see nothing to contradict the good execution of the worke: I desire the mason to sett on more hands that we may complete with expedition the two wings, and to do that will require another kill [i.e., kiln] for Lime. The coals come hard but now is the season to gett them in which I hope your Lp will order not to be wanting for now I shall wish the conclusion of the worke as earnestly as I was for opposing the beginning of it. I shall give your Lp a farther acct the next post.[22]

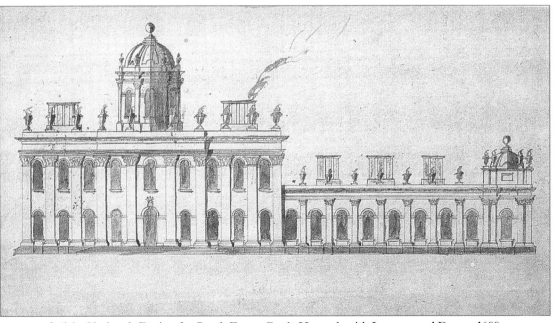

2. John Vanbrugh, Design for South Front, Castle Howard, with Lantern and Dome, *1699.*

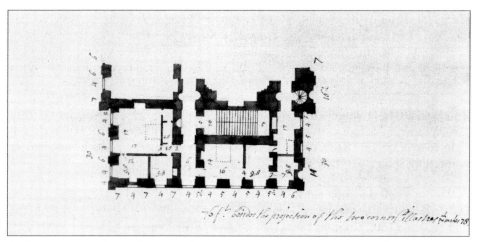

3. John Vanbrugh, Ground Plan of the North-east Angle of the Main Block for Castle Howard, *1699.*

Some of the workmen were already going into errors and difficulties because preliminary or infrastructure work had been in progress for a whole year.

So the essence of today's great house was on paper *in the summer of 1699.* That leaves the question of Hawksmoor's part in it. 'If the argument is judged to be sound, Vanbrugh emerges a more limited artist than the general opinion has allowed, and Hawksmoor a more capable one. . . . It is agreeable, then, to be of help in making tardy restitution to Hawksmoor.' That was Whistler's conclusion to his 1954 book.[23] Here was the Vanbrugh expert giving it all away! Everything I have written has been guided by the belief that Whistler's judgment, though well meant, was simplistic, and that in a unique partnership, the architect of Castle Howard was Vanbrugh. In about April 1700 he thought it was time to introduce his colleague *officially* to Carlisle, so that he could be not only recognized but also paid:

> I wish't I cou'd possibly have stay'd . . . till tuesday, that I might have seen yr Ldship, and known whether you are come to an agreement with the Mason & Carpenter. I talk't a great deal to 'em both, the morning I came away; but found 'em very unwilling to come to any abatement. They made a world of protestations of its being impossible, without letting the work pay for't: they say'd they believ'd yr Ldship might expect some abatement from their proposall as a thing of course; but that Mr Hawksmoor had persuaded 'em to make no provision for that, but to make the lowest offer they cou'd possibly work for, and do it well. I ask't Mr Hawksmoor alone, what he really thought on't; He said they were indeed come as low, as he ever expected to bring 'em; and yet perhaps it was not impossible for 'em to work lower, and that since they so positively declar'd, they cou'd not do the best work lower, and that if they lessen'd their rates, they must save themselves in the performance, it was to be fear'd (unless they have more honesty than is reasonable to expect) they might take this pretence, to performe the work ten per Cent: worse for five per Cent: they were reduc't. since there was no direct form of Workmanship cou'd be

agreed on, when once they had got loose from being oblig'd to the best. So that this wou'd give 'em a loophole to play the Rogue very much, and one cou'd not tell how to redress it: wheras, if they have the rates they have propos'd, they own themselves engag'd to do as good work as that they receive twice as much for, at London, and by consequence they have no room left for evasion . . .

I spoak to Mr Hawksmoor about his perticular concern and found him as he us'd to be. so he intended to ask yr Ldship fourty pound a year Sallary & fifty each journey wch mounts to £100 clear. I hope he'll deserve it, and that all will go to yr Ldships satisfaction. for I shou'd be very sorry to have meddled in anything shou'd do otherwise.[24]

We can place this undated letter here, just a year before Hawksmoor's, because the first recorded payment to Hawksmoor, on 25 May 1701, the day before his site report, was £150: two journeys at £50 each, a year's salary at £40, and surely £10 for contingencies. In his letter Hawksmoor speaks as the expert consultant manager; in all the Vanbrugh letters quoted it is the architect who speaks. On 25 May 1716 he told the Duke of Marlborough, faced with completing Blenheim at his own expense, of the virtues of direct labour:

Out of the Several Proposals the Masons have given in, I have collected the Lowest price put to each Article in each Mans proposall, And so made the enclosed Scheme of Prices, to offer to them, which upon the whole, is therefore a good deal Lower than any one of their distinct offers . . .

I have farther look'd over the rates my Lord Carlisle pays in Yorkshire; and find them within a Small matter the Same with these, tho' the work is by no means so good, and the Country vastly Cheaper than Oxfordshire: And yet my Lord has, during the whole Course of his Building managed all that part himself, with the greatest care; And tho' he began with ignorant Masons at Lower Rates, he soon found there was good reason to give more, in order to have his work tollerably done.[25]

Vanbrugh was also proud of the warmth, economy and convenience he had provided. On 29 October 1713 he told James Craggs:

I am much pleased here (amongst other things) to find Lord Carlisle so thoroughly convinced of the Conveniencys of his new house, now he has had a years tryall of it: And I am the more pleas'd with it, because I have now a proof, that the Dutchess of Marlborough must find the same conveniency in Blenheim, if ever She comes to try it (as I still believe she will in spite of all these black Clouds.) For my Lord Carlisle was pretty much under the same Apprehensions with her, about long Passages, high Rooms &c. But he finds what I told him to be true. That those Passages woud be so far from gathering & drawing wind as he feared, that a Candle wou'd not flare in them; of this he has lately had the proof, by bitter stormy nights in which not one Candle wanted to be put into a Lanthorn, not even in the Hall, which is as high (tho not indeed so big) as that at Blenheim. He likewise finds, that all his Rooms, with moderate fires Are Ovens, And that this Great House, do's not require above One pound of wax, and two of Tallow Candles a Night to light it, more than his house at London.[26]

Moreover, he believed his methods to be generally applicable. On 4 January 1719 he wrote, again from Castle Howard, to the young Duke of Newcastle, for whom he was refurbishing Nottingham Castle:

> At least to encourage you, let me acquaint you, that this Place where I am now, has since I remember been Shiver'd at, when Nam'd for a Winter habitation. And yet, is now so very comfortable a One, that in this Sharp Season, there has not past a day, without setting Open Severall times, the door and Windows of the Room My Lord Car: and the Ladys constantly use; it has been so much too hot: And all the rest of the house, is so in proportion. And so may Nottingham Castle be made, by the Same care and Methods.[27]

And what of Lord Carlisle? Saumarez Smith concluded that, by the time he had finished with it, Castle Howard had changed from 'an instrument of power and self-aggrandisement, a demonstration of personal and political prestige' to 'an expensive retirement home and, as Lady Mary Wortley Montagu described it, a nunnery for Lord Carlisle's unmarried daughters'. He found 'a curious irony in comparing the great lavishness of the Castle Howard interiors with the third Earl's life of modest domesticity, of gossip and conversation, and long winter evenings without company, as he grew old and lame'.[28]

When the inscription on the great obelisk was put up in 1731 Carlisle was sixty-two, about the age at which Rembrandt and Rubens and Vanbrugh died; he would live to be sixty-nine. The rhyming epigraph is about the plantations; these, with the 'faithful pillar', are to be his memorial (as opposed to the Mausoleum, the dynastic burial place). Castle Howard itself, the 'out-works' and monuments and (again) the plantations are mentioned, as his creations, in the prose lines that conclude the inscription. What sort of man – and what sort of artistic patron – was he?

John Macky described Carlisle as 'a gentleman of great interest in the Country and very zealous for its welfare; hath a fine estate and a very good understanding, with a grave deportment'.[29] His views on religion and the afterlife were not entirely orthodox, but they had a part to play in the creation of the Mausoleum.[30] He bought and commissioned pictures and other works of art. He had made the Grand Tour in his early twenties, and it must have been in Rome that he acquired a knowledge of, and a taste for, the landscape paintings of Claude Lorrain which so many writers have seen as one of the factors in the landscape of Castle Howard; for Claude's paintings – though perhaps not his etchings – were still little known in England. In his Roman notebook Carlisle identified the 'right' artists;[31] on his travels he made the 'right' purchases. It is reasonable to suppose that the subjects of the sculptures and mural paintings he commissioned had some meaning for him, even if the sea-horses on the south frieze of the house may be there only because the carver brought his pattern-book from Chatsworth. But the range of references is that of an educated man, not a learned one; that Castle Howard has an integrated symbolic programme is yet to be proved, and there is no hint of it in either his daughter's poem or his own literary attempts.[32] The poems only become specific in references to Ray Wood, Lady Irwin's being consciously Virgilian and her father's racily closer to Ovid. But atmosphere and the *genius loci* do not depend on an iconographer's handbook. Carlisle's aims, associations and taste were, it seems, those not of a philosopher or connoisseur but of a politician or magnate. And those were his characteristics.

The rehabilitation of Hawksmoor is now a fact, and it is gratifying to have played a part in it. But in my first book I quoted Sir John Summerson writing at about the same time as Whistler. 'The truth', he wrote, 'can only be that *both* Hawksmoor *and* Vanbrugh were very exceptional men.'[33] So, I might add, and in his fashion, was the 3rd Earl of Carlisle.

TWO

Estate Management and Landscape Design

Tom Williamson

Designed landscapes are always complex and problematic: their form and meaning change ceaselessly, responding to a whole range of influences and pressures – social, economic, political, ideological. Those of Vanbrugh's age changed particularly rapidly, as geometric gardens passed through a series of fashionable phases, and as landowners keenly displayed their interest in contemporary taste and their ability to make the necessary improvements.[1] The famous and familiar illustrations published by Kip and Knyff in *Britannia Illustrata* (1707) thus present a misleading impression of stasis, of completion. At Chatsworth, for example (fig. 4) the parterre shown to the south of the house, created by George London and Henry Wise, was less than six years old in 1700 when the drawing was made. It was a comprehensive remodelling of an earlier layout, which had itself probably been in existence for less than a decade. It was for this, rather than for the London and Wise design, that the famous *Triton and Sea-horses* fountain by C.G. Cibber had originally been carved.[2] Further changes were under way in the garden even as Kip's engraving was being produced. In 1702–3 the canal – usually referred to today as the Canal Pond – was laid out to the south of the great parterre, on the same alignment as the house, and the figure of *Flora* (just visible on the engraving) was accordingly removed to a new home in the Bowling Green House, several hundred yards to the west.[3] The Cascade on the rising ground to the east of the house had only been completed in 1696, but it was realigned (and probably extended) between 1703 and 1708, when John Ingham and Thomas Harris were paid 'Ye remaining part in full of their bill for 1277 yards 2 feet of paving in ye 23 spaces or falls of water in the cascade'. The Cascade House at its summit was built to a French design by Thomas Archer during these same years.[4]

And many more changes were made to the surroundings of the great house in the first two decades of the eighteenth century. There was a slight pause in activity in the mid-1720s; but then the gardens seem to have been radically transformed in line with the vogue for a simpler geometric style – with an emphasis on turf and gravel – that was becoming fashionable, activity that culminated between 1732, when 2,200 trees were felled in the gardens, and 1734, when Thomas Pennistone and partners were paid for cutting down 'all the fir

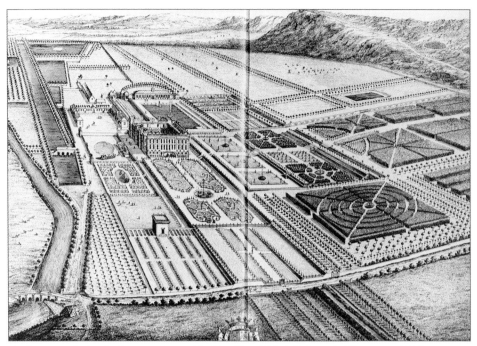

4. Chatsworth, Derbyshire, as depicted in Knyff and Kip's Britannia Illustrata, *1707.*

trees' there.[5] Rapid change on this grand scale was not unusual in the age of Vanbrugh, at least at the exalted social level of families like the Devonshires. Close examination of estate archives often reveals this kind of intense, restless activity, almost as if the *doing* – the planning and execution of a design – was as important as its actual completion.[6]

Engravings like this are thus snapshots – one frame of a moving film. And of course, no-one ever saw Chatsworth, or any of the other great seats depicted in *Britannia Illustrata*, like this. The impossible aerial perspective adopted not only by Kip and Knyff but by most fashionable illustrators of the day, is itself worthy of some consideration. It is a tradition that stops, abruptly enough, when more 'naturalistic' styles of garden design become current in the middle and later decades of the eighteenth century. No one ever thought of portraying a Capability Brown landscape from the air. The design would simply have dissolved into an undifferentiated, undistinguished hotchpotch of water, turf and trees. An aerial view, in contrast, was almost essential for gardens designed in the grand manner. It allowed the full magnificence of the geometry to be displayed; and served to tie the architecture of the house firmly into that framework. But such views also – like the estate maps being produced in ever-increasing numbers in this same period – usually located the house and its garden within their wider context, that of the working estate.

The fields, farms, and woods towards the margins of such pictures were not just the 'economic background' to the aesthetic landscape – the source of the cash that paid for the frenetic activity at places like Chatsworth. Nor were they simply a static backdrop to the gardens of grandeur. They, too, were in a state of rapid change and flux; and they too contributed to the overall design. At times they might be hidden, and form an implied contrast with the designed landscape; at times they might be included in the view, and thus form an extension of it. Either way, the complex relationship between the productive estate land and the designed 'core' are of crucial importance for understanding the aesthetic landscapes of any period, although such matters are frequently neglected in studies of garden history. Most emphasize instead the complex allusions and symbolism that elite gardens contain, their references to classical mythology, to Renaissance Italy, to politics and philosophy. These are unquestionably important matters: but it is arguable that their centrality in most discussions (to the virtual exclusion of other perspectives) reflects the fact that many garden historians have trained in art history or comparative literature. In contrast, I would like to draw attention to some other kinds of message and symbolism embedded in landscapes of Vanbrugh's period, which referenced instead aspects of everyday agricultural and domestic production. Such allusions, references, contrasts and connections were more easily understood by contemporaries than they are by modern commentators. The former, unlike the latter, lived in a world in which farming, forestry and food production were central to the lives of most people, from aristocrat to labourer, even if the extent of their *direct* involvement in such matters varied considerably.

The primary aim of all large landowners in the seventeenth and eighteenth centuries was to maintain or improve their rental incomes. Most kept a proportion of their estates 'in hand' – plantations, home farms, sometimes a park – and these were managed with varying degrees of enthusiasm and involvement. The greater part, however, was occupied by tenant farms. The income from this tenanted land could be increased in two main ways: by improving its quality and hence the rents it could command, principally through the enclosure of open-fields; or by expanding the area of the estate, through enclosure and reclamation of common land and (above all) the purchase of neighbouring farms and estates.

The wider economic background is important here. The period of Kip and Knyff, and of London and Wise, was a time of agricultural recession. Demographic growth, rapid in the early seventeenth century, levelled off in the period after 1650, and England's population remained static, or even fell, until *c.* 1750.[7] As a consequence, grain prices, in particular, remained low; and so too, in consequence, did both the income from the home farm and, more importantly, that derived from agricultural rents. In addition, the fortunes of landowners were adversely effected by the institution of the Land Tax in 1691 to pay for King William's war in Flanders, and for the conflicts that followed. Not all landowners suffered equally from these circumstances, however. In general, the local gentry fared worse than the great landowners – that is, those owning estates of 10,000 acres or more. Many of this latter group had alternative sources of income – from government office, from urban or industrial rents. They thus tended to prosper at the expense of lesser landowners, especially small freeholders or minor gentry. Their share of the landed 'cake' may have increased, as Thompson suggested, from around 15 per cent to *c.* 24 per cent in the century after *c.* 1650. The smallest landowners, in contrast – those owning less than 300 acres – may have lost some 30 per cent of their land in the same period.[8]

There were a number of other reasons why large estates tended to expand. The development and elaboration of entails and strict settlements in the course of the seventeenth century ensured that large estates remained intact (if increasingly encumbered, in many cases, by debt). More important, though, were the fundamental political changes that had occurred in the course of the century. In medieval, Tudor and early Stuart times, large estates had been vulnerable to the political decisions of their owners, who might back the wrong side in dynastic struggles, religious conflicts, or civil war. The Revolution of the 1640s and '50s and the Settlement of 1688, however, ensured that property was now much more secure, protected as it was by a parliament of the propertied. This was, in a very real sense, a post-Revolutionary era, and in the final analysis it was the security of landed property provided by the new political dispensation that allowed great estates like Chatsworth to flourish. The gardens laid out around such seats were confident, arrogant assertions of power by those who had benefited most from the eventual outcome of the constitutional upheavals, and who were benefiting most from the immediate economic circumstances – the great landowners. Yet at the same time such men carried with them, to the end of the seventeenth century and beyond, keen memories of the upheavals of the Civil Wars and their immediate aftermath, when estates had been ruined and when, at times, the threat of real social revolution had loomed. Such memories were heightened by the crises of 1685 and 1688, and by rumours of plots, real or imaginary, hatched by disaffected Jacobites.

Most large estates thus grew steadily in this period. But expansion was normally greatest in their heartlands. Land close to the centre of the estate might be bought at any price. As one land agent commented, concerning the proposed purchase of a neighbouring farm:

> If we cannot purchase on terms we would, we must purchase on the terms we can, as from its contiguity [the farm in question] is extremely desirable, and to have a disagreeable neighbour, so near, would be superlatively vexatious.[9]

Consolidation brought a number of practical benefits. Monopoly of ownership within a township or parish allowed any surviving areas of arable open field or common grazing to be enclosed, and the latter to be 'improved' and put to new uses. Debate continues about the chronology of enclosure in England, but many historians agree that enclosure by parliamentary act after 1750 affected less than a quarter of the land area of England and that the period from 1650 to 1750 may have been of equal or greater importance, in terms of open-field enclosure at least. Enclosed land invariably brought in higher rents than open, and landowners were particularly keen to maximize their rental income in these hard times. Moreover, the agricultural recession tended to trouble grain producers more than livestock farmers, and this gave particular impetus to the spread of enclosure, especially on the heavier soils of the Midlands: it was impossible to expand livestock production in a landscape of small, intermingled open-field strips.

Consolidation of ownership also had important effects on the development of settlement. In this period of demographic stagnation, parishes wholly or largely under the control of a single owner – 'closed' parishes – tended to lose their inhabitants, while 'open' parishes in multiple ownership usually displayed at least sluggish growth. There were a number of reasons for these divergent demographic regimes. Landowners and their agents preferred to deal with a small number of large tenants, able to weather the storms of recession, rather than with a plethora of smallholders. An estate with fewer tenants, moreover, required less management and demanded lower repair and maintenance costs than one with innumerable small farms.[10] In addition, large numbers of cottages meant large numbers of labourers and their families, all potential claimants for Poor Relief through sickness, old age or the burden of illegitimate offspring. As the Poor rates were paid by the landowners and principal tenants in a parish, monopoly landowners had an understandable interest in limiting or even reducing the size of villages, while large numbers of cottages, once again, meant high repair costs.[11] In 1730 Sir Marmaduke Constable of Everingham in the East Riding of Yorkshire typically described to his steward how he 'would rather have my cottages diminished, than increased, though I am now in Everingham at or about the number I would be at'. Ten years later he noted that 'Few houses and good is what I propose at Everingham'. Like that of many neighbouring villages, the population of Everingham fell fast in this period. There were 57 households there in 1672, but only 27 in 1743.[12]

All landowners thus aspired to the same essential ideal: a property that was extensive, compact and continuous, without the vexatious presence of 'disagreeable neighbours'; one that was entirely enclosed, i.e., in which intermixed open-field arable, and common pastures, heaths or moors, had been eradicated; and one in which, especially in the vicinity of the mansion, the number of farms and cottages were few in number. And because this was an ideal to which all aspired, its achievement was to be celebrated and flaunted, its existence visually expressed in the landscape. Such a property would then give

5. Dovecote at Rougham Hall, Norfolk, designed by Roger North in the 1690s.

more aesthetic pleasure than the most elaborate of parterres, the most complex of waterworks.

Agricultural recession of the decades around 1700 had other effects besides encouraging the growth of large estates, and some of these have a direct bearing on the appearance of estate landscapes. As Joan Thirsk has argued, this was a period of diversification, in which landowners sought to augment their incomes with new enterprises and new forms of land use, both on their home farms and on the poor, marginal ground of the unenclosed commons.[13] One marked development was the burgeoning interest in forestry, which was becoming a more attractive form of medium- and long-term investment. There is little doubt that the area under woodland in England began to increase in the period after 1660, following at least 800 years of steady decline: a decline that had accelerated during the Civil Wars and Interregnum, when large-scale fellings had taken place in the royal parks and forests, and on the sequestered estates of Royalists. In the period of stability following the Restoration, landowners had the confidence to replant on a lavish scale.[14] It is no coincidence that Evelyn's *Sylva* appeared when it did, in 1664.[15] Passing through many editions, it was an almost indispensable text in the libraries of the nobility and gentry, imitated and shamelessly plagiarized by others – most notably, perhaps, by Batty Langley in his *A Sure Method of Improving Estates, by Plantations of Oak, Elm, Ash, Beech and Other Timber Trees, Coppice Woods &c.* of 1728.

New forms of livestock production were also embraced by landowners on their home farms and on the manorial wastes. Of particular importance was the resurgence of interest in semi-domesticated animals – deer, rabbits, fish, pigeons and the like.[16] Most of these were old, indeed ancient, forms of food production, closely associated with the social elite, which have their own distinctive archaeology. Rabbits for example, were introduced soon after the Norman Conquest and had been farmed in enclosed warrens throughout the Middle Ages, often housed in long, low mounds (complete with purpose-built burrow-systems), which archaeologists usually term 'pillow mounds'.[17] Deer parks – principally housing another Norman import, the fallow deer – had become a common feature of the English landscape by the thirteenth century. They functioned as carefully managed venison farms as much as hunting grounds. Fishponds containing carp (again, a medieval introduction) were widespread by the same period, while dovecotes, or *columbaria*, were to be found beside most manor houses.

Archaeologists sometimes assume that these were all essentially medieval forms of production, but they continued to be important in post-medieval times and, more particularly, all appear to have experienced a notable revival in the period after 1660. Thus, in Thirsk's words, 'the gentry seem to have lost much of their interest in deer keeping and deer parks in the course of the late sixteenth and early seventeenth centuries. Their enthusiasm revived after 1660.' The keeping of pigeons likewise 'aroused fresh interest after 1660': the majority of surviving dovecotes appear to have been erected between *c.* 1680 and 1740 (fig. 5).[18] Fishponds were also of considerable importance in this period, and no less a person than Roger North – lawyer, historian, architect – published a comprehensive book on the subject, the *Discourse of Fish and Fish Ponds*, in 1713.[19]

In addition, entirely new forms of animal exploitation were developed by landowners in this period, most notably duck decoys, which were introduced into

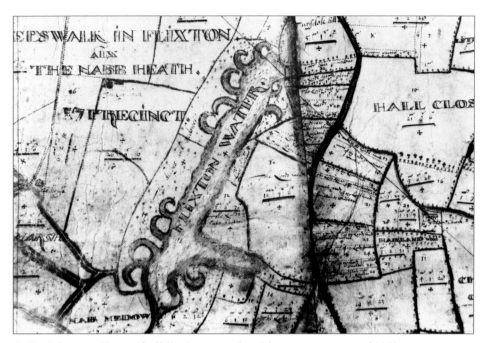

6. Duck decoy at Flixton, Suffolk, shown in a detail from an estate map of 1652.

England at the start of the seventeenth century but proliferated rapidly in the decades after 1660 (fig. 6). Few survive intact, but the one at Boarstall in Buckinghamshire is maintained in working condition by the National Trust. Decoys were sometimes a feature of home farms, used to produce meat for domestic consumption. But many were large commercial enterprises, often established on the manorial waste, that were leased out to professional wildfowlers. Daniel Defoe, writing of the decoys he had seen in the East Anglian Fenland in 1722, remarked that:

> it is incredible what quantities of wild-fowl of all sorts, duck, mallard, teal, widgeon, &c. they take in these duckoys every week, during the season; it may indeed be guess'd at a little by this, that there is a duckoy not far from Ely . . . from which duckoy alone they assured me at St Ives . . . that they generally sen[d] up [to London] three thousand couple a week.[20]

We can look at all these activities in purely economic terms, as forms of diversification in a climate of recession. But we might also consider their wider, social and ideological significance. In this post-revolutionary society, all had a symbolic meaning, as well as an economic importance. This is perhaps most obvious in the case of forestry. Royalist propaganda after the Restoration had exaggerated the extent of felling in royal parks and on Royalist estates, and this had fostered an association between felling and republicanism – and conversely, between planting and loyalty to the restored monarchy. But in a more general sense, planting showed confidence in the new political dispensation: long-term investments were safer now that the right to private property was guaranteed by a parliament of the propertied. Planting was also a patriotic duty, providing timber for the navy that would protect Protestant Britain and its trading interests from enemies and rivals at a time when England was frequently at war – points repeatedly emphasized by Evelyn, Langley and the rest. But in a time of equally aggressive estate aggrandizement, woods and plantations had another significance. They symbolized the ownership of land by large landowners, and confidence in the continuity of that ownership. As Worlidge in 1669 explained: 'What can be more pleasant than to have the bounds and limits of your property preserved and continued from age to age by the testimony of such living and growing witnesses?'[21]

A small freeholder might plant a few trees in his hedgerows, but on a farm of 100 acres it was impossible to put aside ten acres or more for forestry. Only those with broad acres could tie up land in this way for perhaps two generations. Contemporaries read the landscape in this light, understanding well that most basic equation of the eighteenth century: 'plantations equals gentlemen'. Moreover, trees could only be established on enclosed ground. Planting on commons, or within unenclosed open-fields, was impossible, because of the rights enjoyed by the local community to forage over them. Livestock would simply uproot the young trees, or destroy them through grazing. Hence the second essential rule of the eighteenth-century landscape: 'plantations equals enclosure'. Trees were so closely associated with these things that in some districts they were almost a sign of civilization, with plantations clustering close to the house and open, unenclosed heath or moor, as yet only partly under the control of the landowner, stretching beyond. In the light

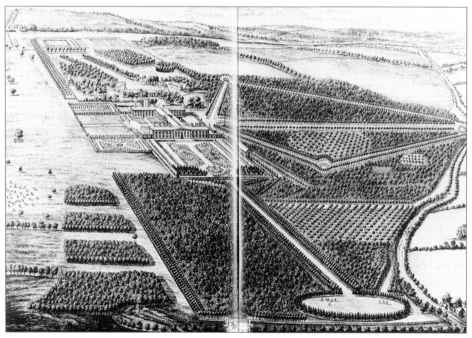

7. *Cassiobury, Hertfordshire, from Knyff and Kip's* Britannia Illustrata, *1707; Moses Cook's plantations form a major part of the design.*

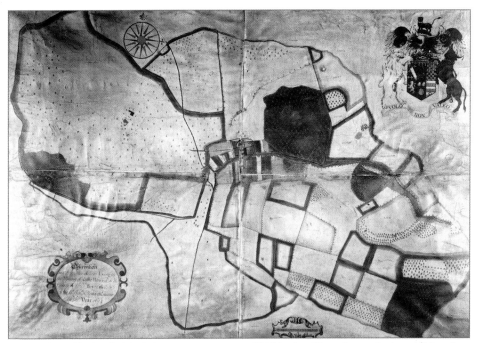

8. Henderskelfe Castle, Yorkshire, an estate map of 1694; the old castle stands, in traditional fashion, to one side of the deer park.

of all this it is not surprising to find that woods and trees were a frequent target for vandalism on the part of the disaffected and the poor, as at Cassiobury in Hertfordshire in the 1670s where trees planted by Moses Cook were damaged 'by base men or boys' (fig. 7)[22]. Successive acts of parliament from the 1720s sought to protect trees growing in both pleasure grounds and plantations.

The burgeoning interest in fishponds, deer, warrens and dovecotes also had a deeper significance. All these forms of production had, since medieval times, been the preserve of the landed gentry and aristocracy. Ponds and parks were expensive to construct and maintain, while the erection of dovecotes was actually restricted by law to the manorial gentry. Pigeons fed indiscriminately on the grain of owners and neighbours alike, and were naturally considered the preserve of the hereditary elite. During the Civil Wars and Interregnum, all had come under sustained attack, in part for what they symbolized – established rank and privilege. Thus a group of Parliamentary soldiers, stationed at Leamington, did considerable damage to Baron Trevor's dovecote. When their commanding officer remonstrated with them, their reply was that

> Pigeons were fowls of the air given to the sons of men, and all men had a common right in them that could get them, and they were as much theirs as the barons, and therefore they would kill them . . . and not part from their right: upon which the captain said he was so convinced by their arguments he could not answer them, and so came away, letting them do as they would.[23]

9. Anon., Averham Park, Nottinghamshire, *c. 1730; the house was built as a secondary residence within an existing deer park.*

In the 1640s, when parliament debated the abolition of the manorial monopoly on the keeping of pigeons, one commentator argued that it would be a 'Blemish of government that the enferior sort of people should assume that power and libertye wch in reason and policye of state ought to belonge to great estates and persons of qualitye and commission.'[24] Deer parks in particular were both a target for generalized vandalism on the part of army radicals, and of more systematic asset-stripping on the part of the revolutionary government. Hardly surprising, then, that in the period of stability following the Restoration, such traditional symbols of status enjoyed renewed popularity, and were proudly displayed in the immediate vicinity of high-status residences.

Deer parks are particularly interesting in this respect. In early medieval times most had been located at a distance from the owner's principal residence, in some area of residual wood-pasture or waste. Many were supplied with a lodge, which served as a home for the park-keeper and/or as accommodation for the owner during hunting trips. But since the fifteenth century, such isolated venison farms and hunting grounds had been in steady decline, and parks had increasingly been laid out *adjacent to* the big country houses. This tendency seems to have accelerated in the period after 1660, and by the early eighteenth century almost all parks formed a prestigious adjunct to a country house, although often at this stage attached to one side of the residence, as at Henderskelfe (fig. 8), rather than surrounding it on all sides.[25] Indeed, where isolated parks were maintained, the lodge sometimes mutated into a full-blown secondary residence, as at Averham Park in Nottinghamshire, built *c.* 1725 (fig. 9)[26]. This fundamental change in the rôle of the park was accompanied by important alterations in its appearance. Medieval parks had, for the most part, comprised densely timbered pastures, with only limited areas of more open grounds, called 'laundes'. As the aesthetic rôle of parks increased, however – as they came to be located next to mansions – the density of trees within them was reduced, and vistas steadily opened up.

Parks were the most prestigious adjunct to a country house, but the structures associated with certain other forms of 'intermediate exploitation'[27] might also be proudly displayed. Dovecotes were often prominently positioned, sometimes within the main areas of ornamental garden. They were usually elaborate structures, their fine architectural detailing proclaiming their more than utilitarian significance, such as the magnificent example built before 1750 that stands within the walled garden at Felbrigg in Norfolk. And fishponds, too, were objects of beauty as much as production. Roger North recommended that they be positioned within the gardens 'Because the Fish are fenc'd from Robbers, and your journey to them is short and easy, and . . . they will be an Ornament to the Walks.'[28] As Christopher Currie has shown, most of the ornamental canals and basins that were such a feature of the gardens of Vanbrugh's age also served as fish stews.[29]

In contrast to parks, most dovecotes, fishponds, warrens and decoys were located at some distance from the main residential complex. Rabbits and gardens do not mix well, and decoys need extreme quiet to work effectively. Nevertheless, these facilities might also be ornamental, as much as productive, features of the estate landscape. In 1681 John Evelyn visited Mr Denzil Onslow of Pyrford in Surrey and described

> Such an extraordinary feast . . . there was not any thing, save what his estate about it did afford: as Venison, rabbits, hares, pheasants, partridges, pigeons, all sorts of fowle in season (from his own decoy near his house), all sorts of fresh fish. After dinner we went to see sport at the decoy . . .[30]

The passage illustrates well the concept of estate self-sufficiency that was the practical counterpart, in the real world, of the 'rural retirement' theme that is so prominent in the poetry of the age. It extended to other aspects of domestic production, and in particular to the maintenance of orchards and the nurture of fruit trees, subjects that loom large in the writings of Stephen Switzer and Batty Langley, among others. Roger North's garden, according to one contemporary account, contained 'every kind of fruit tree known'.[31] Many estate archives are more explicit, describing in meticulous detail the varieties of fruit in garden and orchard. Typical is the list from East Turnbull in Berkshire, where the orchard and garden planted in 1696 contained 450 fruit trees, in all more than 90 different varieties of apples, pears, nectarines, apricots and quinces.[32]

These various aspects of estate production cannot be divorced from the aesthetics of landscape, and of landscape design, for among the things that men find most attractive are those that make them money and express their social superiority. Enclosure, control of settlement, forestry, and particular aspects of domestic production thus provided some of the crucial building blocks out of which a contemporary landscape aesthetics was constructed. But because the interests, activities and fortunes of different strata of the landowning class differed in this period, as we have seen, not all of the various activities outlined above were equally prominent on all landed estates, or had the same aesthetic appeal to all men of property.

10. Badminton,
Gloucestershire, as shown in
Knyff and Kip's Britannia
Illustrata, *1707.*
The house sits at the centre of
a complex web of avenues.

Some, certainly, were shared by all landowners of any substance – in particular, an interest in tree-planting. One notable aspect of this was the great vogue for avenues that characterized the period. Avenues had been planted in England since at least the sixteenth century, but there is no doubt that their numbers increased massively after the Restoration. They remained fashionable into the 1720s and beyond, and it is no exaggeration to describe them as the quintessential landscape statement of Vanbrugh's age. Minor local squires often had only one avenue, focused on the main façade of the house; the residences of the greatest landowners, in contrast, might sit at the centre of a vast and elaborate web. The popularity of avenues is often explained as a manifestation of 'French influence';[33] it is, perhaps, better understood in terms of the principal interests and aspirations of landowners, and the imperative to express their attainment. For the individual avenue demonstrated complete ownership of the *enclosed* ground over which it passed, while a complex web proclaimed monopoly ownership of all the land in the vicinity of a big house. The main axial avenue served to tie the strict symmetry of the fashionable compact mansion to that of the gardens and grounds; the wider mesh expressed power and control – naked and unashamed – over the surrounding landscape (fig. 10).

Great magnates, like the Devonshires at Chatsworth or the Howards at Castle Howard, planted avenues as they did woods – on a large scale. Local squires did so more modestly. These were matters of degree, necessary variations – the consequence of differences in wealth and in the extent of ownership – on the same shared aesthetic theme. But there were some important distinctions between the grounds of the great landowners and those of the local gentry that are not so easily explained, and that became more marked in the years around 1700. These were related to differences in lifestyle, which were, it appears, growing more acute in this period. Great landowners were involved in national political life, sharply aware of their rank and status; they had little direct involvement in the management of their estates, and had less and less in common with the surrounding local communities. The gentry, in contrast, were – by inclination as much as by necessity – more likely to be actively involved in agriculture and domestic production. Their homes were generally associated with a wide range of productive facilities and enclosures, often not very clearly segregated from the 'ornamental' areas (fig. 11). Gardens, kitchen-gardens, orchards, nut grounds, fishponds, dovecotes, stable-yards, farmyards, barns and areas for recreation (especially bowling-greens) all jostled for space around the walls of the house. Within each of these areas, moreover, 'beauty' and 'utility' might, to varying extents, be combined. Fruit trees were espaliered along the walls of all enclosed gardens, even those containing ornamental parterres; sometimes, as at Stow Bardolph in Norfolk in 1712, wildernesses might contain apples, pears and other fruits.[34] Contemporary descriptions, perhaps more than plans and illustrations, emphasize this rich mixture of aesthetics, production and recreation. At Croft Hall in Yorkshire, for example, the head gardener was eventually forced to nail up

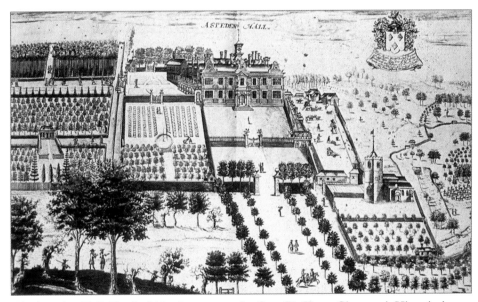

11. Aspenden Hall, Hertfordshire, in an engraving from Sir Henry Chauncey's Historical Antiquities of Hertfordshire, *1700.*

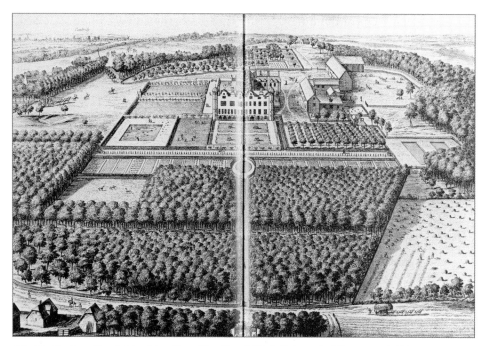

12. Madingley, Cambridgeshire, from Knyff and Kip's Britannia Illustrata, *1707.*

the door leading from the main ornamental gardens to the bowling-green because visitors were in the habit of helping themselves to the gooseberries growing in the borders around the latter (to no avail: the visitors continued to pilfer the fruit, according to the gardener, 'though he looked very narrowly to 'em').[35]

All this was more than simply an expression of practical convenience on a small estate, for a much greater degree of segregation of the 'productive' and the 'aesthetic' could have been attempted, and generally was in the second half of the eighteenth century. The cluster of productive facilities proclaimed that the owner was actively involved in the farming and management of his estate – was at home in his 'country'. It also proclaimed that, in a world still dogged by dearth, he ate more food, and more varied food, than most of his neighbours. Yet this message, though powerful, was a simple one that the local population of tenants and freehold farmers could easily understand. It was an assertion of superiority, but not of exclusivity.

Among the great landowners, in contrast, there was a greater segregation of production and aesthetics. This was not just because of the greater area occupied by the house and domestic complex. Indeed, the degree of separation increased noticeably in the period under discussion. When Kip and Knyff published *Britannia Illustrata*, most of the greatest landowners had, like the Devonshires at Chatsworth, already banished productive facilities so that their houses could sit within landscapes of ostentatious luxury. But there were still some great houses, like Madingley (fig. 12), where barns, farmyards and the rest remained in full view. By the 1720s this had changed. Houses of this social status were seldom, if ever, associated with humdrum aspects of domestic production. Isolated kitchen-gardens were beginning to appear, barns and farmyards were banished, even orchards were placed in increasingly marginal positions. The great gardens illustrated in Colen Campbell's *Vitruvius Britannicus* volume of 1725 display few obvious traces of productive facilities, and the land beyond the gardens is often shown not as productive fields but as open grazing.[36]

In the decades around 1700, great landowners thus rejected some of the traditional symbols of elite production. But at the same time, their landscapes emphasized others. Not only were their demesnes more lavishly planted than those of the gentry; they were also more likely to include a deer park, a luxury beyond the reach of many landowners. There was, moreover, a clear tendency for these to grow in size in the period after 1660; and whereas in the early seventeenth century houses had often been located near the edge of deer parks, they were now often positioned towards the centre – as at Nostell Priory in Yorkshire, where, in the mid-1730s, Sir Rowland Winn and Stephen Switzer intended diverting the Doncaster road in order, as Switzer put it, 'to place ye House in ye Middle of ye Park'.[37] Nor was it just roads that might be moved. It is probable that more villages were destroyed, shifted or truncated to make way for parks and designed landscapes between *c*. 1660 and 1740 than in any previous, or subsequent, period.[38]

Every great landowner aspired to a property free of troublesome neighbours, to an estate that – at least at its most visible and public core – ostentatiously kept the number of inhabitants to a minimum. But only the most wealthy were able to take this desire to its ultimate conclusion – removing the village altogether so that the mansion could stand entirely alone. At this social level, moreover, exclusion and exclusivity took more subtle forms. Increasingly parks, and demesne land more generally, were filled not only with those two ancient symbols of status – timber and deer – but with elaborate garden buildings of no practical purpose and designed in a range of exotic, foreign styles: temples, obelisks, triumphal arches and the like. Their meaning was reserved to those with the correct knowledge, education and 'taste'. Exotic buildings had existed in earlier gardens, but seldom on the scale of the early eighteenth century, and seldom out in the wider landscape of park and demesne.

The landscape created by Vanbrugh and Charles Howard at Castle Howard in the first twenty-five years of the eighteenth century was in many ways new and innovatory. London's proposals for the site were rejected by Carlisle, and as a result the grounds were less axially organized than most designs of the period – i.e., they were not laid out around the main avenues focused on the principal elevations of the house – and they featured elements, such as the great terrace, that, while not quite of serpentine form, were nevertheless less rigidly rectilinear, more alert to natural topography than was usual at the time. In these respects the landscape of Castle Howard perhaps pointed the way towards the stylistic developments of the mid-eighteenth century. However, in many ways it echoed themes common in the estates of other great landowners of the day, and needs to be understood in these terms. Thus, in particular, although Ray Wood and some other small areas of woodland already existed when the 3rd Earl inherited in 1692, the woods and plantations were steadily extended thereafter in an orgy of planting, and a network of avenues was established in the parkland to the west and south of the house. The inscription added to Vanbrugh's obelisk in 1731 typically associated landownership, confidence in family succession, and planting:

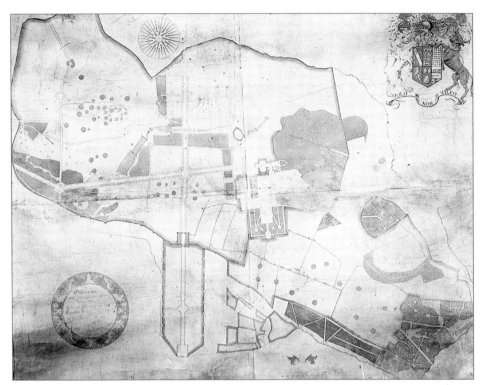

13. Castle Howard, Yorkshire, an estate map of 1727. To the east of the house is Ray Wood; Vanbrugh's Temple of the Four Winds stands just beyond the Wood's most southern point.

IF TO PERFECTION THESE PLANTATIONS RISE
IF THEY AGREEABLY MY HEIRS SURPRISE
THIS FAITHFUL PILLAR WILL THEIR AGE DECLARE
AS LONG AS TIME THESE CHARACTERS SHALL SPARE . . .

The plantations were, in effect, stored capital, money in the bank for future generations. The inscription concludes with the boast that, together with building the new house, Carlisle had 'likewise made the plantations in this park and all the out-works, monuments and other plantations'. In line with many other great seats at the time, these 'monuments' included buildings in a range of eclectic styles – Gothic, Renaissance, Romano-Egyptian – as well as structures whose form was loosely derived from that of contemporary military fortifications. These essentially alien constructions would have contrasted sharply with the vernacular architecture of the farms and cottages of the village of Henderskelfe had this been suffered to survive. It was not: Carlisle demolished it, cleared its site, and the village street – its line modified slightly – became the great terrace, leading from the house to the Temple of the Four Winds.

Although the deer park itself was not extended to encircle the house on all sides, the areas to the south and east comprised ornamental farmland with ornamental buildings and much aesthetic planting (fig. 13). The views in this area, especially that from the Temple of the Four Winds, would have been over enclosed, improved farmland. But this working landscape – as at other comparable sites in this period – was observed from the Temple, or across the bastioned haha, as a picture at one remove from the habitation of gentility. Fields and farming – if carried out in an appropriately enclosed and improved landscape – might make a suitable object for distant contemplation. But there was no attempt to emphasize the practical involvement of the landowner in agrarian production. No barns, stalls or rick-yards complemented the elegant façade of Castle Howard. In all these ways, a landscape of aristocratic taste had come to dominate Henderskelfe and its surroundings.

The great aristocratic landscapes of the late seventeenth and early eighteenth centuries – whether Baroque extravaganzas in the Chatsworth fashion, or more innovatory formal and symbolic designs like Castle Howard – thus embodied contemporary ideals of elite estate management. They also reflected the key social and economic developments of the period. Great magnates prospered, while the decline of the small landowner both encouraged and allowed the spatial distancing of the great landowners from the surrounding communities, as landscapes of 'taste' were wrapped around their houses, excluding everyone else in ways both obvious and subtle. These superior landscapes emphasized certain key forms of production traditionally associated with landowners (deer, timber, wood, enclosed farmland), but also added new features – alien architectural intrusions whose full significance could only be appreciated by those with the correct education and knowledge, although their sheer scale, and that of the landscapes in which they were set, were clearly intended to overawe in more basic ways. The gentry, by contrast, continued for the most part to surround their homes not only with ornamental gardens but also with those features (orchards, fishponds, dovecotes, barns stuffed with wheat) that proclaimed their superiority and prestige in an accessible way to those who dwelt in their more local worlds.

This dichotomy is drawn too sharply, of course; and I will not further over-simplify by identifying the extremes on this spectrum with those problematic terms Whig and Tory – shifting and dangerous labels. Landscapes of ostentatious grandeur in whatever style could be, and were, laid out around the homes of great men of all political persuasions, although their particular choices of buildings or garden figures might proclaim particular affiliations. Yet many of the individuals who began to challenge the landscapes of elite exclusivity in the first three decades of the eighteenth century did have broadly 'Tory' sympathies: Alexander Pope, with his parody of 'Timon's Villa';[39] Lord Bolingbroke, who – on his return from exile in 1725 – laid out an ostentatious little landscape at Dawley in Middlesex, with a mesh of avenues running through farmland; or Lord Bathurst, who created something similar at Richings, ten miles away, which included a wilderness containing areas 'for sowing of corn, Turnips etc and for feeding cattle'.[40] Nevertheless, it was Joseph Addison, a man with rather different political affiliations, who famously urged that whole estates might be thrown into 'a kind of garden, by frequent plantations, that may turn as much to the Profit as the Pleasure of the Owner'.[41] Clearly, in the early eighteenth century there was growing opposition to existing modes of elite garden design that to some extent transcended conventional political categories.

These individuals have often been seen as early advocates of more 'natural' styles of garden design, but this is to oversimplify, and to misunderstand. In reality, they were making a plea for a less exclusive, less ostentatious and more *practical* form of garden and landscape design, one which both great landowners, and local gentry, could practise: a form of large-scale aesthetic landscaping that was more fully integrated with agricultural production than those currently undertaken at the highest and most fashionable social levels. This is, in particular, the context within which we should understand the writings of Stephen Switzer, whose *Nobleman, Gentleman and Gardener's Recreation* appeared in 1715, later becoming the first volume in his *Ichnographia Rustica* of 1718.[42] Switzer, too, is often paraded as one of those familiar stepping-stones on the road to Capability Brown. But his own designs – like that for Caversham in Berkshire of 1718 (fig. 14) – were highly geometric in character.[43] More importantly, even a cursory reading of *Ichnographia* makes it clear that it was not serpentine lines or 'nature' that Switzer wanted, but 'magnificent gardens, statues, waterworks'.[44] His geometric designs were firmly in the French tradition (which he clearly admired). The majority of English landowners – the local gentry – could not afford great gardens in the Baroque manner. But they could, by combining beauty and utility, ornament and production, lay their whole estates out as designed landscapes; this was 'extensive gardening', to use Switzer's phrase. The main lines of an 'inner garden' – designed in the increasingly simplified geometric form of the 1710s – should (Switzer urged) be extended out as rides or avenues through working farmland interspersed with plantations 'as far as Liberty of Planting will allow', so that the whole 'Would appear as a part, and add to the Beauty and Magnificence of the Gardens in the View, tho not in the expense of keeping' (fig. 15).[45] Interestingly, the second edition of Switzer's *Ichnographia* (1741–2) included a description of Richings and Dawley, which are described as *fermes ornées*.

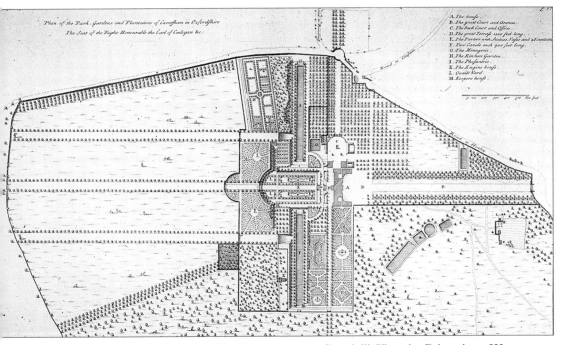

14. *Switzer's design for Caversham, Berkshire, as shown in Campbell's* Vitruvius Britannicus, *III, 1725. The contract for this work was made in 1718, the year* Ichnographia Rustica *was published.*

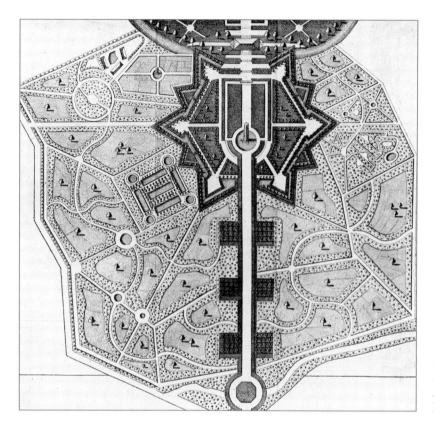

15. The idealized landscape of Paston Manor, from Switzer's Ichnographia Rustica, *1718.*

The implication of Switzer's argument is clearly that a more socially unified form of landscape design should be developed. If his advice were to be followed, great landowners would have less exclusive landscapes, be less divorced from agricultural production; while local gentry, by planting their estates more lavishly, would narrow the gap in the other direction. Looking at the way in which landscape design actually developed though the 1720s, '30s and '40s, it is clear that the social realities expressed by the dichotomy in landscape design were not to be easily overcome. Only in the second half of the eighteenth century did a style emerge capable of unifying the various levels of landed society, with the landscape parks of Lancelot 'Capability' Brown, Nathaniel Richmond and the rest. These landscapes, however, achieved this aim by emphatically abjuring the kind of overtly productive landscape beloved of Switzer. But that is another story that takes us into a very different world, a long way from Vanbrugh and his age.[46] I do not mean to suggest that political and economic circumstances, or attitudes to production and estate management, were the only – or even the major – influences on the development of landscape design in the late seventeenth and early eighteenth centuries. But such things did unquestionably have an influence. As in all periods, the essential qualities of a garden cannot be understood without considering what was happening in the wider world – the real world – beyond the garden wall, or across the bastioned haha.

THREE

The Formal Garden

David Jacques

Formal gardens of the late seventeenth and early eighteenth centuries in England have not received their due. Too often they have been viewed collectively as a somewhat inert genre, worth mentioning only in order to provide a foil to the triumph of the landscape garden of the 1730s. But during the reigns of William III, Anne and George I, they went through a series of radical and well-defined transformations, and – notably in the decade 1710–20, the phase under consideration in this essay – developed in ways that were wholly distinct from contemporary continental garden-making, France's in particular.[1] French design had come to dominate western Europe by the 1680s; thus, when recording the death of André Le Nôtre in 1700, the Duc de Saint-Simon was able to add that 'the fine gardens that adorn all France' made by that celebrated master 'have so lowered the reputation of Italian gardens (which are really nothing by comparison) that the most famous landscape architects of Italy now come to France to study and admire'.[2] English estate owners and their gardeners went to France too. As early as 1680, gardens in England were beginning to display *plates-bandes*, carved figures, *jets d'eaux*, geometric pools and canals, and many other features made familiar by the French. The accession in 1689 of William of Orange, a keen exponent of the French style, strengthened the trend.

Hostilities during the War of the Spanish Succession (1702–13) do not seem to have diminished respect for the French approach. In England there was continuing curiosity concerning recent developments abroad, fuelled by hints, such as Joseph Addison's in 1712, that French, as well as Italian, gardens 'represent every where an artificial Rudeness, much more charming than the Neatness and Elegancy which we meet with in those of our own Country'.[3] Three years later Stephen Switzer wrote of 'that magnificence that is easily discoverable from the *French* Designs', and complained that 'the Misfortune that most of my Profession are under, in not having been abroad, is certainly great'.[4] He even adopted a few quasi-French terms, some ungrammatical, such as *La Grand Manier*, and, *c.* 1730, *anfilade* and *ferme ornée*.[5] And in the very year the war ended, one of the Duke of Marlborough's commanders, Lord Orkney, requested designs from Claude Desgots, Louis XIV's chief gardener, for a parterre for Cliveden, Buckinghamshire.[6]

Because the Succession War so swiftly followed King William's War (1689–97), England's cultural contacts with France were more or less severed for a quarter-century, save for a five-year interlude. Though the prevalent style in English

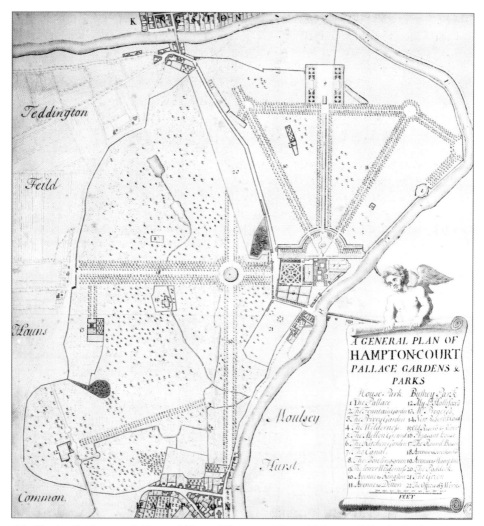

16. *Charles Bridgeman*, A General Plan of Hampton Court Palace and Bushy Park, *c. 1712, showing how both parks were embellished with avenues intersecting at circles.*

gardens in the first decade of the eighteenth century remained the frenchified William III style, English gardenists increasingly established their own insular variants, not least with regard to avenues, forecourts, garden walls, parterres and wildernesses.

The wider and longer avenues that were established aggrandized the approach through the grounds to the house. Reflecting basins, set within circles of trees, were introduced to the grandest avenues at about the two-thirds point; George London was responsible for several, including the one made *c.* 1700 for the Chestnut Avenue in Bushy Park, Middlesex (fig. 16). If the wind was negligible, reflections from these basins provided an inverted view of the destination. The Williamite fashion for 'carved' ironwork gates began to subside at exactly the same moment, partly as a result of the demise of the broad walk in favour of the carriage sweep.[7] Hawksmoor at Easton Neston, Northamptonshire, and he and Vanbrugh at Castle Howard and Blenheim (fig. 17), preferred their forecourts to be parades around which offices, stables and quasi-military structures could be arranged.

New gardens were still generally walled about, and grates (or *grilles*) were frequently built into them to allow 'vistos'. Even so, experiments to improve the range and variety of prospects continued. *Grilles*, if the landowner could afford the undertaking, were extended as iron fences ('palisades'), on occasion along the whole side of a garden.[8] A new form of enclosure, consisting of military-style bastion walls, was introduced by Vanbrugh in 1705 to encase the hexagonal wilderness at Blenheim, which he repeated for Ray Wood at Castle Howard.

Within the parterre, after 1710 there were no more attempts at *broderie*, but *parterres à l'angloise* (i.e., grass plats with flower borders) continued. Pyramid and round-headed evergreens were never more popular, and these expensive items could be seen at several places. Scrollwork borders, which became prominent after

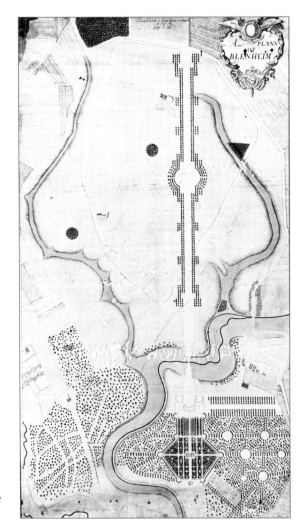

17. *Charles Bridgeman,* A Plan of Blenheim, *1709. A scrollwork parterre positioned next to the garden front led into a huge hexagonal wilderness within bastioned walls. The rectangular kitchen-garden lies to the south-east of the hexagon.*

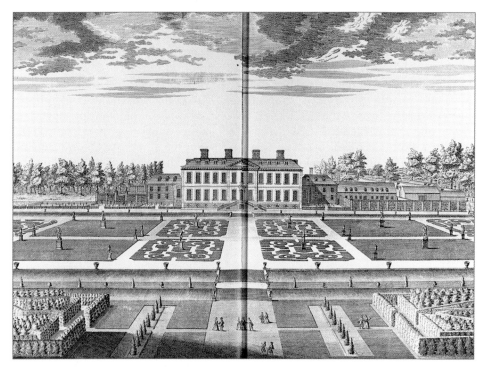

18. 'The East Prospect and Garden Front of Kiveton House', c. 1710, an engraving from Badeslade and Rocque's Vitruvius Britannicus, *IV, 1739. This huge parterre was partly grass plats and partly cutwork.*

the Privy Garden at Hampton Court Palace was embellished with them in 1701, were reproduced in the next decade. In contrast, Queen Anne herself transformed the Fountain Garden parterre at Hampton Court from *broderie* and intricate borders to simple but noble grass plats, and there had always been a demand by owners (perhaps of a Puritanical bent) for grass plats without any decorative borders, even in the height of fashion for such borders in the 1690s. Cutwork in grass continued in favour, as at Kiveton (fig. 18). Possibly also in imitation of Hampton Court, lead, stone and marble urns were introduced at many gardens as an alternative to cast and carved gods and goddesses. All kinds of terrace were still made, though breast walls were discontinued in favour of *glacis* slopes.[9] But interest in tunnel arbours, like the one constructed at Hampton Court in 1691, was not sustained.

Wildernesses with gravel paths continued to be planted out in geometric patterns after 1700, but 'forest gardens' (as we may term them), many associated with George London, were slowly beginning to make their appearance.[10] These were more extensive and less finished than the traditional wilderness; for example, carpet (i.e., grass) walks were acceptable instead of gravel. The gardens at Boughton, Northamptonshire, were extended in the early 1710s by means of several curious wilderness designs with carpet walks between hedges. Some forest gardens, like those at Wanstead, Essex, and at Waldershare (fig. 19), were huge in scale, dominating the estates. Asymmetry was an acceptable solution for an irregular site: in Surrey at Chargate (known as 'Claremont' after October 1714), Vanbrugh's asymmetric layout of *c.* 1711 was cut from woodland to suit the precipitate topography (fig. 20);[11] the wilderness at Knole in Kent was refurbished as an irregular layout *c.* 1712 (a design perhaps by Thomas Acres), as the plate in Dr John Harris's *History of Kent* (1719) shows. Other owners converted coppice or coppice-with-standard woodland (which had a diminishing value, thanks to the fact that the use of coal was spreading steadily through the country), with the intent of keeping older trees. Thus, at Castle Howard, the irregular layout of Ray Wood (*c.* 1705–10) was decided on in order to retain the large beech trees, a solution that worked too for Thomas Coke at Melbourne Hall, Derbyshire, and for the Earl of Portland at Bulstrode Park, Buckinghamshire.[12]

The rupture with France during the Succession War had another, less obvious by-product. This was the emergence, sometimes re-emergence, of a number of themes in garden-related literature that in retrospect had peculiarly English interpretations. Two of great consequence for garden design were the rhetoric of the 'rural' and the mesmeric influence of Antiquity.

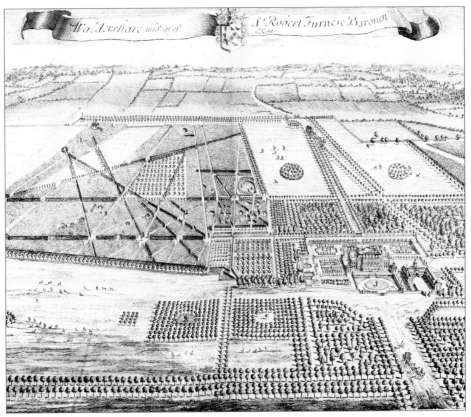

19. *Badeslade and Kip's view of Waldershare, Kent, from Dr John Harris's* A History of Kent, *1719, possibly a late design by George London.*

According to seventeenth-century popular belief grounded in Christian teaching, common nature (i.e., fields, moors, hills and dales, etc.) had degenerated following the Fall and was made further ruinous by the Flood. But the supposition that there existed a higher form of nature – *la belle nature* – was also current. And *la belle nature*, it was argued, might in some sense be realizable: the world of common nature was improvable by the intervention of high art, whether that of the painter, say, or the garden designer. Charles Alphonse du Fresnoy, for example, argued in *De Arte graphica* (1668) that art pleased by imitation of the beautiful ideal in nature. The complementary rôles of art and nature were upheld in science too: Robert Boyle wrote persuasively on common nature and ideal nature (or 'particular' versus 'general').[13] John Evelyn's advice in successive editions of *Sylva* (first published in 1664) on setting out planting, illustrated how 'natural' had become synonymous with 'irregular' and 'rural', and 'artificial' with 'regular' and 'ornamental': 'trees . . . may be sown promiscuously, which is the most natural and Rural; or in straight and even lines, for Hedge-rows, Avenues, and Walks, which is the more Ornamental'.[14]

Towards the end of the seventeenth century, though, confidence in the superiority of artificial beauty was less assured. Newtonian science was providing strong arguments that an ideal nature of sorts did underlie the actual, and the

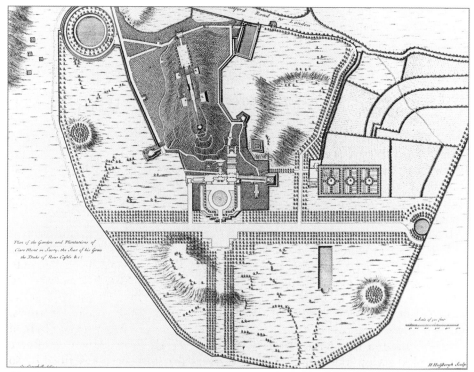

20. *The gardens and plantations at Claremont, Surrey, c. 1717, as shown in Campbell's* Vitruvius Britannicus, III, 1725. *The clumps and peripheral planting in the newly enclosed park gave Claremont a medieval air.*

realization that ideal nature could be approached through the hidden order in common nature encouraged a fresh respect for the latter. Common nature could be beautiful, and be the object of taste. Addison, among others, argued that 'Nature appears in the greatest Perfection' in the country.[15] He and Lord Shaftesbury recovered beauty in the wildness of nature.[16] The implication of this was that landowners should capitalize on the natural scenery within and beyond their estates, for, as Addison pointed out in 1712, 'the Works of *Nature* . . . afford so great an Entertainment to the Mind of the Beholder'.[17] This meant extended layouts with plantations and walks, giving 'an agreeable mixture of Garden and Forest, which represent every where an artificial Rudeness', for in his *Spectator* essay Addison considered 'our *English* Gardens' – neat and elegant though they might be – were 'not so entertaining to the Fancy as those in *France* and *Italy*'. Indeed, Addison criticized 'Our *British* Gardeners', who 'instead of humouring Nature, love to deviate from it as much as possible', and cited as evidence their adherence to clipping trees into unnatural shapes.

Among Addison's supporters was Alexander Pope, who in *The Guardian* the following year ridiculed figurative topiary,[18] and Samuel Molyneux, an admirer of the rustic cascade at Bushy Park's Upper Lodge and the forest garden at New Park near Richmond, Surrey.[19] Addison's most enthusiastic follower, however, was Switzer, first in Switzer's *The Nobleman, Gentleman, and Gardener's Recreation* of 1715.[20] This was a book aimed at estate owners, not town gardeners, and Switzer described 'the general distribution . . . into Rural and Extensive Gardens, Parks, Paddocks, &c.'. No doubt struck by Addison's admiration for France's forest parks, he explained his new system as '*Forest*, or, in a more easie Stile, *Rural Gard'ning*'.[21] For the enlarged edition, published in 1718, Switzer selected the title *Ichnographia Rustica* ('design of the country'). A decade later, a competitive Batty Langley, though clearly an imitator of Switzer, announced that his own *New Principles of Gardening* contained a 'method . . . entirely *New*, as well as most *grand and rural*'.[22] Subtitled 'The laying out and Planting Parterres, Groves, Wildernesses, Labyrinths, Avenues, Parks, &c. After a more Grand and Rural Manner than has been done before', *New Principles* included fourteen plates of 'a rural garden after the new manner' and others laid out in similar style. Meandering walks were referred to as 'Rural walks'.[23] In the same year that Langley's *New Principles* appeared, Robert Castell published his *Villas of the Ancients Delineated*, in which he identified three types of garden design – the 'rough', the 'regular', and '*imitatio ruris*'.[24]

It was a disappointment for garden writers that biblical, Greek and Roman authors wrote of fruits and vegetables rather than design when they touched on gardens;[25] hence John James complained that 'the Reading of whom, tho' good in itself, has, however, been of no great Service to me in this Case'[26] when working on his translation of Dézallier. Even so, appreciative, if oblique, remarks on the countryside and on gardens could be gleaned from some classical authors. Addison, for example, had reread Virgil and Horace before departing for Italy in 1702.[27] He found his greatest pleasure there on a journey made between Rome and Naples, seeing 'the fields, towns and rivers that have been described by so many classic authors'. His ally Pope agreed that unadorned nature provided a more exalted kind of pleasure than the nicer scenes of art. Further: 'This was the Taste of the Ancients in their Gardens, as we may discover from the Descriptions

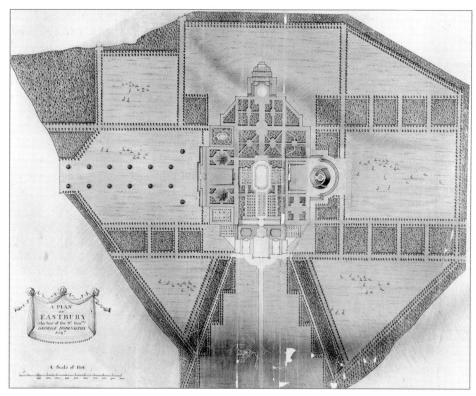

21. Eastbury in Dorset, a huge forest garden in a plan attributed to Charles Bridgeman, c. 1718.

. . . extant of them.'[28] Switzer speculated that 'the Romans had doubtless the same extensive kind of Gardens'[29] as did those owners of the fashionable forest gardens of Cassiobury in Hertfordshire, New Park and Castle Howard. Even Vanbrugh's fortified garden at Blenheim was, Switzer supposed, 'after the ancient *Roman* Manner' (fig. 17).[30] And it was Castell's conclusions that spurred Switzer to assert that rural gardening 'was the Method used by the Romans of old, [as] the curious Drafts and Accounts of the Ancient Villa's . . . fully evince'.[31] Furthermore: 'the Roman genius, which was once the Admiration of the World, is now making great advances in Britain also'.

The Treaty of Utrecht in 1713 that ended hostilities between France and 'Britain' (as England and Scotland had become with the Union in 1707) aided these 'great advances' by setting off a tremendous burst of financial confidence that lasted into the 1730s. A number of *nouveaux riches* acquired their own new country seats or handsome villa residences. Lauded military commanders, such as Stowe's Sir Richard Temple (Baron Cobham from 1715), came home from the wars with the intention of enhancing their estates (the building boom for country houses peaked in the early 1720s), and war profiteers spent extravagantly too, not least James Brydges, Duke of Chandos, on his palace and grounds at Canons near Edgware. There was also greater cultural confidence. Lord Shaftesbury detected the 'rising Genius of our Nation', and in 1712 had prophesied that when the

Succession War ended, '*united* Britain' would be 'the principal Seat of Arts'.[32] He felt that an improved 'national Taste' was forming because 'almost every-one now becomes concern'd, and interests himself' in both public and major private projects. He was at pains to show that, despite France's great achievements under absolutism, the English genius, under a parliamentary system, promised even greater. The potential for England to surpass France was foreseen by gardenists too. John James remarked that

> we may hope to see, ere long, our English Pleasure-Gardens in greater Perfection, than any the most renowned, in France, or Italy, since our Woods and Groves, our Grass and Gravel . . . are allowed to surpass in Verdure and natural Beauty, whatever is to be found in those Countries.[33]

Actually, this claim for the superiority of English grass was not new, or even English. However, James's point emboldened Switzer to hope that 'we . . . may excel the so-much-boasted Gardens of France, and . . . make that great Nation give way to superior Beauties'.[34]

If Addison's article in *The Spectator* in 1712 was a manifesto for a fresh approach to garden style based on the ideology of the 'rural', the taste of the Ancients, and of English genius in the arts, *The Nobleman, Gentleman, and Gardener's Recreation* was Switzer's attempt to give it more concrete application. Switzer and Charles Bridgeman represented a new generation of garden designers in the ascendant following London's death in 1714. They sought to re-evaluate old forms and adopt new ones, and when Dézallier's *La Théorie et la pratique du jardinage* of 1709 was translated by James as *The Theory and Practice of Gardening* (1712), a new range of forms became widely available in England.

Addison's ideas on extensiveness were reflected by the wholesale removal of walls, a process that started in the late 1710s.[35] Iron fences provided one alternative, but they were expensive, and not entirely satisfactory when it came to opening up the view. They declined at country houses after the most magnificent example – at Canons – was set up in 1714,[36] though they remained appropriate in towns. Often much could be achieved by removing internal walls. At Thoresby, Nottinghamshire, in the mid-1710s, it was proposed that the gardens and forecourt east of the house be suppressed.[37] The north gardens at Chiswick villa were opened up *c.* 1718.[38] But the uncertainty one could suffer in this phase of changing fashions regarding walled or unwalled gardens is wonderfully revealed in John Bromley's will of 1718, in which Bromley specified that his gardens at Horseheath Hall in Cambridgeshire had to 'be finished according to plan, unless they would be better contrived with garden walls, iron gates and all other things necessary'.[39]

Vanbrugh continued in the 1710s to experiment with fortified walls, for example along the northerly edges of the wooded garden at Claremont (fig. 20), and works of this kind were imitated in Buckinghamshire at Hall Barn and Hartwell House.[40] In the late 1710s more modest walled fosses without raised terraces or bastions, later referred to as hahas, were tried at Chiswick by Burlington, at Houghton, Norfolk, by Bridgeman, and at Eastbury by Vanbrugh and Bridgeman (fig. 21).[41] And with increasingly lengthy fosses being dug, often very large areas were absorbed within gardens. Some, for example Boughton's and

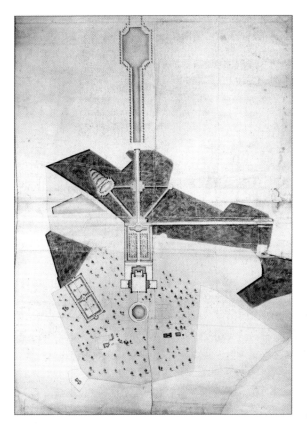

22. A plan of Sacombe,
Hertfordshire, attributed to
Charles Bridgeman, c. 1715,
showing what was probably an
early garden by Bridgeman and
Vanbrugh's detached kitchen-
garden at lower left.

one at Canons, were over 100 acres in size. Even Switzer suspected that the
explosion in scale had got a little out of hand as a result of Bridgeman's influence:
'This aiming at an incomprehensible Vastness, and attempting at Things beyond
the reach of Nature, is in great measure owing to a late eminent Designer in
Gardening, whose Fancy could not be bounded . . .'.[42]

One of the consequences of the fashion for extent and prospect gaining force in
the 1710s was that the siting of walled kitchen- and fruit-gardens became less and
less acceptable close to the house, as Switzer argued:

> the Method that has been us'd some Years since, in walling the Parterre with an
> high Wall, what could be more ridiculous, or expensive? It may be alledg'd,
> these Walls are for Fruit; but these Fruit-Gardens ought to be detach'd from
> the House, separate and private.[43]

This, indeed, had already begun to happen. At Blenheim in 1705 the kitchen-
garden was positioned at a skew to the fortified wilderness. Vanbrugh afterwards
sited his awesomely walled kitchen-gardens at Claremont and Sacombe (fig. 22),
both c. 1715, away from the principal gardens and vistas, and they were dealt with
similarly at Bramham in Yorkshire and, c. 1710, by Thomas Archer at Heythrop,
Oxfordshire.[44] From c. 1715, most new kitchen-gardens were detached from the

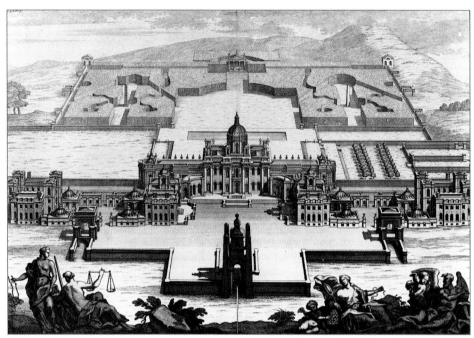

23. *A bird's-eye view of c. 1715 that includes the planned south gardens for Castle Howard, Yorkshire, from Campbell's* Vitruvius Britannicus, *III, 1725.*

garden enclosure. Orchards, too, disappeared from the vicinity of the house, partly because of the new insistence on prospect, and partly because dwarf fruit-trees were replaced by espaliered fruits within kitchen-gardens. As Philip Miller recalled in the 1730s, dwarf fruit-trees 'were formerly in much greater Request than they are at present; . . . and since the introducing of Espaliers into the English Gardens, Dwarf-Trees have been destroy'd in most good Gardens'.[45]

As for parterres, the principle of Antique noble simplicity argued for the 'plain' parterre, with minimal gravel and the demise of ornamentation, such as *jets d'eaux*, pyramid or shaped evergreens, borders and scrollwork. In effect, this meant a return to the old grass plats, though with larger areas of grass and less gravel. Indeed, some owners with old *parterres à l'angloise* simplified them to achieve the effect. Switzer wrote of, and illustrated, his preference for the plain parterre in *Ichnographia Rustica*. Bridgeman did not immediately cast aside his inheritance from George London, for he made scrollwork parterres and planted many pyramid yews in the 1710s. However, the advance of the fashion for the plain parterre was inexorable. The one for Castle Howard may have remained unmade for as long as its intended position was a building site (fig. 23), but there is no evidence that borders, figures or *jets d'eaux* were ever planned for it, and it seems from the outset to have been conceived as plain grass. Soon, other examples were set out below garden fronts, as at Compton Verney (Warwickshire), Worksop Priory (Nottinghamshire), Shotover (Oxfordshire) and Stowe,[46] and then at most new gardens from 1717 onwards.

Bodies of water became extremely common in the 1710s. The first example of a basin significantly larger than was needed for a fountain had been constructed at

Boughton *c*. 1694.[47] Worthy successors were the circular basin at Claremont *c*. 1715 (fig. 20),[48] and the octagon pool with *giulio* at Stowe, *c*. 1719. Basins could also be attached to axial canals, as they were at Wanstead, *c*. 1701,[49] and Worksop Priory, *c*. 1715, and then by Bridgeman in several of his designs until the mid-1720s. But water features took many forms, and a great variety of shapes gradually filled the halls of forest gardens.

Axial canals were an acceptable embellishment of plain parterres, as at Shotover and Hurstbourne Priors, Hampshire (fig. 24). A variant on the axial canal theme, where the fall of water could be managed, was to extend it with a staircase of shallow cascades. From below, the cumulative effect was of a continuous cascade, a 'rural' feature not out of place in view from a plain parterre. Examples include the cascades at Ebberston Hall, North Yorkshire, of *c*. 1718,[50] and those made at Shireoaks, Nottinghamshire, soon after (see pp. 165–6). While some cascades might be of regular architectural form, they could also thus be viewed as 'rural'. One was made at the end of the canal at Lord Lymington's Hurstbourne Priors. Switzer observed that Lymington 'seems to take the Model of one he has' there from a cascade at the Villa Aldobrandini, Frascati,[51] and he admired the original's side arches and 'Rurality of Trees . . . on each Side of the Cascade', reckoning the ensemble to be 'one of the best Copies of Nature imaginable'. This Aldobrandini cascade may, in fact, have been the principal model for William Kent's rustic cascades at Chiswick, Rousham in Oxfordshire, and elsewhere. Dézallier mentioned the '*Rustick Order* of a Grot or Cascade', and also that high hedges pierced through with arches composed 'a kind of Order of Rural Architecture'.[52] 'Rural architecture' meant arcades in clipped yew. Dézallier's plates, copied for James's edition, included a 'cloister gallery' (his plate 9C), which sparked a short-lived fashion for topiary arcades enclosing

24. John Griffier II, Hurstbourne Priors: A View of the Canal and Cascade from the House, *1748, showing the distant cascade modelled on those at the Villa Aldobrandini,*

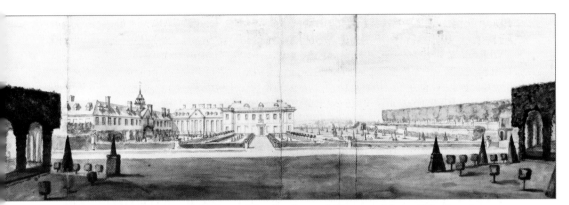

25. *Peter Tillemans (attrib.)*, A View of the Garden and House at Upper Winchendon, Buckinghamshire, *late 1720s. The Marquess of Wharton's parterres were surrounded by arcades after Dézallier d'Argenville's designs.*

parterres in England. Switzer saw the early example at Winchendon (fig. 25), and it had contemporaries at Forde Abbey in Dorset and Stowe.[53] Over a dozen other examples followed.

The traditional geometric wilderness with gravel paths and hedges remained in vogue until *c*. 1730, although its popularity was fading and there was an increasing preference for asymmetry. Meanwhile the looser form, the forest garden, developed tremendously, both in number and in size. In the 1710s it still generally had gravelled principal walks flanked by hedges. The minor paths were often unhedged carpet walks, however, and the overall arrangement was increasingly complex and asymmetric: walks, cabinets, halls, water, groves, temples and earthworks jostled for position within enlarged perimeters generally set by field or property boundaries. Horace Walpole recollected that Bridgeman had 'disdained to make every division tally to its opposite, and though he still adhered much to strait walks with high clipped hedges, they were only his great lines; the rest he diversified by wilderness, and with loose groves of oak, though still within surrounding hedges'.[54]

The attention to detail and complexity formerly lavished on the parterre was now transferred to the forest garden. The interior arrangement of forest gardens was an amalgam of several forms. The traditional vocabulary of straight gravel walks in crosses and *pattes d'oie*, hedgework and *cabinets* in *bosquets*, and the very recent innovation of meandering walks, were retained among them. *Patte d'oie* arrangements were set out at Sacombe, Chiswick and Hartwell, and became a frequent element from the late 1710s. The more private *cabinets* could be entered by just one walk, as at Belton where a bewildering number of tiny ones were designed into the wildernesses of *c*. 1713 (fig. 26). More often, though, they formed nodes at the junction of two or more walks. They were generally circular, and occasionally embellished with *jets d'eaux*.

These *cabinets* could also be strung along winding walks. These were occasionally found prior to 1710 in France,[55] and serpentine walks were threaded through the perimeter planting of the vast woodwork at Blenheim, set out *c*. 1709, presumably to confuse its bounds (fig. 17). The association between such meanders and a 'rural' feel was obvious. Langley was later to recommend them as 'not a small help to invention in designing gardening after that rural manner'. His plates show winding walks that could hardly be described as 'rural', but they symbolized the idea of it. The Chiswick meanders of c. 1720 (illustrated in Rocque's plan of 1736) were so elaborate that the adjective 'intestinal' can be applied; perhaps they were the model for Langley's. There also seemed to be sanction from the Ancients for meandering walks: Castell reckoned that 'the Manner of [their] more regular Gardens' is revealed 'by the Care used in regulating the turning and winding Walks'.[56]

Switzer admired the way that existing openings within Castle Howard's Ray Wood were chosen where possible as *cabinets*, and meanders had been managed so as to avoid the trees.[57] In describing a plate in *Ichnographia Rustica* (1718), unfortunately missing from the publication, he noted how the open circle at the summit of Ray Wood would have been the obvious centre for a formal design, and that 'Mr London design'd a Star' for the wood. However its 'Distribution and Figure . . . is by no means Regular' because 'his Lordship . . . has given it that Labyrinth diverting Model we now see it'.[58] The Earl of Carlisle's response had been, in Switzer's words: 'by no means cut it out into a Star, or any Mathematical Figure; but follow Nature, and where-ever we find natural Openings and Glades, there, to make our Lawns and Walks, be they either strait, or Serpentine, still humouring, and not straining, the Place by Art'.[59] A visitor in 1712 or thereabouts

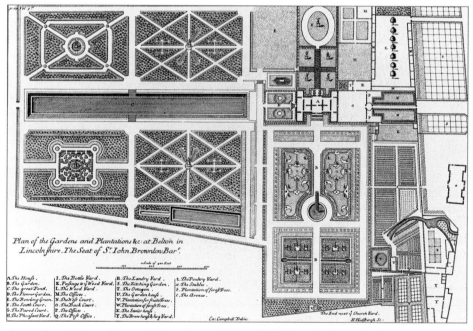

26. A plan of the gardens and plantations at Belton Hall, Lincolnshire, c. 1717, from Campbell's Vitruvius Britannicus, III, 1725, in part a traditional layout with gravel walks, high hedges and cabinets, but incorporating a flower-garden in a 'hall' after d'Argenville.

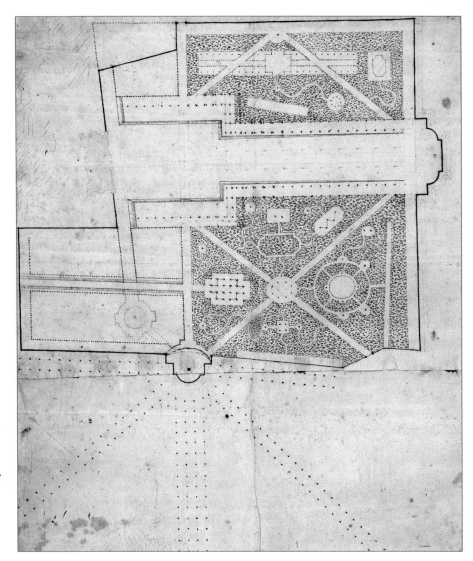

*27. Charles
Bridgeman's*
Proposal for the
Gardens at
Houghton,
*Norfolk, c. 1717,
shows how he
sought to introduce
complexity to the
wilderness by
means of
meandering paths
and 'halls'.*

confirmed that several 'winding mazes' linked a number of circular or square openings irregularly disposed about the Wood.[60] For Bramham, not far from Castle Howard, freeform paths are shown on a pre-1713 estate survey. Bridgeman was using them by 1717 at Houghton (fig. 27). At Hall Barn, Lord Percival observed of the reforming of the coppice in the late 1710s that 'the narrow winding walks and paths cut in it are innumerable'.[61]

Dézallier's *La Théorie et la pratique du jardinage* of 1709 provided James for his English-language edition with twelve elaborate designs for *cabinets* that offered variety in size and form to the openings within forest gardens (fig. 28).[62] Switzer considered the book 'the best that has appeared in this or any other Language, and seems to be the best-laid Design, and carried on with the most Judgement'.[63] He commented enviously that the originator of 'Mr. *James's* Translation . . . has

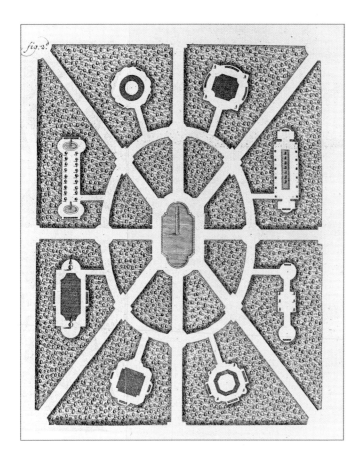

28. 'A Great Wood of
Forrest trees Cut into
Single Star with
Cabinets', from James's
The Theory and
Practice of Gardening,
1712, a pattern-book for
owners of forest gardens.

had the most magnificent Gardens in all France to view, and he has certainly
chose the very Marrow and Beauty of all those excellent Designs'.[64] Switzer
discovered that many suitable designs for *bosquets* 'may be collected out of
Mr. *James*'s Book'.[65] And several owners did just that. The plate (6B) of a *parterre
de pièces coupées pour des fleurs* was copied *c.* 1713 for a flower garden in a 'hall' (a
large opening) in the wilderness at Belton (fig. 29). The figure in another plate
(8C) showing a 'hall' was reproduced at Southill, Bedfordshire, *c.* 1720.[66] The
plate (10C) of a spiral labyrinth was copied at Cholmondeley, Cheshire, and at
Wentworth Woodhouse in Yorkshire.[67]

Nevertheless, admiration did not prevent Switzer from attempting to upstage
Dézallier. He took the plan for a quincunx and bettered it with his own quincunx
formation.[68] His own hall of horse-chestnuts appears to have been an elaborated
version of one in Dézallier.[69] Bridgeman, too, was clearly working to expand his
range of designs of this sort. From *c.* 1715, those for Eastbury, Stowe, Houghton,
Rousham and Sacombe incorporated canted, niched and compound squares,
rectangles, circles and other shapes along the meandering walks.[70]

Burlington, meanwhile, introduced elements into his Chiswick garden that he
had probably seen in Rome, no doubt considering them Antique in spirit. By the
late 1710s these included, besides meanders, the use of buildings to terminate
vistas and a high-stemmed grove by the house,[71] and by 1720 Bridgeman was

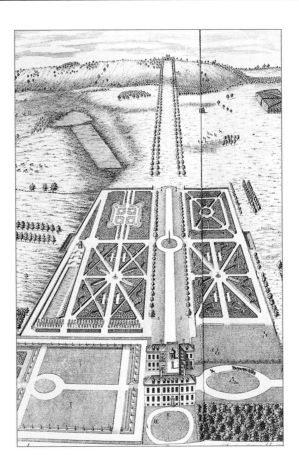

29. Belton in Lincolnshire, c. 1725, from Badeslade and Rocque's Vitruvius Britannicus, *IV, 1739, showing Lord Brownlow's fashionable improvements to his wilderness: meandering paths, an obelisk, hahas and a small amphitheatre.*

filling some of his own halls with grovework. Other Antique features introduced in the period 1700–1720 were garden pavilions in temple form, i.e., with columns and porticoes, and obelisks. The amphitheatre was also understood as Antique. Meanwhile, if sculptured figures were banished from the plain parterre, they were often found a niche in a wilderness.

Although great terraces, side terraces and *glacis* slopes of all kinds were now out of favour, as were terraced orangery gardens, the complex earthworks called 'amphitheatres' that were in vogue from the late 1710s had evolved from terraced orangery gardens. The term had new meaning in gardens after Dézallier described how a hillside could be contrived into 'Landing-Places, or Rests, at several Heights, and easy Ascents and Flights of Steps for Communication . . . called Amphitheatres'.[72] It came to embrace all complex earthworks, not just concave ones. Bridgeman was a prolific designer, generally placing his amphitheatres within halls of forest gardens, from his works at Sacombe (fig. 22), Stowe, Eastbury and Rousham onwards.

Emparkment had continued throughout the seventeenth century and into the 1710s. However, in that decade their planting became not simply grandiose avenues, such as at Hampton Court, but an attempt to suggest the impression of older parkland through replicating the sort of planting found there. A 'clump', otherwise a 'plump', is an old English word for an unordered cluster or tuft of objects. A number of tree clumps, in this pure sense, can be seen in the Knyff and Kip view of the ancient park at Stansted in Sussex. The roundels, seemingly randomly placed, in the park at Blenheim in the 1700s are marked as 'Nurseries for trees' on a map of *c*. 1710.[73] Other clumps planted about this time included the Earl of Portland's 'Star Clump' on a knoll in Moat Park at Windsor.[74] Symmetrically placed circular clumps were also planted on the rising hill at Waldershare *c*. 1710, as Harris's *History of Kent* reveals (fig. 19). Within a few years several other places had them. Presumably clumps were hedged or palisaded around – screens that were intended to be removed, or at least thinned, over time. The purpose of these clumps was probably more scenic than silvicultural, though. Frequently they were found on knolls, emphasizing the form of the ground, and Switzer directed that 'Clumps of Trees' should be placed on 'Eminences'.[75]

Peripheral planting was often required too. Back in 1676, Cassiobury's garden-master, Moses Cook, had advised that a 'single Rowe, to bound a Lawn round . . . would be mighty obliging to the Noblest Sense'.[76] Actual examples were few until the late 1710s, when, for example, some were established at Claremont (fig. 20). A new form of peripheral planting, the belt, appeared at Houghton *c*. 1717 and at Eastbury *c*. 1718 (fig. 21). Ridings, as the name implies, were for racing along, either on horseback or in a calash. For example, a 'new riding' had been set out at Windsor in 1703 to cross the park that Queen Anne, aboard her chaise, hunted in.[77] Cirencester Park's vast plantations were later intersected by the 'Seven Rides' and the 'Ten Rides'.[78] When the belts at Houghton were set out *c*. 1717, broad tracks down their centres created a forest ride in miniature.

By 1720, then, after a decade of experiment and change, English garden style had diverged quite unpredictably from the international style headed by the French. The years of isolation brought about by two long wars had squeezed the English into experimentation, and then the remarkable concatenation of Addison's *Spectator* article on rural gardening in 1712, the translation into English that same year of Dézallier's book, the promotion of a fresh ideology of artistic superiority, and a construction boom from 1713, all encouraged English gardenists to find their own course. And a correct reading of the transformation that really occurred between *c*. 1710 and *c*. 1720 resolves today's paradoxical, and wholly erroneous, interpretation of those times – i.e., that the seminal literature by Addison, Switzer and others was published twenty years before the advent of the landscape garden, and was therefore at odds with its own times. As this essay makes clear, it was not.

FOUR

Fortified Gardens

Robert Williams

Why fortify a garden? When, in 1728, Sir Matthew Decker visited Sacombe Park, Hertfordshire (fig. 22), he was amazed to find that the 3-acre kitchen-garden designed by Vanbrugh *c*. 1715 boasted walls and towers 'so strongly built' that it was 'as if they were to defend a City'.[1] Had Decker gone instead to Claremont, Surrey, he would have discovered that its 7-acre version by Vanbrugh, also *c*. 1715 (fig. 20), 'with its entrance arch between supports heavily battered, and its square bastions climbing the slope', was even more impressive.[2] But perhaps the most striking of all Vanbrugh's kitchen-gardens is in the Park at Blenheim in Oxfordshire. Built 1705–7, the imposing walls – 14 feet high and strengthened with four huge semicircular bastions – enclose no less than 8 acres of cultivated ground (fig. 17).

The primary reason for these stern Brobdingnagian walls was that they rebuffed chill winds and kept out greedy rabbits, rats and thieves. In addition, being brick-built, they absorbed the heat of the sun, slowly releasing warmth at night, which contributed to the micro-climate within. And it was from their high, warm inner faces that espaliered fruits could safely be dangled. Blenheim's walls proved themselves immediately. By the summer of 1707 the 'success' in the garden of its many varieties of peach and pear, as well as the nectarines, plums, figs and other fruits, was 'greater than I or any one else could reasonably expect', so Henry Wise was pleased to inform the Duke of Marlborough.[3] A few years more and Vanbrugh was telling the Duchess with some pride that the garden 'in full vigour and full of fruit, is really an astonishing sight. All I ever saw in England or abroad of the kind, are trifles to it.'[4]

The new kitchen-gardens of the early eighteenth century – often standing at some distance from the house, and stuffed as they were with choice produce – had to be kept under watchful eyes by day and locked at night. As one authority – Stephen Switzer – warned, although high-walled 'Fruit-Gardens ought to be detach'd from the House', they must be kept 'private; since by this Means no Body dare walk but the Owner himself, for Fear of losing his Fruit.'[5] It seems, though, to have been difficult to monitor house guests, who had the bad habit of slipping into the gardens and helping themselves. Worst were the poets. In Lord Burlington's garden at Chiswick, for example,

> Where Pope unloads the boughs within his reach,
> Of purple vine, blue plum, and blushing peach,[6]

the corpulent seasonal glutton James Thomson was actually spotted on one occasion 'lounging around . . . with his hands in his waistcoat pockets, biting off the sunny sides of the peaches'.[7]

Fortified kitchen-gardens – within which English nurserymen sought to catch up with recent French and Dutch horticultural advances – were built with talismanic bastions and other military detailing in order that they proclaim with some wit their protective power. No doubt it amused architects, estate owners and even tourists to understand them in this way. But what of *pleasure* gardens? Why were they on occasion constructed in, or afterwards embellished with, a defensible format? Some, certainly, were made in jest – light-hearted architectural flourishes that handsomely set off old soldiers' country seats. Others served as sites for war-games and pageants. There were, too, those made or planted out to commemorate martial successes in distant wars.[8] But in the seventeenth century there had often been a deeper, more pressing reason than any of these. The fact that this was so complicates a response to the question, not least because, although the prominence of the fortified garden in the early eighteenth century – and Vanbrugh's and Switzer's rôles in promoting it – are well known, the circumstances that ushered it in are unclear. To determine why gardens in those days were sometimes fortified, their historical moment must first be recovered. It was a time when the science of fortification was at its zenith.

30. Switzer's design for an octagonal kitchen-garden in The Practical Kitchen Gardiner, *1727, a defensible site with bastions and a moat.*

In Europe and its colonies, war followed war. Both facts bear strongly on the subject. And to investigate those and other contributory causes we can do no better than to begin at what for Switzer *was* the beginning – Blenheim.

On 18 June 1705 'the Garden wall was set agoing the same day with the House'.[9] Not Blenheim's kitchen-garden wall, however, but the one for the hexagonal pleasure garden. This hexagon was several times larger than the kitchen-garden (fig. 17). And it was fortified. According to Switzer, it was the first real example in England of 'reducing Fortification into Gardening'.[10] Switzer knew Blenheim well, having spent several years on site from 1705, working by turn in the quarries, on the Grand Bridge's foundations and the projected canals, and as manager in the gardens. But what intrigued him most was Vanbrugh's idea of designing a garden as if it were a fort. 'It seems', he wrote, 'somewhat of Wonder, that it has not been made Use of before now', and he anticipated that such a novelty would soon be taken up by 'all the martial Genius's of our Country'.[11] His one qualification concerning Blenheim's example was that it was 'after the ancient *Roman* Manner',[12] by which, presumably, he meant Vanbrugh's retardatory circular bastions at the angles. Evidently, Switzer reckoned that trend-setting ideas ought to be up-to-date in their realized forms. As he later took pains to point out, when illustrating a fortified design of his own displaying angled bastions in *The Practical Kitchen Gardiner* (1727) – 'D are bastions, after the latest manner' (fig. 30).[13]

The angled bastion – Switzer's preference – had been invented in Italy shortly before 1500 in response to developments in siege artillery. The advantages it had over the round bastion were threefold: it was less easy to hit, it stood a good chance of deflecting the shot that did strike, and there was no adjacent dead ground hidden from the defenders' enfilading crossfire. As a result, on the continent over the next two centuries emaciated medieval curtain walls, with their series of rectangular or round towers, encircling countless forts, ports and inland cities were gradually replaced by ever more complex systems of defence in depth – low, slope-walled, aggressively profiled saw-tooth constellations capable of withstanding better and longer both withering artillery fire and massed assaults, while supplying defenders with ramparts for their own cannon. Tilbury Fort on the Thames, downriver from the London it was built to defend from enemy shipping, is the finest surviving example in England of late-seventeenth-century military architecture (fig. 31). Designed by the engineer Sir Bernard de Gomme, a Royalist veteran of the Civil Wars, Tilbury was conceived as a double-moated artillery platform able to cannonade anything afloat, yet remain hard to storm. Its original means of access (across the moats at lower-right) was protected by a triangular redan, an arrowhead ravelin in the inner moat and an ingeniously exposed sequence of drawbridges.[14]

The individual to whom much of the credit was given for turning fortification into the compelling subject it became was Sébastien LePrestre de Vauban, a Marshal of France and the acknowledged authority on systems of both attack and defence, who between the 1660s and his death in 1707 provided France's frontiers and coastlines with the most sophisticated series of fortified cities and batteries ever seen in Europe.[15] (As a participant in the bloody repulse of English assault troops at Camaret Bay near Brest in June 1694, Captain Vanbrugh had first-hand experience of Vauban's talents.)[16] Louis XIV so prized the accurately detailed

31. Tilbury Fort, Essex, a Thames-side artillery fort built 1670–83 by Sir Bernard de Gomme to protect London from naval attacks by the Dutch.

1:600 scale models of the 100 or more cities and other defence works Vauban refortified that he treasured these three-dimensional state secrets – which is exactly what they were – under lock and key in the Louvre's grandest gallery. (About thirty survive, and can be seen today in Paris at the Musée des Plans-Reliefs in the Invalides.) Vauban transformed siege warfare into an up-to-date science, which in both practice and theory dwarfed the achievements of the classical and medieval worlds.

Inevitably, then, on examining the intellectual affray concerning the superiority of classical or of contemporary culture that was waged either side of 1700 between the so-called Ancients and Moderns, Defoe noted in *The Compleat English Gentleman* that 'We find the Moderns begin to gain upon the Antients extremely', not least because of 'improvements in mathematicks, fortification, incampments, intrenchings, military discipline, besieging and defending towns, in all of which the knowledge and experience of the present age is infinitely beyond what ever went before them'.[17]

Few of Defoe's contemporaries would have disagreed. Switzer, for example, surely promoted fortified gardens because he identified them as avant-garde structures keyed to a science that was at the cutting edge of applied mathematics and non-Euclidean geometry. Indeed, as he asserted, 'much may be borrow'd, both of Terms and actual Directions in the designing and laying out gardens, from military and civil Architecture'.[18]

Swift, therefore, was backing the wrong side when he sought to deride the fortificatory achievements of the Moderns in *The Battle of the Books in St James's*

Palace Library, written in 1697 in support of his employer, the diehard Ancient Sir William Temple. In the Modern Spider versus the Ancient Bee episode in this satire, the vainglorious arachnid's website is all too easily surfed to shreds by the errant antique hymenopter. Interestingly, even Swift's description of the Spider's fortified web is insidiously managed by means of the cant terms swopped by Ordnance engineers, terms that were increasingly to be 'borrow'd', as Switzer guessed they would be, by landscape architects:

> The Avenues to his Castle were guarded with Turn-pikes and Palissadoes, all after the *Modern* way of Fortification. After you had passed several Courts, you came to the Center, wherein you might behold the *Constable* himself in his own Lodgings, which had Windows fronting to each Avenue, and Ports to sally out upon all Occasions of Prey or Defence.[19]

The turnpikes Swift had in mind were not toll-road booths, they were heavy gates bristling with spikes and other sharp obstructions that served to impede cross-country cavalry. A palissado, or palisade, was an upright fence of close-set pointed stakes – the very thing, in fact, that the Stuart loyalist William Blundell was desperate to see the capital ringed with during the panic of November and December 1688 when the Protestant Anglo-Dutch army led by William, Prince of Orange, was bearing down on London.[20] Only in a *garden* would one have expected to see a palisade composed of decoratively shaped iron railings or hedges of trimmed yew or beech.

As a committed Modern, Switzer based his schemes for fortified gardens on illustrated accounts in books on military architecture and warfare. Though unexecuted, his own best-known design in this vein is the Paston Manor project of 1718, its heart a moated starburst comprising arrowhead ravelins and bastions (fig. 15).[21] The plan, or *trace* (the military term), copies the fortified garden he had initiated in 1711 at Grimsthorpe in Lincolnshire for the Bertie family (fig. 32). Both Grimsthorpe and Paston were conceived as moated and bastioned polyangles. At Grimsthorpe Switzer had 'cut out into Gardens'[22] the four rectangular plantations established some thirty years earlier by Elizabeth Bertie, Countess of Lindsey. Her successor there, Jane, Duchess of Ancaster, seems to have been fond of one of Switzer's ramparts in particular, which became known as the Duchess's Bastion (fig. 33). Here she, too, could sally out on all occasions of prey or defence. It has been suggested that Switzer's mock fort was 'conceived on the plan of a Vauban fortress',[23] but in reality earthen ramparts and floodable ditches were the particular favourite of Vauban's Dutch rival, Menno van Coehoorn (1641–1704), for they were both cheap and appropriate for the low-lying Netherlands.[24] What William Stukeley's Grimsthorpe sketches record are an English Modern's fortified garden in the Dutch, not the French, manner.

Switzer's imitative designs were his response to the strong profile military architecture then had. Some earlier garden-makers on the continent had reacted in much the same way, for example Josef Furttenbach the elder during the Thirty Years War (1618–48) and André Le Nôtre in the course of Louis XIV's Dutch War (1672–8) and 'King William's War' (the Nine Years War of 1689–97).[25] Switzer's own introduction – at Blenheim – to the toy fort came at a time when 'Queen Anne's War' – the long War of the Spanish Succession (1702–13) – was in

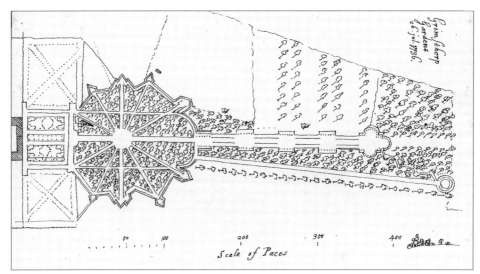

*32. William Stukeley's plan of Grimsthorpe, Lincolnshire, 1736, the fortified garden
constructed by Switzer over twenty years earlier.*

*33. The Duchess's Bastion at Grimsthorpe, drawn by Stukeley in 1736, and revealing the
planting profile established there by Switzer.*

progress, in which Britain, the Dutch United Provinces and lesser states sought
to prevent the union of the French and Spanish crowns. The cockpit was
Flanders in the Spanish Netherlands, although there was fighting in Spain itself,
on France's borders, in parts of Germany and Italy, in New England and Quebec,
and elsewhere. The Succession War is best remembered for the four great set-
piece battles won by the 1st Duke of Marlborough, John Churchill: Blenheim
(1704), Ramillies (1706), Oudenaarde (1708) and Malplaquet (1709). But year in,

year out, most of the campaigning involved one siege after another of fortresses and cities, many of which had been strengthened under Vauban's direction. Marlborough undertook no fewer than thirty sieges in the course of the war. They were often painfully slow and costly. Lille in 1708, for example, although ultimately successful, took four months; in the process Marlborough's allied armies (the Confederates) suffered 15,000 casualties.[26]

The Succession War was a grinding process of attrition, just as King William's War had been; most of William's had been fought in Flanders too (the oppressive Land Tax act of 1691 was passed to help pay for it). Sieges were usually undertaken in the summer months, when foodstuffs and fodder were more plentiful; winter rains made roads all but impassable for heavy equipment, and downpours flooded out the camps and trenches. The besieging force would open its investment by digging protective anti-sortie lines of counter-circumvallation, cutting off the city or fortress from relief. Huge artillery trains brought in howitzers, cannon and mortars, which were set up on timber platforms in gun parks behind the counter-circumvallations. Once the heavy bombardment began – a relentless cascade of red-hot shot and fused mortar bombs – the engineers, sappers and miners began digging the first parallel trench forward of the counter-circumvallation. This tightened the noose. (Siege warfare was to a large extent trench warfare, for the defending troops at the salients were also busy digging their own webs, from which to sally forth to frustrate the investment.) To advance to the ground selected for the first parallel, zig-zag trenches were opened – zig-zag rather than straight, so that defenders could not enfilade their whole length with cannon fire. The process was repeated for the second and subsequent parallels. Troops and *matériel* poured into the final one to be made, the guns rolled forward, the defenders' walls were mined or breached, and the assailing army hurled itself in.[27] No wonder, then, that the glorious science of Military Architecture is imaged (to the right of the *Blenheim* man-of-war, gun-ports open) in the vast allegorical mural by Thornhill – the *Triumph of Peace and Plenty* (1708–17) – that gives the Painted Hall at Greenwich Hospital its name.

The *Gazette* and other newspapers and periodicals kept those at home in England fully up to date with the latest sieges under way across the Channel. 'Few of this generation can remember any thing but war and taxes', moaned Swift, a Tory Peace-at-any-cost propagandist, in the autumn of 1711.[28] In August of that year, in the Douai–Arras–Cambrai triangle, Marlborough, in a brilliant tactical coup, had pushed his armies through a weakened section of the defensive Ne Plus Ultra lines established by the French. Switzer, on site in Lincolnshire that same August, no doubt heard the exciting news within days.

The technical jargon used in the newspapers and by Ordnance engineers must have penetrated beyond Switzer and others like him. Indeed, Martha Pollak has suggested that, by the end of the seventeenth century, the 'proliferation of fortification elements had had a great and general linguistic influence, and the names of the parts were fully ensconced in the imagination of a general public'.[29] Maybe so, but when a certain Captain Toby Shandy, who had been wounded in the course of the second siege of Namur in 1695, sought to explain that 'when a ravelin . . . stands before the curtin, it is a ravelin; and when a ravelin stands before a bastion, then the ravelin is not a ravelin; it is a half-moon', he succeeded only in confusing his audience.[30] Sergeant Kite, in Farquhar's *The Recruiting*

Officer (1706), equally befuddled a Shrewsbury man with his martial talk of ravelins and palisadoes (Act III, scene i). And some years later Roderick Random was to witness a row break out in a crowded London coffee-house over the exact meaning of *épaulement* in connection with Namur's first siege in 1692.[31] Certainly, when Ephraim Chambers published his *Cyclopaedie* in 1728 – the first encyclopaedia in English – he ensured it included an extensive, illustrated glossary of fortification terms, *épaulement* among them.

On the continent, a familiarity with the science of military architecture and its terminology had been part of a gentleman's education since the Renaissance, hence Sir Henry Wotton's reason for studying the subject while in Venice early in the seventeenth century. In time, English courtesy books, for example Richard Blome's *The Gentleman's Recreation* (1686), included it in their bundle of improving topics; thus, when the young Sir John Percival spent six months of 1705–6 as a student in Utrecht, he was there 'to perfect his knowledge of fortifications, drawing, music and fencing'.[32] It also engrossed mathematicians and architectural writers. Christopher Wren researched fortification before taking up architecture, which is why in 1661 Charles II approached him – the monarch was rebuffed – to undertake repairs to the newly acquired Mediterranean fortress of Tangier.[33] The paucity of coverage of the subject in English provoked, albeit without much success, William Winde, Dean Henry Aldrich and others to carry their manuscripts to a state of completion fit for the printer.[34] Landowners, such as William Paston, 2nd Earl of Yarmouth,[35] as well as architects,[36] collected books on warfare and fortification for their libraries, although, inevitably, most were in French, Dutch, German or Italian. James Gibbs's library, none the less, included Ruse's *The Strengthening of Strongholds* in an English edition.[37] Henry Wise and George London had no more than two or three military works between them,[38] whereas their friend Thomas Coke of Melbourne Hall, Derbyshire, could show a more impressive collection.[39] But Coke's was nothing like the Earl of Burlington's. The latter had so many housed in the basement library at Chiswick villa, that they were separately shelved and given their own category – *Fortification* – in the in-house catalogue.[40]

Following Vanbrugh's and Switzer's apparent lead,[41] Charles Bridgeman experimented with bastions and other defensive items at several sites. At Westbury in Hampshire, for example, designed for Admiral Philip Cavendish in the 1720s, he edged the formal gardens with a line of bastioned walling, providing a viewing platform from which to overlook the fields.[42] Yet if Switzer in 1718 could wonder why fortifications had 'not been made Use of before now' in garden design, clearly he had not read Marvell's 'Upon Appleton House', published in 1681 but describing the gardens of the Yorkshire country house belonging to the Parliamentary war hero General Sir Thomas Fairfax as they were in the early 1650s. Fairfax:

> . . . when retirèd here to peace,
> His warlike studies could not cease;
> But laid these gardens out in sport
> In the just figure of a fort;
> And with five bastions it did fence,
> As aiming one for every sense.[43]

Half a century before Fairfax measured out his new pentagon, the virtuoso courtier Sir Henry Fanshawe had made a garden fort, albeit short-lived, 'with rampar[t]s, bulwarkes, counterscarpes, and all other appertenances' at Ware Park in Hertfordshire.[44] Tourneys and mock-battles in parks and gardens were not uncommon either. John Evelyn has described how Windsor Castle's slopes and meadow were used in August 1674 for a public re-enactment of the successful Anglo-French siege of Maastricht the previous year:

> There was approches, & a formal seige, against a Work with *Bastions*, Bullwarks, Ramparts, Palizads, . . . hornworks, Conterscarps &c: in imitation of the Citty of *Maestrict* . . . They made their approches, opened trenches, raised batteries, [took] the Counterscarp, Ravelin, after a stout Defence. Greate Gunns fir'd on both sides, Granados shot, mines Sprung, parties sent out, attempts of raising the seige, prisoners taken, Parlies, & in short all the Circumstances of a formal seige.[45]

The toy forts, and their placement, built by Fanshawe, Fairfax and others indicate that Switzer's claim for Vanbrugh as the originator of the fortified garden in England needs qualification: Vanbrugh on occasion made the *garden* a fort, whereas these Jacobean and Cromwellian forerunners of his work seem in each case to have been a small fort *within* the garden. They are early examples of a distinct strand in the history of the fortified garden; in Vanbrugh's day this strand included the moated pentagon with its battlemented tower constructed within the water-gardens at Wanstead in Essex (*c.* 1720),[46] and Batty Langley's design for 'An Arbor in a Fortified Island' (Langley's plate 18) in *New Principles of Gardening* (1728). The scale and ambition of Blenheim's hexagon – a defensible garden connected to the house and within a park – is of a wholly different order. The same is true of Vanbrugh's fortified gardens at Castle Howard, Claremont and Seaton Delaval. Not that he seems to have been the first to undertake schemes of this sort. At Levens Hall, Westmorland, Colonel James Grahme – with help from his French gardener, Guillaume Beaumont – constructed a run of ditch and bastioned wall on the western edge of his gardens overlooking the park in 1692. Grahme, Keeper of the Royal Buckhounds until James II's sudden flight to France in December 1688, and Beaumont, apparently a sometime Surrey nurseryman who supplied Hampton Court Palace's gardens, were perhaps consoling themselves in bucolic retirement over the loss of their master.[47]

Switzer evidently knew nothing of this undertaking in faraway Westmorland, because in 1718 he suggested that the garden ditch, or *foss* 'was first deliver'd to us by a Gentleman, that is deservedly honour'd with some considerable Posts belonging to the Architectural Province, &c. in his Majesty's Works', i.e., Vanbrugh.[48] Here, surely, Switzer was recollecting the one dug in 1705 at Blenheim for the hexagon garden. After Blenheim, Vanbrugh's preoccupation with fortifying either a garden, or a garden and house together, led him to adopt one strategy after another, from curtain walling to an artillery platform. The 'Wall built in the Fortification way with several Bastions' noticed by John Tracy Atkyns at Castle Howard while on a visit there in 1732 was begun in 1706,[49] when the labour force was set to work 'making ye Ditch Round Wraywood'.[50] The most prominent bastions in this run of ditch-and-wall are on the north-west edge of

Ray Wood, the only section visible from the approach avenue to the house (fig. 13). These round bastions are consciously scenic, even picturesque, devices, whereas north-easterly sections of the wall – running towards the site of Hawksmoor's later Temple of Venus (1731–5) – were given nothing more than rather meaningless rectangular projections. The open ground north and north-east of Ray Wood was for cattle or deer, not for visitors, hence there was no need to add any pleasing visual accents to that section of the walling.

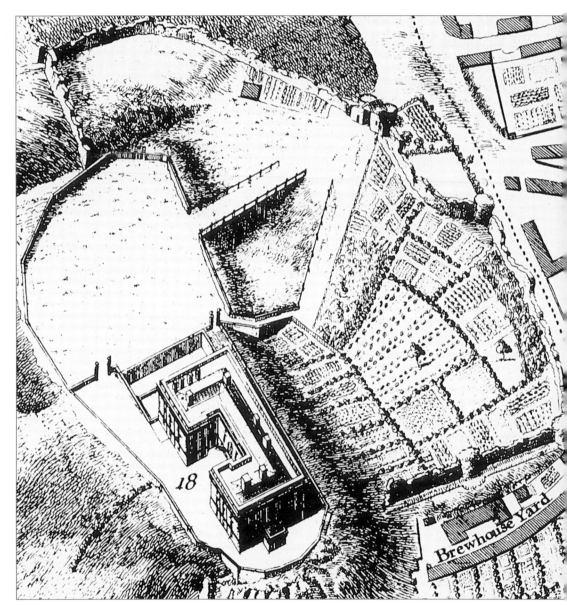

34. Nottingham Castle, the new mansion within its medieval curtain walls, as shown in a city map of 1744.

Ray Wood's line of fortifications was continued south from the Temple of Venus site to that of the Temple of the Four Winds (built from 1725); the line then crossed the brook to link up with the Wilderness walls south of the house. The wall then continued south-west until it struck the impressive east–west line of curtain walling built in the early 1720s – the best-known of all Vanbrugh's defensive works (fig. 58). So the defences – starting at the house's north courtyard, and from there reaching around Ray Wood, across the brook, past the Wilderness and then, finally, west to the far end of the curtain wall – were approximately two and a half miles in length, a remarkable distance.[51] The curtain walling was itself in the front line: it was the first section of Vanbrugh's outworks to greet visitors travelling to Castle Howard from York. By April 1722 Colonel James Tyrrell of Shotover, Oxfordshire, was giving people 'a mighty good Acc[oun]t of . . . the out Works'.[52] In August of the following year Vanbrugh bragged to the Duke of Newcastle that 'I think all that come here, are Supris'd at their Magnificent Effect'.[53] 'They are all vastly Surprised and taken with the Walls and their Towers, which they talk much of', he later enthused to Carlisle; 'I always thought we were Sure of that Card'.[54]

Even so, Vanbrugh never repeated mock-medieval walling of this kind elsewhere. It suited this site particularly well because Castle Howard itself was built to replace the burnt-out Henderskelfe Castle, whose reduced wreck was still visible immediately west of the new house when the curtain wall was built. (Henderskelfe may have been the source for some of the wall's stone.) Vanbrugh's scenic screen stood for the ancestry of the place: here at Castle Howard was a new ancestral home behind protective walls that seemingly had been standing guard for centuries. He may have hit on this picturesque strategy while working at Nottingham Castle, one of the Duke of Newcastle's properties. The castle – held for Parliament by Colonel John Hutchinson in the Civil Wars – had been slighted in 1651 to render it unusable in the case of further conflict. Following the Restoration in 1660 it passed to William Cavendish, 1st Duke of Newcastle, who swept away the blasted core and built on the site a nine-bay mansion in a fashionable classicist idiom, although he retained the enclosing curtain walling (fig. 34). Vanbrugh refitted the mansion's interiors in 1719, but he also seems to have ensured that the damaged curtain wall was sympathetically attended to, comparing it favourably with the feeble outworks recently constructed at Belvoir Castle, Rutland, which 'looks all like past[e]board work'.[55] Nottingham Castle was a new home on an ancient site behind old walls. Why not Castle Howard too?

Claremont in Surrey, where Vanbrugh had built a small house for himself (Chargate) in 1709, selling it five years later to Thomas Pelham-Holles, Earl of Clare (afterwards Duke of Newcastle), was not the site of an ancestral seat. Vanbrugh hugely extended the house for Newcastle and, concurrently with Castle Howard's curtain wall, oversaw construction of a defensive wall along the northern edge of Claremont's woody hill crowned by his embattled belvedere of c. 1715 (fig. 20). But either because Claremont had no baronial history to capitalize on, or because the precipitate wooded garden west of the house when seen at a distance was similar in visual effect to Ray Wood, he opted for a more modern system, complete with a diamond bastion.[56] Those travelling south from Esher on the road to Guildford (a section of the busy London–Portsmouth highway) saw to their left across Claremont's open pasture a substantial ditch-and-earthwork

35. John Vanbrugh's Seaton Delaval, Northumbria, 1719–26, as seen from the road to Seaton Sluice.

(possibly brick-faced) sequence of outworks protecting the gardens and house. This scenic arrangement also worked for visitors, who in Vanbrugh's day left the public road and crossed the pasture towards the house with the uninterrupted fortified wall always on their right until they reached the front (east) courtyard.

On at least two occasions Vanbrugh sought to tie fortifications more closely to the house. The annotated measured drawings (*c.* 1718) from his office for the unexecuted pyramid-gate forecourt for Kings Weston near Bristol are of masonry walls set deep into a 'fossee' – a ditch-and-wall combination that would have defended the house from the south-west side of the park, through which the approach avenue ran.[57] At Seaton Delaval, Northumbria, however, Vanbrugh's more extensive project was realized. He began the house for Admiral George Delaval in 1719; it was a powerful, atmospheric composition that kept a firm grip on a romantic feudal past despite the neo-Palladian format of extended wings (fig. 35) and a portico on the garden front (fig. 91). This is a house that looks like it was designed to put up a fight. And so it was. Sited midway along the northern edge of a massive rectangle (400 yards across) where it meets a smaller, ramped rectangle sloping down from the house to the road (fig. 36), the house is contained within an ambitious configuration walled in stone and deeply ditched; at the four main angles, circular bastions are positioned (fig. 37). No other house by Vanbrugh was ever protected like this one. It sits within what has been called a haha, but it is much more than that: this was surely conceived as an artillery platform, one that could defend the house and cover the road.

It is not readily apparent why Vanbrugh suggested – or why the Admiral accepted – such an uncompromising form of landscape architecture. But work began at Seaton Delaval around the same time that Vanbrugh became involved at

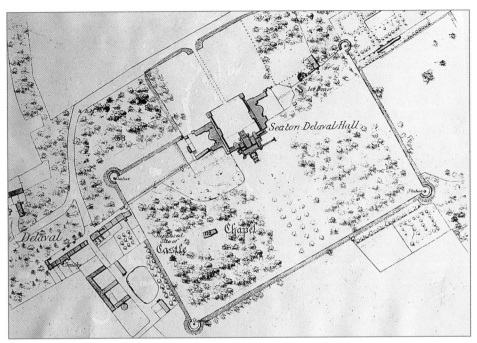

36. *Seaton Delaval and its bastioned platform, in a detail from a Victorian map.*

37. *The ditch, platform and north-west bastion at Seaton Delaval, their original aggressive contouring softened by time and nature.*

Stowe, Buckinghamshire, and maybe they are related in motive as well as effect. The situation at Stowe is complicated by the fact that we do not know who was responsible for its fortifications; perhaps they were designed by committee – Vanbrugh, Bridgeman and Stowe's owner, Lord Cobham. According to John, Viscount Percival (the same Percival, now elevated, who had studied in Utrecht), who visited Stowe in August 1724, 'Bridgman laid out the ground and plan[ne]d the whole'.[58] This implies – although Percival may not have meant it to – that the recently constructed line of bulwarks he encountered separating the gardens from the Home Park were by Bridgeman. But most of the buildings this line defends – the Temple of Bacchus, the Rotondo, the Lake Pavilions – are Vanbrugh's, and indeed the bulwarks may have been designed by him too.

The probable year in which Vanbrugh began at Stowe – 1719 – was certainly the year in which Lord Cobham had been at war abroad. A career soldier, and a veteran of Marlborough's campaigns in Flanders, in September 1719 he had sailed with a strong expeditionary force to attack Coruña, just one episode in the barely remembered War of the Quadruple Alliance against Spain. Although Coruña proved to be too strong for assault, Cobham voyaged on, bombarding, and then taking, Vigo and a few other towns round about. And either just before he departed for Spain, or shortly after his triumphant return, he approved the introduction of stormpoles along the western edge of the raised gardens fringed by the Home Park, running from Lee's Bastion to Gurnet's Walk, south of the Rotondo, a section of which can be seen in Rigaud's engraving (fig. 38).[59] Fang-like rows of sharpened stakes of this sort were set horizontally in fortified walls in order to obstruct assailants; Cobham would have encountered them in Flanders, at Vigo, and elsewhere.

It is easy to imagine that Stowe's lengthy stormpoled platform and other defensive works like it – Seaton Delaval's, for example – were no more than droll attempts by veterans to lighten the trauma of remembered combat. This

38. *A detail from Jacques Rigaud's 'View of the Queen's Theatre from the Rotunda', 1739, with the stormpoled walling discernible at the far right.*

39. *James Bretherton's engraving after Henry William Bunbury,* The Siege of Namur by Captain Shandy and Corporal Trim, *1773, a Shandy Hall siege not in fact mentioned in* Tristram Shandy.

explanation certainly fits in the case of the makers of the best-known military garden in English fiction – Shandy Hall, a few miles from York, a parody of Switzer's Grimsthorpe, Cobham's Stowe and other fortified gardens of the eighteenth century. Having received a debilitating wound in Flanders during the second siege of Namur (1695) while serving under William III, Captain Toby Shandy spent several years convalescing in London (during which he began collecting books and prints on fortification) before, in 1701,[60] Corporal Trim and he moved to Yorkshire in order to use Shandy Hall's garden as a site for great sieges (fig. 39). From 1702 until the Peace of Utrecht in 1713 and the dismantling of Ostend's menacing defences, while Vanbrugh and Hawksmoor laboured on at nearby Castle Howard, at Shandy Hall the pair kept pace with Marlborough's campaigns, throwing up midget fortified cities and then tearing them down in parallel with the latest assaults underway in Flanders and northern France. Perhaps they were encouraged in this compulsive repetition by Defoe, who in 1697 had published his proposals for setting up a military academy, where cadets could be trained 'to cast bombs, to raise regular works, as batteries, bastions, half-moons, redoubts, horn-works, ports, and the like . . . [with] room to fire great shot at a distance, to canonade a camp, to throw all sorts of fire-works and machines, that are or shall be invented.'[61] But no college for instruction in warfare and military architecture was to be established in England until 1720, when the Royal Military Academy was founded at Woolwich by a group of Ordnance engineers that included Vanbrugh's good friend, Brigadier-General Michael Richards.

Wholly fictional though the Shandy Hall extravaganza is, old soldiers do seem to have enjoyed undertakings of this sort, and not just in the eighteenth century. Take Captain Edward Jekyll and Colonel Hamilton, for example, who in the mid-1850s together dug out a huge Shandyesque earthwork model of 'part of the enceinte of a fortified town on the modern French system, with bastions, curtains, ravelins and covered way complete' across 40 yards of lawn at Bramley House near Guildford, Surrey.[62] Captain Jekyll (Grenadiers, Retd), a pyromaniac by all accounts, had become obsessed by the Crimean War (1854–6) then under way, and during hostilities gave lectures on the conflict in village halls to anyone who would listen. According to one of his own brisk debriefings, 'I discoursed my audience for one hour and a half, and never did I hear a more breathless silence'; having demonstrated 'the attack and defence of a Citadel; my enlarged plan of Sevastapol explained our position and the defences of that place'.[63] His beleaguered audience at home included a shy, garden-loving, eleven-year-old daughter named Gertrude.

An earlier Yorkshire garden, Sir Henry Goodricke's Ribston Hall (fig. 40), might at first be supposed to have been undertaken in the spirit that was to infect Shandy Hall and Bramley House. In a letter of 1688 Charles Bertie reported to George Legge, Lord Dartmouth, that he, Lord Drumblane and Thomas Osborne, Earl of Danby, were all at Ribston, where Goodricke, a former soldier, was at work 'environing his garden with a kind of fortification, and has already finished 2 bastions, and hopes when Lord Dartmouth visits the northern forts, he will be pleased to reckon this among the number'.[64] But this letter to Dartmouth, one of James's commanders, was sent in *September* 1688. Bertie was a committed Stuart loyalist; so was Dartmouth. Goodricke, however, was a crypto-Williamite. Did Bertie know that? Was this communication to Dartmouth a warning? In the

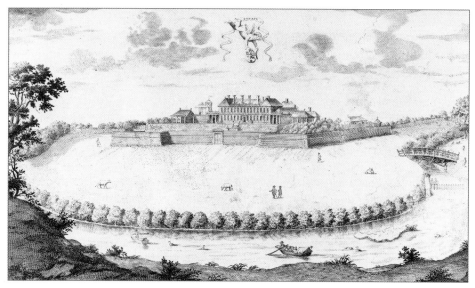

40. An anonymous sketch of Ribston Hall, Yorkshire, c. 1688–90, showing the new bastioned garden Sir Henry Goodricke suddenly wanted for himself.

month it was written, William, Prince of Orange, was in Holland urgently fitting out a huge invasion fleet and hiring extra regiments. James's commitment to the Catholic cause, and the unexpected birth of his male heir in June 1688, had finally forced leading Protestant Whigs in England into desperate measures. In late June they had sent a coded letter to William, inviting him to invade and rescue England from an encroaching Catholic absolutism. By the autumn Lord Danby, the Duke of Devonshire and others were busy plotting at the Cock & Pynot inn (now 'Revolution House') near Chesterfield. Once William had safely landed his Anglo-Dutch armies at Torbay in Devon on 5 November and begun his cautious advance on London, the plotters gathered their armed followers and seized the major cities on his behalf. Devonshire, for example, took Nottingham; Goodricke and the Earl of Danby seized York; by December Richard Lumley, 1st Earl of Scarborough, had established his supremacy over the north-east. And as the invasion force advanced on the capital, James's commanders (John Churchill among them) deserted to William; little by little James's disillusioned regiments melted away. By the end of December James was in flight to France; the following April, William III and his wife Mary II (one of James's daughters, but a committed Protestant) were crowned jointly in Westminster Abbey.

The reason, then, that Goodricke was busy 'environing his garden with a kind of fortification' in the summer of 1688 was because he, like everyone else, knew that a fresh civil war was brewing. The crushed Protestant Monmouth Rebellion of 1685, with its failed supportive rising in Scotland, was the sign of things to come. And when the next insurrection came, either James or William would win outright, or England would probably have to endure years of bitter campaigning, as had happened in the 1640s. Goodricke, and surely others, were busy in the meanwhile making their homes defensible. Everyone knows the names of the great battles of the Civil Wars – Edgehill, Marston Moor, Naseby and the rest – and of Cromwell's brutal campaigns in Scotland and Ireland, but little attention has been given to the countless sieges and skirmishes that pockmarked the 1640s. Country houses of every kind were fortified, fought over, burnt out. While De Gomme was constructing huge earthwork defences for Royalist Oxford (the King's headquarters), other commanders in Charles I's army were encircling the city with 'almost a score of garrisons, most of them in country houses and castles within fifteen miles'.[65] Among them was Woodstock Manor. A defensible country house packed with troops and munitions could control its surrounding district and frustrate the enemy's lines of communication; to maintain such garrisons, the local farms and towns were coerced into supplying provisions and cash. For example, the 300 or so Royalists that garrisoned Basing House in Hampshire, who included Wenceslaus Hollar and Inigo Jones, harassed the neighbourhood and the important London–Portsmouth road for years until Cromwell's Ironsides were finally able to cannonade the property and overrun the substantial earthwork defences in October 1645, slaughtering many of the defenders and wrecking the house beyond repair.[66]

Hillesden House in Buckinghamshire had suffered the same fate eighteen months earlier (March 1644). Cromwell's troopers stormed over the earthworks, killing every soldier that resisted and destroying the house. When Celia Fiennes visited the rebuilt Hillesden exactly fifty years later she found charming 'gardens which are neatly kept'; there was 'grass and gravel walkes with dwarfs and flower

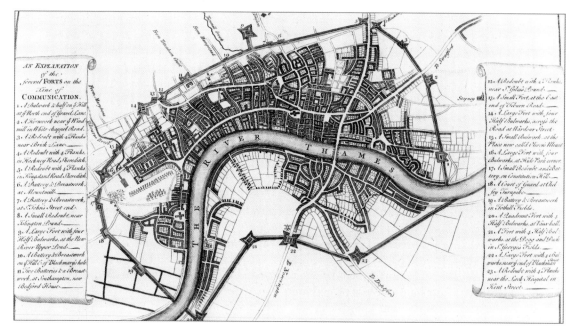

41. George Vertue's 'London as Fortified in the Years 1642 and 1643', a historical record of the
fortified capital measured and drawn for Maitland's History of London, 1739.

trees and much fruit; the prospect is fine all over the gardens and parkes and the
river and woods beyond them'.[67] But the 'prospect' over the park was enjoyed
from the remains of the Royalist ditch-and-bastion sequence that had enabled the
terracing for the post-Civil Wars garden. Hillesden's fortified garden was an
authentic one, not a Switzer-like toy.

So, too, was the one built for Southampton House in London's Bloomsbury
district in 1642–3, when Parliament encased the capital with the most ambitious
defensive system constructed during the Civil Wars – eleven miles of ditch and
ramparts, punctuated by twenty-three stormpoled forts and redoubts (fig. 41).[68]
These were the defences that the architect John Webb spied on, secretly sending
'to the King at Oxford the designes of all the fortifications about London, their
proportions, the number of Gunns mounted on them, how many Souldyers
would man them, how they might bee attempted & carried and all particulars
relating thereto in writing'.[69] Southampton House's north-facing garden
(marked no. 11 on Vertue's map) was in the front line, boasting a pair of artillery
platforms in the form of arrowhead bastions linked by a breastwork 3 yards thick
and 18 feet high, the whole fronted with a palisaded double ditch (fig. 42).[70] This
deep ditch is confirmation that the haha, though pseudonymously so, was an
item in English garden design seventy years – and perhaps there are earlier
examples – before John James translated into English A.-J. Dézallier
d'Argenville's La Théorie et la pratique du jardinage (1709). The property itself,
renamed Bedford House after 1669, survived until 1800; the outline of the
bastioned garden – clearly marked on John Rocque's Plan of the Cities of London

& Westminster of 1746 (fig. 81) – continued to be included on maps of London up to 1799.[71]

The examples of Hillesden, Southampton and Basing in the 1640s (many others could be cited) and Ribston in the 1680s confirm that the fortified garden was not always a toy. But as for those made in the half-century after 1688 – what were they? The spectre of civil war that loomed over England, Scotland and Ireland that year was never really driven off until the utter destruction of the Jacobites at Culloden Moor near Inverness in April 1746. One pro-Stuart plot, riot, rising followed another. Rumour was everywhere. The nearer one's home, mine, estate or factory was to the Anglo-Scottish border, the more at risk it was: the failed rising of 1708 and the hard-fought ones of 1715 and 1745–6 all had as an immediate goal the seizure of Newcastle upon Tyne and the region's coalfields in order to cut off London's fuel supplies. This continuing threat and the insecurities it bred shed a strange light on Seaton Delaval and its fortified garden. The house is only 15 miles north-east of central Newcastle. Much of the Delaval money came from the local coalfields the family controlled and worked; their black gold was shipped to London from Seaton Sluice, the privately owned coastal dock barely a mile east of the house. The core of the house itself has been likened to a medieval keep; its octagonal towers and powerfully banded masonry are also remindful of a more violent feudal past. There in the far north, Vanbrugh had learned from the 'many more Valluable and Agreeable things and Places to be Seen, than in the Tame Sneaking South of England'.[72] The remote and hilly landscape in the north and west of the county was peppered with ancient castles, bastle-houses and gaunt, towered residences, the fading world of the Border Reivers – six centuries of cattle-rustling, house-firing, murder and mayhem that only came to an end in the years following the union of the two crowns in 1603.[73]

Yet there were the recent times to act as warning too. The Jacobite dream in the summer of 1715 was the overthrow of the new Lutheran king, George I, shipped

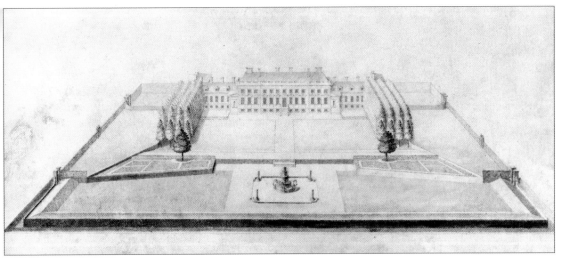

42. The north front of Southampton House (later Bedford House), London, a late seventeenth-century drawing that shows the deep ditch and bastions hurriedly constructed in 1642–3.

in from Hanover by the Whigs, and his replacement with James III, the exiled Stuart born in London in June 1688. It was to be managed thus: the Earl of Mar would lead the Scottish revolt and bring its armies south; Lords Lansdowne and Wyndham with their followers were to hold down the West Country until the Duke of Ormonde landed there with a French army; the Northumbrian Catholics, meanwhile, had to seize Holy Island and contain the county until James and more French got safely ashore in the north.[74]

But the rising – badly planned and ill-led – fell apart. In September, as Mar slowly gathered his army north of the border, the Whig government in London acted swiftly: the West Country lords and army plotters were arrested and their Bristol arms dump seized.[75] Ormonde never arrived. Early in October the French fleet cruising off the Northumbrian coast, having looked in vain for the signals to bring them ashore, sailed away. The Northumbrian Jacobites, abandoned and confused, aimlessly roamed the county, proclaiming James III in the market squares while dodging government troops sent north to crush them. With Mar's route south blocked by the Duke of Argyll's pro-government army, these lost Northumbrians and a force of Lowland Scots were obliged to combine and march west in the hope of picking up recruits in disaffected Lancashire. They beat off the Earl of Carlisle's militia at Penrith Fell (Carlisle was Lord-Lieutenant of Cumberland and Westmorland), and headed south towards Preston. The sudden end to the rising came on Sunday 13 November. In Scotland at Sherriffmuir, Mar, with 10,000 troops, failed to annihilate Argyll's smaller army, and was forced to withdraw into the Highlands, where his followers drifted away into the heather. On the same day in Preston, the Anglo-Scots Jacobites, though still holding the town after fighting off spirited attacks by government troops the day before, saw a large number of fresh regiments suddenly arrive, among them Lord Cobham's dragoons, and take up position. Lord Lumley was there too, and so was the Earl of Carlisle. The 1,500-strong Jacobite army wisely surrendered.

Surely, in a world as volatile as early eighteenth-century Britain, from time to time fortified gardens were built in order to protect families, their houses and possessions?[76] In those days, after all, in the wildernesses of British America, English relatives living in the frontline villages took care to maintain a block-house and palisade in case of attack by roaming French and Indian war bands.[77] Closer to home, in impoverished, wild, Catholic Ireland, where the military 'officer architects' were the chief designers of country houses in the later seventeenth and early eighteenth centuries,[78] defensible houses and outbuildings were the norm for Anglo-Protestant landowners. Not suprisingly, then, the response of the Warwickshire-based Earl of Conway in 1671 to designs by the English architect William Hurlbutt for new stables for Conway's Irish house at Portmore, County Antrim, had been this: he thought the designs 'well sett out, only I dislike the Ovall Figure and have altered it to Sex Angular as the more defensible'.[79] As for the Percival we encountered earlier at Utrecht and Stowe, his keen interest in the science of fortification was no doubt fostered during his childhood years at Burton House, County Cork. This was a handsome Restoration-style box of 1671 by the 'officer architect' Captain William Kenn with neat gardens. The ensemble was protected by massive walls with six castellated square towers at the angles designed by the fort-builder Thomas Smith (who from 1681 redesigned the house).[80] As Smith confided: 'Eyther of the

4 doors of the Maine House may be defended from two Turretts.'[81] But only from small marauding bands. After the Percivals had fled to their Southwell relatives in England at Kings Weston when civil war loomed in 1688, the Jacobite army streaming south following its defeat at the Battle of the Boyne in July 1690 paused long enough to burn Burton House to the ground.

Horror stories from Ireland and America and the continuing pro-Stuart riots and rebellions that threatened to drag England back into the nightmare times of the 1640s all played their part in the resurgence of interest in the fortified garden in Vanbrugh's day. When Vanbrugh began at Seaton Delaval, the 1715 rising was a very recent event. The ringleader of the Northumbrian Catholics – James Radcliffe, 3rd Earl of Derwentwater – had gone to the block for his part in it.[82] And since plots and riots continued unabated, why not protect Seaton Delaval, its coal reserves, the exposed road and the private dock? Its defences are still in place for all to see, but because they were never put to the test in the way that those of the 1640s had been, it is hard to know whether they were decided on in jest or earnest.

The same might be said for an unexecuted project by the architect William Etty. In 1727, having served under Vanbrugh at both Seaton Delaval and Castle Howard as clerk of works, Etty sent designs to George Bowes that included 'bastions'.[83] They were probably for Gibside, a Bowes property 5 miles south-west of Newcastle. What makes Etty's proposal intriguing is the fact that Bowes's huge wealth derived from the coalfields he owned in the region. It was Bowes, no less (a Whig MP for County Durham from 1727), who co-founded the powerful combination of the Durham coal-owners, the martial-sounding 'Grand Allies'. Bowes shipped his coal to London from Tyneside's staithes. Did Etty think Bowes was just the kind of magnate who might one day find himself in serious need of a fortified home? Certainly, when the Forty-Five Rising broke, Bowes, as Deputy Lieutenant for the county, was begging London for more troops to protect 'this unarmed part of the world'.[84] Having just bludgeoned Sir John Cope's army at Prestonpans, east of Edinburgh, in September, Bonnie Prince Charlie's pugnacious Jacobites had the north-east's coalfields as their next goal.

Another case – this time north of the border – is William Adam's fortified garden (c. 1725–30) for Newliston House, west of Edinburgh. Newliston's defences are thoroughly Vanbrughian in the Seaton Delaval manner – a rectangular, stone-walled platform with bastions at the angles.[85] This curious commission was from John Dalrymple, 2nd Earl of Stair, a Flanders veteran who had served under Marlborough.[86] And even the south of England was not always so tame and sneaking. In 1714 or thereabouts, John, 2nd Duke of Montagu, fortified his old Beaulieu Palace upriver from the exposed coast of Hampshire with a moat, curtain wall, towers and drawbridge.[87] Montagu was an inveterate practical joker, a gentleman architect with a taste for embattled designs (and in the 1740s he was twice Master-General of the Ordnance). But was Beaulieu a jest? Everyone knew that a war would quickly follow the death of the sickly and heirless Queen Anne. And after she expired in August 1714, it did.

So why not fortify a garden and thus protect a house and its contents? If, at any point during the reigns of Anne or the first two Georges, England had been suddenly ripped apart by the kind of chronic internecine strife Charles I had caused in the 1640s, we would know today whether the fortified gardens of

Vanbrugh's and Switzer's time were *always* merely ornamental projects, or whether in some cases a more urgent reason lay behind their making. As it is, we are left peering into the past, trying to discern meaning behind the visible product. Uvedale Price did just that at Blenheim around 1790. While gazing at the lakeside décor and arbuscular frippery introduced by the arch-Neoclassicist Capability Brown back in the 1760s, Price decided that

> if those banks above and near the bridge were formed, or even approved of by him, his taste had more of the engineer than the painter; for they have so strong a resemblance to the glacis of a fortification, that it might well be supposed that shape had been given them in compliment to the first duke of Marlborough's campaigns in Flanders.[88]

What Price saw, and all but misattributed to Brown, were in fact the shadowy remains of the bridge and canal earthworks built in Switzer's day that had been augmented in the 1720s by Colonel John Armstrong, a prominent Ordnance engineer who had served in the Flanders wars.[89] Price stared hard. And he asked himself – *Why fortify a garden?* His conclusion was that Blenheim's apparent *glacis* might simply be part of the redolent martial symbolism of the place. But one doubts that this explanation will suffice for every fortified garden made in or after 1688.

FIVE

Antiquaries, Theatre and Early Medievalism

Timothy Mowl

Vanbrugh's career as an architect began at Castle Howard in 1699 with a palatial improvization on the Baroque and ended, in 1725, at Grimsthorpe Castle with a deadly dull Palladian design, mercifully never realized. However, in 1718 for his own family house, Vanbrugh Castle at Greenwich, he built an intensely personal neo-medieval fantasy of towers, walls and battlements (fig. 43). The drawing that William Stukeley made of this exoticism in 1721 may have exaggerated its romantic profile and apparent asymmetry, but Vanbrugh was so pleased with his experiment that he went on to raise a small middle-class housing estate around it, with buildings that came to be known as The Nunnery, Mince-Pie House and the White Towers. There was not a single pointed arch in this whole neo-medieval complex, and Vanbrugh Castle, the sole survivor of the original cluster, reveals not one authentic medieval detail. Raw round arches and gaunt, narrow turrets of brick give only a token profile of the Middle Ages. When Vanbrugh used the term 'Gothic' he meant buildings constructed in rough rubble stone as opposed to ashlar stonework; a rude 'Castle Air' was what he admired, and by that he thought of a structure both dramatic in profile but perfectly habitable.[1]

'Gothic' was still accumulating meanings in 1718, and had not acquired a precise definition. Christopher Wren, when discussing Westminster Abbey, wrote in 1713: 'This we now call the *Gothick* Manner of Architecture';[2] Antony à Wood used the term in 1664 in much the same way when describing Bampton Castle, whose 'gatehouse' had a 'ruined entrance, and an old gothick window over it'.[3] The diarist John Evelyn, who did more than most to establish the word in its common architectural usage, spelled 'Gotiq' in a 1641 *Diary* entry and 'Gothick' in 'An Account of Architects & Architecture', the appendix to his translation of Roland Fréart's *Parallèle de l'architecture antique et de la moderne* of 1664.[4] But the word first appeared in the Preface to the 1611 King James Bible, which speaks of translating 'the Scriptures into the Gothicke tongue'. A more precise definition of Vanbrugh's round-arched, military style, in view of its precosity in the development of the Gothic Revival, would be 'Early Medievalism'.[5]

The interesting question about Vanbrugh's neo-medieval style is how he came to acquire such a taste when he was in no way personally eccentric or odd. He was eminently, in fact, a man of his times, popular, fashionable and entertaining, able

43. William Stukeley's sketch of Vanbrugh Castle, Greenwich, *1721, the neo-medieval fantasy that Vanbrugh had just completed for himself.*

to talk acceptable bawdy with ducal clients: ''tis so bloody Cold, I have almost a mind to Marry to keep myself warm'[6] – and completely at ease with the potent power brokers of his day. 'We remember'd you', he told his publisher friend Jacob Tonson, 'the Night before at Hampton Court, as we were sopping our Arses in the Fountain.'[7] Clearly he fitted in comfortably with the good and the great. If he had reserved his 'castle airs' for a few small villas in Greenwich they could be dismissed as a suburban fantasy. But muted medievalism runs through all his projects, great ones like Castle Howard, Blenheim and Seaton Delaval, as well as the more utilitarian – dock buildings, water-towers, arsenals, even brewhouses (fig. 44).[8] In the two decades between 1700 and 1720 there was a general acceptance by Vanbrugh's clients of his highly personal version of a romantic, towered and fantastic adaptation of continental Baroque. The English, in their usual insular introversion, had shunned the European style for at least half a century. Now, just as the other nations were drifting towards the Rococo, England was on the verge of its own island Baroque – triumphalist, experimental and theatrical – but almost 100 years late.

Vanbrugh's first commission was a courageous gamble by the 3rd Earl of Carlisle, designed to assert his regional eminence and to impress a king, Dutch William, with an eye for prestigious houses and gardens (fig. 45). Castle Howard worked its intended political magic. In December 1701 Carlisle was made First Lord of the Treasury. That the King should have died unexpectedly the following March and Carlisle lose his job in May can only be seen as bad luck. His new house had achieved what it was built to achieve. Vanbrugh's building style was

44. The Old Ordnance Board-room at the Royal Arsenal, Woolwich, 1718–20, attributed to Vanbrugh.

45. Vanbrugh's Castle Howard, built from 1699, seen from the south.

not, however, such a brief candle as Carlisle's political career. The most dramatically towered and castle-like section of Castle Howard, the eastern service range (fig. 46), was not begun until 1710, and by that time Blenheim Palace, or 'Castle' as it was first called, had been entrusted to Vanbrugh's design, virtually unfettered by any stylistic restraint, for five years.

Then in 1715 Vanbrugh began the extraordinary sprawl of Claremont, with its extensive garden layout, for the Duke of Newcastle (fig. 47). Eastbury for George Dodington was under construction from 1718, Seaton Delaval from 1719, and the new north front of Grimsthorpe Castle from 1722. There were also lesser houses, still of aggressive individuality, like Kings Weston, so there does seem to have been a time when the Vanbrughian Baroque-medieval compromise might have been England's architectural future.[9] So what combination of movements and events brought about Vanbrugh's almost effortless rise to eminence, and kept him as a prime-mover in architectural fashions for over two decades?

There are three possible answers: scholarship, the theatre and a longstanding tradition in English architectural design not just of conservatism, but of obstinate insularity and deliberate historicism. The three are so intricately entangled that the only way to follow them through is crude chronology.

If there was ever an exact starting-point for deliberate historicism, it might be the decision by Henry VII in 1486 to name his first-born son Arthur, consciously

46. The eastern service range at Castle Howard, designed by Vanbrugh and built from 1710.

47. Vanbrugh's brick-built Belvedere at Claremont, Surrey, c. 1715, which towered over the original house that stood beyond and below it.

breaking a long run of Henrys, Edwards and Richards in order to evoke the Celtic myth of the 'once and future king' who would return to save his people. The Tudors needed the support of myth and pseudo-history. The Plantagenets had not, though it is interesting to note that some sources indicate the discovery of a much-decayed body, identified as that of King Arthur, in the grounds of the abbey church at Glastonbury, was made in Henry II's lifetime. Other sources give 1190 and 1191, just after Henry's death in 1189.[10] Arthur's grave was neatly authenticated by a leaden cross with the inscription 'HIC IACET SEPULTUS INCLITUS REX ARTURIUS IN INSULA AVALONIA' (Here lies buried the renowned King Arthur in the Isle of Avalon). In the Great Hall of Winchester Castle, the Saxon capital of Wessex, there is a reputed Arthurian round table. In 1522, in advance of a visit to Winchester by Charles V, the newly crowned Holy Roman Emperor, Henry VIII had himself depicted on the table as Arthur, thereby reinforcing Henry's claim to the inheritance of the British kings. And Renaissance-style tomb chests containing the bones of the Anglo-Saxon kings of Wessex were set up in the choir at Winchester a little later, in 1525, by Bishop Fox.[11]

One manifestation of Tudor Celtic-ness was the zoo of Welsh dragons, each one as large as a fox-hound, carved for Henry VIII on the walls of King's College Chapel, Cambridge, the completion of which might in itself be seen as an act of pious historicism to the memory of Henry VI. Then in Edward VI's mercifully brief reign (1547–52) John Thynne supervised the building of Old Somerset House on the Strand in London for the Duke of Somerset, and it looked as though England might at last be about to catch up with the Renaissance, despite the handicaps of the Reformation. Somerset House, as Summerson has noted, 'was the first deliberate attempt to build in England a front composed altogether in the classical taste'.[12] But this was a relatively isolated incident, and the classical moment passed with the accession of Elizabeth in 1558. Soon the Queen was making her 'progresses' and the country was deep in the annual pantomime of the November Accession Day tournaments, when the aristocracy donned armour, adopted obscure mottoes and pretended to tilt at one another.[13]

Towards the end of the sixteenth century, scholarship, theatre and architecture all took a consciously historicist turn. At towered, triangular Longford Castle in Wiltshire, there was an attempt – with some success – to combine a Renaissance loggia with a moat and castellated round towers (fig. 48), but Robert Smythson's design career in the 1570s and 1580s – Longleat, Wollaton, Worksop and Hardwick – marks a determined and hugely impressive adaptation of Perpendicular Gothic forms to create fantasy castles, entirely indefensible,

48. Longford Castle in Wiltshire, built on a triangular plan and completed in 1591.

eminently habitable.[14] Parallel with this conscious evocation of the past in architecture, Spenser's *Faerie Queene* would, if he had completed its twelve projected books, have centred on Prince Arthur as the embodiment of 'Magnificence'. Spenser deliberately used archaic terms, Chaucerian language, to give his poem the air of a medieval epic, and it abounds in castles, hermits, knights and distressed damsels in dark forests – the essence of Gothic material and Arthurian romance.

As for Shakespeare, his plays are so much a part of the current entertainment industry that it requires a little effort to see how far they were, in their day, exercises in historical imagination, fuelling in audiences a spirit of national identity and historic awareness. Shakespeare, like Spenser and Smythson, has to be ranked as a myth-maker, a dreamer of towers, whether Hamlet's or those of besieged French cities.

An island is a natural breeding ground for patriotic myths and also for a deep regard for past movements in architecture. In Elizabeth's reign, scholars and historians were beginning to add their weight to the antiquarian process, but not in anything like the numbers or the consequence of their seventeenth-century successors. William Camden's first *Britannia* came out, in Latin, in 1586, with enlarged English editions between 1587 and 1607. These contained carefully researched and convincing accounts of the mythic British kings Bladud, Lear and Cole. Two of Shakespeare's plays, *King Lear* and *Cymbeline*, are derived from Camden, setting an impressive precedent for using antiquarian writings as a source for drama.

If the Tudor monarchs had both required and inspired antiquarian or historical evidence to support their uncertain claims to the throne, then James I and subsequent Stuarts needed even more to bolster the shaky concept of Great Britain, the very title being pure historicism. In architectural terms, the reigns of Elizabeth and James were a seamless unity. Robert Smythson even left a son, John, to continue his medieval, towered revival with the exquisitely habitable keep of Bolsover Castle, Derbyshire.[15] Jacobean houses, such as Audley End in Essex and Hatfield in Hertfordshire, are romantic stage scenery, turreted, walled and evocative of some nobler, ideal past from a book of hours.

When Vanbrugh came to design his first country house and looked around him for precedents in layout and image, these towered and turreted courtyard houses of the Elizabethan–Jacobean continuum were what he saw, and in far greater numbers than we see now. As B. Sprague Allen has remarked, in the later seventeenth century 'many ancient houses scattered all over England remained unchanged or were only partially modernized'; this suggests 'to what an extent the progress of classicism was delayed by economic necessity or preference for the old style of building.'[16] Vanbrugh's new classical houses – Castle Howard, Blenheim, Seaton Delaval and the rest – were not the prodigious structures they have come to seem to us. They were close in layout and towered impact to older houses surviving all over the country. Lulworth Castle, Dorset (1607), and Ruperra in Wales (1626) illustrate how acceptable the more compact castle image remained for smaller gentry houses (fig. 49).

By the early seventeenth century, antiquarian scholarship was beginning to feed more or less reliable historical information into society, to be picked up and popularized later by the Restoration dramatists and Vanbrugh's generation.[17]

49. Lulworth Castle, Dorset, 1607, a compact gentry castle near the south coast.

William of Malmesbury, a prime source for the Celtic past, had been translated and published in 1598, and in 1605 Richard Verstegan's *Restitution of Decay'd Intelligence in Antiquity* appeared, an uninviting heavyweight among studies but nevertheless a popular and important work, with later editions in 1628, 1634, 1655 and 1673.[18]

It was in July 1606 that a living Goth, Christian IV of Denmark, came to England on an official state visit. Charles I is rarely remembered as having been half-Goth in blood, but he was: James I had married Anne of Denmark. James's amiable, hard-drinking brother-in-law, King Christian, was not officially titled 'King of Denmark'. Like all his forefathers he had been crowned *Gothorum Vandalorum Rex* ('King of the Goths and the Vandals'). During Christian's long and sometimes embarrassingly drunken stay in London, his correct Gothic title would often have been pronounced.[19] The custom that the abstemious Hamlet deplored – of sounding trumpets and firing off guns whenever a toast was drunk at a feast – was not, as he claimed, exclusively Danish, but a tradition at Garter feasts in St George's Hall, Windsor Castle, and is on record as current in Vanbrugh's time.

Seventeenth-century England was obsessed, largely for political, legal and constitutional reasons, with the Saxons.[20] Celtic Arthur was not forgotten, but, with his rôle as a victor in twelve battles against the invading Saxons, he had become an iconographic embarrassment, one that John Dryden was to handle carefully.

By 1640 a lectureship in Anglo-Saxon had been endowed at Cambridge. Funds were subscribed in 1653 to support William Somner in his research, and in 1659 he was able to publish the key to an entire forgotten literature, his Saxon–Latin–English *Dictionary*.[21] As Saxon institutions were believed to validate the primacy of Parliament over a monarch, Saxon studies were particularly favoured under the Commonwealth. But in 1658 a far more poetic and evocative study than Somner's had been published, an anonymous but brilliant translation of the *Compendius History of the Goths, Swedes and Vandals and other Northern Nations*, originally published in 1555 as *Historia de gentibus septentrionalibus* by Olaus Magnus, Archbishop of Sweden. This was a companion volume to the *Historia de omnibus Gothorum Svenonunque regibus* by his brother, Johannes, published posthumously in 1554.[22] This translation, infinitely more than Verstegan's *Restitution* or Bishop Percy's much later *Reliques of Ancient English Poetry* (1765), should be remembered as the true source-spring of dark legend. Suddenly a frightening Gothic world of Norse myth, cold warrior gods and cruel Valkyries was opened up as a counter-attraction to the hackneyed pantheon of classical Greece and Rome. Olaus claimed that the kings of Denmark were descended from the beastly rape of a fair maid by a bear, which, if true, gives the Stuarts, and even Queen Elizabeth II, a measure of bruin blood.[23] The book's chapter headings exude an icy poetry:

> Of the Ports of Iron Rings
> Of the Night dances of Fairies and Ghosts
> Of the Piracy of Famous Virgins
> Of the fight of Frotho and Fridlevus against a Serpent
> Of the dancing of the Bears in Lithuania.

And there is a most chilling account from Iceland of how the dead sometimes returned to fornicate with the living.

Ruperra of 1626 should logically have been the last play-acting castle in Britain, but the genre continued sporadically after the Restoration. The towered wings of that prodigy house of 1598, Westwood Park in Worcestershire, date from 1660–70, while Drayton House, Northamptonshire, was given its impressive

50. Jeffry Wyatville's drawing of the east front of the Upper Ward, Windsor Castle, undertaken by Hugh May in 1675–84, which impressed and influenced Vanbrugh.

castle walls and gatehouse by Henry Mordaunt, 2nd Earl of Peterborough, before 1676, using as his architect John Webb, who can hardly have relished such a Gothic task.[24] But the outstanding medievalist symbol of the Restoration, and Vanbrugh's most important precedent, was Windsor Castle, as rebuilt under Hugh May's supervision. The style devised for the exterior work is best described as a melancholy neo-Norman, yet no attempt was made to create medievalizing interiors. Instead, gloriously riotous Baroque decoration by imported Italians, notably Antonio Verrio, was heaped up. We know the northern and eastern elevations of May's castle-palace from views by Paul Sandby and Jeffry Wyatville, and they do seem to have been actively depressing, with low towers, no lively caps and what doors there were hidden in the side-angles of the towers (fig. 50). But Vanbrugh claimed to admire it, and urged the rebuilt Windsor as an example to follow when, in 1707, he was persuading the Duke of Manchester to accept his gauche scheme for adding a battlemented frill to the otherwise classical elevations of Kimbolton Castle, Huntingdonshire:

> As to the Outside, I thought 'twas absolutely best, to give it Something of the Castle Air, tho' at the Same time to make it regular. . . . This method was practic'd at Windsor in King Charles's time, And has been universally Approv'd, So I hope your Ldship won't be discourag'd, if any Italians you may Shew it to, shou'd find fault that 'tis not Roman, for to have built a Front with Pillasters, and what the Orders require cou'd never have been born with the Rest of the Castle: I'm sure this will make a very Noble and Masculine Shew.[25]

Windsor's expensive recladding is usually blamed on Prince Rupert, who became Constable of the Castle in 1662; but the Prince's private rooms, which John Evelyn described as 'hung with tapisserie, curious & effeminate Pictures',[26] do not suggest a taste for the rugged and the martial. Hugh May began the reconstruction of Windsor in 1675, three years after Elias Ashmole had published *The Institution, Laws and Ceremonies of the Most Noble Order of the Garter* (with further editions in 1693 and 1715), an important revival after the Commonwealth hiatus, and a book that could hardly have failed to draw the spotlight of national attention on the royal castle.[27] The double-page illustrations of the complex are Wenceslaus Hollar's greatest achievement, photographic in their accuracy and amazing in their technical expertise (fig. 51). Every detail of the two wards is laid out in their pre-Hugh May medieval magnificence, while the interior views of St George's Chapel – one looking east, one west – with added illustrations of the screen and chantry chapels, actually make a fine building look more beautiful than it really is, or was. Another illustration shows a feast in progress in St George's Hall, revealing that today's Tudor-style hammerbeam roof (recently raised after the disastrous fire) harks back over two subsequent installations to the original medieval structure shown by Hollar.

Ashmole's text is, of course, painfully scholarly and detailed, but – as in John Ogilby's very similar folio volume of 1662, *The Entertainment of His Most Excellent Majestie Charles II in His Passing through the City of London to His CORONATION* – it is the brilliant quality of the illustrations that must have influenced comparative stylistic thinking. Ogilby shows, full-page again, all four classical triumphal arches raised for the King's procession; one with a great dome

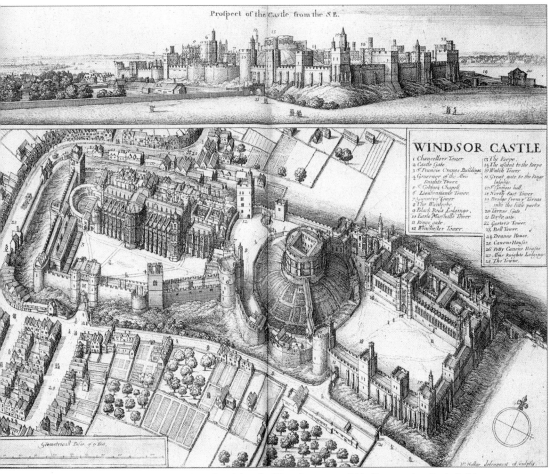

Prospect of the Castle from the S.E.

WINDSOR CASTLE

1 Chancellors Tower
2 Castle Gate
3 S.t Francis Crosses Buildings
4 Gouernor of the Alms Knights Tower
5 S.t Gobryes Chapell
6 Lieutenants Tower
7 Spinners Tower
8 The Wardrobe
9 Black Rods Lodaings
10 Earle Marshalls Tower
11 Pinne gate
12 Winchester Tower
13 The Keepe
14 The ascent to the Keepe
15 Watch Tower
16 Great gate to the lower lodaing
17 S.t Thomas hall
18 North East Tower
19 Bridge from y.e Terras into the little parke
20 Terras Gate
21 Darke ashe
22 Garters Tower
23 Bell Tower
24 Deanes House
25 Canons House
26 Petty Canons House
27 Alms Knights Lodgings
28 The Towne

Geometricall Plan of y.e Bed.

W. Hollar delineavit et sculpsit.

51. Wenceslaus Hollar's 'Windsor Castle', a brilliantly executed bird's-eye view included in
Elias Ashmole's The Institutions, Laws & Ceremonies of the Most Noble Order of the
Garter, 1672.

over precisely delineated classical orders, which, with its theatrical panache, could
well have influenced Vanbrugh (fig. 52). But, despite this parade of pure classical
forms, the most striking is still to come with a resounding illustration of the
moment of Charles's enthronement, when the whole aristocratic throng in
Westminster Abbey is made to look insignificant by the tremendous display of
Gothic arches in the main arcade, triforium and clerestory of the choir (fig. 53). It
would take a conscious effort to forget the potential force of Gothic building after
absorbing that double-page spread.

On a more subdued but still very impressive note are the histories published in
this period. They tend, such was the legal obsessiveness of the time, to end at the
Conquest and give the Saxons their full measure of attention. John Milton's *The
History of Britain* of 1670 covers 'That part especially now call'd ENGLAND From
the first Traditional beginning, continued to the Norman Conquest'. Similarly,

52. A Triumphal Arch raised to line Charles II's coronation procession, from John Ogilby's The Entertainment of His Most Excellent Majestie Charles II in His Passing through the City of London to His Coronation, *1662*

Aylett Sammes's *Britannia Antiqua Illustrata* of 1676 goes into details of the rulers of the Heptarchy kingdoms rarely covered by modern studies.[28] Sammes was much quarried by Dryden for his libretto for Purcell's 'Dramatick Opera' of 1691, *King Arthur*, which will be treated in detail below in its chronological place. One scene of *King Arthur* is drawn directly from an illustration by Sammes of three Saxon gods, namely Thor, Woden and Frea, although Dryden omits the explanation from Sammes that Frea is a bisexual cross-dresser (fig. 54). In his plates Sammes also gives a civilized interpretation of an Ancient Briton to indicate how confident historians of his time were when imagining the appearance of our remote ancestors.

What is almost invariably ignored when Vanbrugh's medieval yearnings are discussed is the real route by which he, a moderately successful playwright and certainly neither a scholar nor architect by training, acquired that sympathy with medieval airs and towered profiles that allowed him to breathe poetic life into Baroque forms just as the Baroque was going out of fashion elsewhere in Europe.[29] It was the contemporary London theatre and his own play-going.

It is important to stress that Vanbrugh never built a true Gothic or pointed arch in his life. His medievalizing was a personal obsession that found expression in projects for his own homes and those of his relatives: Chargate in Surrey and, later, Castle Vanbrugh at Greenwich, together with the other villas around it. These had a convincing castle air, but only when seen from a distance. Then there was the five-eighths of a mile of towered, apparently medieval, walls in the park at Castle Howard. All these are interesting experiments, but Vanbrugh's fame

53. *Charles II's enthronement in Westminster Abbey, from John Ogilby's* The Entertainment of His Most Excellent Majestie Charles II in His Passing through the City of London to His Coronation, *1662.*

rightly rests on the great houses raised in his liberated Baroque style, which have only subliminally medieval airs.

As for the antiquaries, the only one of any intellectual substance in the early eighteenth century was William Stukeley, whose *Itinerarium Curiosum* came out in 1724, too late to have any significant influence on Vanbrugh.[30] The architectural studies of Stukeley's contemporaries are a most unimpressive collection. Of their eight published works, six are studies of large churches: Richard Rawlinson's *Hereford* (1717), Browne Willis's surveys of four Welsh cathedrals (1717) and his surveys of York, Durham, Hereford and Worcester (1727), John Dart's *Westminster Abbey* (1723) and *Canterbury* (1726). Slightly earlier are Thomas Hearne's journey from Windsor to Oxford, published in Leland's *Itinerary* (1711), and Thomas Staveley's *History of Churches in England* (1712). These last two believed that all Saxon churches were built of wood and hence had perished. None of the five authors differentiated Romanesque work from Gothic, but embraced all as 'Gothick'. They evolved no descriptive language of architectural terms, and their only importance is that they indicate a growing interest in ecclesiastical monuments of the past.

It was popular movements that really influenced Vanbrugh not to be Gothic, but Romantic. Would his incarceration in the Bastille and, earlier, at Vincennes have given him a taste for towers? Possibly. His boyhood in Chester, a romantically

54. Thor, Woden and Frea, three of the Saxon gods illustrated in Aylett Sammes's Britannia Antiqua Illustrata, *1676.*

walled city, must surely have been of more seminal influence. In the late seventeenth century most English towns still retained their medieval walls and gatehouses; for example, Newcastle, Shrewsbury, Worcester, Bristol, Exeter, Chichester, Winchester, Norwich, even Bath, were still guarded by fortifications. Celia Fiennes visited Carlisle in 1698 and pronounced that 'the walls of the town and battlements and towers are in very good repair and looks well'.[31] Vanbrugh's youthful years had no doubt given him a predisposition towards historic towns, and possibly an aesthetic preference for the north of England. As he revealingly declared in 1721 during a Northern tour: 'Lumley Castle is a Noble thing. . . . If I had good weather in this Expedition, I shou'd have been well enough diverted in it; there being many more Valluable and Agreeable things and Places to be Seen, than in the Tame Sneaking South of England.'[32] He had, then, a natural feeling for dramatic irregularities, in landscape as well as in buildings. However, his modernizing of the asymmetrical courtyard ranges of fourteenth-century Lumley eventually made the castle more regular by the imposition of symmetrical façades. This was still a very classical response to an historic building.[33]

What propelled Vanbrugh most towards historic pomps and fraught romances was his background of play-going. Here we must rethink our selective twentieth-century perceptions of Restoration theatre. Today we encounter only inexpensive revivals of the comedies by men like Wycherley, Congreve and, of course, Vanbrugh, where adultery is all too often the theme and cuckoldry the goal. Such comedies certainly had their place, though Vanbrugh's only two real successes in a string of such writings both came at the very end of that period when theatrical immorality was fashionable. But throughout the last forty years of the seventeenth century, running parallel with cynical comedy, had been what might be termed the Theatre of Honour, essentially an English version of French drama, with epic plays after Racine and semi-operas by Dryden, Aphra Behn, William Davenant, Thomas Otway, Nathaniel Lee and Elkanah Settle packing the theatres with battles, escapades and solemn romantic love scenes. Dryden's *The Indian Emperour* (1665), *Aureng-Zebe* (1675), *Albion and Albanius* (1685), Davenant's *The Cruelty of the Spaniards in Peru* (1658), Settle's *The Empress of Morocco* (1673), Lee's *Caesar Borgia* (1679) are just a few of the titles; there are thirty or forty more.[34]

Dryden – exotic, military and grandiose in his themes, romantic in plotting – was the towering dramatist of Vanbrugh's youth and maturity, not smutty Wycherley or Congreve. But we tend to ignore Dryden, and as a result we miss what Vanbrugh and his generation absorbed – a bizarre mix of battles, majestic pomps and noble posturing. And these plays had elaborate painted scenery.[35] The prologue to Shadwell's *The Tempest* of 1674 declared:

> We, as the fathers of the Stage have said,
> To treat you here, a vast expense have made.

The transformation scene at the end of Dryden's *Albion and Albanius* had scenes, first of 'that part of Windsor, which faces Eaton', then the Terrace Walk with the King's Lodgings, St George's Chapel, the Keep and the Upper Ward, while 'In the Air is a Vision of the Honours of the Garter; the Knights in Procession and the King under a Canopy'. All this was clearly a memory of Hollar's superb illustrations to Ashmole's book, not a memory of real events. In other plays there were grottoes, a 'Temple of the Sun', a 'Street of Palaces', a grove of trees. Extravagantly painted backcloths or side-flats bearing depictions of these scenes that were pushed out on grooves from either side of the stage could be admired or criticized by the play-goers. One direction in Dryden's *Albion and Albanius* reads: 'the great Arch is open, and the view is continued through the open part of the Exchange, to the Arch on the other side, and thence to as much of the Street beyond, as could properly be taken'. Cross that complexity with a Temple of the Sun, as in *The Indian Emperour, or, The Conquest of Mexico by the Spaniards* of 1665, and we begin to see the visual sources of Blenheim.[36] Elsewhere in the same text, 'Part of the Scene disappears and the Four Triumphal Arches erected at his Majesties Coronation are seen'.

It was this familiarity with exotic heights of drama, added to their military successes abroad, that allowed the triumphant Whigs – Carlisle, Marlborough, Manchester – to accept impossible palaces as no more than their due. They could take romantic grandiosity in their stride. Castle Howard was to have been littered with triumphal arches (the bird's-eye view in volume three of *Vitruvius Britannicus*, 1725, is proof of this), and still retains quite a number. Even though Vanbrugh gives no hint of having read the antiquaries at first hand, he would have been familiar, as a Herald, with some of this material.[37] But he had no need to study antiquarian literature too deeply, for as one of the men about town, a member of the Kit Cat Club, how many first nights at the theatre had he missed? Surely very few. It was the Theatre of Honour, its scenery and its ethos, that liberated his visual imagination, hence the absolute *in*authenticity of his creations in medieval terms.

Let us consider Vanbrugh's first three successes in life, all packed into a mere three years. First, in 1696, *The Relapse*, and in 1697 *The Provok'd Wife*; then after these predictabilities comes Castle Howard, begun 1699. Does the sequence make sense? Is there any kind of connection? Seemingly none at all. But take Purcell's *King Arthur, or, The British Worthy*, with libretto by Dryden, presented in June 1691 at the Dorset Garden Theatre by Vanbrugh's patron Sir Thomas Skipwith, and the contemporary influences begin to connect.[38] With King William's War then raging in Flanders, Ireland and New England, and with the War of the Spanish Succession (1702–13) soon to follow, it was an intensely jingoistic age of military successes, so Dryden's theme is predictably war and battles. The opening of one scene reveals 'A Battle supposed to be given behind the Scenes, with Drums, Trumpets, and Military shouts and Excursions: After which, the *Britons*, expressing their Joy for the Victory, sing this Song of Triumph'. If, for King Arthur, we substitute General John Churchill, then Earl (but later Duke) of Marlborough, we have the atmosphere of the future Blenheim Palace:

Come if you dare, *our Trumpets sound,*
Come if you dare, *the Foes rebound:*
We come, we come, we come, we come,
Says the double double double Beat of the Thund'ring Drum.
    Now they charge on amain,
    Now they rally again:
The Gods from above the Mad Labour behold,
And pity Mankind that will perish for Gold. [39]

This catches the national mood. Vanbrugh devised an architecture for a second imperial age, only this time England had not been saved, as in Elizabeth's reign against the Spaniards, by luck and bad weather. England was now a new super-power, and from 1704 onwards its armies were trampling on the French and their allies with exhilarating regularity. That was why Castle Howard, after 1710, like a new stage-set being pushed out, gained unconvincing but dramatic towers on its eastern service range. Not only were these intended to give the complex a military air, they may also have been a conscious historicist gesture towards the old Henderskelfe Castle, still *in situ* then, which Leland had described as 'a fair quadrant of stone having 4 toures builded castelle like'.[40] The nation's triumphal militarist mood also accounts for the line of fortified walls set up in the next decade to straddle the approach to Castle Howard. England was at last a main player on the continental and American stages. This explains why Blenheim, unlike Castle Howard, was towered from the start, but not convincingly towered, only a stage designer's towers, tricked out with trophies of lions savaging cockerels, and cannon-balls and flaming grenades, not unlike the trophies on the Invalides with which the French, a little earlier, had celebrated their victories. And Blenheim has a castle-style moat like virtually every seventeenth-century French château, and is approached on the east via an almost medieval gatehouse. Vanbrugh even gave the formal garden and the kitchen-garden, both to the south of the house, huge bastioned walls (fig. 17).[41] So the castle-palace ends up looking like King Arthur's Camelot, but from a picturesque distance (fig. 55).

55. The main (north) front of Blenheim Palace, Oxfordshire, a Vanbrughian Camelot built from 1705.

Naturally the Whigs, who had invited William over to England from the United Provinces and had thus set off the train of martial successes, were eager to take the credit and build a super-power's super houses. The new Protestant monarch is evoked in the finale of Purcell's *King Arthur*, although the scene is set in the Dark Ages with King Arthur. But Arthur's Britons, like Elias Ashmole, are celebrating the Order of the Garter, which of course was not instituted until 1349, another instance of a lack of interest in historical accuracy. They tell William of Orange how lucky he is to have got away from miserable little Holland and become king of a real country, England:

> Saint George the Patron of our Isle!
> A Soldier and a Saint,
> On that Auspicious Order smile,
> Which Love and Arms will plant.
>
> Our Natives not alone appear
> To Court this Martial Prize;
> But Foreign Kings adopted here,
> Their Crowns at Home despise.
>
> Our Soveraign High in Aweful State,
> His Honours shall bestow;
> And see his Sceptr'd Subjects wait
> On his Commands below.[42]

When we consider the arrogance of Dryden's vocabulary, we begin to understand the spirit of the architecture: 'Foreign Kings *adopted* here . . . their Crowns at Home *despise*'; or 'his *Sceptr'd* Subjects'. Monarchs normally carried sceptres as symbols of their power, but now the subjects are consciously, proudly sceptred. These were the early, intoxicating years, when the aristocratic club that was to run Britain for the next century first took over. It was their mood of ebullient jingoism – confident, extrovert, innovative – that created Blenheim, and Blenheim was unique. Classical rules and precedents did not allow for it, but the great Tudor and Jacobean castles did.

Three men brought this sculptural prodigy of a building into existence between 1705 and 1709 by trial and error, argument and model-making. There was Vanbrugh with his sense of theatre and his fascination with the presentation of episodes from history on the contemporary stage, Hawksmoor with the technical expertise acquired while working on the west towers of St Paul's with Wren, and the Duke of Marlborough with a successful commander's sense of self-importance and swagger. Vanbrugh thought up the panache, Hawksmoor realized his ideas and made them practicable by his structural drawings, Marlborough urged them on and carted a giant trophy of Louis XIV and stone banners back from Tournai to crown a parapet at his new palace. As Kerry Downes has perceptively written, this colossal bust was intended as 'a perpetual version of the traditional head upon a stake'.[43]

Possibly the most revealing episode in Vanbrugh's building career was his desperate attempt to rescue what was left of Woodstock Manor, the old Plantagenet hunting palace adjacent to Rosamond's Well in Blenheim's park, from the Duchess of Marlborough, who was determined to pull it down and who eventually succeeded.[44] The longstanding battle to preserve or demolish the Manor was one reason why the Duchess sacked Vanbrugh in 1716. He had reroofed and repaved the Manor, not just to secure for himself a house near the building works, but because theatrically it was a hot property. '*Are there any that do not run eagerly to See* what Ancient Remains are to be found of Rosamonds Bower?', he demanded in 1709.[45]

All that can be seen today is the unimpressive flow of Rosamond's Well. In its prime it was surrounded by a cloister of Norman arches built by Henry II to create a love-nest for his mistress Rosamond (real name Jane Clifford).[46] Much still survived in Vanbrugh's day, and the reason he was excited by it was that in 1692 John Bancroft had written *Henry II, King of England; with the Death of Rosamond*, followed in 1707 by Joseph Addison and Thomas Clayton's semi-opera *Rosamond*. Bancroft's version of the tale of Rosamond anticipates every feature of the eighteenth-century Gothic novel – wicked monks, evil queens, languishing death-bed heroines. Poor Rosamond chooses poison rather than the dagger so that she can live a few minutes more and bid Henry an affecting farewell. That was why Vanbrugh wanted to preserve the Manor: it was a piece of history, and a piece of theatre. Also, it was towered and rugged. 'I have set the Oxford Masons upon the offices in the Kitchen Court', he told the Duchess in one of his more ingratiating letters, 'and do promise your Grace I will have the homely simplicity of the Antient Manor in my constant thoughts for a guide in what remains to be done, in all the inferior Buildings'.[47] We have to accept the castellated round-arched loggias of Blenheim's kitchen-court, together with its overwhelming carriage arch, as Vanbrugh's idea of 'homely simplicity' (fig. 56). One of the features of his design career that we find most difficult to grasp is that his was the last generation sublimely indifferent to what we would call historical authenticity.

At the start of Purcell and Dryden's *King Arthur* there is a dramatic anticipation of Wagnerian opera. Dryden had done his research into Aylett Sammes and found the plate (fig. 54) of Woden in fifteenth-century armour, Thor in Roman toga and Frea looking like an all-in wrestler. From this plate, he and Purcell built up an atmospheric opening scene in which six Saxon warriors, hypnotized by an evil spirit named Grimbald, volunteer to be sacrificed. Then, to make victory doubly sure, the Saxons sacrifice a holocaust of beasts to all three gods: it is a real precursor of Frazer's *Golden Bough* as well as Wagner's Ring cycle. In addition to his debt to Sammes, which he admits, Dryden has taken evil Grimbald and Merlin's good spirit Philidel from the enchanted Baltic world of Olaus Magnus. All these Saxon warriors, in addition to their theatrical costumes, would have been wearing their fashionable periwigs, just as everyone in Hollar's

56. Vanbrugh's East Gate at Blenheim Palace.

57. Shirburn Castle, Oxfordshire, 1716–25, the fourteenth-century wreck bought by a Lord Chancellor and transformed into a romantic retreat.

depiction of Charles II's coronation procession wears the tall-brimmed hat of the period, as a flourish to their robes of office: it is as if every man at Queen Elizabeth II's coronation in 1953 had worn a trilby. Upper-class characters in all these exotic plays of the Theatre of Honour, whether Aztec Mexicans or fifteenth-century Moors, wore periwigs.[48] That is how we should be thinking of Blenheim: a castle-palace with periwigs.

The next stage towards authenticity, the doffing, as it were, of the periwig and the adoption of convincing battlements, came in 1716: that was the year when Vanbrugh was sacked unceremoniously from Blenheim, and when Robert Parker, an up-and-coming lawyer and a most unscrupulous man who was soon to be Lord Chancellor and Earl of Macclesfield, bought the wreck of a fourteenth-century castle at Shirburn in Oxfordshire. Whereas Blenheim was built on a new site ignoring the potentially influential remains of Woodstock Manor, Shirburn was built firmly on the foundations of the old castle and within the limits of a moated site. It was completed in 1725, a romantic prodigy (fig. 57).[49] Virtually everything we can see of Shirburn today dates from the eighteenth century, and it is built of brick rendered over. Only one fourteenth-century entrance arch survives. Can Shirburn be described, with all its round-arched windows, as neo-Norman on a genuine Gothic base? The arches have no Norman-style capitals, but neither do they have classical keystones. Still the home of a fiercely private Lord Macclesfield, Shirburn has never been given its due of stylistic originality in the Gothic Revival.[50] The acclaim always goes to Clearwell Castle in Gloucestershire's Forest of Dean, designed in 1728 by Roger Morris for Thomas Wyndham. Clearwell is a typical product from a classically trained architect constrained by his patron to give an otherwise Palladian format a castle air; it is very close in style to Vanbrugh's remodelled Lumley Castle.[51] Clearwell is a stolid, unromantic building when compared with Shirburn in its swan-haunted moat, still crossed by a functioning Regency drawbridge. It is true that Shirburn was not built *de novo*, but we must consider its visual beauty, nearness to London, 1716–25 date, and the fact that it was the seat of a Lord Chancellor. In the 1720s, that decade of stylistic uncertainty when Baroque and Palladian were fighting it out, Gothic of a kind was waiting in the wings.

Vanbrugh and his tutor, advisor, clerk of works and successor, Nicholas Hawksmoor, were both caught, like other architects of the time – William Kent and James Gibbs, for instance – on this cusp of authenticity. But unlike Vanbrugh and Hawksmoor, who were both essentially insular architects, Kent and Gibbs were men of a younger generation, with study in Italy as part of their training. As a consequence they were able to make more of the style, and work with Gothic in a different manner. When, between 1719 and 1725, Vanbrugh was raising that extraordinary five-eighths of a mile of towered walls in the park at Castle Howard, he cited an English precedent for the military authenticity of its detail (fig. 58).

58. Vanbrugh's mock fortification walls at Castle Howard, built 1719–25.

William Etty, the clerk of works in charge, was proposing spirelets to cap the towers. But Vanbrugh strongly disapproved. 'Towers upon Walls', he wrote to Lord Carlisle on 10 December 1724, 'are Suited to them as part of the Fortifications, and are Suppos'd to be lodgings or Storehouses, and as Such only require a Covering, which may however be in a degree ornamental, but shou'd not look too light and trifling'.[52] A few weeks earlier, on 21 November 1723, he had written urging a simple cap: 'I have seen one upon a round Tower on the Walls of Chester, that I thought did extreamly well'.[53]

This joint exercise in designing is just one instance in a long career that proves Vanbrugh was not a lone architect, but one half of a brilliant partnership. Vanbrugh, the confident amateur, influenced Hawksmoor, the hesitant, retiring professional, rather than the other way round. From Vanbrugh, Hawksmoor picked up that trick of designing every detail *fortissimo*. His East End of London church towers are powerful, heightened versions of Blenheim's theatrical Baroque. But Hawksmoor, who survived Vanbrugh by ten years, edged further into archaeological accuracy. Far ahead of his unenterprising contemporary antiquaries, he had observed and made stylistic definitions, naming them 'Monastick' (Norman), 'Saracenic' (Early English), 'Tracery' (Decorated) and 'Filigrane' (Perpendicular).[54] Although he was building pure stage-scenery towers at All Souls College, Oxford, from 1716, Hawksmoor made a significant practical advance towards scholarly revivalism in his works of 1716–20 at Beverley Minster. There he supplied the crossing with a convex cap, and produced elegant details of carved Gothic woodwork derived from the early fourteenth-century Percy tomb.[55] And finally, at Westminster Abbey, he found a distressfully clumsy, half-finished composition of the late fourteenth century by Henry Yvele, and designed in 1734 the eminently tactful part-Gothic, part-classical west front that we all find satisfying enough.

By 1733, seven years after Vanbrugh's death, William Kent had completed Esher Place in Surrey, his first major building, in what was, at the time, termed the 'Gothick' style. Whereas Vanbrugh's 'Early Mediaevalism' had been ruggedly military and theatrical, a masculine reinterpretation of the Middle Ages, Kent's new 'Gothick' was a fusion of classical motifs with the intensely feminine forms of ecclesiastical Gothic. Neither was authentic, but both were necessary stages towards the revival of true medieval architecture. Esher Place was designed, like Shirburn Castle, around an authentic medieval Gothic core, a fifteenth-century gatehouse.[56] It was Henry Pelham's suburban London seat for the entire nine years of his term as First Lord of the Treasury, initially as a successful warlord, then later as a much appreciated taxcutter. Surrounded by an enchanting Rococo park, its Gothick towers and rooms of entertainment, all a mere 9 miles from London, meant that medievalism – not subliminal as at Blenheim, and not yet scholarly in its details, but charming, surprising and unashamed – was coming into its own. Pelham's only mistake was that, being a busy minister, he had no time, unlike Horace Walpole fifteen years later, to write and boast about his originality.

SIX

Exotics and Botanical Illustration

Mark Laird

On 30 March 1717 the Kit Cat Club convened what seems to have been its final gathering. The Duke of Newcastle was in the chair. Kerry Downes tells us:

> This may have been in the nature of a discreet stag party for the Duke, who was married three days later. Did they perhaps regale themselves with Sir John's cup? Pope told Spence that it consisted of 'Water or small beer; mead; port – two glasses each; rum, saffron – a very little of each; nutmeg, poker, orange or lemon-peel in winter; balm etc. in summer.[1]

Sir John Vanbrugh certainly knew how to enjoy himself with Kit Cat chums: toasting beauties in 'Bumpers';[2] or 'sopping our Arses in the Fountain' at Hampton Court Palace.[3] Likewise he appreciated, as much as liqueurs and spices from the Indies, the good things that came out of the earth: 'currants red as blood . . . and gooseberrys, peaches, pairs, apples, and plumbs to gripe the gutts [?] of a nation'.[4] He responded to kitchen-gardens bursting with apricots and grapes. And, in the wider landscape, he embraced scenes of licentious as much as controlled planting: espalier hedges trimmed to perfection; parterres of obelisks that recalled the skylines of Constantinople and London; and picturesque ruins embosomed in a thicket of promiscuous yews and hollies.[5] Yet how much did Vanbrugh cherish the delicate beauty of flowers? Did he understand the allure of exotics beyond taste and intoxication? Or does this casual reference in a letter written at Blenheim on 18 July 1709 indicate a dismissive, perhaps even martial, view of Flora:

> Nor will there be so pleasant a Room for View Nor so cool (yet all the same Gay and light) in the Whole house, as that Greenhouse or Detach'd Gallery, for that indeed is what I take it to be, And not a Magazine for a parcell of foolish Plants.[6]

In the same year as that final gathering of the Kit Cat Club, William Sherard (fig. 59) – a man who had devoted himself entirely to the science of 'foolish Plants' – was on his way back to London from Smyrna (Izmir). Sherard was Vanbrugh's contemporary but not, in all likelihood, his acquaintance; he had spent the past fourteen years as Consul in the Turkish port. Now, at the age of fifty-eight, he was coming home to catch up on lost years. Like Vanbrugh, he

59. Anon., William Sherard, *before 1728, a leading botanist and supporter of horticultural advances in the early eighteenth century.*

had known convivial days in London, in Sherard's case among a circle of botanists and horticulturists who gathered at the Temple Coffee House to examine exotics. He had briefly tasted thrills and good fortune – working with Joseph Pitton de Tournefort in Paris; helping the Duchess of Beaufort to enlarge her plant collections at Badminton. But unlike Vanbrugh, who from the age of thirty-two seemed to enjoy one theatrical or architectural triumph after another, Sherard failed to find immediate rewards through his passion for botany. In fact, he would never achieve his main goal in life: revising Caspar Bauhin's *Pinax* of 1623, a comprehensive but by then outdated index of plant names.

And yet Sherard's life, always at the mercy of contingencies, was a success story. He is, in fact, no less than the *éminence grise* of English botany and horticulture in the age of Vanbrugh: a sponsor helping Mark Catesby to undertake a second voyage to North America; a facilitator bringing Johannes Jacobus Dillenius from Giessen to London to work on his revision of Bauhin's *Pinax* and thereby his brother's *Hortus Elthamensis*, which Blanche Henrey has called the 'most important book to be published in England during the eighteenth century on the plants growing in a private garden';[7] and, finally, of course, a benefactor, founding the Sherardian Chair of Botany at Oxford with an endowment of £3,000. Indeed, without him, the flowering of the English landscape garden might never have been quite so remarkable, nor the planting so manic. In this sense, the path from Baroque horticulture to Picturesque planting design can be interpreted as the convergence *and* divergence of two dramatically contrasting worlds represented by architect and botanist – Vanbrugh, confident in knowing that life had dealt him a good hand of cards; Sherard, less consequential, but just as assured in his final acts of turning worldly wealth into art and science.

Let us take up Sherard's story at St John's College, Oxford, in 1678. It is the year after his matriculation, and coincidentally the year that Vanbrugh's father was writing to Henry Compton, Bishop of London, in the wake of the Titus Oates revelations. It was also the year that the Revd John Banister reached Virginia and began collecting plants for Compton. While studying law until 1683, Sherard must have encountered Dr Robert Morison at the Oxford Physic Garden. Doubtless benefiting from the reputation in the natural sciences that St John's College had, his inclinations turned to botany. By the mid-1680s he was studying under Tournefort in Paris and Paul Hermann in Leiden. By 1688, Tournefort's proposal of working on Bauhin's *Pinax* was uppermost in Sherard's mind; his mood must have been buoyant. On his return to England that season – just as Vanbrugh was being led to prison in Calais – Sherard was catching up on developments in the world of horticulture in London. Interesting things were happening in a garden in Fulham.

Henry Compton, the sixth son of the 2nd Earl of Northampton, became Bishop of London in 1675. Due to the enforced retirement to Fulham Palace that came with his political allegiances, Bishop Compton had plenty of time to devote to his greatest passion: a 'Genius for Botanism'.[8] As Stephen Switzer later observed, Compton was:

> one of the first that encouraged the Importation, Raising, and Increase of Exoticks, in which he was the most curious Man in that Time . . . and by the Recommendation of Chaplains into foreign Parts, had likewise greater Advantages of improving it than any other Gentleman could.[9]

The Revd John Banister was one such chaplain. He reached Virginia in 1678, and on two occasions sent consignments of plants to Fulham for Compton (who was, incidentally, Bishop of Virginia too): the first arrived in 1683, and the second in 1688. Banister's untimely death in 1692 in a shooting accident near the Roanoke River prevented him from publishing the record of plants observed in the wild. Yet, as the Ewans have documented in *John Banister and his Natural History of Virginia*,[10] the impact of his unpublished work on later nomenclature – and notably Linnaeus's binomials – was enormous. His delicate drawings remain among the earliest impressions, however fugitive, of a new North American flora. It was to be another half century before Mark Catesby brought that flora of 'foreign Parts' to prominence in English gardening circles through his *Natural History of Carolina, Florida, and the Bahama Islands*.[11]

Banister's immediate impact was at Fulham Palace, where the new immigrants had a first home. A few years ago Sandra Morris, with the help of the late John Harvey, compiled lists of plants grown by Bishop Compton. The list of woody

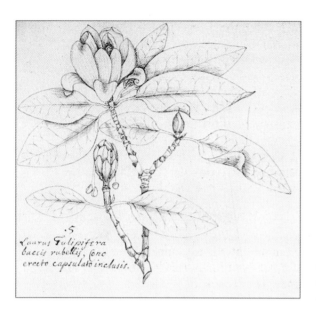

Laurus Tulipifera
baccis rubellis, (one
erecto capsulato inclusis.

60. John Banister, Magnolia virginiana, c. *1688,*
one of a number of plants collected in Virginia by
Banister and sent to Fulham Palace, London.

species suggests that, well before Catesby and John Bartram, the influx from the
colonies had begun in earnest. Banister's first consignment of 1683 almost
certainly included *Baccharis halimifolia, Cornus amomum, Crataegus pedicellata,
Lindera benzoin* and *Liquidambar styraciflua*.[12] The second contained *Acer
negundo, Aralia spinosa, Rhus copallina* and the very significant *Magnolia
virginiana* (fig. 60) – the first magnolia to reach Europe. Introductions linked to
Banister's endeavours (sometimes posthumously) also include *Physocarpus
opulifolius* in 1687, *Quercus coccinea* and *Rhododendron viscosum* in 1691, possibly
Ostrya virginiana in 1691, *Picea mariana* in 1693, possibly *Myrica cerifera* in 1699,
and possibly *Rubus odoratus* in 1700. The list of non-woody species is also
impressive: *Dicentra cucullaria* (fig. 61), *Trillium sessile* and *Viola pedata* in 1688,
Gillenia trifoliata in 1690, *Dodecatheon meadia* (fig. 62) in 1692, *Sisyrinchium
angustifolium* in 1693 and *Echinacea purpurea* and *Mertensia virginica* in 1699.[13]
     There is very little documentation on how these plants were grown at Fulham,
but it seems reasonable to assume that they formed a scientific collection,
formally organized for classification in *pulvilli* or order beds. Banister's imports
were grown in the open air to test for hardiness. Once propagated, a new plant
might be passed to another collector or into the nursery trade through Compton's
one-time gardener, George London. But wider dispersal did not guarantee
permanent status as nursery stock. It was a haphazard process.
     John Harvey's 'The English Nursery Flora, 1677–1723' provides a convenient
way of checking the rate of dispersal.[14] Of the sixteen trees and shrubs associated
with Banister, only two made it into the nursery trade: *Baccharis halimifolia* and
Physocarpus opulifolius (fig. 74). Of the eight non-woody species, only *Echinacea
purpurea* turns up in nurseries before 1723. In other words, a mere
12 or 13 per cent of the Banister imports to Fulham had succeeded in becoming
widely available commodities. Of course, earlier introductions made through the
Tradescants had already established secure positions within nursery catalogues:

the tulip tree (*Liriodendron tulipifera*) of 1638, for example, or the Virginian bladder-nut (*Staphylea trifolia*, fig. 78) of 1640. However, the slow dispersal rate for the Banister introductions suggests that until the Bartram/Collinson imports of the 1730s, the North American flora was only sporadically entering the English commercial market.

The likelihood is that most exotics remained for some time objects of scientific and artistic interest among relatively small groups of 'curious' collectors. This is where William Sherard enters the scene once again, for he appears at the centre of a significant but elusive group who gathered at the Temple Coffee House to examine and exchange plants. Sherard had spent a good part of the 1690s in the rôle of tutor.[15] From June 1690 he educated Sir Arthur Rawdon's son at Moira, County Down, where he collected many botanical specimens. Then, after three and a half years, Sherard escaped the isolation of Ireland to spend 1693–4 in London and Oxford, just as Vanbrugh was finally able to return to England after his release from the Bastille. The next appointment was as companion to Charles, Viscount Townsend, on a tour of the continent until late in 1697; and finally, he was tutor to Wriothesley Russell, Marquess of Tavistock (2nd Duke of Bedford from 1700). Thus, while Sherard was only in London on a limited basis, he remained in contact with members of that loosely constituted 'Temple Coffee House Botanic Club'. This club seems to have been the epicentre of curious collecting in Vanbrugh's England.

61. John Banister, Dicentra cucullaria, *c. 1688.*

62. John Banister, Dodecatheon meadia, *c. 1690.*

On 24 July 1698 William Vernon wrote to Hans Sloane:

I met severall Curious parts of Naturall knowledge, which I'd rather refer to you in ye Temple Coffe-House, yn in Scriptis. I've a collection of plants for you & any other part of my Collection is at yr Service. When I return, which I expect will be ye later End of October, I shall bring every Fryday night a collection of plants to be discussed by you, & yt Honourable Club, to whom my Service.[16]

David Elliston Allen, in his book *The Naturalist in Britain*, propagated the notion first entertained by George Pasti Jr in 1950 that this 'Temple Coffee House Botanic Club' was 'the earliest natural history society in Britain and probably in the world'.[17] He viewed it as an 'unofficial outgrowth' of the Royal Society, claiming its members included Hans Sloane, Tancred Robinson, Nehemiah Grew, William Sherard, James Petiver, Adam Buddle, Samuel Doody, Leonard Plukenet, Samuel Dale, Charles Du Bois, William Vernon and Henry Compton.

Les Jessop of the Natural History Museum in London has effectively downplayed such claims.[18] He argues that only two things are certain: some form of club met at the Temple Coffee House in 1698 to discuss plants; and its membership and activities are unrecorded. Even the identity of the coffee house seems in question, since there were several of that name. As just one example, an undated letter from David Krieg to James Petiver supports Vernon's letter of 1698 in alluding to 'the noble club att the Temple Coffe house', but leaves unclear the club's precise business. Moreover, the fact that Humphrey Wanley wrote to Sloane on 2 February 1702 to inform Sloane that he had arrived at the 'Temple-Coffee-house' just too late to catch him, implies nothing about a 'club'; it only confirms that one of the two coffee houses off Fleet Street near the Temple was a convenient meeting place. It certainly does not corroborate the continued activities of the so-called 'Temple Coffee House Botanic Club' throughout the reign of Queen Anne.

Despite this, there is more than enough circumstantial evidence that botanists and horticulturists were meeting at coffee houses from the 1690s to the 1720s. Leonard Plukenet clearly regarded the Rainbow near Temple Bar as a good place to meet (if only temporarily) when he informed William Byrd I in December 1687 that

Dr Lister has engaged me to give you notice that he wil be ready to meet you & Mr. North at the Rainbow Coffeehouse by Temple-Barr at eleven a clock at farthest on Thursday next, & that you be not disappointed in the view of those raritys [previously referred to as 'the celebrated collection of nature'] the doctor will send his man to Mr. Charlton who upon that notice wil not faile to be at his chamber to receive you. Sir you may be sure that neither I nor Mr. Doody pretend to so much self denyal as not to awayte your coming at the same time and place and I believe Dr. Robinson wil not be wanting to assist at our meeting.[19]

Informal clubs were certainly springing up in London too, even if they cannot be indentified with the 'Temple Coffee House Botanic Club' as such. Take, for example, the earliest reference, dated 1 July 1690. Edward Lhwyd is writing to Martin Lister:

Mr Sherard tells me yt ye Botanic Club in London have entertain'd some thoughts of Sending me to the Carnarie Ilands to make what Discovereies I can in Plants. If they contineue their resolution; I should be very forward to undertake ye Voyage.[20]

On 11 May 1691, William Charleton wrote to William Sherard:

I wisht [*wish we could have had* crossed out] yow at our club ye other night for an Hower or 2 to have had a sight of a curious book of plants (of ye Cape of good Hope) in miniature presented by ye States to ye Bishop of London. there were to ye number of 40 — & as [*ye learned said not* crossed out] our cheif Botantists said most of ym not described.[21]

On 11 June 1692 Sherard wrote to Hans Sloane about 'ye clubb' and referred to William Charleton, Tancred Robinson and Samuel Doody in that context. On 25 October 1694, and again in 1698, Sherard was penning notes to Sloane in which 'ye Clubb' was associated with Charles Hatton and Sir John Hoskins respectively. On 7 October 1699, Sherard told Sloane that he would have something to show him at 'yr clubb' after his return to London. Sherard had come home after the third tour with the Marquess of Tavistock, and at the age of forty he must have been worried at his lack of steady employment.

If the club, society or coffee-house group formed one nexus, there was also the informal connection of class and kinship. Mary, Duchess of Beaufort, provides the best example of a collector who would not have operated directly through the 'Temple Coffee House Botanic Club', but who had contacts all the same – from William Sherard to George London. She started with the advantage that horticulture and botany were both in her blood. Born in 1630, she was the eldest daughter of Arthur Capel, Baron Hadham.[22] She is included in Cornelius Johnson's famous portrait (National Portrait Gallery, London) of the Capel family seen in the foreground of an Italianate garden. Next to her is the eldest son, Arthur, who as Earl of Essex would create the 'forest' garden of Cassiobury in the early 1670s. Arthur's gardener, Moses Cook, went on to found the Brompton Nursery with George London; Arthur's daughter Anne married Charles Howard, 3rd Earl of Carlisle, of Castle Howard.

Mary's other brother, Henry, who became Lord Capel of Tewkesbury, cultivated many newly imported exotics in his garden at Kew. He was thus a first source of rare plants when she began serious collecting in the 1690s. On the evidence of Hendrik Danckerts's painting of the north front of Badminton (the Beaufort seat in Gloucestershire), tentatively dated to 1669 or 1670, the gardens seem to have been largely formed by 1670.[23] In other words, this was well before the family's acquisition in 1681–2 of the town-house in Chelsea – the mansion subsequently known as Beaufort House.[24] By 1687 the Duchess was already receiving specimens from New England and Virginia through George London. On 14 May 1690, London was providing instructions on how to grow *Magnolia virginiana* (fig. 60), which had arrived at Bishop Compton's garden in Fulham from Banister just two years before.[25] Her gardener also recorded plants seen at London's Brompton Nursery and at Chelsea Physic Garden as a *desiderata* list for the Duchess: for example, 'the Tulip bearing bay' (probably again *Magnolia virginiana*), the 'Benjamin Tree' (*Lindera benzoin* of Banister's 1683 consignment) and 'Angelica tree' (*Aralia spinosa* of the 1688 consignment).[26] This shows the Compton connection as vital in transatlantic importation. But London also had his hands on Chinese, European and South African exotics.[27]

By August 1700, the Duchess had secured the services of William Sherard as tutor to her grandson and as household botanist. Sir Hans Sloane – at once doctor and botanical companion to the Duchess – played a rôle in urging the then somewhat impecunious Sherard to take up the position. Despite failing to extract an annuity from the Duchess, Sherard's initial impressions of Badminton were favourable: 'I was extremely surprised to see the gardens, which out do any in Europe.'[28]

Through family connections and influence, the Duchess had put herself at the centre of collecting circles. Sherard was working closely with John Ray and set about augmenting the gardens: 'I have writ to all my correspond[en]ts to procure what I can for her Grace, who deserves them the best of any body I know; & I doubt not but in a few years here will be the best garden in Europe'.[29] However, the Duke of Beaufort was not always obliging, as Sherard indicated to Sloane in October 1700: 'I never met with any body who has so little genius for learning (or anything else but horses, dogs, & sport) as his Grace'.[30] Evidently the Duchess was alone in her 'Genius for Botanism'.

Sherard fowarded a catalogue of the Badminton gardens to his contacts. In return he got plants; his correspondents abroad furnished seeds from Sicily, Rome, Florence, Nuremberg, Holland and France.[31] Over 1,700 plants were added to the collections, of which Sherard believed 300 to be nondescripts.[32] All this was helpful to his main ambition: updating Bauhin's *Pinax* to provide a comprehensive account of botanical synonyms. But it did not solve the problems of an unruly ward, an uncongenial Duke and a chronically ill Duchess – an insomniac with 'yellowish & greenish Appearances before her eyes during the day'.[33] The employment lasted only a year. By 1703 Sherard was on his way to Smyrna to take up a role as Consul that would undermine his work on the *Pinax* but provide a fortune to underwrite the rest of his life's work.

The Duchess, meanwhile, had other things in mind. From 21 July 1703 she employed a Dutch artist by the name of Everhard(us) Kick, Kik, Kickius or Kychious to paint her exotic collections.[34] Kychious remained at Badminton until 14 July 1705. In two years he painted sixty-eight glorious portraits of groups of plants – typically three in each portrait in stunning juxtapositions of colour and form, roots and all. Many were succulents, a large number came from the Cape, and his plate 61 is directly associated with Sherard's importation from Sicily. Kychious's grandiose, rather larger-than-life 'Amaranthus Globosus' shows the diminutive *Gomphrena globosa* – a half-hardy annual that had come into cultivation in England from India around 1690 (fig. 63). Badminton must have been one of its first homes but, like most of the Banister plants, it did not enter the nursery trade until later in the eighteenth century. It demonstrates once again the slow dispersal rate of some exotics. In contrast, Kychious's 'Apocynum americanum' (fig. 64; now *Asclepias tuberosa*) illustrates an American perennial that found wider distribution after its arrival in 1680. By the 1720s it was probably available through Thomas Fairchild at Hoxton in London.[35] Likewise the *Quamoclit coccinea* (fig. 65) or scarlet convolvulus that stands at the centre of his portrait of three 'convolvulus' on stakes was in the nurseries by the 1720s.

63. *Everhard Kychious*, Gomphrena globosa, *1703–5*.

64. *Everhard Kychious*, Asclepias tuberosa, *1703–5*.

65. *Everhard Kychious*, Quamoclit coccinea, Flanked by Two Other Types of 'Convolvulus', *1703–5*.

66. *Everhard Kychious*, An Auricula (Primula x pubescens) and a Polyanthus (Primula x variabilis) to Either Side of a 'Cynoglossum', *1703–5*.

Supposedly introduced from North America in 1713, this scarlet vine was clearly growing at Badminton and in Compton's Fulham garden by 1705.[36] The fact that it was depicted as trained up tall stakes may suggest something about the methods of cultivation; for here was a plant that could be used in the centres of the decorative *plates-bandes* of the parterre. Indeed, its presence in Henry Wise's list of flowers – assumed to date from after 1712 and probably before 1722–3 – indicates how it had made its way out of the specialized enclosures of Fulham and Badminton into the general domain of ornamental planting design.[37] In contrast, florists' flowers, such as the dwarf auricula and polyanthus of Kychious's marvellous study (fig. 66), remained throughout the eighteenth century confined to specialized horticultural enclosures – and notably the 'auricula theatre', where science and display were uppermost.[38] The Duchess favoured these florists' flowers in her town garden in Chelsea.[39]

Thus, unlike Compton, the Duchess immortalized a portion of her collections in florilegia, thereby combining art and aggrandizement with the science of collecting. Douglas Chambers has described in detail the collecting methods of the meticulous Duchess, who wrote to Sloane of her intoxication for botany: 'When I get into storys of plants I know not how to get out.'[40]

Whether, of course, any of her exotic collections – the *Quamoclit coccinea*, for example – transcended scientific organization, entering the decorative enclosures around Badminton, requires further elaboration. The 1699/1700 Kip and Knyff views certainly suggest developments in the ornamental layout within the framework already evident in Danckerts's painting (?*c*. 1669–70).[41] Most interesting are sketch plans *c*. 1700 – possibly in the hand of Henry Wise rather than George London – for two 'wilderness' gardens and a formal parterre (figs. 67, 68, 69) that correspond to Kip's bird's-eye view of *c*. 1700–2. Whether these were implemented is put in doubt by the two Thomas Smith paintings of *c*. 1708–10, which show a rather different layout of parterre and wilderness.[42] Whatever the attribution for the three proposals, it is clear that London had close links to the household; his daughter, Henrietta London (who married John Peachey in 1706),[43] was evidently engaged in painting or copying flower portraits around the time of Kychious's employment. Kychious may have supervised her along with the Duchess's servant Daniel Frankcom; the results were in both cases much inferior to the master. On balance, it seems most likely the Kychious exotics remained curiosities within the scientific collecting grounds near the hothouse.[44] Their home was still in the *pulvilli*.

The remarkable radiating avenues of Badminton, just as much as the massive architectonic wilderness quarters, are of a scale and purpose that sets the Duchess's garden apart from the compact enclosures of her Chelsea home, Beaufort House. Yet the common organizational principle – compartmentalization – distinguishes Badminton from the pleasure ground of Blenheim (fig. 17), where a thrusting Baroque hexagon with bastions offered viewpoints over the park. Kerry Downes has pointed to the several uses of fortifications in Vanbrugh gardens,[45] a topic that is explored elsewhere in this present book. Perhaps this is reason enough to trace the martial idea to the common hand of Captain Vanbrugh, following Switzer's claim that it was 'after the ancient *Roman Manner*'.[46] Whatever the inspiration, it was Henry Wise who had complete control over decorative and horticultural matters within the hexagonal

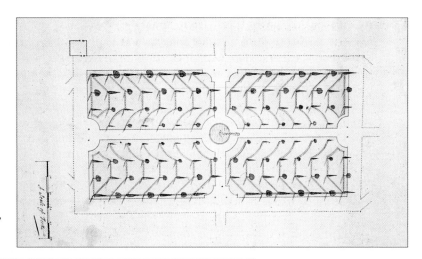

67. 'Draught of a Wilderness',
Badminton House,
Gloucestershire, after 1699.

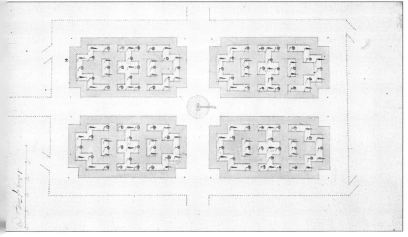

68. 'Draught of a
Wilderness', Badminton
House, Gloucestershire,
after 1699.

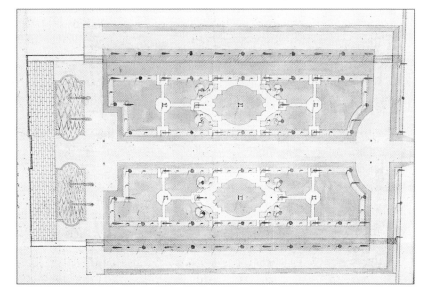

69. 'Draught of the Great
Garden', Badminton
House, Gloucestershire,
after 1699.

wilderness, the rectangular parterre and the Duchess of Marlborough's private flower garden to the east side of the Palace. By 1705, when work began, Wise was fifty-two – experienced enough to handle the operation without George London (who was busy at Wanstead from 1706), but perhaps too set in his ways to experiment with novelties of planting form or horticultural content. By October that year, the clerk of works, Henry Joynes, could report: 'The Bastions that were in hand, some of them are finished . . . Mr. Wise is planting with all expedition.'[47]

The structure of parterre and wilderness are nothing exceptional. The parterre is comparable to the 1701 *parterre à l'angloise* of the Privy Garden at Hampton Court (as Switzer first pointed out) and has none of the intricacy or fantasy that London and Wise introduced the same year into the mannered French layout made for Marshal Tallard at Nottingham. The serpentine walks in the wilderness are notable, but otherwise the intersecting orthogonal and diagonal *allées* are conventional and do little to exploit the daring possibilities that the hexagonal platform opened up within its park setting. It would take another generation or two – notably Stephen Switzer at Grimsthorpe (figs. 32, 33) or Francis Richardson at Lowther (fig. 71) – to see how the Blenheim prototype could be further integrated into the landscape, both in plan and planting profile.

The vocabulary of 'Espalier Standard Limes', of pyramid bays and yews, seems as predictable at Blenheim as the palette of stocks, tulips, carnations and violets in the Duchess's flower garden; such vegetable architecture remained rooted in the

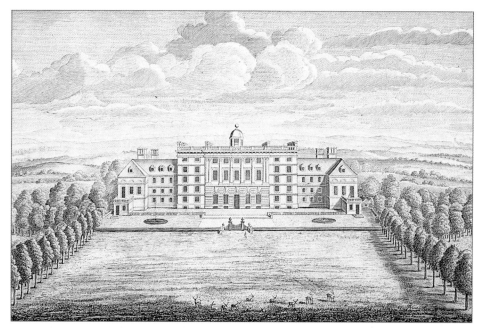

70. Kip's Badminton House, Gloucestershire, *a view from the north across the deer park. The garden designs illustrated in figs. 67–9 were intended for the grounds below the east front of the house.*

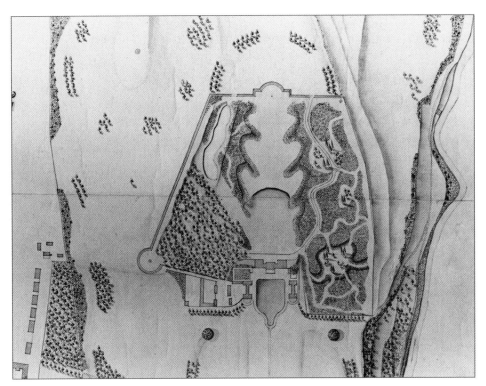

71. Francis Richardson's proposal plan for Lowther Castle, Westmorland, 1754, a development of the design and planting scheme established early in the century at Blenheim.

geometries of the Baroque style.[48] Above all, there is no indication that any of the new exotics grown by Bishop Compton or the Duchess of Beaufort had made their way out of the *pulvilli* of the collector's enclosure. (The '59 Pyramid Swedish Junipers' alone are a novelty, for *Juniperus communis suecica* appears to have been cultivated in England only from 1701 onwards.) The slow rate of exotic dispersal may have been compounded by inherent conservatism in horticultural circles. Leaping the fence (or in this case, the brick walls) would require a critical conjunction of forces that Sherard helped set in motion in the 1720s.

At this point, let us consider the remarkable years of 1721–2. The 58–year-old Sir John is in a new rôle as husband and father. At home in Vanbrugh Castle, he tells his old friend Tonson of the satisfaction of being 'two Boys Strong in the Nursery'.[49] Blenheim – with all its stresses – is behind him, Stowe and Castle Howard are the present and future. In a reflective mood he writes to Lord Carlisle (8 June 1721), explaining that:

I, without the Gout to incline my Philosophy, have every day of my Life Since twenty years old, grown more and more of opinion, that the less one has to do, with what is call'd the World, the more Quiet of mind; and the more Quiet of mind, the more Happyness. All other delights, are but like debauches in Wine, which give three days pain, for three hours pleasure.[50]

Yet, a few weeks later, in a letter of 8 August, Vanbrugh – still ready to outbid any player with a sure card – describes the new vision for Castle Howard:

> Many new Charms open this year, that never appear'd before; And many more will next; that people do not dream of now; If I take in, what a Third will produce, (bar more Southsea Storms) I believe here will be, (beyond all contest), the Top Seat, and Garden of England.[51]

In 1722 Mark Catesby was on his way to Carolina, where the chaos of hurricanes would infect his imagination: deer lodged in high trees; the carcasses of panthers and bears strewn in water.[52] And William Sherard was once again at the centre of things in London. If Vanbrugh seems more introspective, Sherard appears more worldly. In the intervening decades, Sherard had temporarily lost the battle to keep his botanical enthusiam alive. He was preoccupied in plague-ridden Smyrna with protecting his community from Turkish encroachments; in the arid summers, antiquarian pursuits proved easier than botanizing; and with the death of Tournefort in 1708, his main encouragement was gone. By 1713 he could write to James Petiver: 'The strongest heat of passion grows cool without some nouriture to sustain it.'[53] Twenty-five years of being a 'drudg[e] of all the gardens in Europe'[54] had all but finished him. Thus, when he returned from Turkey to find a London without John Ray, Samuel Doody and Leonard Plukenet and with James Petiver ill, it must have taken considerable gumption to continue his botanical work – even to dream of completing the *Pinax*. In the spring of 1720 he wrote to Richard Richardson (1663–1741): 'All my Botanick friends I had here, are dead in my absence, & not one new one sprung up but my Brother [James Sherard] and Mr. Rand, who are both ingaged in business.'[55]

That same spring of 1720, having been elected a Fellow of the Royal Society, Sherard met up with Catesby, recently returned from Virginia. By 12 November 1720 he was writing to Richardson again:

> Mr. Catesby, a gentleman of a small fortune, who liv'd some years in Virginia with a relation, pretty well skilled in Natural History, who designs and paints in water-colors to perfection, is going over with General Nicholson, Governor of Carolina. That gentleman allows him £20 a year; and we are indeavouring to get subscriptions for him, viz. Sir Hans, Mr. Dubois, and myself, who are all that have subscrib'd to him; but I'me in hopes to get the Duke of Chandos, which will be a good help.[56]

Sherard – as Catesby's 'champion among naturalists and collectors'[57] – eventually organized twelve sponsors. From 1722 to 1726 Catesby worked tirelessly in Carolina and the Bahamas, corresponding with Sherard, who often acted as an intermediary to placate the difficult Charles Du Bois or the demanding Sir Hans Sloane. Although Sherard was dead before the first segment of Catesby's *Natural History* appeared in 1729, his rôle in the group of twelve paved the way to the larger sponsorship of 155 subscribers.

Meanwhile Sherard had not given up his *Pinax*. The German botanist Dillenius – recommended to him 'as a person very curious in mushrooms & mosses'[58] – seemed the key to progress. Late in the summer of 1721, Sherard crossed the

72. Jacobus van Huysum's Hibiscus syriacus cvs., *before 1730, one of the portraits he made for the Society of Gardeners'* Catalogus Plantarum.

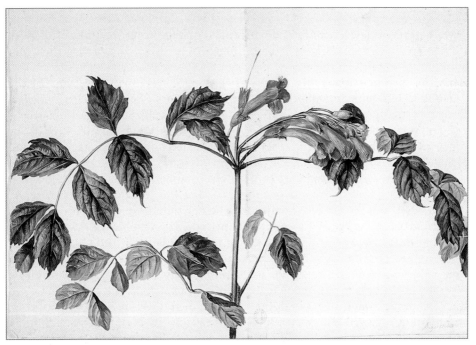

73. Jacobus van Huysum's Campsis radicans, *before 1730.*

Channel to import the moss expert from the University of Giessen. Dillenius's impact in London was immediate (though not entirely positive: Lord Petre dismissed the nervous, thin-skinned workaholic as 'an arrant old woman').[59] In that first season he was already President of the newly founded Botanical Society. John Martyn as Secretary gave a first course of lectures. Interestingly the group met weekly at six at the Rainbow Coffee House in London's Watling Street before they moved into private rooms. The apothecaries John Wilmer and Isaac Rand, along with Philip Miller as gardener to the Society of Apothecaries, were notable members. Unlike the poorly documented activities at the Temple Coffee House, the Society's proceedings are well recorded; it was an aspiring group of surprisingly young men, many in their early twenties (Martyn was only twenty-two), largely middle-class and with medico–botanical interests. Perhaps this age-profile and the preponderant interest of the group in apothecary matters accounts for Sherard's absence. Whatever the reason, he was not one of the members congregating each week with a plant in one hand and a cup of Turkish beverage in the other.

By 1726, perhaps through Martyn's own doings, the Society disbanded.[60] He went on to achieve fame through the *Historia plantarum rariorum* of 1728–37, and Sherard was a vital early subscriber. Most of the plates were made from drawings by another immigrant from the Low Countries who had reached London in 1721: Jacobus van Huysum, brother of the famous Dutch flower painter Jan van Huysum. At first van Huysum lived in Chelsea with Robert Walpole, who employed him in making copies of Old Masters for Houghton, Walpole's seat in Norfolk. But, according to Horace Walpole, he was dismissed after two years for 'drunken dissolute conduct' and his future lay with flowers.[61]

It was also Jacobus van Huysum who received the commission to paint a series of portraits of plants for a publication sponsored by the Society of Gardeners: the *Catalogus Plantarum* of 1730. Founded in 1724, the Society was composed of twenty practising gardeners and nurserymen, including Thomas Fairchild, Robert Furber, Samuel Driver and Christopher Gray. It appears they met monthly at Newall's Coffee House in Chelsea, each member bringing flowers and fruits for examination. Only Philip Miller, as Secretary or 'Clerk', had the standing to bridge the membership of both a gardeners' society and the Botanical Society of the Rainbow Coffee House. Of the many lovely paintings completed by van Huysum, only twenty-one reached publication in the *Catalogus*, such as his remarkable study of hibiscus (fig. 72).[62] Delicate portraits of European and oriental exotics – *Prunus tenella* (introduced 1683), for example, or *Prunus glandulosa roseo-plena* (introduced 1673) – were among those that missed out.

Jacobus van Huysum missed out too. His later life in London is obscure; he died in 1740, and we are left wondering whether the bottle explains his demise. His dramatic rendering of *Campsis radicans* (fig. 73) or his delightful portrait of *Physocarpus opulifolius* (fig. 74) – the same exotic that Banister had sent to Fulham in 1687 – indicates the power the *Catalogus* might have wielded, had the intended four volumes reached the press. Instead, Catesby's *Natural History* can be regarded as the primary stimulus to a new mania for North American shrubs and trees that took hold in England in the 1730s (fig. 75). Catesby's 155 subscribers – and no doubt many besides – were drawn through the tempting plates into an unprecented consumer boom. Thereafter John Bartram would make exotics accessible to English clients in large quantities through the agency of Peter

74. Jacobus van Huysum,
Physocarpus opulifolius, *before
1730.*

Collinson; and, by the middle of the century, the nurseries would turn those rare curiosities into affordable commodities, making the shrubbery available to all.[63]

The *Catalogus* was, in some senses, the practitioner's response to the problem that had bedevilled Sherard's botanical endeavours: the lack of a comprehensive catalogue or 'Pinax' of synonyms. Confusion in the nursery trade had resulted in complaints. The nurserymen were branded as 'Knaves and Blockheads'.[64] Robert Furber's *Twelve Months of Flowers* of 1730 can also be seen as an attempt to produce a systematic illustrated catalogue.[65] Interestingly, the Society's worthy efforts did not escape the ridicule that had afflicted the Kit Cat Club. By 1732, a W. Jones had published *The natural history of the Frutex vulvaria or flowering shrub . . . By Philogynes Clitorides, botanist, and one of the missionaries for propagating knowledge in foreign parts.*[66]

Meanwhile, circumstances still continued to get in the way of Sherard's *Pinax*. Dillenius, admittedly with Sherard's blessing, found himself busy working on a third edition of Ray's *Synopsis*. It appeared in 1724. He was being drawn increasingly, moreover, into the rôle of botanical amanuensis to James Sherard. Like his brother, James had amassed a fortune that went into his favourite pastime, the cultivation of rare and exotic plants in his garden at Eltham, Kent. After William Sherard's death in 1728, the game was well and truly up; illustrating the fabulous *Hortus Elthamensis* for publication in 1732 became the German botanist's preoccupation. As the querulous Dillenius lamented: 'James Sherard hath spoil'd it . . . If the time which hath been spent in composing this work had been employ'd in the *Pinax*, I durst say the *Pinax* was finished.'[67]

Today, the incomplete five-volume *Pinax* lies in Oxford's Bodleian Library. Others would realize Sherard's dream. By the mid-eighteenth century Linnaeus's system of

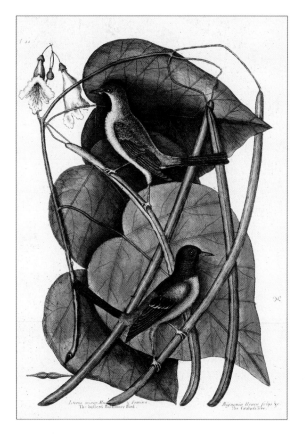

75. Mark Catesby, 'Catalpa bignonioides', from The Natural History of Carolina, Florida, and the Bahama Islands, *1731–43, vol. I, pl. 49.*

binomials would help reduce polynomial confusion, and by the second half of the nineteenth century *Index Kewensis* offered a comprehensive 'pinax' of synonyms.

On his death William Sherard bequeathed his belongings and fortune to the University of Oxford: his library, his herbarium and the new Chair that Dillenius took up in 1734 – the Sherardian Professor of Botany. But his legacy was already established. By 1728 the taste for exotics, nurtured by his various endeavours, was being fed through the medium of lavish books – the *Catalogus Plantarum* and *Twelve Months of Flowers* of 1730, Catesby's *Natural History*, whose first plates appeared in 1729, and Dillenius's *Hortus Elthamensis* of 1732. By 1728 Batty Langley was showing the way to display flowering shrubs along the edge of a wilderness; and by the early 1730s Peter Collinson and John Bartram were supplying private clients and the nursery trade with American plants in abundance. The mania for the shrubbery was to take hold after 1750.

Here we should pause to consider that moment in 1734 when Sir Thomas Robinson wrote his now famous letter to the Earl of Carlisle about the 'new taste in gardening' at the Prince of Wales's Carlton House: William Kent's method of laying out 'without line or level'.[68] Something remarkable was happening in planting design in that small patch of land so near to George London's old house in Spring Gardens (figs. 76, 77).[69] The Virginia Groundsel Tree (*Baccharis halimifolia*) and Benjamin Tree (*Lindera benzoin*) that Bishop

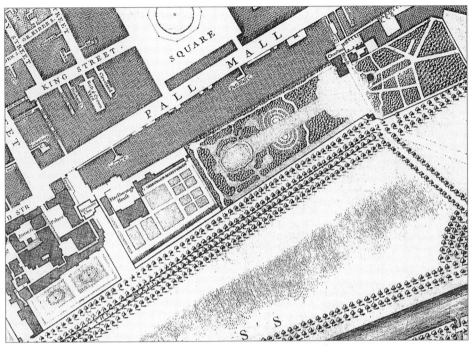

76. *The garden at Carlton House, on the north side of St James's Park, London, shown in a detail from Rocque's* Plan of the Cities of London and Westminster, *1746.*

77. *William Woollett's* Carlton House Garden, London, *an engraving of 1760 that shows Kent's garden and the temple he designed for it.*

Compton had grown at Fulham in the 1680s were being planted alongside Tradescant exotics such as *Staphylea trifolia* (fig. 78). More importantly, the most recent arrivals from America – the *Symphoricarpos orbiculatus* (fig. 79) of 1727, for example, which Dillenius had illustrated in his *Hortus Elthamensis* – were making an appearance too. Even *Catalpa bignonioides* (fig. 75), which Catesby had introduced into cultivation on his return to London in 1726, and which the Society of Gardeners' *Catalogus Plantarum* still described as 'very little known in England' in 1730,[70] made a showing at Carlton House. It was a 13-foot specimen costing 3 guineas.[71] Only the Prince of Wales's resources allowed for the use of rarities in such number and of such size. There was a huge tulip tree transferred from Robert Furber's nursery for the enormous sum of £21.

It is not entirely clear how these exotics were used within the hedges and standards of Carlton House's still essentially Baroque layout, or whether, indeed, Kent was involved in their planting. The clipped evergreens of Wise's Blenheim were still in evidence at Carlton House; and the selection of flowers was little changed from 1705.[72] Nevertheless, it seems fair to assume that the Prince of Wales's layout (along with Lord Petre's at Thorndon Hall, Essex) was among the first to incorporate a new exotic flora into proto-Picturesque plantations. No wonder Sir Thomas Robinson saw it as the 'new taste in gardening'; the shrubbery of American plants was just around the corner.

78. *Johannes Jacobus Dillenius,* Staphylea trifolia, *from* Hortus Elthamensis, *1732, tab. CXXII fig. 148.*

79. *Johannes Jacobus Dillenius*,
Symphoricarpos orbiculatus, *from*
Hortus Elthamensis, *1732, tab.*
CCLXXVIII, fig. 360.

At the very same moment, of course, Lord Carlisle's son-in-law, Robinson, was
also putting the finishing touches to a very different landscape at Castle Howard –
correcting Hawksmoor's design for the Mausoleum.[73] Here was a monumental
scene largely devoid of 'foolish' plants – a landscape of plantations, associative
deities, temples and obelisks.[74] While the path that leads from Blenheim to
Grimsthorpe to Lowther Castle brought Mars and Flora together, the august
Castle Howard remained on a path divergent from the new botanical exoticism of
Carlton House or Thorndon Hall. On the Yorkshire estate and at Stowe a
numinous, emblematic Picturesque was to arise that continues to intoxicate us
centuries later. Indeed, today we struggle to remember that other, almost
forgotten, vision of landscape architecture emerging out of Baroque England.
This was the floriferous Picturesque that Bishop Compton and William Sherard
helped create through bringing a 'Genius for Botanism' to the 'Genius of the
Place'. Vanbrugh would no doubt have enjoyed the paradox that, while the
botanists were dreaming of America with the aid of *Coffea arabica*, the great
architect seems to have projected obelisks with the aid of saffron and nutmeg
(*Crocus sativus* and *Myristica fragrans*), and even conceivably a North American
exotic: the 'poker', or pokeweed, of Sir John's cup (*Phytolacca americana?*).[75] It
was perhaps the nearest he ever got to loving the Flora of Foreign Parts.

SEVEN

Vanbrugh's India and his Mausolea for England

Robert Williams

For fifteen months between 1683 and 1685 Vanbrugh lived and worked in India, where he was employed by the London-based East India Company as a factor (a junior merchant) at Surat (fig. 80), an important trading centre on the west coast north of Bombay.[1] Following his return to England he enlisted in the army, spent time in prison in France, joined the marines, began writing plays, and in 1699 turned to architecture and landscaping. But unlike William Chambers, who in the 1740s voyaged once to Bengal and twice to China for the Swedish East India Company before training as an architect and thereafter zealously promoting Chinoiserie, at first glance Vanbrugh seems not to have capitalized on his own foray into distant parts. (No English architect of his day had travelled farther East than Italy.) No features or details in Vanbrugh's drawings or buildings challenge the accepted view that the Indian style in English architecture and garden design was a phenomenon of the late eighteenth century and early nineteenth.[2] This surely means Vanbrugh's sojourn in the Orient had no effect whatsoever on his subsequent designs for country houses or gardens.[3]

But to suppose in such a case as this one that the presence or absence of quintessential non-Western items, such as onion domes, minarets, Elephanta columns, *chatri* or cusped arches, confirms or refutes the idea that India influenced Vanbrugh is to seek out merely the obvious. The whiff of the East that he sought to introduce in England was a subtle one, and not, in fact, wholly Oriental. To identify and explain this, what follows is a brief account of how it was that Vanbrugh came to be in India, and his subsequent attempts to respond to a pressing problem in England for which Mughal India had an answer: the burial of the dead.

Vanbrugh was nineteen when he set off for the East. In 1681–2 he had been employed in London by a cousin in the wines and brandies trade, but the business was suddenly forced into bankruptcy.[4] Obliged to seek a fresh position, he applied for one in the East India Company, a global corporation in which several members of his family and kinsmen had been involved for decades. For example, one uncle, Peter Delboe, had been appointed Chief of the Council at the Company's factory in Taiwan a few years earlier,[5] although unfortunately he died en route at Ayudhya in Siam in 1676;[6] two others, Thomas Breton and Edward Pearce, had

80. 'Surat from the North Bank of the River Tapti', c. 1670, an exotic scene published in
Baldaeus's Beschreibung der ostindischen Kusten Malabar und Coromandel, 1672.

stock in the Company and invested in a number of Eastern ventures.[7] During
1682 Vanbrugh went through the selection and acceptance process for the
position of factor.[8] He was admitted into the 'freedom' of the Company on
9 October 1682; a month later the necessary security of £1,000 was underwritten
by his father Giles and his uncle William Vanbrugh;[9] and on 30 March 1683
Vanbrugh was given permission to lade export freight on the *Scipio Africanus*, an
armed 370-ton East Indiaman.[10] On 4 May of that year the *Scipio*, and the 500-
ton *Success*, both bound for Surat, slipped down the Thames.[11] In Captain
Thomas Woodcock's post-bag aboard the *Scipio* was a letter from the Company's
headquarters in Leadenhall Street to the Surat factory's new President, John
Child, introducing 'Mr John Vanbrugh whom we have also entertain'd
[contracted] as a Factor . . . for 5 years'.[12]

The East India Company had been set up in 1600 by venture capitalists to
finance a flotilla of small ships to the Indies in search of spices and the chance to
trade. A Company factory, that is, a trading-post, was established at Surat in 1612.
The Gujarat region produced high-quality cottons and silks at low prices, hence
the interest in buying there for the European market, but Surat was also an
excellent base from which to trade in various commodities with Persia, Arabia and
the Far East. In the course of the seventeenth century the Company established

factories along the coasts and up navigable rivers from the Red Sea to Japan. The work of its servants based in these distant, often hostile and disease-ridden, outposts was always subject to sudden, at times murderous, shifts in local power. There was, too, fierce competition between the English, Dutch, French and other European trading companies, which on occasion led to bloodshed. For the investors at home, piracy and wild seas substantially added to the financial risks.[13]

The Company's men in the East were there to get rich. Sir John Lewis made enough money in Persia after 1643 to buy Ledston Hall, Yorkshire, on his return a decade later. Sir Josiah Child (no relation to the Surat President), a director and later Company chairman, had bought Wanstead, Essex, in 1673, which under his son Sir Richard Child (Viscount Castlemain from 1718) was transformed by Colen Campbell into *the* Palladian showpiece of the early eighteenth century. In 1688 Sir Thomas Rolt – who began his career in India as a humble writer in 1658, eventually serving as Surat's President in 1678–82 – bought Sacombe Park, Hertfordshire. Elihu Yale engrossed enough while serving at Fort St George (Madras) to found the American university named for him by means of the huge benefit he donated in 1718. That we know so much about these and other servants and their undertakings abroad is a result of the Company's obsession with paperwork and reluctance to throw any of it away. Its headquarters in London's Leadenhall Street (on the site of which Richard Rogers's Lloyd's Building now stands), was gradually filled with a mass of correspondence, minutes, accounts, marine reports, logs, factory records, service records and other documentation of its activities worldwide. Today these documents make a major contribution to the nine miles of shelving comprising the British Library's India Office Records.[14]

The continent Vanbrugh sailed to in 1683 was not *terra incognita*. As a boy he would have heard plenty of stories concerning it from his trading relatives. His class and generation had ready access to printed maps and all kinds of published accounts of faraway lands.[15] Johann Albert von Mandelslo, for example, included a lengthy description of life at Surat in the late 1630s in his *Morgenländische Reyse* (1658), which appeared in John Davies's corrupt English translation in 1662. Philip Baldaeus's detailed study of the Hindi religion on the west coast of India was available in Dutch and German from 1672, although not in English until 1703.[16] The steady growth in imports of Eastern foodstuffs and manufactured goods during the seventeenth century was matched by the increasing interest Europeans showed in Oriental art, architecture, religion, trade and politics. Portraits by Van Dyck – of Sir Robert Shirley (1622; Petworth House) in his Persian dress, complete with turban; of William Feilding, 1st Earl of Denbigh (c. 1635; National Gallery, London), in the pink silk vest and pyjama trousers the Earl brought home from his holiday in India – image the strong interest there was in exotic foreign fabrics and dress in the early seventeenth century, a taste soon to be matched by a demand from upper-class homes for suitably costumed Indian boys and girls as servants.[17]

A voyage to India invariably took five to seven months, the ships slowly working their way out into mid-Atlantic to catch the trade-winds across and down to the Cape of Good Hope; from there they moved up Africa's south-east coast, after which either a north-easterly route was followed across the Indian Ocean or ships headed further north in order to tack along the Arabian coast, with many calls en route to pick up fresh supplies or to load or unload partial cargo or Company servants or soldiers. The *Scipio*, for example, on the occasion Vanbrugh was aboard, had first to pick up 'goods at Calicut and Carwar' on India's Malabar coast before voyaging north 'to land soldiers at Bombay' and so on up to Surat, the *Success*, meanwhile, having swept straight to Surat across the Indian Ocean.[18]

By the close of 1683 Vanbrugh was at work in and around Surat, buying silks, cotton calicoes, painted and dyed chintzes and other fabrics, and overseeing their storage aboard Company ships bound for Europe.[19] Surat at that time was a bustling, cosmopolitan city dinned by a babble of languages. Fortunately, the exotic world he encountered there was recorded in some detail by John Fryer, who returned to England from Surat the year before Vanbrugh set out; by John Ovington, who served there as the Company's chaplain in 1690-3; and by the Scots seaman Alexander Hamilton, who spent the years 1688-91 on India's west coast, visiting Surat for the first time in 1690.[20] There in that Mughal city 'famed for its traffic throughout Asia'[21] and the point of embarkation for the annual pilgrimage to Mecca, the Christian European traders encountered adherants of all manner of religion, sect (Hamilton reckoned there were over 100 sects in Surat),[22] diet, custom and lifestyle, from polygamists, self-torturing Hindi ascetics and the 'Molacks' (a group that endured an annual wife-swapping feast as part of their religious commitment) to psychopathic Thuggees, street-sweepers, so-called 'dancing wenches' and indolent *bhang*-puffers. The narrow streets and crowded marketplaces squeezed together wealthy merchants and penniless beggars, foreign sailors, clinically insane zealots and overloaded carts hauled by asses or camels. In the urban gardens, grapes, pineapples, mangoes, cucumbers and water-melons flourished. Beyond the city lay fly-blown fields of sugar-cane, tobacco and other crops, in which labouring men and women, oxen and water-buffalo sweated together under a burning sun.

According to Fryer, the Company's factory at Surat contained 'upper and lower Galleries, or Terras-Walks; a neat Oratory, a convenient open Place for Meals'; there were also 'spacious Lodgings, noble Rooms for Counsel and Entertainment, pleasant Tanks, Yards, and a Hummum to wash in'.[23] Ovington's account of life there suggests that the arrangements were somewhat collegiate, with the Company's European staff gathering daily for dinner and worship; on days set aside for religious festivals the Europeans went forth in designedly awesome cavalcades of palanquins, coaches and thoroughbreds to dine in shady gardens beyond the city.[24] The staff comprised the Company's President and Council, a chaplain and surgeon, some twenty or so factors and 'writers' (the rank below factor) and a company of European soldiers, plus the Bannians (Hindi brokers) and forty or so *peons*, foot messengers employed to speed far and near on Company business. Since both Surat and its hinterland were feverishly producing textiles to order for the English Company as well as for those of the French, Dutch and others,[25] 'at every place the Factors are sent to oversee the Weavers, buying up the cotton yarn to employ them all the Rains . . . that they may be ready against the Season for the Ships'.[26] At 'Shipping-time' the factory was in 'a continual hurly-burly', Fryer observed: 'the Packers and Warehouse-keepers, together with merchants bringing and receiving Musters' laboured in so frantic and noisy a manner that it reminded him of Billingsgate market in London.[27] Such was Vanbrugh's workaday world.

But factory life didn't suit him, or for that matter Robert Graham, the new writer who had set out for India with Vanbrugh on the *Scipio*. A letter dated 16 February 1685 from Child and three of his Surat Council to the Leadenhall

Street headquarters was carried aboard the *Nathaniel* before it sailed that day from Surat's Swalley Hole anchorage:

> Mr Jn:o Vanburgh & M:r Rob:t Graham take theire passage for England on this ship being quite a weary of these parts, & in bigg expectation of much sooner raiseing theire fortunes in England depending on theire good friends to put y:m into places of great proffit, Cred:t and ease, they are a Couple of young men, very fitt for businesse, and a few yeares more being over theire heades, may doe y.m a greate deale of good, we heartily wish y.m both well, for theire worthey relations sakes, and have argued w:th them all we could, to perswade y.m to continue, but all to noe purpose.[28]

The voyage home took almost six months, the *Nathaniel* arriving back in London on 7 August.[29] Fryer's return in 1682, 'though a tedious Voyage of Seven Months', was 'passed away merrily with good Wine, and no bad Musick', the captain feeding the passengers throughout 'with fresh Provisions of Turkies, Geese, Ducks, Hens, sucking Pigs, Sheep, Goats, etc.'.[30] No doubt Vanbrugh had a similar experience three years later. And having reached London, he was obliged to travel north to his parents' house in Chester in order once again to begin the search for a position. That December he wrote a begging letter to the Earl of Huntingdon,[31] and within a month Huntingdon had arranged to make him a serving soldier.

The following twenty-five years need not detain us here. No evidence has come to light that links Vanbrugh's activities for this phase of his life with his time in India. Not until 1711, when the new Tory government that had swept into power the previous year passed the Fifty New Churches Act, did Vanbrugh seek to capitalize on his experiences abroad. The construction of St Paul's Cathedral had largely been financed by taxing coals from Newcastle upon Tyne, and with St Paul's nearing completion the government decided to maintain the tax but redirect the revenue to pay for no fewer than fifty new churches for London and Westminster.[32] Only twelve actually resulted from this overambitious Act, half of them to designs by Hawksmoor. Vanbrugh did submit designs for two projects – St Mary le Strand and St George, Bloomsbury, in 1714 and 1715 respectively – but neither was accepted. However, back in 1711, immediately after the new Act was passed, and having been appointed as one of the Commissioners for the fifty new churches, Vanbrugh submitted a document – his 'Proposals about Building ye New Churches' – that included the following point:

> That they may be free'd from that Inhumane custome of being made Burial Places for the Dead, a Custome in which there is something so very barbarous in itself besides the many ill consequences that attend it; that one cannot enough wonder how it ever has prevail'd amongst the civiliz'd part of mankind. But there is now a sort of happy necessity on this Occasion of breaking through it: Since [because of the cost] there can be no thought of purchasing ground for Church Yards where the churches will be placed.[33]

He then explained that this meant cemeteries would have to be laid out in the fields on the edges of London and Westminster. And:

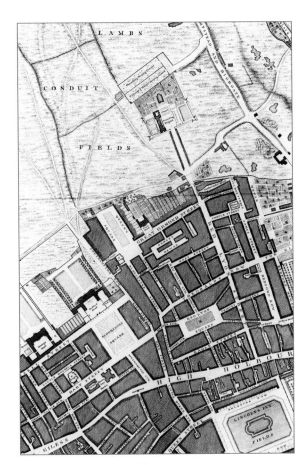

81. *A detail from Rocque's* Plan of
the Cities of London and
Westminster, *1746, showing*
St George, Bloomsbury *(lower
left), and the burial grounds to the
north near the Foundling Hospital.
The bastioned garden of Bedford
(formerly Southampton) House
can also be seen.*

If these Caemitarys be consecrated, Handsomely and regularly wall'd in, and
planted with Trees in such form as to make a Solemn Distinction between one
part and another; there is no doubt, but the Richer sort of People, will think
their Friends and Relations more decently inter'd in these distinguish'd Places,
than they commonly are in the Ailes and under Pews in Churches; And will
think them more honourably remember'd by Lofty and Noble Mausoleums
erected over them in Freestone (which no doubt will soon come into practice)
than by little Tawdry Monuments of Marble, stuck up against Walls and Pillars.

There was growing opposition to the established practice of intramural burial,
primarily because so many of London's churches were literally bursting at the
seams. Out in the rural parishes, churchyards could almost always be expanded
without too much difficulty; in inner London there simply was no available
exterior space and as a result, interiors had slowly been packed with more family
vaults and with more former family members. To have so many bodies
decomposing behind the walls and under the floors of churches that were already
unable to cope with the rise in numbers of their living congregations was an
additional health risk.

Christopher Wren, who was also a Commissioner for a time, had long been opposed to continuing the practice of church burial. 'I could wish that all Burials in Churches might be disallowed',[34] he told one of his colleagues, and, in an explanation that Vanbrugh's Alberti-influenced 'Proposals' echo, advised that the best alternative would be to lay out walled plots planted up with yews as a green belt on the edge of London. These, he said, could be filled with pyramids, busts and statues on pedestals of a modest size, that is, 'regulated' for size and proportion 'by an Architect', while memorials could be attached to the walls. These cemetery projects put forward by Wren and Vanbrugh were not, as it happens, wholly a new idea in 1711. Wren had made similar proposals when much of London had to be rebuilt after the Great Fire of 1666: 'All Church-yards . . . to be plac'd out of the Town';[35] and in *London Revived*, John Evelyn expressed the hope that the rebuilding would offer the opportunity for intramural burial to be curtailed, for burying in churches 'I neither think it decent, nor sufferable'.[36] Evelyn wanted flower- and shrub-filled grounds laid out as an alternative, though none, he thought, should be made within the walls of the City. He and Wren shared the vision of a cemeterial green belt for the capital, Evelyn capitalizing on the suggestion he made in his anti-pollution tract *Fumifugium* (1661) – that a planted and flower-strewn green belt would nourish the capital with pleasing scents.

In November 1711 the Commissioners did agree to refuse to allow vaults to be constructed within the new churches, arguing that burial grounds needed to be established. Each new church either had to be supplied with one adjacent to it or, in those cases where the available plot was too enclosed to be able to include a churchyard, land would purchased beyond the built-up areas.[37] Hawksmoor's project for a new church at Bethnal Green in East London, his 'Basilica after the Primitive Christians', is an example of the first – the adjacent burial ground. He annotated his sketch plan (drawn *c*. November 1711) with the admonition 'No burying in ye church', and indeed the rectangular churchyard is marked on the plan as a separate enclosure beyond the east side of the building. Hawksmoor described it on the plan as the 'cemetery, Sleeping place or place of Sepulture'. Beyond this is an area closed on its eastern edge by a columned hemicycle, and this area he intended should provide the space for vaults and a 'Cloyster for inscriptions'.[38] But at some point after July 1712 the Commissioners declined to buy the site, and 'nothing more is ever recorded of this proposal' in the Minutes.[39]

Hawksmoor's plans for the new church of St George-in-the-East, Wapping (1714–29), were realized, however, and, like the Bethnal Green site, there was space at Wapping to include a burial yard on the east side. There was also space at his best-known contribution to the new churches programme – Christ Church, Spitalfields (also 1714–29). Land was not available, however, for a burial place at St George, Bloomsbury (1716–31), where even the building itself had to be orientated north–south, and so land was purchased half a mile north-east of this overcrowded district. An adjacent pair of plots were laid out in open fields to the north of what was later to become the site for the Foundling Hospital (built 1742–52). These two plots served Hawksmoor's new Bloomsbury church plus nearby St George the Martyr, an old church that was under repair by the architect while he was overseeing construction of the new one (fig. 81).

Despite the fact that the new churches built under the Act of 1711 were either given adjacent graveyards or cemetery plots at a distance, intramural burial did take place in them. Indeed, due to the raised basements that every new building was given – and the avariciousness of the ministers, who could exact a burial fee for every vault established within – 'the churches erected under the Act provided for intramural burial on a scale never seen before in England'.[40] The difficulty of breaking what by then was a long-established practice, explains why even Wren and Vanbrugh – both so opposed to its continuance – were none the less interred in London churches: Wren in his own St Paul's, and Vanbrugh within the family vault in St Stephen Walbrook.

Vanbrugh, of course, might well have preferred to have been laid to rest in 'a Lofty and Noble Mausoleum', the building type he envisaged would in time enrich the kind of cemetery he promoted in his 'Proposals'. He had, in fact, supplied two sketches in his 'Proposals', one a hitherto unremarked ground-plan that is here reproduced for the first time (fig. 82), and an impressionistic elevation

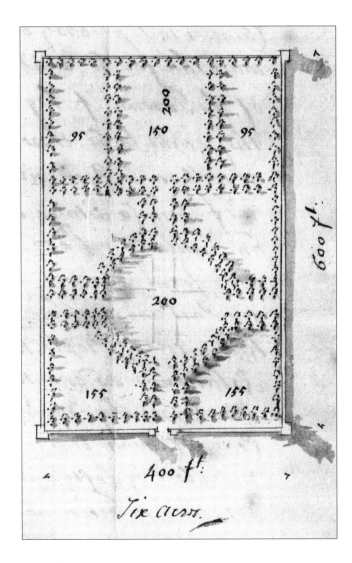

82. Vanbrugh's sketch-plan for a six-acre cemetery, 1711, intended for a site on the edge of London.

83. *Vanbrugh's sketch of the cemetery at Surat, 1711, drawn a quarter-century after his return from India.*

of this design – loosely based on Surat's cemetery – in its imagined future prime (fig. 83). The ground-plan – by far the earliest-known English design for a cemetery, a fact that can only further enhance Vanbrugh's reputation today as a true innovator in landscape architecture – is for a six-acre plot compartmentalized by means of shady avenues. At the angles are rectangular salients that we learn from the elevation sketch are imagined as funerary, stone-built pyramids.[41] The cemetery's boundaries are defined by a planked palisade.

This ideal burial place was to be a tree-filled necropolis packed with massive domed mausolea, towers, colossal pyramids and even lofty, bust-capped columns. The dimensions supplied with the ground-plan allow us to estimate the height of the structures shown in the elevation: the tallest, the bust-topped column to the left, is *c.* 65 feet. This elevation looks more than a little like mid-eighteenth-century Stowe in embryo. But back in 1711 there was no place at all in England that appeared remotely like this visionary drawing. Several more years were to pass before Vanbrugh and Bridgeman joined Lord Cobham to begin work at Stowe, while William Kent's serial interventions there were a decade and more away. In 1711 there were, in fact, *no* freestanding mausolea in non-consecrated settings. There were, as it happened, hardly any mausolea anywhere in England. The earliest known examples are the two that were built in churchyards in 1656, one in Bedfordshire, the other in Devon.[42] Only a handful were in existence by 1711, all of them in churchyards, and more or less all of them physically attached to the church. John Webb's unexecuted design of 1657 for the Isham family in Northamptonshire was indeed envisaged as a freestanding drum, but within a churchyard.[43] Even in Vanbrugh's day, apart from the example of a handful of eccentrics who had insisted on being interred in a garden, in a farmyard, under a hedge or somewhere else, burial outside consecrated ground was more or less unknown.[44]

Thus, when Vanbrugh drew out his ideas in 1711, the freestanding parkland or cemetery mausoleum was still nothing more than an exercise in office draughtsmanship. In 1678 Wren had prepared a design – a dome-capped drum within a circular, colonnaded base – for reinterring Charles I's remains within the grounds of Windsor Castle.[45] Conceivably, Webb's ambitious project of a few years earlier – a stepped, saucer-domed structure within a steeply battered

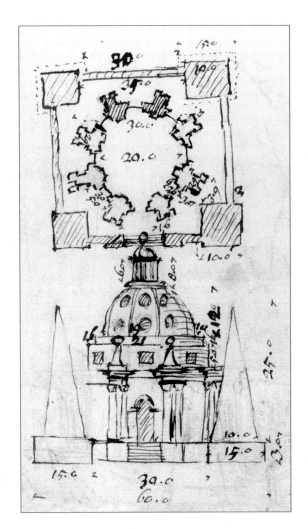

84. *A sketch by Vanbrugh of a projected garden building; its funerary detailing indicates that this is a mausoleum design, perhaps of the 1720s for Castle Howard or Blenheim.*

rectangle of masonry, a design that reminds one of French Neoclassicism a century later – was made with the same Stuart in mind.[46] Neither, of course, was built. Nor was the mausoleum Hawksmoor designed for William III, following Dutch William's sudden death in 1702.[47] Indeed, despite the fact that the park mausoleum did become almost a commonplace in later eighteenth-century England, and was certainly one in the nineteenth, no English or British monarch was laid to rest in such a setting until 1902, when Victoria's remains were interred at Frogmore near Windsor. Before that departure from tradition, deceased kings and queens were deposited either within the Henry VII Chapel at Westminster Abbey or in St George's Chapel at Windsor.

The novelty – and design potential – of the mausoleum as a building type evidently fascinated Vanbrugh; in fact, a number of his freehand sketches that today are catalogued as garden temple projects for sites unknown ought to be reconsidered as probable designs for mausolea (fig. 84). It was Vanbrugh, not Hawksmoor, who from the early 1720s was in discussion with the Earl of Carlisle

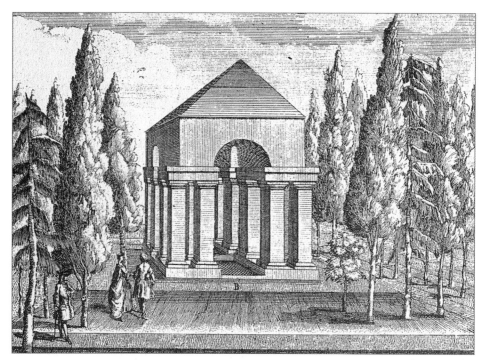

85. Vanbrugh's pyramidal garden temple at Claremont, as shown in Rocque's Plan of Claremont, *1738. This building may have been an experiment in mausolea design.*

about building a mausoleum at Castle Howard.[48] And it was Vanbrugh who, in 1722, sought in vain to persuade the Duchess of Marlborough to lay the Duke somewhere to rest in the park at Blenheim, with, as he explained, a 'plain, but magnificent & durable monument over him'.[49] And a particularly novel feature of Vanbrugh's schemes is that the mausolea he wanted to undertake at Castle Howard, at Blenheim, and doubtless elsewhere too, were to be built in parks, in gardens, not in consecrated churchyards. His visionary project was surely the English landscape cemetery garden.

Perhaps the long-since demolished pavilion he built in the grounds at Claremont, Surrey, for the Duke of Newcastle was intended – either in anticipation or perhaps simply as an architectural exercise – as a mausoleum (fig. 85). Kent, when he made a sketch of this building in its landscape setting in the early 1730s at a time when he was redesigning Claremont's gardens, contrived to record it as a less weighty, more elegant Serliana (fig. 89). But Vanbrugh's original idea of a heavy pyramid supported by columns is notionally close to several canopied tombs for wealthy lawyers that were constructed within the churchyard of S. Francesco, Bologna, in the thirteenth century, evidently in allusion to Roman precedent.[50] Whether Vanbrugh knew of them via reports by travellers is unknown.

It must be acknowledged, however, that Vanbrugh's funerary vision was not wholly his own. As he wrote in the margin of his 'Proposals about Building ye New Churches' against his elevation sketch, 'This manner of Interment has been practic'd by the English at Suratt and is come at last to have this kind of effect.'[51]

Vanbrugh's sketch of Surat's cemetery is the most exciting remembrance we have of his time there, although it is interesting to note that his classicizing rendition bears scant resemblance to the Oriental scene he actually encountered back in the 1680s. One reason he would have been struck by what he found there was the lack of anything remotely similar in England. With no churches in Surat in which to bury their dead, the English, Dutch, French and Armenian traders based there in the seventeenth century had been obliged to lay out their own cemetery plots on the city's edge. They filled them with mausolea, some remarkable for their ambition and commitment to Mughul forms and details. Each nation's traders competed with those of other nations, hoping to win preferential treatment from the ruling power by advertising *their* particular wealth, importance and influence as their state's unofficial ambassadors. In the significance they placed on display, the Europeans followed the Mughul dynasty itself, which built on a scale and extravagance that overawed its subjects at home and enemies abroad. The Taj Mahal at Agra, for example, the mausoleum constructed for the mother of Aurangzeb, the ruler of much of India when Vanbrugh was there, had only been completed in 1654.

The most extraordinary mausoleum in the English cemetery is the massive two-storey example that houses the remains of the Oxinden brothers (fig. 86). Christopher died in 1659, which occasioned its construction in the form of a domed kiosk with angle pinnacles, but when Sir George, Surat's Company President, succumbed to epidemic fever a decade later, he was interred there too, whereupon the structure was given its upper storey and over the dome an open-cross cupola was added – a Christian cross within a Mughal frame.[52] The Company took its leave of the former President in a way that impressed the city:

> At the Funerall for Sr: GEORGE OXINDEN the Streets, Balconys, and tops of the houses were soe full as they could [not] stand one by another. At the Grave after the Corps is enterred, there is Mony throwne and given to the Poore People; and our Burying Place [the English cemetery], which is large and spacious, is adorned with severall great and many handsome Tombs and Monuments, which many of the great Men of the Country esteem worth their Sight.[53]

Over 400 tombs can be seen today in the dusty and decayed English cemetery;[54] they range from the ambitious works undertaken for the Oxindens, for Gerald Aungier, for Samuel Annesley and other chiefs, to the numerous modest table-tombs built over lesser Company servants, many of which date from the days of the Raj. The earliest of the surviving seventeenth-century mausolea is the domed octagon that houses the remains of Francis Breton, who died in Surat on 21 July 1649 (fig. 87). Breton began his career with the Company in 1633, when he was taken on as a factor and sent to Persia, though within two years he was serving on the Council at Surat.[55] In 1644 he became head of the Surat Presidency, and was still serving in that capacity at his death. The long inscription his tomb bears is a variant on the classical formula – *Siste viator* ('Stop, traveller . . .') – encountered on Roman wayside tombs: 'Viator (si saltem Christianus es) siste . . .'.[56]

86. *Later seventeenth-century mausolea set up in the English cemetery at Surat to contain the remains of the East India Company's high-ranking servants; in the foreground looms the prodigy commemorating the Oxinden brothers.*

87. *Francis Breton's Mughal-style mausoleum in Surat cemetery, built from 1649.*

Vanbrugh may have had good reason to pause at this tomb when on his wanderings in the Company's cemetery, for it is probable that this Francis Breton was a distant relative, a suspicion that can only briefly be summarized here. Vanbrugh's mother, Elizabeth, was one of Sir Dudley Carleton's daughters; her sister Lucy married Thomas Breton, a London merchant that Kerry Downes has established was intimately involved in East India Company trade.[57] References to one Breton after another at home and abroad scattered through the Company's Minutes and correspondence from 1634 onwards suggest a family busily enriching itself.[58] By the early 1660s a Thomas Breton was serving as a Committee member (there were twenty-four members in all) at head office in London.[59] Further research in the India Office archives will probably establish that this individual was indeed Vanbrugh's uncle and that Francis Breton was a relation too. (In February 1666 the Thomas Breton who married Lucy Carleton was with her at Morden near London for the baptism of their newborn son, whom they named Francis.)[60]

As for the Edward Pearce who joined the Committee at the same time as Thomas Breton (this Pearce and Breton were hand in glove in one Company venture after another), he is likely to be the same Edward Pearce who, according to Downes, by 1657 was married to Mary Carleton, another of Vanbrugh's aunts.[61] By 1657 the Edward Pearce mentioned in the Minutes and correspondence (several Pearces, surely related, are named time and again in the records) was certainly back in London. Having begun his career in the Company in 1634, when he sailed on the East Indiaman *London* to serve at Bantam (western Java) in the Far East, two years later he was transferred to Surat as a writer, where he was eventually to serve briefly as President (in 1655), before he set out for England for good in January 1656 aboard the *Constantinople Merchant*.[62]

If Francis Breton was a distant relative of Vanbrugh, then Vanbrugh's encounters with Breton's mausoleum, and with the cemetery containing it, would surely have moved him in ways more profound, more affecting, than might otherwise have been the case. His memories of the place, even a quarter-century later when he made his sketches, would have been of an intimate nature. For him in 1711, landscaped cemeteries and mausolea would not have been unfelt possibilities, mere concepts ripe for realization and establishment in England, but sites and structures he had known at first hand, places and things that affected both thoughts and emotions. For him, cemeteries were surely charged with felt meaning.

Vanbrugh's encounters with the Islamic tomb in the landscape that, in Surat and elsewhere in India, had been adopted by Europeans and given a Christian gloss, lie behind his own attempts, made years later in England, to popularize park mausolea and out-of-town cemeteries. He, like many other European traders and travellers in the East in the seventeenth century, saw that Islam dealt with the dead in a way that Christians ought to emulate. As a French traveller to Turkey admiringly pointed out: 'Eastern people know no such evil custom as that of Burying their Dead within the walls of their Churches'.[63] This was indeed true, but *non*-Islamic methods in use in India at the time for disposing of the dead had little appeal to Europeans. Hindis, Buddhists and Jains all practised cremation. John Ovington watched Hindi mourners burn their dead by the River Tapti, and then cast the ashes into the waters.[64] He also saw the way that the *Parsees* (Indians of Persian origin) disposed of their dead in the open fields at their circular Towers of Silence:

> They enclose a small Piece of Ground, with a Wall about 4 Yards high, and place several Benches for the Corps to sit on . . . The Water or Rain carries the putrified Flesh and the Bones to the Earth . . . and the voracious Fowls carry what they can pick into the Air in their Maws.[65]

Hamilton also visited these grim charnel houses, and noticed that after the mourners had departed:

> within the space of a Day or two after, some of the nearest Relatives return again hither, to observe which of the Eyes of their deceased Friend was first pickt out by the hungry Vultures; and if they find that the right Eye was first seis'd on, this abodes undoubted Happiness; if the left, they then are sorrowful, for that's a direful sign of his Misery.[66]

Apart from Buddhist stupa, commemorative funerary monuments were unknown in India prior to the establishment of the Mughal empire.[67] This empire had originated when Babur, an adventurer from central Asia, swept south with his armies in 1526 and seized Delhi. Despite initial setbacks, the invading warlords in time overwhelmed the native Marathas and others and extended their power into India's heartland. In 1573 Babur's grandson, Akbar, captured Surat. The Mughal tide was relentless. By 1707, the year of Aurangzeb's death, all but the southern tip of India had been absorbed. And it was as this empire fractured and slowly fell apart during the eighteenth century that the Europeans began pocketing the pieces. But in the course of the sixteenth and seventeenth centuries, the Indian landscape was gradually ornamented with Mughal mausolea, often, as in the case of the Taj Mahal, constructed in luxurious garden settings, and on occasion within hunting parks.

What Vanbrugh the landscape architect grappled with in 1711 while reflecting on his encounters in India were conceptual, not stylistic, issues. It was the *idea* of the cemetery and the effects monumental mausolea could exert that motivated him to badger the Commissioners and his patrons. Despite these efforts, none of his own designs were ever realized, unless Claremont's temple was indeed a tomb, albeit an empty one, in the landscape. But by the time of his death, the park or garden mausoleum was beginning to be recognized as superior to the church vault by those that could afford to construct the landscape alternative. 'I do design to build a burial place near my seat of Castle Howard, where I desire to be lay'd', the Earl of Carlisle recorded in his will at some date in the early 1720s, when Vanbrugh and he were discussing the subject.[68] Appropriately enough, the Mausoleum Hawksmoor designed and built for Carlisle from 1729 was a very extravagent addition to the Yorkshire estate. On a visit to Castle Howard in 1731 the Duchess of Marlborough was startled to discover that 'My Lord Carlisle is laying out a mint of money in making an extraordinary place to bury his own family in a finer manner than I have ever heard of'.[69] Ovington had already noticed in India that 'The *Moghuls* are very profuse in their Funeral Expences';[70] soon many English at home would be too.

The garden cemetery took longer to establish itself in England. The Rosary in Norwich, reckoned to have been the first, was licensed for 'burial of all denominations' in 1819;[71] in 1830 the General Cemetery Company was set up in London, and, with Kensal Green, Norwood and others, by the close of the 1830s the landscaped cemetery was acknowledged as the way Victorian England would have to manage its dead.[72] No one then knew that Vanbrugh had designed a cemetery more than a century earlier. Similarly, it is unlikely that the architects and landscapists who promoted the Indian style in England at the end of the eighteenth century could have been aware that the Orient had once exerted its influence on him. Conventionally, the rise of Orientalist garden design is traced from the period that includes Chambers's novel undertakings at Kew in the late 1750s and early 1760s through to the temples and other structures at Melchet Park, Hampshire (*c.* 1800), and Sezincote, Gloucestershire (1805), as well as William Beckford's Moorish kiosk (mid-1820s) in the garden of his home in Lansdown Crescent, Bath, and a handful of other examples, whereupon it

88. The Hedges Visnu, *an eleventh-century siltstone image from Sagar Island, West Bengal, which William Hedges shipped to England and gave to the Ashmolean Museum in the mid-1680s.*

faltered.[73] Lutyens's water gardens (1923) for Amport House, Hampshire, are an idiosyncratic coda to the fashion, constructed at a time when he was working on New Delhi. But Oriental architectural details on buildings that date from as early as England's Baroque era do exist, although because they anticipate by several decades the established start date for Eastern influences, they are assumed to be 'neo-Gothic', for example the extraordinary main doorway to 'Preston's Folly' – a house in Settle, Yorkshire. Its paired pillars and cusped arch lights are surely from beyond the Bosphorus. The lintel is dated '1679'.[74]

There are enough examples known concerning dress, interior decoration and other aspects of late-seventeenth-century cultural life in London and provincial cities to suggest that historians of architecture and landscape design might do well to look afresh at the history of Oriental fashions and influences in England. In the Ashmolean Museum in Oxford, for example, there is a siltstone sculpture of Visnu, known as the *Hedges Visnu* (fig. 88), thought to be 'the first major Indian sculpture to have been acquired by a museum in the West'.[75] It was the gift of William Hedges, who in the early 1680s served as the East India Company's Governor of Bengal. On 12 March 1683 Hedges and several companions took boats down the River Hoogley on a holiday outing:

> We went in our Budgeros [river boats] to see ye Pagodas at Sagor, and returned to ye Oyster River, where we got as many Oysters as we desir'd, and lay at ye mouth of ye River.[76]

Saugor (or Sagar) Island, which lies at the mouth of the Ganges, was a major pilgrimage centre for Bengalis, and Hedges seems to have made himself the proprietor of this devout image in the course of his visit that day. Following the revocation of his commission soon after for his lack of tact as Governor, Hedges sailed from Bengal in December 1684 and returned to England via Persia. He appears, though, to have shipped home direct his gift for the Ashmolean, for it reached England in 1685, the very same year that Vanbrugh returned from India. The *Hedges Visnu* is rare physical evidence of a developing interest in non-Western art, a reminder that we should not underestimate the influence the Orient then exerted. It is well known, after all, that Wren and Hawksmoor were both intensely interested in Eastern architecture. That we now know their friend and colleague Vanbrugh had once travelled as far as India and returned to tell the tale ought to encourage a much-needed reassessment of their shared culture and ambition that takes full account of the East's influences in Baroque England.

EIGHT

'After ye Antique': Vanbrugh, Hawksmoor and Kent

Giles Worsley

When it comes to understanding the architecture and landscape design of the early eighteenth century, the indiscriminate use of the term Baroque and the rigid distinction made between Baroque and Palladian have confused far more than they have assisted. Sir John Summerson highlighted that conventional assumption of rigid distinction in his *Architecture in Britain*, placing Hawksmoor, Vanbrugh and Archer in a chapter on the English Baroque and commenting thus in his chapter on the rise of Palladianism: 'The first point to note is that it had nothing to do with Wren, Vanbrugh, Hawksmoor, or Archer except in so far as, by excluding the works of these architects from salvation, it was better able to distinguish its own particular sort of grace.'[1] While Archer is, I suggest, a genuinely Baroque architect, and the others all had Baroque moments, the boundaries cannot be set so rigidly.[2]

If the division really was so absolute, then there should be a complete divide between the work of Vanbrugh and Hawksmoor and that of William Kent. Kent was Burlington's favourite architect, his friend, a member of his household, co-designer of his garden at Chiswick, the man whom he used his influence to have appointed Deputy Surveyor of the Office of Works, to whom he entrusted the publication of Inigo Jones's drawings and, above all, the most important architectural commission of the day – the designs for the new Houses of Parliament. Surely 'Palladian' Kent should be about as far as one can get from the 'Baroque' Vanbrugh and Hawksmoor? So why is it sometimes hard to distinguish between their work?

The paintings of Claremont in Surrey of *c*. 1742–5 by the Master of the Tumbled Chairs highlight the problem.[3] Which buildings are by Vanbrugh (who built a house there – Chargate – for himself and then extended it for the Duke of Newcastle), and which by his successor Kent? Was the lake's island pavilion, with its suspended broken-based pediment, by Vanbrugh (one thinks, for instance, of the pavilions of his house in Whitehall[4] or the centrepiece of his original house at Claremont[5]) or Kent? What about the strange pyramidal temple (fig. 89), whose authorship is passed over in silence by Kerry Downes and Michael Wilson, is

89. William Kent's design sketch for Claremont, Surrey, c. 1730, which shows Vanbrugh's pyramidal temple and beyond it the hilltop Belvedere of c. 1715.

implicitly linked to Kent by John Dixon Hunt, and is forcefully attributed to Vanbrugh by John Harris?[6] And do the staccato rhythms of the Home Farm shown in the painting suggest Kent, as John Harris assumes,[7] or Vanbrugh? Their form and detail seem remarkably close to Vanbrugh's stables at Eastbury, Dorset, and even more so to his stables at Stowe, Buckinghamshire.[8]

Careful analysis of the evidence answers most of the questions, but not all. The engraved plan of Claremont in the third volume of *Vitruvius Britannicus*, published in 1725, long before Kent was involved, clearly shows the four piers of the temple on a curious, stepped, pyramid-like hill.[9] This is confirmed by a drawing of the temple in the Elton Hall collection now in the Victoria and Albert Museum.[10] The pavilion, on the other hand, was part of Kent's remodelling of the lake.[11]

The Home Farm is not shown on either the *Vitruvius Britannicus* plan of 1725 or Rocque's of 1738 in *Vitruvius Britannicus* volume four, but it is shown on Rocque's plan of Claremont of 1750.[12] It is possible that it had been built before 1738 and is just off the edge of the Rocque layout published that year, but improbable. Comparison of the three plans indicates that the Home Farm lay on the site of the original entrance from Esher common, and that its erection followed the extension of the drive and the creation of a new entrance slightly further north. This, and the pair of new lodges, can be seen in the painting of the Home Farm by the Master of the Tumbled Chairs. This suggestion is reinforced by the fact that the obelisk (originally in the centre of Vanbrugh's circular lake) shown in the painting standing next to the Home Farm, is clearly depicted in the 1738 plan in the centre of the semicircle of trees at the entrance from Esher common. It would thus appear that the Home Farm must have been part of the remodelling that happened in the early 1740s, and therefore is presumably by Kent; it is certainly not by Vanbrugh, despite its similarity to Stowe's stables.

If Kent and Vanbrugh are supposed to sit on opposite sides of the stylistic fence, why is it so confusing when trying to decide who designed what? The more their buildings and unexecuted designs are studied, the greater the similarities appear. No proper analysis of the similarities between Vanbrugh's, Hawksmoor's and Kent's work appears to have been undertaken. It deserves to be, for any analysis of this kind sheds light on the difficult concept of Palladianism, shows Vanbrugh not to have been the childless architectural figure he is usually portrayed to be, and helps us understand more fully the unusual place Kent holds in the Palladian canon. Above all, by examining what drove the three architects and what distinguished them from their contemporaries, we gain a fuller understanding of the importance of antiquity and neo-Classicism in the evolution of British architecture and landscape design, and in particular the significance of the Antique and neo-Classicism in the landscape at Castle Howard.

It is principally in their garden buildings that Vanbrugh, Hawksmoor and Kent seem to occupy such similar positions. This is not a question of saying that Kent deliberately imitated certain Vanbrugh and Hawksmoor buildings (the comparisons are not meant to be precise), but that shared influences are at work in their architecture. The similarities are general not specific. Nor are they absolute. It is easy to find buildings where the architects have little in common. But the similarities are marked.

Thus, the island pavilion at Claremont can be compared to Vanbrugh's flanking entrance arches proposed for Castle Howard[13] and Kent's lakeside pavilions at Holkham.[14] The Claremont pavilion suggests a pyramid over a building. Pyramids are a familiar feature in Vanbrugh's work – the Pyramid at Stowe;[15] and in that of Hawksmoor – the Carrmire Gate, the Pyramid cenotaph to Lord William Howard, the pyramid in Pretty Wood, all at Castle Howard; and in Kent – the pyramidal centrepiece to Kent's Temple of British Worthies at Stowe or his earlier design for the exedra at Chiswick.[16] We find it on rooftops in Vanbrugh's work – the Pyramid Gate at Castle Howard, the Kitchen Court at Castle Howard, the entrance pavilions at Eastbury;[17] in that of Hawksmoor – the pyramidal cap to the tower of St George's church, Bloomsbury, and a design for St Anne's, Limehouse;[18] and in that of Kent – Worcester Lodge at Badminton of c. 1745, his proposed design for pyramidal temples at Chatsworth,[19] his suggestion for the triumphal arch at Holkham.[20]

Then there are obelisks. Hawksmoor started the obelisk craze with the one for Ripon market-place in 1702 and later proposed a great obelisk for Blenheim. Vanbrugh followed with one celebrating the Duke of Marlborough at Castle Howard in 1714 and the host that ornamented the south parterre. Kent was responsible for an obelisk at Shotover Park, Oxfordshire, and another at Holkham. The obelisks on the parterre at Castle Howard were presided over by a giant, freestanding, fluted Doric column designed by Vanbrugh. Kent designed another such column at Chiswick. Hawksmoor was probably responsible for a column with a statue of Apollo on it at Easton Neston, Northamptonshire.

There are even times when Kent flirted with the idea of buildings that followed the basic form of Vanbrugh's Temple of the Four Winds, as in his design for Townesend's building at Rousham, Oxfordshire,[22] and in his *capriccio* of

90. A detail from one of William Kent's engraved designs illustrating episodes in a new edition of Edmund Spenser's The Faerie Queene, *published in 1751, showing a hillside house reminiscent of Seaton Delaval.*

Hampton Court and Esher Place, Surrey, with his version of the Temple of the Four Winds perched on a hill midway.[23]

Both Vanbrugh at Castle Howard and Kent at Rousham place statues on heavy plinths casually beside informally curving paths. They share a similar fascination for heavily rusticated primitive buildings, as can be seen in Vanbrugh's Robin Hood's Well, near Doncaster, and Kent's Praeneste at Rousham and his grotto for Horseheath Hall, Cambridgeshire.[24]

One can even find parallels in their larger buildings. Hawksmoor's Castle Howard Mausoleum of 1729 can be seen as a more massive version of Kent's Temple of Ancient Virtue at Stowe and the design (in the British Museum) for an Ionic rotunda.[25] The palace in one of Kent's illustrations for Spenser's *Faerie Queene* (fig. 90), where Guyon 'crosses the Idle Lake with Phaedria' (II, vi),[26] has a very similar feel to the south front of Vanbrugh's Seaton Delaval (fig. 91), whose north front recalls Kent's design for Euston in Suffolk[27] and perhaps even his model for Richmond Palace.

There is a raw vitality to the work of the three architects that sets it apart from more conventional Palladian architects such as Lord Burlington, Lord Herbert, Henry Flitcroft or Roger Morris, but it would be simplistic merely to describe this as Baroque. The key lies in their imaginative rather than literal response both to Classicism – where Burlington and his stricter followers worshipped at the feet of Vitruvius, Vanbrugh, Kent and Hawksmoor were more relaxed about rules – and to Antiquity, where their response can only be described as neo-Classical.

Our understanding of Classical architecture is severely handicapped by the mistaken belief that neo-Classicism – that is, the direct return to Antiquity for inspiration, ignoring Classical traditions developed since the Renaissance – was the invention of the second half of the eighteenth century. This has meant that neo-Classical buildings constructed in the first half of the century have been presented today as incongruous puzzles, in the way Summerson treated Burlington's Assembly Rooms at York and Kent's entrance hall at Holkham.[28]

But a literal neo-Classicism was a fundamental element of the neo-Palladian movement in Britain in the first half of the eighteenth century in the work of amateurs such as Burlington, Sir Thomas Robinson, Sir Francis Dashwood and Thomas Worsley.[29] These Palladian neo-Classicists, all amateur architects, had a very specific response to Antiquity: they sought out the evidence of Antique buildings from literary descriptions, from standing remains, from archaeological excavations and above all from Vitruvius, and tried to reconstruct the result as accurately as they could. The Assembly Rooms at York was a painstaking reconstruction of Vitruvius's Egyptian Hall. As for the sources that lay behind Burlington's Chiswick villa, Richard Hewlings needed over 1,000 footnotes to chart them.[30] The result is a literalness, almost a pedantry, which is particularly characteristic of the eighteenth-century English amateur's approach to design.

Vanbrugh, Hawksmoor and Kent were equally inspired by Antiquity, but theirs was a romantic rather than literal approach. It is perhaps best described as a neo-Classicism of the imagination, inspired more by the bold reconstructions of architects such as Pirro Ligorio, Giambattista Montano, Androuet du Cerceau[31] and the anonymous author of the Chatsworth volume *Antiquae urbis praeclarissima aedificia*[32] in the sixteenth century, or perhaps Fischer von Erlach in the early eighteenth,[33] than by the scrupulous (or comparatively scrupulous) archaeology of Palladio or Desgodetz. (Hawksmoor owned copies of Montano and Fischer von Erlach, as well as of Palladio and Desgodetz.)[34] Above all – and perhaps this is the key – it was not a neo-Classicism hidebound by the constraints of those Vitruvian rules held in such awe by Burlington and his fellow amateurs.[35]

91. The south (garden) front of Vanbrugh's Seaton Delaval, Northumbria, built 1719–26.

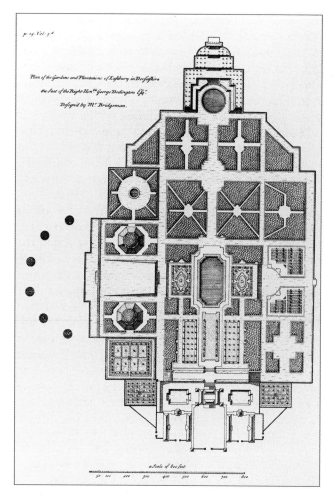

92. *The plan of Eastbury, Dorset, published in Campbell's* Vitruvius Britannicus, *III, 1725, a collaboration between Vanbrugh and Bridgeman, with a reconstruction of the Temple of Fortune at Praeneste at the far end of the garden.*

93. *Pietro da Cortona's* A Reconstruction of Praeneste, *c. 1636, from a scrapbook formerly belonging to John Talman that is now in the Victoria and Albert Museum.*

Vanbrugh's aesthetic motivation is the hardest to gauge because no catalogue of his library survives (the only architectural book we know he used is an edition of Palladio), and his letters, informative and chatty though they are, provide few clues about his architectural thinking. His one statement on architecture, 'Mr Van-Brugg's Proposals about Building ye New Churches',[36] gives no clues about his views on Antiquity. But the buildings and the landscape provide clear primary evidence. There is a strong sense of *Romanitas* in the bastioned garden he created at Blenheim, as Stephen Switzer pointed out when he described it as being 'after the ancient *Roman* Manner',[37] and in Blenheim's bridge built on the scale of a Roman aqueduct.[38] The pyramidal temple at Claremont can be compared to the gate at Albano illustrated in Fréart de Chambray's *Parallèle de l'architecture* (fig. 107) and to a similar pyramidal structure near Vienna illustrated by Montfaucon.[39]

Vanbrugh's buildings at Stowe also have strong Antique overtones. The Pyramid has already been mentioned. The Rotunda[40] owed much to Perrault's reconstruction of Vitruvius's monopteral rotunda.[41] The same is true of the two Lake Pavilions, the parterre temple illustrated in the *Vitruvius Britannicus* bird's-eye view of Castle Howard (fig. 24) and Perrault's reconstruction of the Prostyle Temple.[42]

It is in the garden at Eastbury (where Charles Bridgeman was also involved) that the strongest Antique flavour emerges, as the plan of it in *Vitruvius Britannicus* reveals (fig. 92).[43] At the far (east) end, the series of terraces, two projecting forward, with a huge temple at their summit, is a clear reference to the Temple of Fortune at Praeneste (Palestrina). This, one of the grandest Roman remains, was a favourite subject for Renaissance theorists. Palladio and Pirro Ligorio made reconstructions in the 1550s and 1560s, and reconstructions based on those by Pietro da Cortona (fig. 93) of *c*. 1636 (one of which, now in the Victoria and Albert Museum, was owned by John Talman in the early eighteenth century) appeared frequently in the seventeenth century and the early eighteenth. Examples can be found in Josephus Maria Suares's *Praenestes Antiquae*, published in 1655 and reissued by Graevius in 1723, Athanasius Kircher's *Latium* (1671), Domenico de Rossi's *Romanae Magnitudinis Monumenta* (1699), Bernard de Montfaucon's *L'Antiquité expliquée* (1719 and 1722–4) and Jan Blaeu's *Nouveau Théâtre d'Italie* (1724).[44]

Intriguingly, however, while these followed Pietro da Cortona in capping a hill with a semicircular colonnade, Vanbrugh's version at Eastbury climaxed in a giant hexastyle Corinthian temple (fig. 94), somewhat akin to Palladio's – then unpublished – reconstruction that incorporates a Pantheon-like building (fig. 95). Could Vanbrugh have known this drawing? Exactly which Palladio drawings were owned by Inigo Jones and subsequently by William and John Talman (and sold by the latter to Burlington in 1721), and which were acquired by Burlington in Italy in 1719, is unclear. Certainly Hawksmoor had access to those that Jones had once owned, and so it seems likely that Vanbrugh could have too.

Praeneste, not Bramante's Belvedere at the Vatican, as has been suggested from time to time, was probably also the source for the amphitheatre at Claremont (another collaboration between Vanbrugh and Bridgeman). The concave and convex terracing is a key element in reconstructions of Praeneste, but what gives the game away at Claremont is an engraving of *c*. 1725 that shows a proposed Pantheon-like temple at the summit[45] – as in Palladio's reconstruction.

If these references to Praeneste are correct, they would fit in with Robert Williams's suggestion[46] that the Temple of the Four Winds at Castle Howard (fig. 103) derives

94. *The Temple at Eastbury, probably inspired by Palladio's reconstruction of the Temple of Fortune at Praeneste. It was designed and built by Vanbrugh on a summit at the far end of the garden, as illustrated in Campbell's* Vitruvius Britannicus, *III, 1725.*

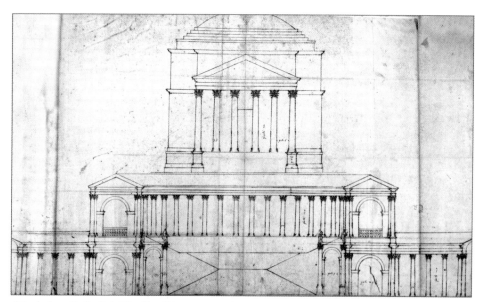

95. *Andrea Palladio's* Idealized Reconstruction of the Upper Terraces and Temple of Fortuna Primigenia, Praeneste *drawn in the late 1560s, which incorporates a Pantheon-like building.*

96. Palladio's Fanciful
Reconstruction of the Forum and
Temple of Fortuna Primigenia,
Praeneste *drawn in the late 1560s,*
showing the design for a temple with
porticos on four sides that he
incorporated in two of his Veneto
projects.

from another of Palladio's Praeneste reconstructions (fig. 96), in which the hill is topped by a temple with porticos on four sides – the inspiration behind Palladio's Villa Rotonda and his projected Villa Trissino at Meledo. And it is at Castle Howard, discussed below, that Vanbrugh's neo-Classical motivation is most clearly expressed.

As for Hawksmoor, you only have to read his defence of his design for the Mausoleum at Castle Howard, look at his drawing for 'The Belvidera' at Castle Howard inscribed 'After ye Antique. Vid Herodotus, Pliny, and M: Varo', see how he used Androuet du Cerceau's reconstructions of Roman temples as inspiration for the City churches, or look at his designs for turning Oxford into a city fit for Augustus, complete with forum, columned temple and domed mausoleum (the Radcliffe Library), to realize he was obsessed by Antiquity.[47] This is confirmed by the sale catalogue of his library, prints and pictures, which included numerous works of Roman architecture, including J.F. Félibien des Avaux's *Maisons de Pline*, Perrault's edition of Vitruvius, Montano's *Architettura*, Serlio, Fontana on the Vatican obelisk, Fischer von Erlach, Desgodetz, Alberti, Palladio, books on Trajan's and Antonine's columns and Sadeler's *Ruins of Rome*.[48]

Kent had an advantage over Hawksmoor in that he had spent ten years in Rome, where he had closely examined and drawn Antique remains and been instrumental in commissioning a series of 158 studies after Antique paintings from Francesco Bartoli for Thomas Coke, later Earl of Leicester. His interest was maintained on his return by studying books of archaeological discoveries. He must have had easy access to Burlington's superlative collection of architectural and archaeological works,[49] and he is known to have borrowed from others. In 1745 he wrote to Burlington that he was reading Bianchini's book on the discoveries on the Palatine Hill, which had been lent to him by the great antiquarian Dr Richard Mead (owner of another important collection of Bartoli drawings).[50] The sale catalogue of Kent's library reveals that he also owned an intriguing collection of such books himself. Among them are a surprising number of sixteenth-century works, including two copies of *Hypnerotomachia Poliphili*, and, most significantly, Montfaucon's multi-volume *L'Antiquité expliquée* of 1722–4, an encyclopaedic collection of Roman and other remains, including buildings.[51]

Among Kent's first important works in England was the *grottesche* ceiling of the Presence Chamber at Kensington Palace of 1724, correctly described by Vertue as 'in imitation of the antient Roman subterranean ornaments', one of the four such ceilings there. His passion for Antiquity is clearest in his designs for gardens: Chiswick with its exedra; the Plinieian layout of the garden at Holkham; and Rousham with its Praeneste. Particularly interesting is Stowe, where Kent was following in Vanbrugh's footsteps.

At Stowe, Kent's Temple of Ancient Virtue would fit happily into Palladio's *Quattro Libri*, and sits comfortably in the conventional run of Palladian garden buildings, but the Temple of British Worthies and the Temple of Venus (fig. 97) do not. Their form and proportions owe nothing to Palladio's careful reconstructions of Roman temples in the *Quattro Libri*. Instead they seem to come straight from the pages of Montano, Pirro Ligorio and the anonymous author of the Chatsworth *Antiquae urbis praeclarissima aedificia* (fig. 98).

The essential similarity between Hawksmoor's and Kent's vision of Antiquity is most apparent when comparing Hawksmoor's dreams for a Classical Oxford – particularly his various schemes for Queen's College[52] – with Kent's grandiloquent designs for the Houses of Parliament.[53] Both reveal a richly Classical imagination only lightly constrained by Vitruvian convention. I suspect that if Hawkmoor's designs for the Houses of Parliament were ever discovered they would not be so far off in aspiration from what Kent sought to achieve.

Then there is the landscape at Castle Howard, whose layout and use of garden buildings is so extraordinary for its date. Here the most plausible explanation for the way the formal garden expands to a heroic scale and then breaks its bounds so that – for the first time in England, and almost the first time in Europe – the garden spreads out into the surrounding countryside to form a landscaped park dotted with buildings, is the deliberate desire to recall, even recapture, Antiquity, and specifically the Roman Campagna.

This may not have been the case when Castle Howard was first planned. The house itself does not seem to have neo-Classical overtones, and Charles Saumarez Smith makes it clear that the landscape at Castle Howard was not built to an original master-plan, but grew and developed over time.[55] But the result only makes sense when seen from an Antique perspective.

Work on the landscape began with the creation of Ray Wood in 1705–10.[56] Instead of accepting George London's radial plan, Lord Carlisle apparently cut informal curving paths into Ray Wood, dotting them with statues and stone seats. The first major structure, the great obelisk at the junction with the road to York, followed in

97. *William Kent's Temple of Venus at Stowe, built before 1731, which owes more to the reconstructions of architects such as G.B. Montano and Pirro Ligorio than it does to Palladio.*

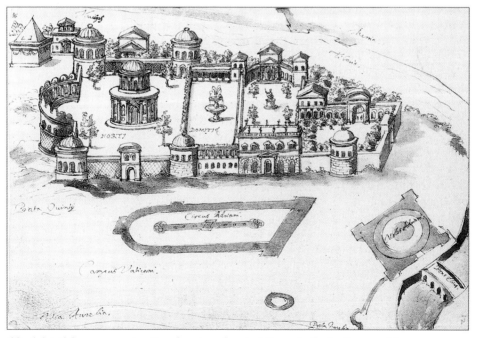

98. *A detail from a reconstruction drawing of ancient Rome in the* Antiquae urbis praeclarissima aedificia, *including a possible model for Kent's Temple of Venus.*

1714. It must have been at about this time that the parterre was designed on the south front of the house. If Nick Savage and Eileen Harris are right, the bird's-eye perspective of Castle Howard (fig. 24) published in the third volume of *Vitruvius Britannicus* (1725) was originally intended for the first volume, and must, therefore, have been drawn by 1715.[57] Although there are some inconsistencies in the topography, the estate map of 1727 reveals the perspective in essence to be accurate (fig. 13). References in letters show the parterre was being laid out in 1719. It comprised a long, wide area of grass enclosed at the south end by the Wilderness, with *bosquets*, straight avenues and curving walks cut into the greenery. In the *Vitruvius Britannicus* plate the Wilderness is shown within rectangular bastioned walls and terminated at its southern end by a Doric temple, but it is unclear whether the temple was built, and it seems unlikely that the bastions were executed.

In 1719 the Pyramid Gate was also under construction, and it was presumably at this date that the road to York was realigned as a long, straight one. Work continued apace. The fortified walls flanking the Pyramid Gate were built by 1723; the Temple of the Four Winds was designed in 1723 or 1724, although not built until 1725–8; work began on the design of the Mausoleum in 1726, although construction did not begin until 1729; the Pyramid was built in 1728; and the Temple of Venus in 1731–5.

This is not a proto-English landscape garden of the Brownian type, although its influence on the landscape garden was undoubtedly strong. Nor should it be seen as an attempt to create a self-consciously Claudian landscape: the Earl of Carlisle does not seem to have been particularly interested in Claude or Poussin, and unlike

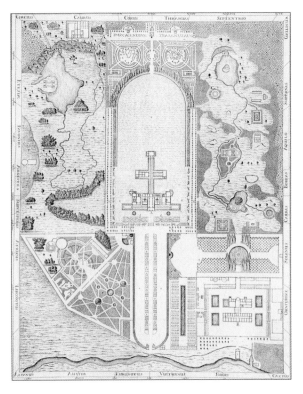

99. The plan of Pliny's Tusculum villa, a reconstruction by Robert Castell published in his Villas of the Ancients, *1728. There are strong parallels with the design of the parterre at Castle Howard.*

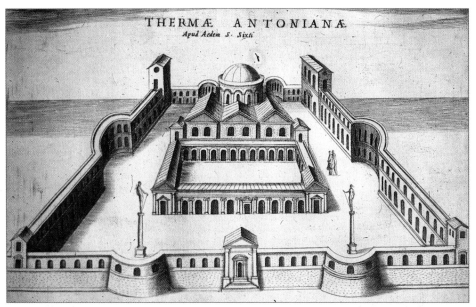

100. A reconstruction of the Thermae Antoninianae of Caracalla, Rome, dedicated in AD 216. Such reconstructions may be the source for the bastions and pavilions proposed by Vanbrugh for the parterre at Castle Howard.

many of his contemporaries he owned none of their pictures. Similarities with the work of Claude, and more particularly Poussin, are noticeable, but these should probably be seen as parallel attempts at the same goal – an evocation of Antiquity. Claude and Poussin may have been guides, but they were not themselves the models.

The key source for Antique gardens was Pliny's description of his Tusculum garden. Consider the Castle Howard parterre in the bird's-eye view (fig. 23). Its extraordinary length has often been commented on, and David Jacques has pointed out how unusual it is for an English parterre before 1715 to be plain grass. Looking at Robert Castell's reconstruction of the Tusculum garden in *The Villas of the Ancients* of 1728 (fig. 99), one sees exactly the same features, a long expanse of grass enclosed by what can be described as a wilderness cut through by paths, with a temple on axis at the end, all within a rigid rectangular framework. The Castle Howard parterre should probably be read as a similar reconstruction. Of course, Castell's edition of Pliny's villas was not published until after the Castle Howard parterre had been laid out and Ray Wood fashioned, but the close similarity is unlikely to be coincidence. Both reconstructions grew out of the ferment of interest in Antiquity in these years, and show their authors reaching similar conclusions from the same source material.

Nor is it just in the parterre that parallels can be made between Castle Howard and Castell's Tusculum. The landscape shown surrounding Pliny's villa is dotted with informally placed buildings – here an obelisk, there a colonnaded rotunda or a square temple on what would appear to be a mount. Many of these features can be found at Castle Howard. Water also plays an important part in the Plineian

101. Nicholas Hawksmoor's colonnaded Mausoleum at Castle Howard, built 1729–36.

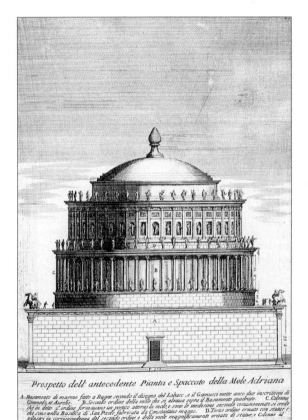

Prospetto dell' antecedente Pianta e Spaccato della Mole Adriana

102. A reconstruction of the Mausoleum of Hadrian, Rome, dedicated in AD 142. Hawksmoor's Mausolem was modelled on such reconstructions of colonnaded Roman mausolea.

landscape, as at Castle Howard, where there were once extensive water features in Ray Wood and a large belt of water to the east of the parterre.

The individual features in the Castle Howard landscape can all be seen as having specifically Roman overtones. The bastioned walls with their corner pavilions proposed for the parterre (fig. 23) bear strong resemblence to the enclosing walls and pavilions of reconstructions of Roman temples and baths, such as that of the Thermae Antoninianae (fig. 100). The importance of the obelisk in ancient Rome had been emphasized by Domenico Fontana's re-erection of the obelisk in the Piazza di San Pietro in 1586, published in a sumptuous folio. The significance of the Mausoleum is also unmistakable (fig. 101). Hawksmoor carefully followed the form of a traditional Roman mausoleum with a square base and circular drum. In this case it is surrounded by a colonnade – the sign, as at the Mausoleum of Hadrian, now the Castel Sant'Angelo, of a mausoleum of the highest status (fig. 102). Temples in the landscape, such as the Temple of the Four Winds (fig. 103) and the Temple of Venus, were considered archetypally Roman. As Robert Morris explained in his *Lectures on Architecture* of 1734–6: 'The ancient *Romans* planted their Plots in this *rural* manner and their *Temples*, dedicated to their peculiar GODS, were dispersed among the *Groves* and Woods, which Art or Nature had made, with *Vistas* to them.'[58] The temple at Tivoli was a well-known example. Pliny's *Natural History* and Pliny the Younger's letters show

103. Vanbrugh's Temple of the Four Winds at Castle Howard, built 1725–8.

104. *A monumental portrait bust of Lord William Howard in Hawksmoor's Pyramid at Castle Howard. It could be the bust of a Roman emperor.*

105. *Vanbrugh's mock fortification walls at Castle Howard, built 1719–25, with Hawksmoor's Pyramid of 1728 seen in the distance.*

that sculpture was also important in Roman gardens – as it was at Castle Howard – with the gardens of rich connoisseurs such as Servilius or Asinius Pollio forming virtual outdoor museums.[59] Perrault's reconstruction of the Clepsydre of Ctesibius in his edition of *Vitruvius* seems to have been the source for the grandest of the pedestals for the statues at Castle Howard.[60] As for the extraordinary colossal bust of Lord William Howard (the 3rd Earl's great-great-great-grandfather, founder of the Castle Howard branch of the family), portrayed as a Roman emperor, in the Pyramid (fig. 104), had that been dug up in York and declared to date from the time of Constantine, no one would have been surprised.

But what about the Pyramid (fig. 105) and Pyramid Gate (fig. 106), whose association, surely, is Egyptian, and the castle walls, usually assumed to be Gothic, an evocation of the Middle Ages?[61] For the Pyramid Gate one might look at the illustration in Fréart's *Parallèle de l'architecture* – one of the key books on architecture translated into English in the seventeenth century, and reprinted in 1707, 1722, 1723 and 1733 – of the pyramid gate at Albano (fig. 107).[62] As for the Pyramid, one of the most famous of all Roman tombs was the tomb of Caius Cestius (fig. 108), a pyramid lying just beyond Rome's walls outside the Lateran Gate, much as the Castle Howard Pyramid, a memorial to Lord William Howard, lies outside the walls. These walls in their turn should probably not be seen as

106. Vanbrugh's Pyramid Gate at Castle Howard, built in 1719, with the wings added later in the eighteenth century.

107. 'The Albano Gate', an engraving from Roland Fréart de Chambray's Parallèle de l'architecture, *1650, which could have inspired the Pyramid Gate at Castle Howard.*

108. *The Walls of Rome and the Mausoleum of Caius Cestius, probably the inspiration for the fortified walls and Pyramid at Castle Howard.*

109. The Avenue at Castle Howard, a striking example of the influence of Rome.

evocations of medieval England – of Chester or York, say – but of Rome itself. The ancient walls of Rome remain deeply impressive, even today. In the seventeenth century, when they were surrounded by fields marking the bounds of a much-shrunken city, they must have seemed all the more remarkable. If Vanbrugh needed any reminder of the solidly Roman associations of battlemented walls, Perrault provided him with one in his translation of Vitruvius.[63]

There is also that most striking feature of Castle Howard, which tends to be forgotten as part of the deliberately created landscape, that remarkably straight road (fig. 109). In England the Romans have always been associated with straight roads, good examples of which can be found not far from Castle Howard at Lord Burlington's estate at Londesborough and on the North Yorkshire Moors. At Stowe, part of a genuine Roman road was pressed into service as the approach to the house, despite the fact that it was off-axis.

The complicated question of Ray Wood (and also perhaps Pretty Wood) is also probably best understood as a homage to ancient Rome. Ray Wood remains problematic. Although we have Switzer's description of its informality, the first clear record of its appearance comes from an estate map of 1773. Assuming that the wiggling paths shown are original, which seems probable, then the thinking behind them is likely to be Roman, as it was commonly believed that Pliny's gardens had included informally curving paths. But Ray Wood may also provide a clue to the intellectual background behind the Antique leanings at Castle Howard.

It has been argued that the immediate inspiration for the informally curving paths of Ray Wood were the similar ones in the Bosquet de Louveciennes at Marly, the apparent informality of which is exceptional for their date. Marly, the most advanced garden of the leading patron of garden design in Europe, was eagerly visited by the English and others after the Treaty of Ryswick was signed in September 1697 (we know that George London, the Earl of Portland and the Scot Alexander Edward all went there), and it seems to have had a strong influence on English gardens.

Betsy Rosasco has argued that Marly's gardens – their bones largely laid out by 1686 but their *bosquets* only elaborated in the early 1690s – are best understood as a reinvention of the ancient gardens of the Augustan age.[64] Her analysis of Marly did not include the curving paths in the Bosquet de Louveciennes, but if her broader argument is accepted then it would make sense that these should be part of that wider Antique recreation, given the common interpretation of Pliny's gardens.

The Augustan gardens at Marly did not arise in an intellectual vacuum. The considered attempt to understand Roman antiquity had been a central part of a certain circle of French intellectuals since Sublet de Noyers, Surintendant des Bâtiments from 1638 to 1643, gathered a small group of 'Intelligents' around him whose goal was to purify French architecture after the excesses of Jacques du Cerceau and to protect it from the licence of the contemporary Roman Baroque. Fréart de Chambray's translation of Palladio's *Quattro Libri* and his publication of the *Parallèle de l'architecture* were both part of this campaign, as were Claude Perrault's translation of Vitruvius, Jean Marot's reconstructions of the temple of Baalbek, Antoine Desgodetz's detailed surveys of Roman buildings in *Les Edifices Antiques de Rome* of 1682, and Félibien's translation of Pirro Ligorio's sixteenth-century description of Hadrian's villa at Tivoli[65] and his reconstruction of Pliny's villas in *Les Plans et les descriptions de deux des plus belles maisons de campagne de Pline le consul*. This last was published in Paris in 1699 and Amsterdam in 1706, the second edition being distributed in London in 1707.[66]

The circle had intimate connections in Rome, where Fréart's friend Poussin made a close study of Antiquity for his paintings and where the director of the French Academy commissioned a manuscript copy of Flaminio Vacca's sixteenth-century account of archaeological finds made in Rome for the Marquis of Louvois, Surintendant des Bâtiments from 1684 to 1691. Here such activity centred around Poussin's patron, Cassiano dal Pozzo, whose passion for exploring Antiquity led to the formation of at least twenty-three volumes of drawings of Classical remains, including those of the Praeneste reconstruction made by his friend Pietro da Cortona.[67]

This interest grew in the early eighteenth century. The 1998 exhibition in Lyon, 'La Fascination de L'Antique, 1700–1770: Rome Découverte, Rome Inventée',[68] provided intriguing evidence of the ferment of Antique investigation that swept Rome in the first half of the eighteenth century – at exactly the same time that similar interest was being shown in England. Far from the rise of neo-Classicism being sparked by the discoveries of Herculaneum and Pompeii (as popular myth would have it), or by the arrival of Winckelmann in 1755 (as the Germans argue), or by the 'discovery' of Greece (as the philhellenes believe), twelve important excavations in Rome between 1704 and 1737 – which built on the earlier work of Cassiano dal Pozzo and his circle – provided the solid foundation from which it grew.

This, perhaps, should be seen as the intellectual background to what happened at Castle Howard. Nor was it extraordinary that Castle Howard should have been the scene of an attempt to recreate Antiquity in the second and third decades of the eighteenth century. Classically educated men living in the north of England were all too well aware that it had once been a Roman province. Edward Gibson's greatly enlarged edition of Camden's *Britannia* was published in 1695, Alexander

Gordon's study of Roman ruins in Scotland and the north of England, *Itinerarium Septentrionale*, in 1726 and John Horsley's *Britannia Romana* in 1732. In 1722 William Stukeley created the (short-lived) Society of Roman Knights, whose aim was 'to adorn and preserve the truly noble monuments of the Romans in Britain' and 'to search for and illustrate the Roman monuments in the Brittanic Isles'.[69]

At Naworth Castle in Cumbria the Earl of Carlisle kept an extensive collection of Roman remains found on Hadrian's Wall. Roman roads ran across Yorkshire. One, known as The Street, passed only a few miles north of Castle Howard along the edge of the Vale of Pickering. Above all, York had once been a Roman capital, as Francis Drake stressed in his history of the city, tellingly entitled *Eboracum: The History and Antiquities of the City of York*, published in 1736. Two emperors had died in the city. A third may have been born there. Drake conjured up 'that Praetorian palace, once in old EBORACUM' and specifically compared it to Burlington's new Assembly Rooms of 1731–2: '[it] must, if now standing, have given place to your *Egyptian* hall in our present *York*'. Burlington even suggested to Drake that York's Micklegate Bar was of Roman origin.[70]

Castell's *Villas of the Ancients* was only one example of wide-ranging scholarly interest in trying to create a model for Antiquity during the critical years that the Castle Howard landscape was being formed. This scholarship included the publication of Jonathan Richardson's *An Account of some Statues, Bas-reliefs, Drawings and Pictures in Italy* in 1722 – the first modern study to give due emphasis to the significance of Antique sculptures that had been lost; the delivery by Dr Mead, a keen antiquarian, of his Harveian Oration in 1723 on the position of the physician in the ancient world; and the publication in 1725 of Richard Bradley's *A Survey of the Ancient Husbandry and Gardening, Collected from Cato, Varro, Columella, Virgil, and others the most eminent Writers among the Greeks and Romans*. These years also saw the creation of Richard Topham's remarkable paper museum of Roman remains to accompany his extensive library devoted to Antiquity, which by his death in 1730 totalled about 4,000 books.

Nor did such thinking arise in a political vacuum. Philip Ayres has skilfully charted the way that members of the English ruling class, in the wake of the Revolution of 1688, wrapped themselves up in the rhetoric and arts of Antiquity, self-consciously identifying themselves with the Roman ideals of 'liberty' and 'civic virtue'.[71] Such parallels both justified the attempt to recreate Antique buildings and landscapes in England and gave those recreations a strong political charge. Absolutist rule made such parallels hard to establish on the continent, making Marly exceptional in its neo-Classical inspiration. Perhaps this explains why neo-Classicism flourished in England in the first half of the eighteenth century, but only became popular on the continent after 1750.

So who lay behind the attempt to create Rome in the Yorkshire countryside? Hawksmoor's enthusiasm and scholarship is undeniable and must have been important, but one never gets the feeling that he was a driving force at Castle Howard. Vanbrugh remained the dominant architectural figure. It is his eye that lies behind most of the critical buildings. He was also probably the key figure in the creation of the landscape. As early as 1703 Vanbrugh was accepted as a landscape designer – we know this from comments made that year by Sir Godfrey Copley concerning Vanbrugh's visit to the Duke of Newcastle's Welbeck, where Vanbrugh 'set out' a 40-acre lake.[72]

But Vanbrugh was clearly not the sole motivating force at Castle Howard. Had he been, the programme would have ground to a halt at his death in 1726 instead of continuing strongly for at least another decade, only really coming to an end with Carlisle's death in 1738. This suggests the importance of the Earl himself (as does the fact that, unusually among Vanbrugh's works, there is little evidence of Elizabethan overtones at Castle Howard). After all, of the three he was the only one who had actually visited Rome. Notes from his commonplace book reveal that while there he took a direct interest in Antiquity. His reference to 'John Piter Bellori Antiquario del Papa, a great vertuoso, he hath a very good closet', suggests he was aware of the writings of the key antiquary Gian Pietro Bellori. Equally revealing is the note 'Mon sig. Fabretti a vertuoso at Rome is about puting out a book of all ye Triumphal arches at Rome'.[73] One of the drafts of his will illustrates his continuing interest in Roman thinking: 'ye practice of ye Romans was very right in erecting ye Monuments they raised for their dead near ye highways & ye most frequented places in order I suppose yt ye living might thereby be put in mind of ye worthy actions of their Ancestors & likewise of their Mortality.'

The answer is that Castle Howard and its landscape were probably the creation of all three men. Design by committee was not exceptional. It certainly seems to have been the way Holkham was created by Lord Burlington and the Earl of Leicester with William Kent and Matthew Brettingham. It would be interesting to know who else was consulted. Burlington, a fellow Yorkshire landowner, was certainly involved with the Mausoleum in the 1730s. Had he been consulted earlier? It is likely that there was more communication at this time between architects of supposedly different persuasions than we realize. Lord Burlington was probably aware of the proto-Palladian work of George Clarke and Hawksmoor at Oxford. Certainly there are remarkable similarities between Hawksmoor's proposed entrance front for Worcester College and Burlington's façade for Old Chiswick House.[74] We also know that Burlington looked at Hawksmoor's plans for the Houses of Parliament, and perhaps not, as is usually assumed, because he wanted to sabotage the work of a rival, but rather from a shared passion.

After Hawksmoor's death in 1736 Sir Thomas Robinson suggested bringing in Kent to complete the Mausoleum at Castle Howard – at a cost of 30 guineas plus expenses. It would have been an appropriate act, for Vanbrugh's influence on Kent's landscape gardening through Castle Howard and Claremont is undeniable. Horace Walpole famously declared that Kent 'leaped the fence, and saw that all Nature was a Garden', but Vanbrugh had been there first.

Of all English landscape gardens, it is probably Kent's at Rousham (fig. 110) that most clearly develops the feeling of Antiquity which permeates Castle Howard. The scale may be much smaller, and there are none of the monumental buildings that so distinguish Castle Howard, but Kent's work from 1737 to 1741, remodelling an earlier scheme of the 1720s by Charles Bridgeman, condenses the intense sense of Roman antiquity found in Vanbrugh's landscape. As at Castle Howard there are echoes of Roman buildings (the Praeneste terrace; Townesend's Building), wandering paths, scattered statues on plinths, and glimpses out into the landscape beyond. Horace Walpole captured its atmosphere perfectly: 'the whole is as elegant and antique as if the emperor Julian had selected the most pleasing solitude about Daphne to enjoy a philosophic retirement'. In a letter to George Montagu of 1760 he noted that the 'garden is Daphne in little; the

110. William Kent's Vale of Venus at Rousham in Oxfordshire, with the cascades he incorporated in the garden c. *1740.*

sweetest little groves, streams, glades, porticoes, cascades, and river imaginable; all the scenes are perfectly classic'.[75] Remove the word *little*, and he could be describing Castle Howard.

The conventional divisions between Baroque and Palladian break down when one examines together the work of Vanbrugh, Hawksmoor and Kent. At times it seems that there is more in common between them than there is between Burlington and Kent. Burlington, like his fellow amateur Palladian neo-Classicists, was obsessed with Vitruvian precedent. Kent, like Hawksmoor and Vanbrugh, felt no such constraint. He used the Palladian vocabulary extensively, but with great freedom. It is in this that he feels so close to Vanbrugh and Hawksmoor, whose architectural heir he should rightly be considered quite as much as he is Burlington's. But ultimately even these divisions melt in the realization that what drove them all was a fascination with Antiquity and a desire to recreate it in the English landscape, nowhere more so than at Castle Howard.

NINE

Stephen Switzer and Water Gardens

Judith Roberts

In his account of the Renaissance garden in England published twenty years ago, Roy Strong rightly drew attention to the impact of the hydraulics engineers Salomon and Isaac de Caus on the structure and iconography of gardens in the early seventeenth century.[1] But there has been no comparable assessment of the contribution of such engineers for the period that reaches from the Restoration to the supposed advent of the landscape garden in the 1730s. Stephen Switzer (1683–1745) – garden designer, author, surveyor, seedsman[2] – was a leading 'hydrostatician' (his term) in the early eighteenth century, and his two-volume *Introduction to a General System of Hydrostaticks and Hydraulicks, Philosophical and Practical* (London, 1729) immediately established itself as the most authoritative directory on the subject for estate owners and landscapists.

Switzer had begun his career in horticulture and landscape projects in 1698, when he entered into an apprenticeship with London and Wise at their Brompton nursery. He was engaged under them on a number of garden commissions over the next few years, notably at the palaces of Kensington (1704–5) and Blenheim (1705–*c*. 1710). It was at Blenheim that Switzer and Vanbrugh first became closely acquainted, and numerous references to the architect made by Switzer in his later books indicate the esteem in which Switzer held him. From *c*. 1711, when he began the fortified, moated garden at Grimsthorpe Castle, Lincolnshire (figs. 32, 33), a design strongly influenced by Vanbrugh's bastion garden at Blenheim, Switzer had his own independent practice as a designer,[3] and subsequently he established a lucrative business as a seedsman. However, it was as a writer and publicist that he was most influential – in Ireland and British America as well as in England and Scotland[4] – and is best remembered. His singular contribution was his revolutionary vision of scale and the interconnectedness of the garden and agricultural landscape, ideas first promoted in 1715 in the *Nobleman, Gentleman, and Gardener's Recreation*, and expanded in the three-volume *Ichnographia Rustica* of 1718, republished with minor revisions in 1741–2.

By the time *Hydrostaticks* appeared in 1729, Switzer had been in independent practice for almost twenty years, and had acquired a degree of practical experience in constructing a wide range of water features for both the ornamental and the productive landscape. For the Earl of Coningsby at Hampton Court, Herefordshire,

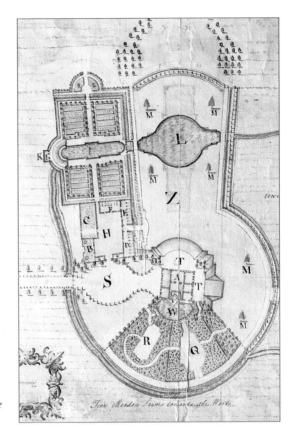

111. Stephen Switzer's Design for Beaumanor, Leicestershire, 1737, showing the watercourses and canal he remodelled for the site.

Switzer's main contribution (made at some date before 1718) was the construction of a 'carriage' (a canal) to irrigate and improve the quality and value of grazing land.[5] By 1724 – the year he was involved in a major survey of the Fens in connection with a drainage project[6] – he had built a cascade for Anne Baynton Rolt, Lady Somerville, at Spye Park, Wiltshire; and by 1727 he had laid out a water garden for her stepbrother, William Greville, 7th Baron Brooke, at Breamore in Hampshire.[7] In 1732 he designed cascades and a lake at Exton Park in Rutland for the Earl of Gainsborough. He then began an extensive undertaking for Sir Rowland Winn at Nostell Priory, Yorkshire (c. 1733–5), which included an irregularly shaped 30–acre lake. The creation of this lake depended on the construction of a dam from which there were views of a serpentine river.[8] And in 1737 he created a new landscape for William Herrick at Beaumanor, Leicestershire, around the new house built to John Westley's design in 1725–7.[9] Switzer retained parts of the existing moat close to the new house, but redirected an old water-course via a conduit house in a nearby field to supply a formal canal (which acted as a reflector and directed the view to the neighbouring church), to create a sheet of water in the kitchen-garden, and to act as a winding water-fence for part of the garden. The water was then channelled back into the fields via an aqueduct (fig. 111).

Hydrostaticks, just one of many specialist guidebooks and manuals produced for an expanding country house market, was written in response to the demand for

practical information on water management and landscape features, and although
it includes designs, it is much more than just a design guide. Switzer was
concerned with the whole estate, and *Hydrostaticks* is a practical manual through
which he promoted a thorough understanding of the properties of water and the
necessary systems for controlling it. His work also introduced the dramatic
progress pumping technology was then making, technology he hoped would
revolutionize water supply.

A great deal of *Hydrostaticks* is taken up with tables, many translated from
French authors, to enable the hydrostatician to calculate more accurately rates of
flow, and the dimensions of pipes and quantities of water required to supply both
the cascades and fountains in the garden and the domestic requirements of the
household. Switzer's main argument was, quite reasonably, that if the calculations
were done correctly, construction costs and failure rates would be reduced. Much
of the information in his chapters on drains, pipes and conduits had already been
published by others elsewhere, but Switzer included useful local knowledge. He
drew on his experience in 'the West', especially at Marston in Somerset, where
much of his book was written,[10] and incorporated information on suppliers of clay
and lead pipes.[11] This sensitivity to site in the choice and costing of water
features, the availability of drainage pipes, the relative merits of various materials
(oak, elm, lead or clay), and the cost of making conduits was fundamental to the
successful and efficient management of water on the estate. What Switzer was
aiming for was a thorough understanding of the infrastructure supporting the
supply of water to cascades and fountains, adapted to suit the conditions of local
topography.

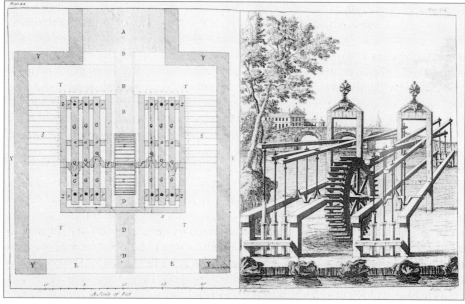

112. The Pumping Engine at Blenheim designed by Robert Aldersley, as illustrated in Switzer's
Hydrostaticks *of 1729.*

For this reason he drew attention to the technological advances occasioned not by the need to supply gardens, but by the demand for clean and reliable supplies of water for expanding towns and by the requirement for efficient pumps for the coalmining industry. These were not recent necessities, for there was already a long history of water-supply schemes and pumping technology harnessed to the extractive industries throughout western Europe.[12] What made early eighteenth-century England different was the high rate of urban expansion (particularly London's), the rapidly escalating demand for fuel, and the Industrial Revolution's move towards mechanization. These new forces put pressure on existing technology, creating a climate for experimentation to solve problems of demand. In *Hydrostaticks* Switzer drew attention to the link between technological advance, urban expansion and trade and industry. He pointed to schemes that successfully supplied Plymouth with clean water,[13] and to the New River built by Sir Hugh Middleton that gave areas of London and Westminster fresh water carried south from springs in Hertfordshire.

Among the pumps Switzer had seen in action was the huge overshot water-wheel, 28 feet in diameter, in use at the mines on the Lumley Castle estate in County Durham.[14] The most famous pumping engine of the time was undoubtedly that at Marly, constructed in 1678 as part of a programme to augment the supply to the gardens at Versailles by pumping water from the Seine. The work required to raise the water about 500 feet above the level of the Seine and transport it over a distance of approximately 1 mile was done in stages, with water being pumped to reservoirs at heights of 150 feet and 325 feet in a network of aqueducts, windmills and water-towers that included 259 pumps.[15] Switzer commented adversely on the scheme in his discussion of the relative cost and reliability of aqueducts and engines.[16] Marly's pump probably raised only about 1 million gallons of water a day, merely a quarter of what the New River's civil engineering works supplied daily to the English capital.

In *Hydrostaticks*, Switzer – pressed for space – confined himself to the most common types of pump and to the new ones powered by steam. In his observations on contemporary technology he drew on considerable personal experience. He had, for example, been involved *c.* 1705–10 in the initial construction of Vanbrugh's bridge across the Glyme at Blenheim, and had constructed the 'carriage' there that supplied water to the pumping engine designed by Robert Aldersey (fig. 112). He failed to mention where or whether he used pumping engines in any of his own commissions, but his comments on the advantages and defects of those he saw in operation, and his enthusiastic and detailed descriptions, provide us with information gleaned at first hand on the range of mechanisms to be found in English estates in the early eighteenth century.

The Archimedean screw was one of the most simple, hand-powered, machines and could be used both for raising water to fill canals and ponds and for emptying them to allow for cleaning as part of a fish-management programme. Here again we see an easy transfer of simple technology between designed and productive landscapes, agricultural use and construction work. The Archimedean screw was used in draining the Fens and to assist in the irrigation of water meadows in Oxfordshire, and Switzer had himself employed it for drainage when constructing the foundations for the bridge at Blenheim.[17] Many of the descriptions of larger, principally water-powered, engines relate to actual machines he was familiar with on a number of estates. He cited examples of chain pumps in operation at the Duke of Queensberry's Amesbury, Wiltshire, and at George Dodington's Eastbury in Dorset, a house that Vanbrugh began in 1717. Eastbury's gardens (and those at Amesbury) were by Bridgeman, whose layout included a formal canal in front of the house. This may have been the piece of water seen by Robert Andrew in 1752, when he discovered that 'the Gardens contain about 46 Acres & are prettily disposed in Walks with Clumps of Trees, & some Water raised with ye utmost difficulty'.[18]

The house at Eastbury stood above the watercourses of the area; Richard Grenville, Earl Temple, the owner of Stowe in Buckinghamshire who inherited Eastbury in 1762, described the site as 'a very dry country'.[19] Switzer supplied no indication of the actual siting of the pump there, nor did he say whether the water was pumped directly to the gardens or if it was intended to supply the house first. He did, however, explain that engines of this sort could be powered by horse or by water. Occasionally, pumping mechanisms were set up very close to the garden: a small bucket-wheel design raised water from the canalized section of the River Stour to fill the formal canal in Sir William Temple's garden at Moor Park, Surrey, as John Loveday discovered on his visit in 1736:

> Not far behind the Canal is the River Stoure that supplies it by a very simple Machine; the Water of the River moves a large Wheel that is in it; on one side of the Wheel at convenient distances all round, are fastened small Wooden Buckets, which, as the Wheel turns down, fill themselves with Water and again on the rotation of the Wheel empty themselves into a Receiver, out of which are Pipes leading to the Canal.[20]

Temple had died in 1699, and it is not clear whether this or a similar sort of mechanism for raising water was in place back in the 1690s, but the engine Loveday describes was certainly of a type that Switzer dismissed as 'out of Date'.[21]

Switzer's objection to many of the pumps he saw was the amount of timber required for their construction, the noise they made during operation and their unreliability, and he was keen to include information in *Hydrostaticks* on the best and the latest machines. He enthusiastically recommended the 'multiplying Wheel Bucket Engine . . . lately invented' by George Gerves, who was working at Sir John Chester's Chicheley Hall in Buckinghamshire, as the very best chain pump, requiring only a limited supply of water as a source of power.[22] Switzer followed a similar pattern of discussion when outlining the developments in the design of 'Crank Work' engines, notably Aldersey's, built into the northern arch of Blenheim's bridge (fig. 112), which supplied water to parts of the Palace. The water channelled via Switzer's 'carriage' turned the wheels that powered the pumps, which in turn raised the water that was to be stored in rooftop tanks.[23] This engine was in operation by the end of June 1706.[24] Aldersey also undertook a number of hydraulic projects at Hampton Court Palace, and his designs were later adapted by John Rowley, Master Mechanic to the King, for the engine he designed for the Chelsea Water Company to raise water from the Thames at London Bridge.[25] But the decline in the use of water-wheel pumps as a means of raising water from rivers was signalled by the atmospheric pumping engine. Switzer claimed a long acquaintance with the 'ingenious' Captain Savery, inventor of the 'Engine for raising water by fire', and it is Savery's engine and the refinements made to it by Thomas Newcomen that concludes Switzer's review of pumping engines in *Hydrostaticks*. Switzer took his illustration of the engine from Savery's own publication, *The Miner's Friend*, and based his description of its working system on the explanation in Richard Bradley's *New Improvements of Planting and Gardening* (1717–18). He closed his account with an illustration of Newcomen's improvements to Savery's engine, which he recommended as 'undoubtedly the beautifullest and most useful Engine that any Age or Country ever yet produc'd'.

Switzer's reason for supporting the idea of introducing steam power to the country estate was the 'Command of Water' these new machines promised, and their comparative cheapness. He discussed the potential they had for large-scale drainage projects (not least for brewing and washing), and for securing water for garden features. Here he gave the example of the engine placed under the banqueting house at Sion Hill that pumped water up to a cistern from whence it was released to play the fountain.[26] How successful he was in his promotion of the new technology is not clear. At Cusworth Park, Yorkshire, in the 1760s, for example, wind-pumps rather than steam-powered ones solved the problem of raising water to supply part of the serpentine lake system in the new landscape park.[27] At about the same time, Thomas Goldney III was using a Newcomen engine to secure an adequate supply of water for the grotto in his garden at Goldney Hall in Bristol.[28] Pumping engines, however powered, clearly became an integral, and visible, part of the designed landscape in the eighteenth century, and were admired both for their mechanical ingenuity and for their manipulation of water. A visitor to Stourhead, Wiltshire, in 1749 was amazed by the machine he saw in action there, which carried water to Henry Hoare II's hilltop Palladian villa from the new-made lake below:

> See yonder engine! Mark each curious part
> Where nature's pow'r is overpower'd by art!
> Water that downward tends its boisterous tide
> Wondrous! Ascends a lofty mountain's side.[29]

In *Hydrostaticks* Switzer was also concerned with the nature and construction of cascades and fountains, and the way in which water was used and deployed in the designed landscape. Taking his book as a starting-point, we can trace changes in the design of water features from the last decades of the seventeenth century and compare Switzer's suggested designs with surviving examples of his own and other contemporary work.

Switzer's contribution to the development of water features in gardens and parks was one element in a long-established tradition of publications on garden-making, which included sections on fountains, cascades and grottoes, or on combining fishponds and orchards to create water mazes.[30] But Switzer opened his discussion of water features in *Hydrostaticks* with what he did not like, and with what he considered to be out of date – grottoes and automata. Water-tricks and automata were still to be seen in the late seventeenth century and early eighteenth, survivors of what might be called the de Caus tradition. At Chatsworth in 1697, for example, Celia Fiennes discovered that there is another green walke and about the middle of it by the Grove stands a fine Willow tree, the leaves barke and all looks very naturall, the roote is full of rubbish or great stones to appearance, and all on a sudden by turning a sluce it raines from each leafe and from the branches like a shower, it being made of brass and pipes to each leafe but in appearance is exactly like a Willow.[31]

The following year at Bretby, also in Derbyshire, she particularly admired the extensive use of water in the garden, and the remarkable clock 'which by the water worke is moved and strikes the hours and chimes the quarters, and when they please play[s] Lilibolaro on the Chymes – all this I heard when I was there'.[32] Switzer was alert to this hydraulic tradition. In *Hydraulicks* he commented on the range of effects created by Thomas Bushell at Enstone in Oxfordshire in the 1630s, the so-called 'Enstone Marvels',[33] and he included a chapter on automata with plates and descriptions taken verbatim from Salomon de Caus's *Les Raisons des forces mouvantes*.[34] However, the water devices that had so impressed Fiennes were the remnants of a fading tradition, and Switzer had no real interest in, or understanding of, such automata or the world view they represented.

Similarly, the grotto had a limited rôle in Switzer's schemes for using water in the garden. What he disliked in particular about an elaborate shell grotto he had 'seen in Holland' was its excessive decoration, which 'made it appear like a tinsell'd hobby Horse, rather than a work of Nature', and the £1,100 it cost to

113. Cibber's Triton and Sea-horses Fountain at Chatsworth, c. 1690. The drop of c. 50 feet from the cascade to this fountain generates the pressure.

make (well over £100,000 in today's money). In his reaction to it he summarized the two strands of the design approach he championed throughout *Hydrostaticks*: the nearer a design appears to be to Nature 'the better it is'; and the economy and efficiency of construction. The empirical science championed by the Royal Society, and reported on in *Hydrostaticks*, was forging a new understanding of the properties of water and a new interpretation of the natural world. In garden design a new phase had begun in which the overwhelming influence was that of the French court and the gardens at Versailles.

Over a period of fifty years of development and reworking, the gardens of Versailles had been fitted out with a range of water features that were copied throughout Europe. Sheets of reflective water carried the eye through Le Nôtre's axial layout and gave depth to the design; basins acted as reservoirs for jets that shot water many metres into the air; and associated sculpture programmes reinforced the image of Louis XIV as Apollo, and Versailles as the centre both of the political and natural landscape of France. Water features were at their most intimate and complex in the *bosquets*. There, water was used almost structurally and three-dimensionally to furnish garden rooms, to produce sound and light to guide the viewer, and, when manipulated through sculpture and trelliswork, to reflect colour in a verdant setting.

The water features at Versailles gained wide currency through the publication of prints and illustrated books of the sort borrowed from by Switzer, in particular A.-J. Dézallier d'Argenville's *La Théorie et la pratique du jardinage* (1709), translated into English by John James as *The Theory and Practice of Gardening* (1712), the edition Switzer used.[35] The influence of the French formal system (much tempered by local topography, individual circumstances and personal preference) and the explosion in garden- and estate-making that followed the Restoration are evident in the parks and gardens illustrated by Leonard Knyff and Jan Kip in *Britannia Illustrata* (1707).[36]

Of all the water features presented in *Britannia Illustrata*, basins occur most frequently. The majority were round, but octagonal and semicircular ones were relatively common, and occasionally more elaborate designs were used. Circular basins, either singly or in pairs, sometimes with single jets, were occasionally used to ornament the main entrance to a country house, as they were at Longleat, Wiltshire (1683), and Badminton, Gloucestershire (1690s). In a less formal arrangement, pairs of rectangular reflecting basins were set on either side of the approach. The greatest groupings of basins, frequently enlivened with statues or jets, were usually found in the parterres close to the house: they formed the centre-point of elaborate designs – for example, at Chatsworth – or articulated the subdivisions or changes in the nature of a layout, as at New Park, Surrey (1692), or were the chief decorative element of a grass parterre, as at Wrest, Bedfordshire (1687), Stansted, Sussex (1686), or Temple Newsam, Yorkshire (1699). In parterres, basins could be viewed from the upper rooms of the house, while contributing sound and light at ground level. Basins were also used in *bosquets* and groves, and here the reflective and aural qualities of water were greatly amplified by the setting:

> 'tis a double Satisfaction: Water there being, as it were, in its Center; besides, the Verdure of the Trees serves as a Ground to set it off, and improves the very Whiteness of the Water; the Purling and Murmur of it strike the Ear too the more agreeably with the Stilness and Echo that reigns in the Woods.[37]

A single basin with a jet was often the main, and sometimes the only, water feature in an ornamental garden. Nevertheless, even a single feature was a powerful indicator of taste and capital outlay. Following his visits to Versailles in 1695 and his subsequent one to Chatsworth, Sir Godfrey Copley was so much taken with the water features and fountains that were 'now ye mode', that he installed a huge circular basin and jet in the gardens of Sprotbrough Hall, Yorkshire, to complement the remodelled house.[38]

Jets were the most common form of 'spouting water',[39] and ranged from very simple single shoots, such as those in the groves at Melbourne Hall, Derbyshire (*c.* 1704), to the giant columns achieved by grouping several jets. Occasionally, perimeters of basins were enlivened by rings of jets feeding back into a central pool, as at Hutton-in-the-Forest, Cumberland (*c.* 1685), and Wollaton Hall, Nottinghamshire (1690s). Much less common was any form of sculptural fountain work; the most elaborate examples of these were at Longleat and Chatsworth. The figures for the *Triton and Sea-horses* fountain at Chatsworth were carved by Caius Gabriel Cibber and his assistants, Samuel Watson, Nadauld and Richard Osgood as part of the impressive scheme for water features directed by Grillet, an obscure French designer (fig. 113). The *Triton and Sea-horses* fountain, like the rest of the hydraulic system, was supplied by water collected

114. The Neptune fountain at Hampton Court, shown in a detail from John Stevens's oil painting, The South Prospect of Hampton Court, Herefordshire, *c. 1705.*

from the moors high above and beyond the garden and piped down through a considerable fall, thus creating the pressure necessary for such a spectacular display. In the fountain itself the water is the dynamic sculptural element in the composition, but few sites could equal the topographical configuration, or the family the finances, that made such a spectacle possible. The compromise made elsewhere was, in effect, to shift the balance of the elements from the water to the stone, allowing a carved fountain to compensate for a more limited flow of water, as was the case with the commanding *Neptune* fountain at Hampton Court, Herefordshire (fig. 114). At Dyrham, Gloucestershire, the original 20 foot high jet at the top of the 'cataract' of steps (the finest in England after Chatsworth's) was replaced by 1711 with a *Neptune* fountain, which relied for its effect on swirls of water from the mouths of attendant fish. One of the most unusual fountains was that at Staunton Harold, Leicestershire, where the height of the jet was enhanced by the water being thrown from, and then spilled down over, a prominent stone column, not unlike the *giulio* in the octagon lake at Stowe.

Larger displays of water – as axial, cross and boundary canals – reflected light within the garden boundary and, framed by ranks of trees, helped carry the view out across the park or into the fields, as at Westbury Court, Gloucestershire. The axial canal was a central feature of the design system developed by Le Nôtre, so it is perhaps surprising that there are not more examples recorded in *Britannia Illustrata*. There was an axial canal at Melton Constable, Norfolk (*c.* 1685), while at Eaton Hall, Cheshire (*c.* 1675), and Acklam Hall, Yorkshire (*c.* 1684), the effect of an axial canal was achieved by formalizing sheets of water in the park and aligning them on the centre of the house. There were cross canals at Haigh Hall, Lancashire, and at Swillington House, Yorkshire (both 1690s), and at Longleat discontinuous pieces of water running across the main parterre were visually connected at ground level to create the impression of one vast sheet. Canals were also used as boundary 'fences' around the garden or to mark divisions within the design, or to separate pleasure ground and park. The water system as it was developed at Wrest Park by the mid-1720s included all these elements.[40] By the 1730s, however, these arrangements of formal sheets of water were beginning to give way to serpentine and irregular lakes.[41]

Water features played a prominent rôle in the formal, designed landscape, but this was just one part of what was frequently a far more complex picture. Many of the estates included in *Britannia Illustrata* show a more marked preference for lateral design, with the canal, or at least an extended piece of water, running along the side, frequently the service side, of the house. Formalized but irregular ponds were often grouped around the service areas of the house, and were probably primarily utilitarian, providing water for washing, cleaning and watering, but arranged in such a way that they contributed to, and helped integrate, the overall design of the areas close to the house. Indeed, many water features had a long history of their own, for example old fishponds that were retained within – but redesigned to fit – a formal setting. The pools and ponds of the productive areas and the wider parkland were frequently incorporated both into the design and into a much broader appreciation of the enjoyment of the estate as a whole. The inter-connectedness of the parts and the function of water within the estate were very much part of Switzer's concept of an ideal country estate. In his description of 1718 of the 'beautiful Rural Garden' commissioned by William Blathwayt at Dyrham, much of it George London's work,

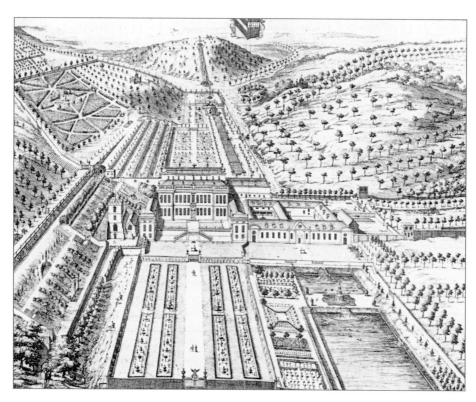

115. *A detail from Kip's 'Dyrham, Gloucestershire', published in Sir Robert Atkyns's* The Ancient and Present State of Gloucestershire, *1712. The jet at the top of the cascade has been replaced by the Neptune fountain.*

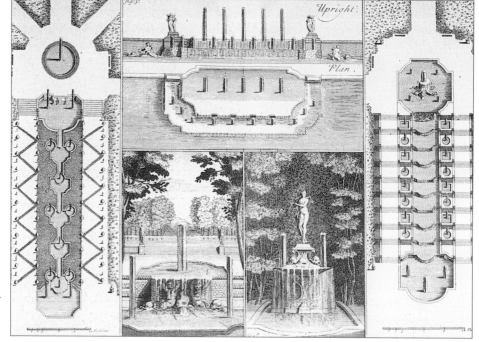

116. *A cascade design from John James's* The Theory and Practice of Gardening, *1712.*

his delight in water features was clearly enhanced by the fact that the pools were also well stocked with fish for the table. In the canal fronting the greenhouse were trout, perch and carp, and at the top of the hill, placed where 'you may sail a Ship on a Mountain . . .',[42] the reservoir supplying the cascade and fountains was equally well stocked both with fish and water-fowl (fig. 115).

The relatively limited use of fountains in the late seventeenth century and the early eighteenth was due only in part to technical difficulties, for the enthusiasm for them was slowly ebbing away. There was, none the less, a sustained interest in cascades, although their structural forms began to change radically, a change both recorded and promoted in *Hydrostaticks*. Cascades fascinated Switzer, and by comparing a number of cascades of this period, including some of Switzer's own, the evolution both of design and approaches to the use and display of water in the landscape can be traced.

John James's English edition of Dézallier's *Théorie* includes a copy of a design for a cascade to suit the estate of a private gentleman (fig. 116). This cascade follows the descent of a gentle slope, there are walks that radiate through woods surrounding a large basin or reservoir at the head of the cascade, and the length of the fall is interrupted or punctuated by smaller basins between the cascade steps. In the more elaborate versions of this design, these basins acted as miniature reservoirs, feeding small fountains set to the sides of the cascade steps. The cascade is framed between lines of clipped yew, holly and horse-chestnuts, and the colouring of the space is enhanced by urns and pots of flowers. The one constructed by Sir Thomas Hewett in the grounds of Shireoaks Hall, Nottinghamshire, in 1791 is, in fact, reminiscent of this design style.[43] This cascade includes thirty-four varied steps punctuated at intervals by twelve oval or circular basins (fig. 117). The cascade feeds a canal aligned on the house,

117. A view looking up the length of the cascade at Shireoaks, Nottinghamshire.

118. A view across the canal to the cascade at Stanway, Gloucestershire.

and is supplied from a large circular reservoir at its head. There are walks around the reservoir, which acts as a giant reflector and focuses the view – originally framed by alternating yews and limes – back to the house standing at the bottom of the slope.

The design is highly architectural and set within a tightly and geometrically articulated frame of trees to accentuate the colour of the water and to amplify its sound. The quality of sound changes at various points along the cascade; for example, the two basins just over midway along the cascade slope reflect the sky and calm the sound, in contrast to the lower stretch, where water tumbles rapidly over closely grouped basins and steps. At Shireoaks the canal and cascade are positioned axially on the house, whereas at Stanway in Gloucestershire the canal and the cascade are at right-angles to each other.[44] Stanway's canal and extensive system of water features were made *c.* 1730, and may have been inspired by Bridgeman's water features for the Dormer family at Rousham.[45] Stanway's grounds included the canal and the main cascade (rising 114 feet above the canal), a smaller, steeper upper cascade, a series of pools, and a network of feeder conduits that ran back into the surrounding hillside. A small pavilion topped with a Vanbrugh-style pyramid was built at the summit of the cascade in 1750 in memory of John Tracy, and there may have been some re-landscaping of the upper pool at that time (fig. 118).

At Stanway the cascade runs rapidly down to the canal without any punctuation by reflector pools or basins. Its setting incorporates a system of walks and earthworks that cross and recross the cascade and link the water features with the parkland and views out to the wider countryside beyond.[46] The earthwork ramps cut into the hillside below the canal contribute to the overall design of the garden and to its entertainments and surprises, since the canal, not visible from the parterre below, comes into view only after a fairly steep climb. Stanway is a relatively compact version of a trend, particularly strong in the 1720s, for linking formal earthworks and water in sometimes extensive designs that stretched across the landscape, such as the one designed in 1721 by Peter Bourguignon for Sir Thomas Lister at Gisburn Park, Yorkshire (fig. 119).[47] As Batty Langley commented, cleverly constructed walks and ramps of earthworks could distort perspective, and, enhanced by the visual depth of reflective water, could make a site look much larger than it actually was.[48] It was this concern with scale and proportion, for example, that prompted Switzer to suggest improvements to the water features of Bridgeman's design at Claremont.[49]

But what does *Hydrostaticks* tell us about Switzer's own approach to cascades and his rôle in their development? In the commentary on the plates of cascades that conclude the book, Switzer made it clear that he held reservations about many of the French designs, finding them too artificial and not sufficiently rural or 'grotesque'. He reserved his praise for the cascades of Italian villa gardens,

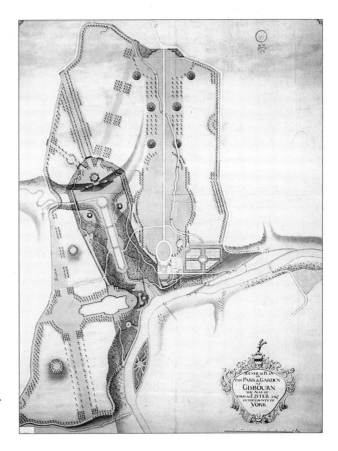

119. Peter Bourguignon's design of 1721 for the park and garden at Gisburn, in Yorkshire's West Riding.

120. An ideal cascade illustrated in Switzer's Hydrostaticks, *1729, incorporating many of the characteristics he praised in the cascades of Italian villa gardens and rivers in the English countryside.*

particularly those of D'Este at Tivoli and Aldobrandini at Frascati. The types of cascade he preferred were those with white water issuing from – and dashing over – rocks framed by tall trees and substantial planting. He was keen on 'rude stones', water running with great violence, water dashed to pieces over rocks; on the 'rurality' of tall trees and on the 'copies of nature' that he recognized as the 'peculiar Genius of Italy'.[50] However, prints of Italian gardens were not the only, or indeed the prime, source for Switzer; rather, he interpreted them as reflections of a rugged English countryside – the landscape he promoted as the basis of rural gardening.

It was the countryside enclosing the Earl of Coningsby's estate at Hampton Court, Herefordshire, and the river landscapes of Herefordshire, Worcestershire, Gloucestershire and Warwickshire, that inspired him. The Wye, the Lugg, the Severn and the Avon meander and break themselves into cascades beneath natural amphitheatres of beech, 'reaching in Appearance to the Skies, in many Places a Quarter of a Mile high, and generally full of Springs'. Switzer described the nobleness of these rivers as equal to, if not excelling, 'the so-much-talked-of Tyber'. He peopled these landscapes in his imagination with valiant Saxons and with characters from the romances of the Middle Ages.[51] The cascades he praised most were not those of Italy, but English ones, for the most part in dramatic country – at Chatsworth and at Dyrham, and, for Switzer, the most stupendous of them all: 'those fine Falls of Water belonging to Mr Aislaby in the North' at Studley Royal, Yorkshire.[52] In *Hydrostaticks* he included a design for a cascade (fig. 120) that, were the water just a little rougher, would be equal to any of those produced by the French or the Italians. The similarities in formal arrangement shown in this design and the general effect of Studley Royal's cascade, with its paired Fishing Pavilions, are noticeable (fig. 121). Together they suggest Switzer's kind of realizable cascade design, one 'very agreeable to the Rural Way', a clear acknowledgement of the brilliance of the scheme commissioned by John Aislabie in the early 1720s at Studley Royal. But how was this ideal mobilized at the sites at which Switzer was employed?

As we have seen, Switzer had some considerable experience in working with water in both the landscaped and agricultural parts of the estate, and in *Hydrostaticks* he included a cascade design of his own that was similar to the one he had made at Spye Park before 1724, and which represented his re-interpretation of the Italian examples illustrated in his book (fig 122). Spye's cascade had a 30–40 feet fall, and the water was sent 'over Steps and rough Work of different Kinds and different Heights'.[53] The design in *Hydrostaticks* shares many of the characteristics of that illustrated in both James and Dézallier, but there is a greater emphasis on earthworks, rockwork and broken water, and a much looser framework of mature or semi-mature trees. The whole effect must have been more robust, and the qualities of light, shade and sound very different. The cascades and ponds at Ebberston Hall in North Yorkshire, although of a more architectural quality, reflect something of the spirit of this approach, and the situation – a steep-sided valley – would have appealed to Switzer.[54]

At Exton Park, where Switzer was employed from 1732 by Baptist Noel, Earl of Gainsborough, the situation was less dramatic, but the scope for rockwork, elaborate construction and broken water was much greater.[55] The park is to the south and east of Exton Hall, and includes an extensive area of woodland, Tunnely Wood, which was gradually formalized from *c.* 1709 in a series of rides; the irregular lake and water features on the boundary furthest from the house were also extended, probably during the same period when he was making the dam for the lake at Nostell Priory in Yorkshire.[56] Here a brook was dammed to

121. The cascade and the pair of Fishing Pavilions at Studley Royal, Yorkshire, built for John Aislabie in the 1720s.

122. A cascade design from Switzer's Hydrostaticks *of 1729, similar to the cascade he constructed at Spye Park, Wiltshire, before 1724.*

123. Francis Vivares's The Lower Cascade at Exton Park, Rutland, *one of a pair of coloured engravings with etching of c. 1739.*

124. A detail from Francis Vivares's The Upper Cascade at Exton Park, Rutland, *coloured engraving with etching, c. 1739.*

create a second piece of water, at first roughly oblong but soon expanded into an irregular lake; between these two lakes were two cascades very different in style.[57] Switzer prepared drawings for a cascade at Exton in 1732,[58] and although the full extent of his contribution to the final scheme is unclear, the cascades reflect many of the characteristics he praised in *Hydrostaticks*. The two cascades are quite different; the lower one (fig. 123) is a simple set of roughly cut rocks arranged in a way that appears to throw the water in several directions as it falls from the second lake to the stream, which channels it away from the park. The upper cascade (fig. 124) is far more architectural, with a massive superstructure rising above the dam between the two lakes. Water shoots through a number of conduits over a two-tier cascade and falls in broken sheets to the second lake. There is no visible evidence remaining to confirm that the towered superstructure of this cascade – as seen in the engraving – was ever built, and today water leaves the upper lake through a single conduit at one side. There are, however, the remains of a number of stone arches in the face of the dam, although they are blocked and overgrown at present, and it is not clear how water could have run through them. This astonishing set of cascades and lakes at Exton illustrates a shift in the focus of water features away from the house to less formal settings within the parkland.

What emerges from *Hydrostaticks* and Switzer's related cascade designs is a new appreciation of water in the landscape and a very different approach to the way in which water should be displayed – moving faster, dashing over rocks with a roaring sound and framed by tall, informally planted trees. The cascades Switzer associated with gardening 'in the Rural Way' were quite unlike – not only in design but in the colour, movement and sound of the water they produced – the designs associated with the formal gardens of *Theory and Practice*. The lakes and cascades at Exton are forerunners of the serpentine lakes of the landscape park, while the spirit of Switzer's remodelling anticipates some of the rugged drama of the Picturesque.

TEN

Rethinking the Picturesque

Christopher Ridgway

'The picture he drew . . . was false'.[1] So wrote Sarah, Duchess of Marlborough, in 1709, dismissing Vanbrugh's 'Reasons' to preserve the manor house that stood in Woodstock Park across the River Glyme from Blenheim Palace. If the Picturesque in England can be said to have been born in the summer of 1709, then it must be acknowledged that its birth was hardly an auspicious one: Vanbrugh's arguments fell on deaf ears; he was accused of trickery and deceit by the Duchess; his relations with her worsened until he parted company with the Marlboroughs and the Palace in 1716; and, in 1723, the Manor was finally demolished.

The facts behind this small Oxfordshire drama are straightforward enough. In August 1704 the Grand Alliance forces led by John Churchill, 1st Duke of Marlborough, pulverized Marshal Tallard's French and Bavarian armies at the Battle of Blenheim on the banks of the Danube in Bavaria. On 17 January 1705, as a reward for his stunning victory, Queen Anne and Parliament proposed to grant Woodstock Manor to the Marlboroughs and pay out of the Civil List for a new mansion in the Park – Blenheim Palace. A month later Marlborough visited Woodstock with Vanbrugh; by the summer Vanbrugh was confirmed as Surveyor in charge of the project. In June the foundation stone was laid, and by August, notwithstanding alterations to the plans, the foundations of the main pile were completed. By the summer of 1706, however, it was clear that the cost of the building was greatly exceeding the funds allotted by the Treasury, and the vexed issue of money began to poison the entire undertaking.[2] The Duchess claimed that she fell out with Vanbrugh over 'constant disputes . . . to prevent his extravagance',[3] but these frictions were exacerbated by Vanbrugh's desire to preserve the Manor and build a massive bridge on the approach road to the Palace, both of which the Duchess strongly disapproved.

A royal palace since Saxon times, the emparked Manor was a cluster of buildings – originally a hunting lodge – on rising ground above the Glyme.[4] (The small town of Woodstock is to the east of the Park.) The Manor had been Henry II's favourite residence: he held councils there, and in 1186, during his reign, it was the setting for a royal wedding (fig. 125). But Woodstock Park is chiefly remembered as home to Henry's mistress, Rosamond Clifford, who lodged barely 200 yards west of the Manor house in the pleasaunce known as Everswell ('Rosamond's Bower'). This site was renowned for its enclosed gardens and series of pools fed by a spring, remembered in tradition as Rosamond's Well and Spring. In 1554 Princess Elizabeth spent twelve months under house arrest in the Manor during the bloody reign of her

125. Anon., The Old Palace in Woodstock Park, *c. 1714, an engraving after a drawing by an unknown artist made shortly before the Manor was demolished.*

sister Mary I; after Elizabeth's accession in 1558, royal entertainments were held there. In the first half of the seventeenth century both James I and Charles I visited the Manor regularly.[5] Garrisoned by Royalist forces at the outbreak of the Civil Wars, it was surrendered to Parliamentary troops following a bombardment in 1646. A Parliamentary survey records that the Manor was 'much out of repair' in 1650, but rather than demolish the building it was suggested that it be divided up into smaller dwellings.[6] By the beginning of the eighteenth century, however, it had fallen into a semi-derelict, barely habitable condition. Yet this was the building that obsessed Vanbrugh, and which he took so much trouble to preserve.

Vanbrugh's famous Memorandum of 11 June 1709 – 'Reasons Offer'd for Preserving some Part of the Old Manor' (see Appendix)[7] – has much to say about his own thinking on certain aesthetic and historical issues, as well as representing a celebrated early formulation of some of the arguments that developed into the principal tenets of the Picturesque debate as it evolved in the later eighteenth century. The arguments Vanbrugh adduced were varied and cogent. There was value in ancient buildings, with their 'magnificence' and 'Curious workmanship', as well as in their ability to prompt 'lively and Pleasing reflections'. Buildings can become historical aids, they can embody human narratives – who built them, who lived in them, what events occurred within them. And when turning the clock forward to contemplate the future history of Blenheim Palace, Vanbrugh claimed that, while the fabric of the building and the skill of the builder might not inspire visitors, the occasion of its construction certainly would, for 'they will find Wonder enough in the Story'. This is what Vanbrugh meant by the 'Historicall

126. Blenheim Park, with the site of Woodstock Manor to the north of the foreground water.

Argument', but to strengthen his case he offered further reasons that may be described as aesthetic and economic.

It would, Vanbrugh suggested, be desirable to achieve a degree of variety in the landscape, through the successful combination of buildings and plantations, allowing masonry and vegetation to mix in an agreeable fashion. Adopting a painterly analogy, he declared that the ensuing composition would satisfy some of the formal criteria of landscape painting, and here he had an eye on the treatment of terrain, paying attention to contour, perspective, light and shade, hard and soft edges. Finally, Vanbrugh argued the economics of the matter, claiming that were the Manor removed, all that would remain would be 'an Irregular, Ragged Ungovernable Hill, the deformitys of which are not to be cured but *by a Vast Expence*'. Some commentators on the Picturesque have seen this as evidence of Vanbrugh anticipating William Gilpin's fully fledged pleasure in variety and irregularity later in the eighteenth century, but it is clear that Vanbrugh did not see the bare hill itself as offering anything pictorially satisfying: for him it was precisely the combination of terrain, vegetation and structure that offered the most promising kind of 'Landskip'.[8]

The theoretical side of the Memorandum appears wholly plausible and reasonable, yet Vanbrugh's accompanying letters to the Duchess and to Lord Godolphin reveal an uncharacteristic hesitancy. Barely two weeks earlier, on 31 May he had written to Godolphin expressing his fears over any hasty decision on the future of the Manor, adding: 'but before tis gone too far I will desire your Lordship will give yourself the trouble of looking upon a picture, I have made of it, which will at one view explain the whole design, much better than a thousand words'.[9] In one sense this was an adroit course of action – to proffer a topographical sketch of how things might look. Yet it is curious that this accomplished playwright and man of the theatre, this witty and urbane member of the Kit Cat Club, who, it seems, could talk his way into almost any enterprise, should confess a lack of faith in words.[10]

Ten days later (9 June), Vanbrugh had recourse to the same argument when writing to the Duchess: 'I was preparing a little Picture of what had been in general propos'd to be done . . . which I feard was not perfectly Understood by any explanation I had been Able to make of it by words'. And he concluded by reiterating 'I have no designe . . . but only in Silent Paint to lay before, and explain to you, what I fear I have not done by other Means'.[11] For an articulate dramatist, this is an odd statement; it is as if Vanbrugh had been rendered speechless, unable to express his wishes other than through a sketch that was to serve as a speaking picture. In all likelihood the sketch, alas untraced, offered a prospect from the site of Blenheim Palace, looking across the valley of the Glyme towards the Manor on the hilltop a few hundred yards away (fig. 126).

Woodstock was famous at this time for one further feature – its echo. An illustrated account of it was included in Robert Plot's *Natural History of Oxfordshire*, first published in 1677 with a second edition in 1705.[12] In the first chapter, dealing with natural phenomena in the Heavens and Air, Plot described what he called a 'Polysyllabical articulate Echo' in the Glyme valley, capable of returning seventeen syllables in the daytime, and twenty at night. After discussing the various phonic effects, Plot conducted a series of experiments to find the optimum spot, or Centrum Phonicum, from where to project one's utterance and receive it back again. In the accompanying engraving the Centrum Phonicum is marked as being within the Park, but quite close to the dwelling in the town known as Chaucer's House. The voice is projected across the Glyme valley to the object of the echo, the Centrum Phonocampticum, half a mile away to the east (fig. 127).[13] Whatever spirit of scientific enquiry motivated Plot, his view includes

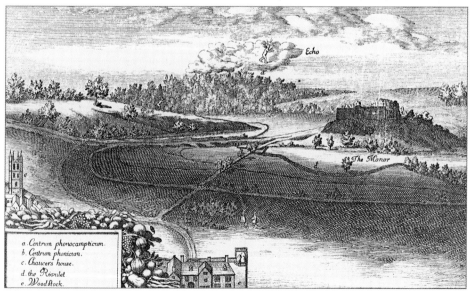

127. *The Vale of Woodstock, looking west across the Park from the town of Woodstock, with the Manor visible on the hilltop, from Robert Plot's* The Natural History of Oxfordshire, *1677.*

two tiny representations of the figures of Pan and Echo, the latter the transformed nymph able to repeat only the last words she hears. Evidently Plot's acoustical arena still preserved its mythological origins as recorded in Ovid.[14] But in the middle of this terrain stands the Manor, and it is intriguing to think that within four years of the second edition of Plot's *History*, a second exchange would float over the valley – this time not from east to west, but from south to north.

For in one sense Blenheim Palace should be seen as a reverberation of Woodstock Manor – a visual and historical response rather than an acoustical one. Just as the Manor deserved to be celebrated as having been the dwelling of 'One of the Bravest and most Warlike of the English Kings', so Blenheim would in the future embody the martial triumphs of Marlborough, and visitors would 'find Wonder enough in the Story'. Indeed, while dismissing most of Vanbrugh's arguments as false and ridiculous, the Duchess conceded this point, scribbling 'I think there is something material in it concerning the occasion of building Blenheim' on the Memorandum.[15] However, Vanbrugh did not assist his case by alluding to Henry's amorous dalliances at Woodstock, 'the Scene of his Affections'. Seven years later, when the Duke suggested siting an obelisk to the north of the house near the Manor, and noting that it 'would please Sr John best, because it would give an opportunity for mentioning that King whose Scenes of Love He was so much pleas'd with', the Duchess annotated acidly: 'but if there were obelisks to bee made of what all our Kings have don of that sort the countrey would bee Stuffed with very odd things'.[16]

In 1707 Joseph Addison and Thomas Clayton used Woodstock Park as the setting for their opera *Rosamond*, and at the beginning of Act III two guardian angels descend to present a vision of war and peace to the sleeping King Henry.[17] As the first angel sings of how 'after long revolving years' Rosamond's ruinous bower will grace 'the future prospect of the place', a scene-change reveals 'the plan of Blenheim castle'. Medieval Woodstock was transformed into contemporary Blenheim:

> Behold the glorious pile ascending!
> Columns swelling, arches bending . . .

This scene-change must have offered to most of the London audience its earliest opportunity to view the Duke's projected palace.[18] But spectacle aside, the opera makes great play with the idea of time – it is a drama set in the remote past but containing a scene that foretells future events, i.e., the present moment: 1707. In Act III, scene ii, Henry awakes from this vision and muses on

> A thousand glorious deeds that lie
> In deep futurity obscure,
> Fights and triumps immature,
> Heroes immers'd in time's dark womb
> Ripening for mighty years to come . . .

This idea of time past, present and future merging into a single action, or visionary moment, also lies at the heart of Vanbrugh's later historical arguments on Woodstock at the beginning of his Memorandum. It has been proposed that Vanbrugh himself suggested the topic of Rosamond and Woodstock to Addison, possibly when the two men journeyed together to Hanover in the summer of 1706;[19] but Vanbrugh's own arguments against the Manor's destruction specifically echo these ideas of futurity and 'time's dark womb', especially where he considers 'Travellers many ages hence' who may visit Blenheim.

Addison had opened his drama with an allusion to Woodstock Park's famous echo, when Queen Elinor, describing Woodstock to her Page, comments 'As o'er the hollow vaults we walk / A Hundred echos round us talk' (I, i); presumably this effect was exploited musically in the same way Purcell had done with the device of echo in Act II of *The Faerie Queene* (1692). And four years after *Rosamond* was first staged, echoes and ruins preoccupied Addison once more: in an essay in *The Spectator*, he describes his visit to a ruined abbey inhabited by rooks and crows, and reputedly haunted:

> There is such an Eccho among the old Ruins and Vaults, that if you stamp but a little louder than ordinary you hear the Sound Repeated. At the same Time the Walk of Elms, with the Croaking of the Ravens which from time to time are heard from the Tops of them, looks exceeding solemn and venerable. These objects naturally raise Seriousness and Attention.

The scene prompted Addison to reflect on Locke's theory of the Association of Ideas, and on how 'an Idea often introduces into the Mind a whole Set [of ideas] that bear no Resemblance to one another in the nature of things'.[20] In Addison's opera, Woodstock's special acoustic properties gave rise to 'a hundred echoes', where 'not a single word is lost'. In the theatre these echoes could be either musical or verbal – notes and chords, or words spoken and sung. But echoes are more than simply fragments of sound, mere phonemes; echoes are also words that can denote thoughts and ideas; and Associationism is essentially a free-play of ideas and thoughts that connect and extend over time and space. It is exactly this sort of imaginative resonance that is central to Vanbrugh's musings on the Manor and the Palace, and for him the connections between the two buildings were complex and varied. Plot had discovered that the echo across the valley worked in one direction only, from east to west, but for Vanbrugh the historical and aesthetic associations between the two buildings operated in both directions.[21] The new Palace had specific martial associations offering prompts for the future interpretation of the house. His lost sketch presumably presented the view from the Palace, a landscape 'varied, irregular, evocative of a past age and ready-made for the artist'.[22] By good fortune a reciprocal view survives (fig. 128), a sketch made in 1724 by that indefatigable antiquary William Stukeley that shows the Palace from the site of Rosamond's Bower, slightly to the west of the site of the Manor, which had been erased the year before.

Vanbrugh wished earnestly to use Woodstock Manor as a home from home. His reasons were no doubt mixed, and if pressed he would probably have been hard put to isolate them. But even if we accept the objective force of his statements on the associative and aesthetic importance of ruins, there still remains the question of how disinterested he was over the fate of the building. Claiming that all he wished for was an 'agreeable Lodging',[23] Vanbrugh spent considerable sums of his own money on making it habitable – repairing a roof in 1708, paving the floors with a coarse stone, and carrying out other 'little necessary things'.[24] In April 1713, a few

128. William Stukeley's sketch of Rosamond's Well in Woodstock Park, which he made while on a visit in 1724.

months after the Marlboroughs had vanished into exile following their fall from grace, Vanbrugh was dismissed from the Comptrollership of the Office of Works, reportedly for making remarks in support of the Duke. Affairs at Blenheim came to a standstill: the Palace was roofed, but unfinished within; the gardens were partially complete; the causeway and bridge were incomplete; the architect had been dismissed; the money was exhausted (and creditors were clamouring for payment); and the workforce, at one point numbering between 1,000 and 1,500 men, had been laid off, with only a skeleton staff retained.

It was at this moment that Vanbrugh moved from a bailiff's house in the Park into the Manor.[25] The move had little to do with playing king of the castle, but it was certainly more convenient, for the Manor was nearer to the Palace, enabling him to keep an eye on the latter while work lay suspended. Certainly Vanbrugh had always lived close by when construction was in progress, and there is a telling phrase in a letter of July 1708 in which he reported that, at Blenheim, he would typically 'Avoid all Company, And haunt the Building like a Ghost, from the Time the Workmen leave off at Six a Clock, till tis quite dark'.[26] In 1713, living in the Manor, just across the Glyme from the empty Palace, Vanbrugh could be forgiven for feeling haunted by the spectre of failure. (Perhaps, too, the Marlboroughs felt haunted by their extravagant architect.) Moreover, looking out from his own dwelling, it might well have seemed to him that he was gazing at a *ruined* Palace, for within it was neither ceiled nor floored, and building debris lay scattered outside 'in a most disagreeable confusion'.[27] There is a curious paradox here: one structure had been going up just when the other should have been coming down. The two buildings exchanged rôles on more than one occasion, in fact, for when the Palace was under construction, from time to time parts of it were torn down in order to accommodate revisions; meanwhile, across the Glyme, Vanbrugh was shoring up and repairing parts of the Manor while making a show of pulling other sections down. At times it must have been hard to distinguish between the inchoate Palace and the authentic ruin.

Vanbrugh was not the first protective spirit to hover over Woodstock. The Manor itself had witnessed one, when, during the Civil Wars, a troop of commissioners had been dispatched from London in 1649 by the Long Parliament to occupy the Manor and 'efface all the emblems of royalty about it'. But once the commissioners began desecrating the Manor (in which they lodged), for a period of two weeks they were unexpectedly subject to a succession of frightening experiences – strange noises, mysterious footsteps, apparitions; the disappearance of some of their clothes and bedding; furniture, plates and dishes that moved inexplicably – until, convinced that Woodstock was in the grip of 'the powers of evil', they fled back to London. It turns out that one of the commissioners was a crypto–Royalist who had grown up there, and so had been able to exploit the Manor's concealed passages and doorways to unnerving effect in his determination to protect the house and its contents.[28] It would be nice to think that Vanbrugh knew of this haunting, for it would certainly have added to his arguments about 'Wonder enough in the Story' of this ancient building. If he did, perhaps he saw himself as a second spectre, battling to preserve both Palace and Manor in the face of adversity.

Vanbrugh's reflections on ancient buildings are in a tradition originating at least half a century earlier, with antiquaries such as William Dugdale, Anthony à Wood, John Evelyn and John Aubrey.[29] Closer to Vanbrugh's time, Thomas Hearne and Stukeley both displayed a learned and sentimental interest in old buildings. Hearne, who frequently walked out from Oxford to Woodstock and Blenheim, was struck by the old Manor as well as the gardens and pools around Rosamond's Bower, and on more than one occasion noted that the size of the Manor and its environs exceeded that of the Palace. He also lamented the destruction wrought 'by the rebells in the civil wars', and recorded the belief that were the Manor 'wholly destroyed', misfortune would descend on the Duke or his heirs.[30] Stukeley, as a boy, accompanied his father to the Lincoln Assizes, but instead of 'attending the Judges' he would spend his time viewing old monuments, ruins and 'Reliques of Antiquity in the Town'. In 1707 he recorded how he 'began to conceive a passionate Love for Antiquitys', and 'frequently took a walk to sigh over the Ruins of Barnwell Abbey' in Northamptonshire.[31] This response is akin to that which Anthony à Wood experienced when visiting the ruins of Malmesbury Abbey, Wiltshire, nearly thirty years earlier in 1687: 'When I entered into the church I had a strange veneration come upon me to see the ruins of such a majestic and gigantic pile.'[32]

Closer still in time and spirit to Vanbrugh's arguments over Woodstock Manor are some of Hawksmoor's comments to Dr George Clarke concerning the building projects at All Souls College, Oxford. In February 1715 in a long memorandum known as the 'Explanation', Hawksmoor argued 'for the preservation of Antient durable Publick Buildings, that are strong and usfull, instead of erecting fantasticall perishable Trash, or altering and Wounding ye Old buy unskillful knavish Workmen'.[33] On another occasion he offered a robust defence of ancient buildings, asserting that 'it is an affront to History to race out the Monuments and Fabricks of former times'.[34] And in 1721 he battled to have St Albans Abbey repaired, where he had recourse to the same tactic as Vanbrugh, writing to the Bishop of London and enclosing a 'Landskip' sketch, which he said was intended to 'Support this venerable pile from being Martyr'd by ye Neglect of a Slouthfull generation'.[35]

Hawksmoor's arguments were not always successful, just as Vanbrugh's pleas fell on deaf ears. Vanbrugh's correspondence with the Duchess in 1709, and again during the course of 1716, when he was living in Woodstock Manor, has a refrain to it, as indeed have the Duchess's comments. Vanbrugh repeated that he did not mean to frustrate her; that he would move out if she wished; and that the costs incurred had been footed by himself. She repeated that his comments seemed ridiculous; that there was 'artifice' in them; and that he was causing trouble. It is hard with these two not to see a parallel with the fates of Narcissus and Echo, who, unfulfilled in their desires, were condemned for ever to exchange empty words. As adversaries, Vanbrugh and the Duchess engaged in riposte and rejoinder, but essentially, neither gave up repeating the same arguments.

The Marlboroughs proved themselves immune to Vanbrugh's Associationist arguments over the Manor, and in the end it was probably on grounds of cost alone that the building was demolished in 1723, not least because it represented a valuable source of stone to be used in building projects in and around the park. The paradox here is that Vanbrugh's Grand Bridge, with its sequence of interior chambers that were to disappear with the formation of Capability Brown's lake in 1765, had already had its lower walls protected, prior to flooding, by extra layers of stone taken from the ruins of the Manor: thus parts of Vanbrugh's two great projects in the larger landscape at Woodstock were effectively drowned together in one operation.[36]

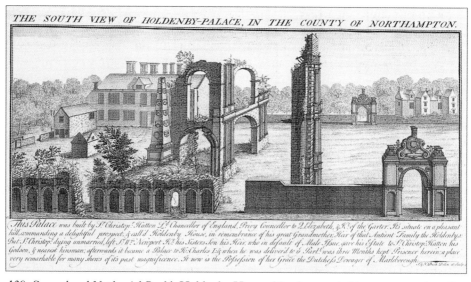

129. Samuel and Nathaniel Buck's Holdenby House, Northamptonshire, *an engraving of 1729 of a ruined Elizabethan palace.*

Since the Duchess was appalled by Vanbrugh's Memorandum regarding the ruinous Manor, it is surprising to discover that in 1709, the very year the Memorandum was written, the Marlboroughs acquired derelict Holdenby, 40 miles away in Northamptonshire, once the home of Sir Christopher Hatton, Chancellor to Elizabeth I. Completed in 1583, Holdenby was one of the great Elizabethan 'prodigy houses', and its south front, 350 feet in length, was a spectacular façade of fenestration. Charles I was held prisoner at Holdenby during 1647, but after an escape attempt he was taken into custody by Cornet Joyce at the head of 500 dragoons and carried off to Newmarket. Holdenby was then bought by a Parliamentary officer, Captain Adam Baynes, who began to demolish the house in order to sell off the stone. He retained the kitchen wing for his own dwelling, and the surrounding area was left to decay (fig. 129).[37]

Here was a country house redolent with history and human narrative, and although the fabric only survived in fragments – principally the two great courtyard arches – there was sufficient remaining for people to 'find Wonder enough in'. An early visitor after Holdenby's wrecking was John Evelyn, who in July 1675 noted that the house, 'which being demolished in the late civil wars, shows like a Roman ruin, shaded by the trees about it, a stately, solemn and pleasing view'.[38] The topographical artist Peter Tillemans visited in 1719–20, and made three drawings of the ruins.[39] The surviving fragments, notably the two archways, are still impressive today, and prompt one to try to recreate the missing entity in one's own mind in an attempt to reconstruct the 'Beauty of the Fabrick', which must have displayed 'Magnificence' and 'Curious Workmanship'. But such responses are only half of the affair, for these ruins would surely have provoked 'more lively and pleasing Reflections' of a historical, Associationist nature. And around 1720 one passer-by was stimulated into just such a series of musings:

> The melancholy reflection of the imprisonment of King Charles the First in this house, and his being violently taken hence again by the mutinous rebels, has cast a kind of odium upon the place, so that it has been, as it were, foresaken and uninhabited. The house and estate has been lately purchas'd by the Dutchess of Marlborough; but we do not see that the house is like to be built or repair'd, as was at first discours'd; on the contrary it goes daily to decay.

So wrote Daniel Defoe, filling a wrecked building with a pattern of thoughts.[40] Where Evelyn had concluded his observation with some brief remarks on the effects of the ruin, Defoe constructed his description around 'melancholy reflection', recounting, to use Vanbrugh's words, 'Remarkable things which ha[d] been transacted' at Holdenby. The fortuitous conjunction of Tillemans's drawings and Defoe's account, as well as the Bucks' engraving of a few years later, enables us to reconstruct something of the appearance and historical perception of Holdenby in the early eighteenth century. It becomes clear, too, that in submitting a sketch with his Memorandum for Woodstock Manor, in combining 'silent paint' and written argument, Vanbrugh intended to present the strongest case possible for the preservation of the medieval structure by using an image to prompt thoughts.

Expert knowledge of, and appreciation for, ruins and their histories could be gleaned while out on the road, and in more detail in a well-furnished library. The flurry of county histories dating from the second half of the seventeenth century

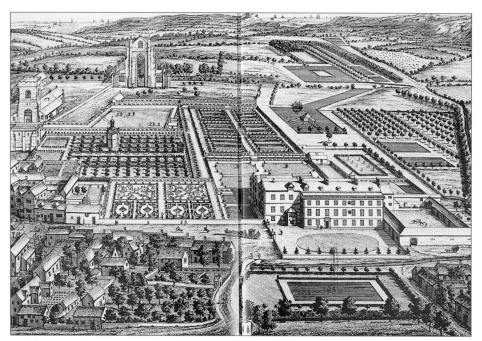

130. Guisborough, North Yorkshire, an engraving from Knyff and Kyp's Britannia Illustrata, *1707.*

enlarged society's geographical, historical and mental horizons. Antiquities, topography, buildings, family histories, the recent and ancient past – many of these topics were addressed to some degree or another in publications by Plot, William Dugdale, William Somner and others; and in the first two decades of the eighteenth century further historical publications appeared, whose authors included Charles Leigh, Robert Atkyns and John Morton. Nor should one forget the many county histories that existed in half-finished or in manuscript form.[41] There were at this time, too, the great illustrated volumes, an expanding record of buildings, towns and landscapes, and in 1711 Samuel Buck began his series of views of sites in England and Wales. Ruins had featured in the background in one or two of Knyff and Kip's prints in *Britannia Illustrata* (fig. 130), but they were prominent among the 400 or so plates that Buck – assisted by his brother Nathaniel from 1727 – produced of castles, abbeys, towns and monuments (fig. 131).

Images of England, therefore, were commonplace, either as maps, engraved views of particular towns and places, or in more detailed prints of houses, castles and ruins. Plates, especially in the folio histories of counties and towns, were often augmented by historical accounts. But armchair knowledge was not sufficient of itself. In 1714, for example, Bishop Berkeley wrote to Alexander Pope from Italy, musing on the value of travel, and on whether 'it might not be worth a poet's while to travel, in order to store his mind with strong images of nature'.[42] Unless one had travelled and observed at first-hand, knowledge of a country (whether historical, topographical, mineralogical, genealogical or whatever) remained partial. There was a crucial empirical value in touring, discovering, observing, recording, and collating – witness Plot's experiments with the echo in Woodstock Park. Discovery involved travel, just as much as it did the accumulation of details from written, visual, even oral sources. For example, Defoe, when visiting York, travelled out to the Civil War battlefield of Marston Moor in the company of an old soldier who gave him 'a compleat account of the action from his father's relation, who, he said, had served in it'. Defoe remarked that he 'described it in so lively a manner to me, that I thought it was as if I had just now seen the two armies engaging'.[43]

Travel meant discovery, and discovery meant knowledge. In this respect travel became a 'mental accumulation' of ideas, images, narratives and connections, and from this one could, if one so chose, build up a broader comprehension of place, history, architecture.[44] The conjunction of geographical progress and historical awareness meant that whatever terrain one travelled through – principal highway, city street, rural lane, or uncharted wilderness – the process was not simply one of voyaging through space (whether known or unknown, empty or filled), for travel also encompassed a fourth dimension – *time*. But time does not mean simply the hours expended on a journey (the pedestrian or equestrian duration), for it also embraces exposure to the past, to a series of histories and narratives particular to specific places.

Today's scholarly assessments of Picturesque travel have focused almost exclusively on the late eighteenth century, when the remoter areas of the British Isles – the Lake District, North Wales, the Wye Valley and the Highlands – were explored for the first time. There was an aesthetic imperative behind many of these tours, as the travellers, equipped with the fashionable vocabulary of the Picturesque and the Sublime, and an array of instruments – Claude glasses, paintboxes, perhaps a camera obscura – could formulate a particularized response to examples of untouched nature.[45]

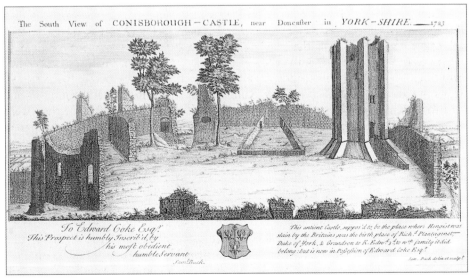

131. *Samuel and Nathaniel Buck's* Conisborough Castle, South Yorkshire, *an engraving of 1728.*

The real and mental geography of late seventeenth- and early eighteenth-century England was somewhat different. A sense of aesthetic expedition, or of the Picturesque, was far less developed. Antiquaries and topographical artists certainly studied with care the landscapes they encountered and recorded (and they often commented on them too), for example Stukeley, Tillemans and the father of Picturesque tourism, the Yorkshire artist and antiquary Francis Place.[46] What animated most tourists *c.* 1700 were topographical and archaeological subjects, which, as Vanbrugh observed, encouraged reflections on the past and an appreciation for the wonder of stories. And nowhere was this more apparent than in responses to ruins. In this sense, early Picturesque travel might properly be called *time travel.*

But how exactly did people perceive the country in the early eighteenth century? If the average travelling person closed his or her eyes and thought of the country (as opposed to the nation), what image might they have seen? Almost certainly, many people's ideas would have been conditioned by the images of England that existed in maps: maps of England or Great Britain; county maps, which were still largely based on the Elizabethan surveys of Saxton, Norden and Speed; but perhaps chiefly by a more recent cartographic achievement, John Ogilby's *Itinerarium Angliae*, published in 1675.

Comprising 100 whole-sheet copper plates, delineating 85 roads or routes across England and Wales, Ogilby's folio established 'a new standard for map making in England' (fig. 132).[47] He was assisted by Robert Hooke, who championed high standards of scientific mensuration and verification, and these strip maps provided a wealth of information for travellers and country

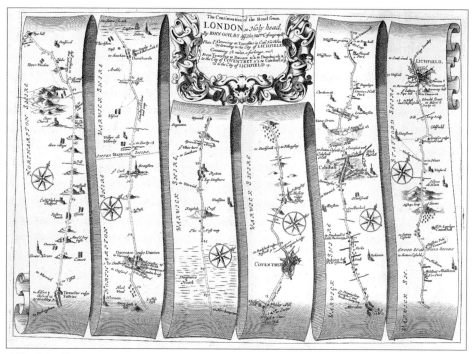

132. A double-page plate from Itinerarium Angliae, *illustrating the second section of the London to Berwick route.*

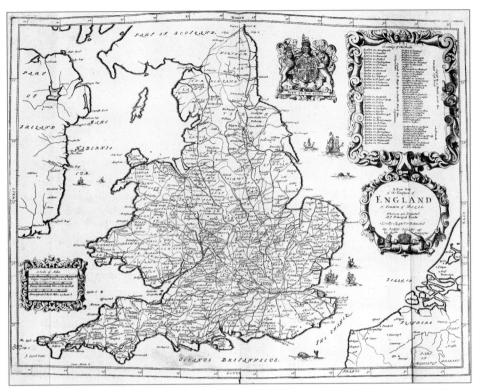

133. Ogilby's prefatory map of England in Itinerarium Angliae, *densely crammed with the principal thoroughfares.*

landowners, many of whom cut out the strips of their local areas, or of the places to which they were travelling. Ogilby's maps determined to a large extent the mental geography of England in Vanbrugh's day. The prefatory map of England and Wales, much as any road map of today, showed a large network of routes that traversed the country, with London as 'the prime Center of the Kingdom' (fig. 133). Each road was 'projected upon Imaginary Scrolls', with, on average, six or seven scrolls to a double page. The longer routes occupied three or four whole plates; shorter journeys fitted onto a single plate. Later editions of the maps supplied commentaries on various towns and features.

To compare the prefatory map of England and Wales with one of the strip maps is to experience two entirely different ways of perceiving the country. The first, small in size and cramped with a dense network of roads, offers a broad, generalized view, and a rough sense of place relative to other locations. London is at the centre, but any journey from London – to York, say – allows the traveller a basic geographical comprehension of the land, with Cambridge to the east and Nottingham to the west of the principal route, the Great North Road. The traveller would also be able to gauge the whereabouts of other places – for example, ports on the east coast, such as Hull or Grimsby, or Liverpool or Bristol to the west. Such lateral perception is harder to achieve when following the strip map, which although clearer to read and filled with a great deal of valuable local information,

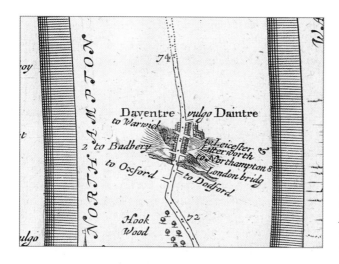

134. A detail from the London to Holyhead route in Itinerarium Angliae, *showing a network of roads from other parts of the country converging at Daventry.*

enforces a kind of tunnel vision, notwithstanding the signs at important junctions that point to destinations away from the route in question (fig. 134).

The roads of England *c.* 1700 were in fact filled with travellers, although, of course, Vanbrugh was not a tourist in the sense that Celia Fiennes, James Brome, John Macky or Daniel Defoe were.[48] He seems never to have undertaken a trip just for the sake of travel, although he did manage one in 1699 purely with the intention of seeing 'most of the great houses in the North'.[49] But what of his other travels in England? As a practising architect with a network of important clients and influential friends, many of whom had seats in the provinces, just how often was Vanbrugh on the road? We know that he drove a calash, a light two-wheeled carriage with a removable hood, and in later life owned several other vehicles.[50]

In and around London, Vanbrugh travelled regularly to Greenwich, Esher, Hampton Court and Windsor (these places would not then have been perceived as the fringes of Greater London they are today). On that first house-tour north in 1699, he visited Burley-on-the-Hill, Kiveton, Chatsworth and Henderskelfe. Thereafter he travelled north most years, and en route to Yorkshire he visited St Albans, Kimbolton (1708), Grimsthorpe, Nottingham (1718, 1719), Londesborough (1700) and Scarborough (1715); then further north still to Lumley and Seaton Delaval. Other commissions took him in a south-westerly direction – to Bath (1716, 1717), Bristol, Eastbury (1725) and Salisbury (1722). There were frequent journeys to Oxford and Stowe; visits to Chester (1700, 1713); and he travelled into Norfolk (1716) and Suffolk (1719) on separate occasions. His account book is filled with references to the number of nights spent away from home.[51]

How did Vanbrugh travel in his calash? Did he follow Ogilby's strip maps dedicatedly, or did he meander away from the highways, exploring and observing in a more serendipitous fashion? We cannot know for certain, but there can be little doubt that his travels across England would have added greatly to his stock of mental images as he passed by houses and ruins, and through towns and places of special interest or renown. Ogilby's strip maps marked in a few tourist attractions close to his route. Travelling north from London, Vanbrugh would have noted the Earl of Manchester's Kimbolton

Castle a short distance from the highway (fig. 135). If he had taken the road from Cambridge to Coventry, or joined part of it near Northampton, he would have seen that Holdenby was not far off. And a journey from Kings Weston to Eastbury would almost certainly have carried him past the spectacular abbey ruins at Glastonbury (fig. 136).

Approaching Henderskelfe, Ogilby's map would not have told Vanbrugh a great deal about houses or ruins in the vicinity of York, but it is unlikely that he could have been unaware of the concentration of old castles and abbeys in the area: castles at Sheriff Hutton, Slingsby, Helmsley, Gilling and Crayke, and of course Henderskelfe itself; abbeys at York, Byland, Rievaulx, Fountains and Kirkham (fig. 137).[52] Even the approach roads north to Yorkshire offered some impressive sights, including the castles at Nottingham, Conisborough, Bolsover, Pomfret and Sandal; and a peculiar place that lodged in Vanbrugh's imagination – Robin Hood's Well in Barnsdale, just north of Doncaster. Robin Hood's Well was an important changing-post on the Great North Road, and Vanbrugh was no doubt familiar with the legends relating to the medieval outlaw, for in 1719 he undertook the interior reconstruction of Nottingham Castle. On journeys north from Nottingham he may even have experienced (or endured) some of the customs enacted at the Well, which included drinking from it and being placed in a chair and crowned with a cap. To commemorate the spot Vanbrugh built a well-house (c. 1720), reportedly paid for by Lord Carlisle (fig. 138).[53]

Vanbrugh would certainly have admired or studied castles, houses and other structures while on his travels. His architect's eye would have observed form, structure, mass and detail; his painterly eye may have considered these in relation to the landscapes they occupied. But he would also have noted the effect of these buildings, and made mental connections. Not only would he have remarked on their 'workmanship', he would have indulged in 'pleasing reflections' of an Associative kind. In the celebrated series of papers published in *The Spectator* in 1712 on 'The Pleasures of the Imagination', Addison had distinguished between primary and secondary pleasures: primary proceeding 'from such Objects as are

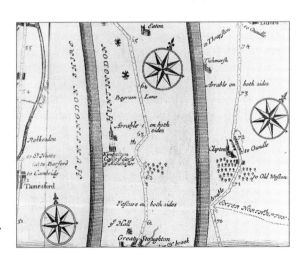

135. A detail from the London to St Neots route in Itinerarium Angliae, *marking Kimbolton on the second strip.*

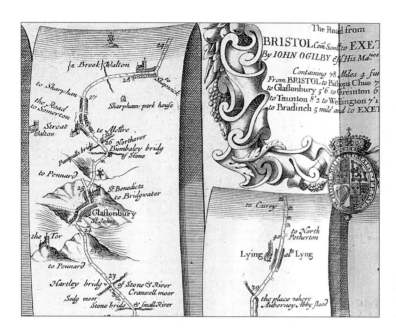

136. *A detail from the Bristol to Exeter route in* Itinerarium Angliae, *marking Glastonbury and the Tor.*

before our Eyes'; secondary deriving 'from the Ideas of visible objects'.[54] Vanbrugh would have recognized these distinctions, for his arguments over Woodstock Manor had been built on such layers of perception; furthermore he would have concurred with Addison's belief that sight (or in his own case, sightseeing) filled the mind with 'the largest variety of Ideas'.[55] Addison had also commented on the limitations of a fixed or single point of view, stressing instead the value of mobility: 'our thoughts', he observed, grow 'agitated and relieved at the sight of such Objects as are ever in motion'.[56] Vanbrugh in his calash, travelling through England, would have found his mind stimulated by the variety of objects he encountered.

It is more than likely that Vanbrugh would have left the main highway on occasions to visit and inspect places; he was, surely, not a traveller bound by the limited horizons of the strip map. Some of his journeys might have followed radiating, or serendipitous, routes, and any measure of physical ranging would have prompted mental voyaging. Vanbrugh was receptive to influences, connections and associations; his was an expanding and radiating mind, a mind always in motion. Indeed, one might adapt Hobbes's famous metaphor of the imagination as a spaniel ranging through the landscape, and consider Vanbrugh in his calash ranging widely through parts of England, visiting real places that were sites of history and memory, his geographical mobility indicative of a mental motion.[57] And this returns the argument to Woodstock Manor, and to Vanbrugh as an early exponent of the Picturesque. In his Memorandum he ranged widely in history, but he also invoked a painterly analogy that is important in terms of the visual and aesthetic arguments he was making with regard to the Manor.

But the term *Picturesque* at the beginning of the eighteenth century had more to do with painting than landscape. As Pope employed it in his translations of

137. Samuel and Nathaniel Buck's Kirkham Abbey, North Yorkshire, *an engraving of a much-visited Cistercian settlement dissolved in 1539.*

The Iliad, the term referred to what was proper or typical for inclusion in a painting. Dryden used it in the same way in his 'Parallel of Poetry and Painting', which forms the preface to his translation of Du Fresnoy's *De Arte graphica*. In this, a reformulation of Horace's famous dictum *Ut pictura poesis*, Dryden affirmed that painting should conform to the precedents of the Ancients.[58] Consequently, painting that imitated heroic or historical action drawn from classical or biblical sources was deemed correct, and superior to other genres. Historical emphasis was the primary focus because only by imitating 'the customs and the times' of the Ancients could art elevate and teach.[59] It is surely possible, then, to suppose that in offering his Memorandum and his sketch for the preservation of the Manor, Vanbrugh felt he was arguing wholly within the decorum of painterly and historical Picturesque. He was, in short, presenting the Manor as a three-dimensional history painting, a 'landskip' that was imbued with history, association and 'Wonder enough in the Story' before all else. These associations were of greater importance than the purely visual impact of ruin and vegetation.

But it is essential not to romanticize Vanbrugh's position with regard to Woodstock Manor. After all, here was an individual who was quite happy to oversee the demolition of the medieval castle of Henderskelfe, even though Vanbrugh must have taken satisfaction in the knowledge that some of the masonry was to be recycled and refashioned, physically and historically, for the mock fortification walls in Castle Howard's park. Equally, one must avoid any teleological interpretation of the Woodstock Memorandum and see it as some sort of finished document prefiguring the Picturesque debate of the late eighteenth century. The Memorandum was not a manifesto in any sense, it was a hastily prepared argument relative to a particular moment and place, although no doubt Vanbrugh was articulating certain closely held beliefs. With this caveat in mind, it is appropriate to consider it in the light of some remarks on Vanbrugh made by that shrewdest and most perceptive of English critics – William Hazlitt. In his *Lectures on Comic Writers* of 1818, Hazlitt reviewed Vanbrugh's dramatic oeuvre:

138. William Stukeley's sketch of Robin Hood's Well on the Great North Road, drawn in 1725, a masonry well-head that Vanbrugh designed c. *1720, and construction of which was probably financed by the Earl of Carlisle.*

He works out scene after scene, on the spur of the occasion, and from the immediate hold they take of his imagination at the moment. . . . He has a masterly eye to the advantages which certain accidental situations . . . present to him on the spot . . . his genius flags and grows dull when it is not put into action, and wants the stimulus of sudden emergency, or the fortuitous collision of different motives to call out all its force and vivacity. . . . The train of his associations . . . lies in following the suggestions of his fancy into every possible connexion of cause and effect. . . .[60]

In these remarks Hazlitt has caught the essence of Vanbrugh and the Woodstock Manor affair: the accidental, the fortuitous, the urgent; the drama of character, the import of history and the pleasures of the imagination; but, above all, the radiating mind.

APPENDIX

REASONS OFFER'D FOR PRESERVING SOME PART
OF THE OLD MANOR, 11 JUNE 1709

There is perhaps no one thing, which the most Polite part of Mankind have more universally agreed in; than the Vallue they have ever set upon the Remains of distant Times Nor amongst the Severall kinds of those Antiquitys, are there any so much regarded, as those of Buildings; Some for their Magnificence, or Curious Workmanship; And others; as they move more lively and pleasing Reflections (than History without their Aid can do) On the Persons who have Inhabited them; On the Remarkable things which have been transacted in them, Or the extraordinary Occasions of Erecting them. *As I believe it cannot be doubted, but if Travellers many Ages hence, shall be shewn The Very House in which so great a Man Dwelt, as they will then read the Duke of Marlborough in Story; And that they Shall be told, it was not only his Favourite Habitation, but was Erected for him by the Bounty of the Queen And with the Approbation of the People, As a Monument of the Greatest Services and Honours, that any Subject had ever done his Country: I believe, tho' they may not find Art enough in the* Builder, to make them *Admire the Beauty of the Fabrick* they will find Wonder enough in the Story, to make 'em pleas'd with the Sight of it.

I hope I may be forgiven, if I make some faint Application of what I say of Blenheim, to the Small Remains of ancient Woodstock Manour.

It can't indeed be said, it was Erected on so Noble nor on So justifiable an Occasion, But it was rais'd by One of the Bravest and most Warlike of the English Kings; And tho' it has not been Fam'd, as a Monument of his Arms, *it has been tenderly regarded* as the Scene of his Affections. Nor amongst the *Multitude of People who come daily to View what is raising to the Memory of the Great Battle of Blenheim; Are there any that do not run eagerly to See* what Ancient Remains are to be found of Rosamonds Bower. *It may perhaps be worth some Little Reflection Upon what may be said, if the Very footsteps of it Are no more to be found.*

But if the Historicall Argument Stands in need of Assistance; there is Still much to be said on Other Considerations.

That Part of the Park which is Seen from the North Front of the New Building, has Little Variety of Objects Nor dos the Country beyond it Afford any of Vallue, It therefore Stands in Need of all the helps that can be given, which are only Five; Buildings, And Plantations[.] These rightly dispos'd will indeed Supply all the wants of Nature in that Place. And the Most Agreable Disposition is to Mix them: in which this Old Manour *gives so happy an Occasion* for; that were the inclosure filld with Trees (principally Fine Yews and Hollys) Promiscuously Set to grow up in a Wild Thicket. So that all the Building left, (which is only the Habitable Part and the Chappel) might Appear in Two Risings amongst 'em, it wou'd make One of the Most Agreable Objects that the best of Landskip Painters can invent. And if on the Contrary this Building is taken away; there then remains nothing but an Irregular, Ragged Ungovernable Hill, the deformitys of which are not to be cured *but by a Vast Expence; And that at last will only remove an Ill Object* but not produce a good One, whereas to finish the present Wall for the Inclosures, to forme the Sloops and make the Plantation (which is all that is now wanting to Compleat the Whole Designe) wou'd not Cost Two Hundred pounds.

I take the Liberty to offer this Paper with a Picture to Explain what I endeavour to Describe, That if the Present Direction for destroying the Building, shou'd happen hereafter to be Repented of, I may not be blam'd for Neglecting to set in the truest Light I cou'd, a Thing that Seem'd at least to me so very Matteriall.

J VANBRUGH

ELEVEN

Remembering Vanbrugh

Derek Linstrum

> Under this stone, reader, survey
> Dead Sir John Vanbrugh's house of clay;
> Lie heavy on him, Earth, for he
> Laid many a heavy load on thee.[1]

This notorious epitaph by the Revd Abel Evans (1679–1737), a not altogether impartial protégé of Vanbrugh's enemy Sarah, Duchess of Marlborough, cannot be avoided when remembering the man whose 'genius', according to Swift, 'without thought or lecture, / [was] hugely turned to architecture' in addition to all his other activities.[2] There is no denying the amount and weight of stone used at Blenheim, Castle Howard, Seaton Delaval and Grimsthorpe Castle, although, as Gervase Jackson-Stops has suggested, 'Vanbrugh would surely have seen the joke' of Evans's epitaph.[3] But how has Vanbrugh's work been regarded more widely since his death in 1726? How has he been remembered?

In the 1881 edition of Joseph Gwilt's *Encyclopaedia of Architecture*, Vanbrugh was described as having

> a stronger claim on our notice as an inventor than any of his predecessors . . .
> his buildings are the result of a combination of forms and anticipation of
> effects, originating solely from himself; effects which none before had seen nor
> contemplated. As a wit, he was inferior to none that levelled its shafts at him,
> and hence his novel compositions in architecture became among the
> professional critics of the day so much an object of derision as, in their puny
> notions, his only assailable point.[4]

By the 1880s, as we shall see, Vanbrugh's star was in the ascendant, but it had not always been so. During his lifetime he had to endure criticism of his work for its clumsiness, heaviness and eccentricity. This ranged from the barbed verses of Swift and Pope to the Gallic superiority of Voltaire, who thought that if the apartments at Blenheim were 'but as spacious as the walls are thick, the Castle would be commodious enough'.[5] The lack of a good-sized room in the planning of both Blenheim and Castle Howard was an oft-repeated criticism. Sir Thomas Hewett (1656–1726), who, with little justification, held the appointment of Surveyor-General of the King's Works during the last seven years of Vanbrugh's life, made known his disapproval of the architect's 'strange Bulky Buildings

139. Robert Adam's Seton House, East Lothian, built 1790–1, which has been described as 'a Vanbrughian legacy'.

composed of Towers, Breaks, Rustic key stones etc., out of all manner of proportion & reason'.[6] True, there were some words of praise. James Bramston confessed in *The Man of Taste* (1733) that 'Substantial walls and heavy walls I like, / 'Tis Vanbrug's structures that my fancy strikes'.[7] But more common were opinions such as that of John Dodd, who wrote in 1735 of Blenheim:

> its Beauties, & Absurdities are so blended, that while you are expatiating upon one, you are checked by the intervening Ideas of the other. . . . Who can admire the Largeness and Magnificence of the House, & not deplore the absence of Beauty and Taste from this Place?[8]

In the following year, Horace Walpole, who thought Blenheim 'execrable within, without, & almost all round', described the house in the vein of Swift and Pope as 'a quarry of stone that looked at a distance like a great house'.[9] Mounting a conventional Palladian rostrum in 1742, John Gwynn (1713–86) attacked Vanbrugh's and Hawksmoor's work in *The Art of Architecture*: 'The same *unmeaning Dress*, in every Place, / The same *wild Heap* of inconsistent Things'. Later in his verses, Gwynn obediently followed the Palladian party line, expressing suprise that

> V[AN]B[RUG]H was admir'd, in *Anna's* Days,
> And even his Blenheim, would excite some praise . . .
> But BOYLE and PEMBROKE, have the art restor'd;
> And distant Ages will their Fame record.[10]

Another admirer of Burlingtonian Palladianism was James Rivers, Under-Secretary of State, who wrote after visiting Castle Howard in 1735 that although it was 'in a noble position', he was 'disappointed in the house, the body of which, & one wing, are an unwielding, unmeaning pile of Sir J. Vanbrugh, with not one grand room in it'. He much preferred the later Palladian west wing designed by Sir Thomas Robinson (c. 1702–77), and compared 'the absurdity of the old part & the elegance of the new'.[11] In 1769 the agriculturalist Arthur Young dismissed Castle Howard as 'so heavy and clumsy . . . as to be perfectly disgusting', having previously described Vanbrugh as 'a miserable architect'.[12] But by what criteria were such judgements being made? Were critics simply repeating the view that Vanbrugh had failed to follow the rules and dared to be original? It might be thought that this was because there had been a change in taste, from the freedom of the Baroque to the rules of Palladianism, and that when he made his final design for the Castle Howard estate in 1725 and looked to Villa Capra's domed and four-porticoed form as a model for his Temple of the Four Winds, Vanbrugh himself was acknowledging it. Of this building, Hawksmoor wrote to the Earl of Carlisle, 'What Sr. John proposes is very well, and founded upon ye Rules of ye Ancients'.[13] But, in fact, from the very beginning of his architectural career, Vanbrugh revealed a knowledge of Palladio's *Quattro libri*. There was no need to wait for 1715 and Leoni's translation.

As Giles Worsley has pointed out, even the plan of Vanbrugh's first undertaking, Castle Howard, owes several features to Palladio, while there are similarities between the ground-plan of Villa Poiana and an unexecuted design for Eastbury.[14] One might even see a debt to the Venetian church of Il Redentore in the central section of Blenheim's entrance front, while Vanbrugh's designs for garden buildings at Stowe and Duncombe Park, Yorkshire, and the proposed garden temple to face Castle Howard's south front (fig. 23) could all be said to have been 'founded upon ye Rules of ye Ancients', from which Palladio derived his own. It should not be forgotten that the three volumes of *Vitruvius Britannicus* (1715–25), comprising Colen Campbell's Palladian manifesto, devoted a considerable number of plates to Vanbrugh's designs, although Laurence Whistler was probably right in thinking that Campbell 'privately shuddered at the "damned gusto" of certain vast unruly buildings that he had to extol; but they were too big, and Vanbrugh was too eminent, for anything but eulogy to be appropriate'.[15] His very eminence provoked envy, which probably accounts for much of the criticism.

In *Vitruvius Britannicus* Blenheim and Castle Howard figured prominently, and other major Vanbrugh houses illustrated are Eastbury, Grimsthorpe, Kings Weston and Seaton Delaval, while Claremont featured in Badeslade and Rocque's volume four in 1739. In remembering Vanbrugh, it is useful to recall what happened to these houses. Castle Howard and Grimsthorpe were not completed to Vanbrugh's designs. Seaton Delaval and Castle Howard were partly damaged by fire, the former on more than one occasion (its main block is now an empty shell). Eastbury was completed after Vanbrugh's death by Roger Morris, but it was destroyed in 1775 and only one wing remains. Kings Weston was completed externally, but many of the interiors are Robert Mylne's and date from the 1760s. Claremont was built (as 'Chargate') in 1709, and extended soon after, but it was demolished and replaced in the 1770s with a villa designed by Lancelot Brown and Henry Holland. Blenheim was completed, but, as at Stowe, there has been a succession of changes in the landscape setting of the house and its garden buildings.

There was, however, a change in attitude towards Vanbrugh's buildings in the same decade that Eastbury was blown up and Claremont knocked down. In 1772 Horace Walpole was in Yorkshire, and after visiting Castle Howard he wrote his oft-quoted eulogy of what he encountered 'at one view':

> a palace, a town, a fortified city, temples on high places, woods worthy of being each a metropolis of the Druids, vales connected to hills by other woods, the noblest lawn in the world fenced by half the horizon, and a mausoleum that would tempt one to be buried alive; in short, I have seen gigantic places before, but never a sublime one.[16]

It seems a change of heart in the man who had apparently been content to repeat George Vertue's opinion of Vanbrugh in *Anecdotes of Painting in England* that

> he wanted eyes, he wanted all ideas of proportion, convenience, propriety. He undertook vast designs, and composed heaps of littleness . . . he broke through all rule, and compensated for it by no imagination.[17]

That opinion – probably Vertue's, who died in 1765, rather than Walpole's – was a conventional one, but in 1772 Walpole was so impressed by the total effect of the Castle Howard landscape and its various buildings that he could afford to praise

140. Robert Adam, Design for a Ruined Castle at Osterley Park, Middlesex, *1774, which could be the ruin of a Vanbrugh castle.*

Vanbrugh's architectural skill in a sentence: 'for the house, Vanbrugh has even shown taste in its extent and cupolas, and has mercifully omitted ponderosity'. Altogether, in the 1770s a gradually more favourable interpretation of Vanbrugh's work was being offered as a new generation looked at his buildings in their surroundings with a Picturesque eye. William Gilpin, while acknowledging the value of rules in architectural design, which provided a restraint he had no wish to shake off, nevertheless believed 'we are fettered . . . too much by orders, and proportions. The ancients themselves paid no such close attention to them'. He proceeded, as he wrote, 'to apologize for Vanbrugh' at Blenheim, where he thought the criticism of 'heaviness and enormity' had been applied 'too severely'.[18]

Almost at the same time as Gilpin was on the road recording these impressions, in 1773 Robert and James Adam offered their well-known apologia for Vanbrugh, describing him as

> a great man, whose reputation as an architect has long been carried down the stream by a torrent of undistinguishing prejudice and abuse. Sir John Vanbrugh's genius was of the first class; and, in point of movement, novelty and ingenuity, his works have not been exceeded by anything in modern times.

They amplified their reference to movement, defining it as the expression of 'the rise and fall, the advance and recess, with other diversity of form, in the different parts of a building, so as to add greatly to the picturesque of the composition'. However, they had reservations:

> unluckily for the reputation of this excellent artist, his taste kept no pace with his genius and his works are so crowded with barbarisms and absurdities, and so borne down by their own preposterous weight, that none but the discerning can separate their merits from their defects.[19]

The appreciation of Vanbrugh and 'movement', with its associations with landscape, light and shade, contrasted convexity and concavity, was carried a considerable step forward by Sir Joshua Reynolds in 1786 in the thirteenth of his Discourses delivered to students at the Royal Academy of Arts. Interestingly, he first singled out a principle he believed architecture held in common with poetry and painting – that of

> affecting the imagination by association of ideas. Thus, for instance, as we have naturally a veneration for antiquity, whatever building brings to our remembrance ancient customs and manners . . . is sure to give this delight. Hence it is that towers and battlements are so often selected by the Painter and Poet, to make a part of the composition of their ideal Landskip.[20]

Vanbrugh had been among the first to recognize this, and not only when he designed the castellated walls and gateways at Castle Howard and his own house at Greenwich. Were the Adams directly influenced in their castellated designs by his example? Alistair Rowan cites a letter of 1766 from Robert Adam to Mrs Montagu about Sir James Lowther's estate that expresses his enthusiasm for the natural landscape of the Lake District and its power to inspire architecture:

cloud capped mountains, extensive lawns, rapid rivers and immense forests so happily jumbled together that nothing . . . can convey a just idea of them. . . . Sir James seems resolved to impose on me the arduous task of placing a castle on this principality.[21]

What sort of a castle? Despite the hyperbole, the resulting Whitehaven Castle (1766–c. 1770), like some other castellated designs supplied by the Adams, notably in Scotland, such as Wedderburn Castle (1771–5) and Mellerstain (c. 1770–78), is castellated only in its trimmings. But other Adam houses in Scotland, such as Culzean (1777–92) and Seton (1790–1), are closer in spirit to Vanbrugh Castle. Seton (fig. 139), apparently a castellated relative of Seaton Delaval, can be seen as what Rowan calls 'a Vanbrughian legacy'.[22]

Like Vanbrugh, the Adam brothers were not designing Gothic buildings. There were no pointed arches, which were associated with ecclesiastical architecture, but instead there was the style of a baronial castle, in which the arches are semicircular-headed. Such historical precedents were to be viewed with 'admiration as sublimely picturesque and beautiful'.[23] They were, indeed, examples of 'the Castle Air' that Vanbrugh had recommended should be given to Kimbolton Castle (1707–10), expressing his conviction that 'this will make a very Noble and Masculine Shew'.[24] If Vanbrugh was a pioneer in this architectural style, he also introduced a precedent in his perception of the qualities inherent in old buildings in his plea for the preservation of Woodstock Manor (reprinted on p. 191). We might regard Robert Adam's design of 1774 for a ruined castle at Osterley as an aspect of Vanbrugh's interest in such architecture (fig. 140). Noting the absence of pointed arches, it could be the ruin of a Vanbrughian castle.[25]

Vanbrugh was 'a Poet as well as an Architect' wrote Reynolds, and hence 'there is a greater display of imagination, than we shall find perhaps in any other':

> To speak then of Vanbrugh in the language of a Painter, he had originality of invention, he understood light and shadow, and had great skill in composition . . . he perfectly understood in *his* Art what is the most difficult in ours, the conduct of the back-ground, by which the design and invention is set off to the greatest advantage. What the back-ground is in Painting, in Architecture is the real ground on which the building is erected; and no Architect took greater care than he that his work should not appear crude and hard: that is, it did not abruptly start out of the ground without expectation or preparation.
>
> This is a tribute, which a Painter owes to an Architect who composed like a Painter.[26]

In his *Analytical Inquiry into the Principles of Taste* (1805), Richard Payne Knight (1750–1824) also considered buildings and their settings in terms of painting. He emphasized the need to consider the views towards the house rather than from it, and the composition of the scenery with Picturesque foregrounds, concluding that 'the middle ground will be the properest situation for it; as will clearly appear from the landscapes of [Claude and the Poussins]'.[27] Having given his general opinion, he looked to the particular and praised Vanbrugh,

141. Stratford Hall, Westmoreland County, Virginia, a plantation home of the late 1730s that was built for the Lee family, perhaps to designs by William Walker.

142. The chimneys at Stratford Hall in Virginia, late 1730s, obviously based on those at Blenheim.

the only architect I know of, who has either planned or placed his houses according to the principle here recommended; and, in his two chief works, Blenheim and Castle Howard, it appears to have been strictly adhered to, at least in the placing of them. The views from the principal fronts of both are bad, and much inferior to what other parts of the ground would have afforded; but the situations of both, as objects to the surrounding scenery, are the best that could have been chosen.[28]

In his *Essays on the Picturesque*, first published in 1794–8 and revised in 1810, Sir Uvedale Price (1747–1829) related that 'when Vanbrugh was consulted about the garden at Blenheim, he said "you must send for a Landscape-painter"; a very natural answer to come from him, who . . . has of all architects most attended to painter-like effects'.[29] Although Price had the usual reservations about Vanbrugh's 'violation of rules . . . neglect of purity and elegance . . . licentious mixture of styles and ornaments [which] ought not to be held up as a model for imitation', he thought that 'an artist who, in any art, produces new and striking effects, well deserves to have their causes investigated':[30]

> It appears to me that at Blenheim, Vanbrugh conceived and executed a very bold and difficult design; that of uniting in one building, the beauty and magnificence of Grecian architecture, the picturesqueness of the Gothic, and the massive grandeur of a castle; and that in spite of the many faults with which he is very justly reproached, he has formed, in a style truly his own, a well-combined whole. . . . His first point seems to have been massiveness, as the foundation of grandeur. Then, to prevent that mass from being a lump, he has made various bold projections of various heights, which from different points serve as foregrounds to the main building. And, lastly, having probably been struck with the variety of outline against the sky in many Gothic and ancient buildings, he has raised on the top of that part, where the slanting roof begins in many houses of the Italian style, a number of decorations [which] if not new in themselves, have at least been applied and combined by him in a new and peculiar manner; and the union of them gives a suprising splendour and magnificence, as well as variety, to the summit of that princely edifice.[31]

Price drew attention to 'the advantage of towers' in creating a varied composition, no doubt having in mind such Vanbrughian examples as the kitchen-court at Castle Howard, the dramatic east and west towers at Seaton Delaval, the military form of the Belvedere at Claremont, and the towers at Grimsthorpe. He wondered at 'the little attention that has been paid to the summits of houses',[32] and admired the striking effects that were revealed in more distant views by the variations and decorations forming the roofline, as at Kings Weston and Eastbury. One plantation owner, Thomas Lee, by the late 1730s had already been inspired, presumably by an engraving of Blenheim, to copy the idea of groups of arched and clustered chimneys for his brick-built Stratford Hall in Westmoreland County, Virginia (figs. 141, 142).[33] Sir John Soane (1753–1837) drew attention in his ninth lecture at the Royal Academy in 1815 to Vanbrugh's having 'given importance to chimney shafts, [making them] contribute materially to the general effect'.[34] The German architect Karl Friedrich Schinkel (1781–1841), who toured Britain in order to report on new buildings under construction, made a similar comment in 1826 when visiting Kings Weston.[35]

The three lectures in which Soane referred to Vanbrugh are important as representing a considered early nineteenth-century assessment by the most thoughtful and best-read architect of his generation, one who was able through his lectures to disseminate his ideas and principles to students. In introducing Vanbrugh in his fifth lecture, Soane spoke of 'the versatility of his talents':

> It is impossible to contemplate Vanbrugh's works without feeling those emotions which the happy efforts of genius alone can produce. In his bold flights of irregular fancy, his powerful mind rises superior to common conceptions, and entitles him to the high distinctive appelation of the Shakespeare of architects.[36]

143. John Soane, Men's Penitentiary Design, *1781. This design, which was not executed, recalls Vanbrugh's military buildings.*

In the eleventh lecture, Soane's enthusiasm for Vanbrugh's architecture reaches its highest point:

> He had all the power of Michael Angelo and Bernini, without any of the elegant softness and classical delicacy of Palladio and his followers. The young architect, by studying the picturesque effects of his works, will learn . . . for himself and acquire a taste of his own.[37]

In contrast to these Soanic eulogies, Sir Robert Smirke (1780–1867) pursued a well-worn path of abuse in insisting that

> Heaviness was the lightest of [Vanbrugh's] faults. . . . The Italian style . . . which he contrived to caricature . . . is apparent in all his works; he helped himself liberally to its vices, contributed many of his own, and by an unfortunate misfortune adding impurity to that which was already greatly impure, left it disgusting and often odious.[38]

Smirke, one of the dullest of architects, can be discounted. It would, however, be interesting to pursue a possible influence of Vanbrugh's 'picturesque effects' on Soane's designs, varying from his early proposal for a men's penitentiary (fig. 143) that recalls Vanbrugh's military buildings[39] to the intricate modelling of the heroic elevations of the Bank of England,[40] while, as Arthur Bolton (1865–1945) noted:

> for all his academic study, [Soane] had an eye for Vanbrugh's dispositions. When called upon for an official report for a Palace for the Duke of Wellington after Waterloo, he takes Blenheim as an example, and his Royal Palace design of 1821 [for a site on London's Constitution Hill] recalls the outline plan of the main block of that example [fig. 144].[41]

Blenheim represented the palatial not only to Soane, but also to his contemporaries. Jeffry Wyatt, later Sir Jeffry Wyatville (1766–1820), used a similar idea in an unexecuted design for a huge mansion at Brocklesby in Lincolnshire in 1820,[42] and so did Benjamin Dean Wyatt (1775–1855) in his idea of a Waterloo Palace (1815–16) intended for a site in Hampshire's New Forest.[43] This member of the Wyatt family had been in India from 1797 to 1802, but he had not yet turned to architecture as a career, although his cousin Charles

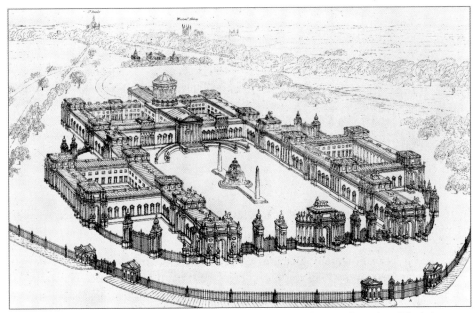

144. John Soane, Design for a Royal Palace, *1821, a design that owed much to Blenheim.*

(1758–1819), who was also in India around the same time, had designed Calcutta's Government House (1799–1804), which was based on James Paine's published design for Kedleston Hall, Derbyshire.[44] This was the time when Calcutta was being developed as 'the city of palaces' with its Anglo-Palladian buildings.[45] Another centre in India of Western-inspired architecture was Lucknow, especially during the reigns of Sa'adat 'Ali Khan (died 1814) and his son Ghazi-ud-din-Haider (died 1827) as nawabs of Avadh (Oudh).[46]

The Banqueting Hall attached to the Lucknow Residency (*c.* 1817) appears to derive from the plate in *Vitruvius Britannicus* that shows the front of Burlington House in London's Piccadilly, except that the single pilasters were doubled.[47] The Darshan Bilas ('Delightful Sight'), a part of the palatial Chattar Manzil complex built 1814–27, incorporates a copy of the Vanbrughian east front of the Dilkusha ('Heart's Delight'), a palace on the eastern outskirts of Lucknow.[48] But it is the Dilkusha (1798–1814) itself that is of particular importance when remembering Vanbrugh, since it was nothing less than a replica of Seaton Delaval, 5,000 miles away. Built by and for the Nawab Sa'adat 'Ali Khan – apparently an amateur architect who relied on the advice of his aide-de-camp, Sir Gore Ouseley (1777–1844)[49] – Dilkusha was enclosed by 'a charming park' filled with 'deer, nil'ga'i, antelopes, bears, tigers, peacocks, and game of all sorts. . . . His Majesty visits the place often for shooting.'[50] The palace, now a ruin, was copied from plates in *Vitruvius Britannicus,* as a watercolour (*c.* 1815) by Sita Ram confirms (fig. 145), although the main elevations were used in reverse, i.e., the garden (south) front of the Northumbrian house (fig. 91) served as the entrance (west) front at the Dilkusha. But the form of the building, the rustication and the coupled, ringed columns were faithful Vanbrughian reproductions. Mid-

145. A detail from Sita Ram's Dilkusha Palace and Park, Lucknow, *1815, a watercolour made soon after the completion of this Vanbrughian palace.*

nineteenth-century photographs (figs. 146, 147) show some later changes were made, notably the addition of kiosks or *chatri*, with gilded conical caps on the octagonal towers and the substitution of a flat balustraded roof for the original pedimented gables of the central block. At right-angles to the east front were paired flanking buildings – the stables and a kitchen block; the former still stands, but as a partly restored shell. Once again there was reference to Seaton Delaval, but not to its wings, which had not been illustrated in *Vitruvius Britannicus*; instead the central section of the inner façades of these two buildings reproduced that of the north front of Vanbrugh's house.[51] How surprised Vanbrugh would have been to observe his design translated from Northumbria's forbidding landscape to one of 'groves and orchards of cypress mango, orange, pomegranate, guave, custard apple, peach, nectarine, apricot and date palm – acre after acre of dark green foliage, spreading almost to the rim of the limpid sky', where, in the distance, 'scattered domes, towers and parapets, fretted and curved, painted and gilded . . . caught the sunlight like ornamental galleons becalmed'.[52]

In England, meanwhile, James Malton (1765–1803), best remembered as a provider of designs for Picturesque small houses, had been offering advice when contemplating 'huge edifices [to] be raised among woods and lawns and water'. In such locations he thought Vanbrugh's 'style of architecture better suited to combine with the natural objects of the country, than the elegant but formal forms of Greek and Roman'. In such situations he thought 'Nature must be disturbed'.[53]

146. *Dilkusha Palace, Lucknow, built 1798–1814, a mid-Victorian photograph that shows the entrance front, which in the Northumbrian original served as the garden front.*

147. *Dilkusha Palace's garden front, another of the number of Victorian photographs that exist of this unique Vanbrughian presence in India.*

In 1818 Jeffry Wyatt was summoned to Chatsworth, already a suitably 'huge edifice', where the 6th Duke of Devonshire was embarking on twenty years of improvement that also added a Picturesque quality to the great Baroque house by extending a long wing to the north which terminates in a massive tower (fig. 148).[54] This was a bold and imaginative addition, worthy of Vanbrugh's sense of drama; at its summit is a belvedere storey that opens up the architecture to Nature in a characteristic Picturesque gesture. It also recalls the prominent towers of Elizabethan and Jacobean houses such as Hardwick and Wollaton, houses that Vanbrugh knew, and seems to have admired for their distinctive skylines. Equally, as C.R. Cockerell (1788–1863) perceptively noted when viewing Burghley House in 1822, 'Vanbrugh must have taken his notion of chimneys' from the ornamental ones that 'look like the ruins of Palmyra or Balbek'.[55] David Watkin has noted that Cockerell's comments on Vanbrugh 'anticipate the findings of modern scholars who have shown how, in his search for a heroic architecture, he looked beyond the quiet reticence of Jones' Palladianism to the splendours of the Jacobean past'.[56] A century after Cockerell, Arthur Bolton thought it was 'very good for the student brought up on Chambers . . . to come into contact with the massive nonchalance of Vanbrugh'.[57]

Cockerell admired Vanbrugh for his understanding of the perspective of architecture, as well as for his bearing in mind the designing and placing of buildings in the changing position of the spectator. In fact, he thought his 'whole genius was theatrical',[58] a scene-creating quality that is an essential element in the Picturesque. Sir Reginald Blomfield (1856–1942), who rather grudgingly recognized that Vanbrugh possessed a 'passionate appreciation of the abstract qualities of architecture',[59] also commented on the theatrical nature of his designs, but he thought it his 'weak point', since it emphasized his habit

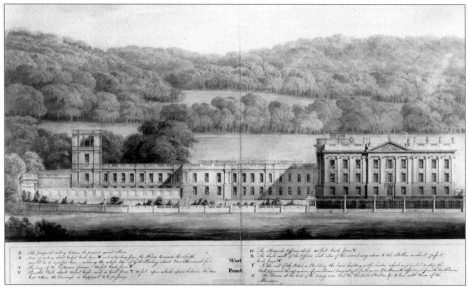

148. *Jeffry Wyatt [aka Wyatville]*, Design for the West Front of Chatsworth, *1818, showing the Vanbrughian effect of the added tower, which reflects his interest in Elizabethan and Jacobean houses.*

of approaching architecture from the point of view of a painter, or rather of a scene painter . . . of considering a building and the parts of a building as simply so much material for effect. . . . It is possible that Vanbrugh's success with stage scenery suggested to him the idea of realizing his canvas palaces in stone.[60]

More recently, Frank McCormick has pointed out that what Vanbrugh's 'contemporary scene designers accomplished with wings, shutters and arched borders, Vanbrugh accomplished through the use of arches, columns, corridors, and wings set at ninety-degree angles from the main block'.[61]

Cockerell himself created theatrically effective outlines, as in the Hanover Chapel (1821–2) in London's Regent Street, with its two towers breaking into the flat skyline of John Nash's street architecture.[62] Apparently, this was not, as one might think, a conscious recalling of Vanbrugh's Town Hall (1714) at Morpeth, Northumbria, for when Cockerell first saw the latter he remarked that it was 'picturesque *like my chapel*'.[63] But a deliberate reference to Vanbrugh must have been meant when Cockerell designed three Bank of England branches for Manchester, Bristol and Liverpool in the 1840s.[64] The Manchester bank employs bold, unfluted Greek Doric columns set against horizontally rusticated walling, and the doorway round the side is set in a frame of heavy voussoirs. The Bristol branch's lower part, with fluted Greek Doric columns, rustication and a heavy entablature, is surmounted by a storey of Vanbrughian semicircular-headed windows and a blank pediment. The finest of the three, that at Liverpool, is also the most indebted to Vanbrugh, with strongly rusticated corner piers, its exaggeratedly deep eaves and its idiosyncratic composition of elements (fig. 149). Cockerell's unsuccessful entry of 1839 for the Royal Exchange in London is another design that seems to owe much to Vanbrugh, with its strongly articulated façade surmounted by large sculptured figures, and its open corner towers with broken pediments and domes.[65]

Charles Fowler (1792–1867), a contemporary of Cockerell, was another architect whose work showed Vanbrughian characteristics.[66] A pair of lodges at Maristow House, Devon (1839), square in plan with a pyramidal roof, recalls Vanbrugh's military architecture and incorporates monumental voussoirs and rustication.[67] Two of his markets, that at Covent Garden, London (1827–30),[68] and the Lower Market, Exeter (1834–7),[69] both feature corner towers of a similar, but larger-scale, character. On the former they are linked by unfluted Doric colonnades, and there is an upper belvedere that responds to Inigo Jones's church of St Paul (1631–3) in Covent Garden and creates a dramatic roofline. On the latter the towers are linked by an arcade of large semicircular-headed openings and a pedimented upper storey. Even more Vanbrughian was Hungerford Market (1831–3), a stone's-throw south from Covent Garden, which incorporated an arcade of semicircular-headed arches above a high rusticated basement storey, the whole crowned by an austere pedimented attic (fig. 150).[70] Another of Fowler's designs, for the great conservatory at Syon House, Middlesex (1827–30), is sufficiently similar in general form and plan to Castle Howard to suggest that he had the Yorkshire house in mind when creating the domed central building with quadrant wings linked to pavilions.[71]

Twenty years later, in 1853, the 22-year-old Richard Norman Shaw (1831–1912) was awarded the Royal Academy Gold Medal for a design for a military college in honour of the Duke of Wellington. It was, observed Henry-

149. C.R. Cockerell's Bank of England, Liverpool, 1844–7.

Russell Hitchcock, 'startling evidence of an early predilection for Vanbrugh-like monumentality'. Only one perspective view has survived of this huge Baroque composition, which included cupolas, campanili and a great dome rising above a central portico (fig. 151).[72] Another Baroque design never to be built was the entry by Cuthbert Brodrick (1821–1905) for a competition of 1861 for the Houses of Parliament in Sydney, New South Wales. It presages great Edwardian public buildings with its domes, spires and towers, which would have created an unforgettable skyline when viewed from the harbour.[73] But Brodrick did see two designs built that reflect a Vanbrughian influence. He had won the 1852 competition for Leeds Town Hall, a building strongly influenced by French Neoclassicism but also by Castle Howard in the repeated bays of two storeys of semicircular-headed windows and pilasters.[74] During the course of construction, a massive domed tower was added that heightened the quality that Hitchcock thought 'recalls in its grandiose scale the Baroque of Vanbrugh'.[75] The similarity was increased by the addition of boldly carved ornaments along the parapets, on the tower itself, and on the pedimented, garlanded ventilation towers (fig. 152). At the same time as Leeds Town Hall was under construction, Brodrick was also working on Wells House, a hydropathic establishment at Ilkley. The almost square rusticated building has corner towers with belvedere attic storeys and a large bow overlooking Wharfedale, all of which creates the effect of a miniature Blenheim (fig. 153), while the entrance doorway reflects that from the courtyard to the east wing at Castle Howard.[76]

Brodrick's two designs were pioneers in the Baroque Revival, and more obviously indebted to Vanbrugh than many that followed, but around the time of their construction in the 1850s there were two significant marks of recognition which confirmed that Vanbrugh had been accorded his place in the English architectural Pantheon. The first occurred in 1856, when the Art Union of England issued a medal

150. Charles Fowler's Design for the Lower Court of Hungerford Market, London, *a watercolour of 1831.*

151. Richard Norman Shaw's design for Wellington College, published in The Illustrated London News *in 1853, an unexpectedly Baroque concept for its date and architect.*

struck in his honour (fig. 154). This was one in a series in which the other architects commemorated were Jones, Wren, Chambers, Barry and Sir George Gilbert Scott.[77] The second was when, in the frieze of 169 portrait figures of 'those men who have excelled in the arts of Poetry, Painting, Architecture and Sculpture' surrounding the podium of Scott's Albert Memorial (1863–72) in London's Kensington Gardens, Vanbrugh was included in a group of eleven English architects, ranging from the twelfth-century William the Englishman to Scott himself (fig. 155).[78]

Such events reflected a firm reassessment of Vanbrugh. Writing in the 1860s, James Fergusson (1808–86) thought the architect had 'never faltered in his career;

152. Cuthbert Brodrick's Town Hall, Leeds, Yorkshire, built 1853–8, which 'recalls in its grandiose scale the Baroque of Vanbrugh'.

and from first to last . . . there is one principle runs through all his designs, and it was a worthy one – a lofty aspiration after grandeur and eternity'.[79] A new appreciation of the work of Wren and Vanbrugh was developing in the 1880s when the 'English Renaissance' became an alternative style. John Brydon, lecturing to the Architectural Association in 1889, described how 'with the advent of Vanbrugh and Hawksmoor and Gibbs begins the later Renaissance . . . characterized by great vigour and picturesqueness, and by a freedom from restraint and an honesty of purpose not always to be found in later Classic'.[80] The identification with the idea of an English national style appealed to the developing imperialism, and the freedom from strict Classical rules as represented by Vanbrugh's work suited the increasingly free versions of Classicism.[81]

Brydon himself worked in an adaptation of early eighteenth-century architecture,[82] as in Bath's Municipal Art Gallery and Museum (1896–7). His design for the large block of Government offices in London's Parliament Square (1898–1912) is, in the commonly held Vanbrughian tradition, a heavy load indeed (fig. 156).[83] However, the building that helped most to establish the Baroque Revival was the Chartered Accountants' Hall in London (1888–93) by John Belcher (1841–1913) and Beresford Pite (1861– 1934).[84] In 1897 it was described as 'one of the most remarkable of modern buildings',[85] and subsequently the Baroque style became virtually the official one for public and commercial buildings. Certainly one can say that Vanbrugh was gratefully remembered at the turn of the century, although there were still those who, like Blomfield, believed quite simply that he 'had no taste',[86] while dismissing the great bridge at Blenheim as 'a standing monument of Vanbrugh's megalomania'.[87]

153. *Brodrick's Wells House, Ilkley, Yorkshire, 1854, which can be described as the central block of Blenheim in miniature.*

Sir Edwin Lutyens (1869–1944) rather ambiguously thought that Vanbrugh had 'used his weighty materials as a pigment, and the sky his canvas, with a brush too wide to allow any niceties of detail'.[88] Nevertheless, Lutyens remembered his predecessor at Heathcote, the house he built at Ilkley in Yorkshire in 1905–7.[89] But surely Vanbrugh's final heir on a scale more heroic than even he had been able to realize must be the great formal layout of New Delhi (1913–31) by Lutyens and Sir Herbert Baker (1862–1946).[90] In its composition can be found movement, light and shade, towers and domes, and a Picturesque variety of changing massings and views, 'whether they be distant, intermediate or near', to quote Sir John Soane.[91]

One might say that the English Baroque came to a magnificent finale in India nearly 250 years after Vanbrugh had reached Surat, and his spirit achieved an apotheosis there, as in a well-constructed play; but at the same time as this was happening, a serious assessment of his work was under way in England. The impetus began with the fourth volume, published in 1928, of the Nonesuch edition of *The Works of Sir John Vanbrugh*, which contains his letters edited by Geoffrey Webb. And in the same year *The Work of Sir John Vanbrugh and his School, 1699–1736*, in the *English Homes* series edited by H. Avray Tipping and

154. *The Art Union Medal, 1856, with a portrait of Sir John Vanbrugh. The central block of Blenheim is shown on the reverse.*

155. *A detail of the Albert Memorial's podium frieze showing the portrait of Sir John Vanbrugh; the Memorial itself was built in London's Kensington Gardens in 1863–72 to a design by Sir George Gilbert Scott.*

156. *John Brydon's Government Offices in Parliament Square, London, built 1898–1912.*

Christopher Hussey, made available current research and a magnificent photographic record. Exactly a decade later Laurence Whistler published *Sir John Vanbrugh: Architect and Dramatist*, a pioneering study based on many hitherto unused sources. 'What an anomaly it seems', marvelled David Green in 1950,

> this steady vogue for Vanbrugh's architecture in times when to build the least of his castles would, even with a thousand permits, be quite out of the question. Yet there the nostalgia is; or should we say the enthusiasm for buildings that are less functional than flamboyant, and altogether more alive, more vigorous and significant than a hundred pretentious monstrosities . . . which have been laid so heavily on us since.[92]

The following year Green himself contributed to the vogue by publishing a detailed study, *Blenheim Palace*; and in 1954 Whistler's *The Imagination of Vanbrugh and his Fellow Artists* brought knowledge of the correspondence and drawings up to date. Meanwhile, Kerry Downes was working on Hawksmoor and Vanbrugh, and his *Vanbrugh* was published in 1977, to be followed ten years later by his biographical *Sir John Vanbrugh*. In 1990 Charles Saumarez Smith's *The Building of Castle Howard* supplied a detailed study of the great house's design and construction, as well as of the patron. Certainly, during these last seventy years Vanbrugh has been well and sympathetically remembered, and, as Kerry Downes wrote, 'his originality has come to be understood and appreciated to an extent greater than in his own lifetime, although no more than is justly due to him'.[93] One can imagine how Vanbrugh, the man of the theatre, would have appreciated Carl Laubin's *capriccio* of the executed and projected buildings at Castle Howard, an architectural display that reflects the Pannini canvases in the house as well as recalling the composite views of Soane's *oeuvre* and Cockerell's *The Professor's Dream*.[94]

Reynolds expressed his appreciation of Vanbrugh's buildings 'in the language of a Painter',[95] and they have offered a rewarding subject for artists to interpret in their personal manner. Within a decade of Vanbrugh's death, Rigaud's fifteen views of Stowe had been drawn and engraved at Bridgeman's invitation.[96] The theme of this earliest set devoted to a single English garden concentrates on Vanbrugh's architectural contribution, largely ignoring Kent's. The view from the domed Rotondo includes Lord and Lady Cobham seated in chairs of state (fig. 38). Lord Cobham is represented in a reflective mood, and George Clarke has supposed that as Cobham 'contemplates Vanbrugh's perfect temple, he remembers how much his garden owes to his dead friend'.[97] Animated groups appear in all these scenes, seated in between Vanbrugh's paired Lake Pavilions, chasing deer along the edge of the lake in front of the house he remodelled, or admiring his Pyramid in the Home Park. Of the Pyramid, Gilbert West, Lord Cobham's nephew, wrote a touching valediction to its designer:

> Lamented Vanbrugh! This thy last Design,
> Among the various Structures, that around,
> Form'd by thy Hand, adorn this happy Ground,
> This, sacred to thy Memory shall stand:
> Cobham, and grateful Friendship so command.[98]

Despite this injunction, however, the Pyramid has not survived.

157. J.M.W. Turner's Blenheim House and Park – Oxford, *a Romantic watercolour of c. 1832.*

158. John Piper's Seaton Delaval, *painted in 1941, a reflection of the theatrical quality of the burnt-out ruin.*

In contrast to the various human and social activities included in Rigaud's views, the four of Castle Howard painted in 1771–2 by William Marlow (1740–1813) are notable for their clarity and the presentation of the house and grounds as architecture and landscaping without any suggestion of life;[99] as John Steegman wrote, 'The great house itself is the point'.[100] Yet another interpretation was placed on the house and its setting by Hendrik de Cort (1742–1810) when he recorded them as Arcadian *vedute* in the Claudean manner, in one of which rustic *staffage* enlivens a landscape dominated by Hawksmoor's Mausoleum.[101] In 1832, or thereabouts, J.M.W. Turner (1775–1851) responded to Blenheim and its park as a panorama in which the bridge is the focus of attention rather than the Palace, while the Woodstock Gate entrance acts as a side-flat in a stage setting, all seen in a golden–blue light (fig. 157).[102]

Both Blenheim and Castle Howard were painted in the 1940s by John Piper (1903–92) as Romantic theatrical settings,[103] but the house that appealed to him most was the dramatic ruin of Seaton Delaval (fig. 158):

> The central block faces down the slight slope of the court, the colonnaded wings embrace it on two other sides. Ochre and flame-licked red, pock-marked and stained in purplish umber and black, the colour is extremely up-to-date; very much of our times. . . . This palace, this drop-scene for melodrama in four dimensions, this vast old war-horse of a house was built with a splendid sense of drama. . . . Vanbrugh the man of the theatre was at least as operative here as Vanbrugh the architect. In this last work he created a rich stage which, when the footlights were turned down and the smart audiences gone, would adapt itself to any kind of bad acting and if necessary would carry on with the play itself.[104]

In the 1980s, following the hugely successful filming of *Brideshead Revisited* at Castle Howard, Felix Kelly (1900–94) painted a series of Vanbrughian fantasies there in interiors commissioned by George (later Lord) Howard to replace those destroyed in the fire of 1940. Julian Bicknell was the architect, and in these rooms, notably the Garden Hall and the Library, Bicknell incorporated giant-order pilasters, broken pediments and large keystones within a proportional system derived from Vanbrugh's work.[105] And in a series of *capricci* Kelly invented houses and garden structures, superhuman in scale, rusticated and vermiculated *in extremis* (fig. 159). In the same decade both Kelly and Bicknell were also involved in the design and construction of Henbury Hall, Cheshire, for Sebastian de Ferranti in the form of a Palladian villa 'such as Vanbrugh himself might have designed in the decade of the Temple of the Four Winds at Castle Howard'.[106] The sequence of its genesis is unusual, as Kelly first painted a picture of how the house might look, and Bicknell then developed it as an architectural project.

'Sir J. Vanbrugh's shade still presides in this neighbourhood', wrote the Hon. John Byng in 1787 after seeing the new Classical tower added to Woodstock church near Blenheim.[107] And his shade might be said to have presided still in the neighbourhood of Castle Howard in 1998 when the Yorkshire businessman Neville Howard (no relation) proposed to construct one of Vanbrugh's unbuilt designs – a drawing now in the Victoria and Albert Museum;[108] the drawing shows a small house set on a basement and topped by urns, obelisks and a pediment, above which rises a monumental composition of chimneys, open arches

159. Felix Kelly's Capriccio of Castle Howard, *painted in 1976.*

and a statue. 'Like a miniature Eastbury', is how Whistler described the design, which he thought 'the least austere and most engaging' of a group of Vanbrugh's drawings for small houses. But the proposal was not to the liking of Richmondshire Council, and early in 1999 planning permission was refused. 'That splendid fellow Vanbrugh', as the Victorian landscape architect William Andrews Nesfield liked to think of him,[109] might well have seen the joke: Vanbrugh had begun Castle Howard exactly 300 years earlier without requiring permits from officialdom, and with not a shred of architectural training to his name. Maybe he could have written a comedy out of the situation.

Notes

1. Vanbrugh over Fifty Years

Most of the assertions not supported by references here will be found either in my *Vanbrugh* monograph (London, 1977) or *Sir John Vanbrugh, a Biography* (London, 1987).

1. Geoffrey Webb (ed.), *The Complete Works of Sir John Vanbrugh, IV: The Letters* (London, 1928).
2. H. Avray Tipping and Christopher Hussey, *English Homes, IV, ii: The Work of Sir John Vanbrugh and his School, 1699–1736* (London, 1928).
3. Laurence Whistler, *Sir John Vanbrugh, Architect and Dramatist* (London, 1938).
4. The third edition was published in 1947.
5. Laurence Whistler, 'Talman and Vanbrugh: Episodes in an Architectural Rivalry', *Country Life*, CXII (21 November 1952), pp. 1648–52; Whistler, 'The Evolution of Castle Howard', *Country Life*, CXIII (30 January 1953), pp. 276–9; the book, of course, was Whistler's *The Imagination of Vanbrugh and his Fellow Artists* (London, 1954).
6. Reprinted in Kerry Downes, *Vanbrugh* (London, 1977); a missing line is supplied in Downes, *Sir John Vanbrugh, a Biography* (London, 1987), p. 505.
7. Published by Zwemmer (London, 1966).
8. Emil Kaufmann, *Architecture in the Age of Reason* (Cambridge, Mass., 1955), p. 13.
9. Webb, *Letters*, p. 149.
10. Kerry Downes, 'Vanbrugh's Heslington Lady', *Burlington Magazine*, CXXIV (1982), pp. 153–5.
11. Kerry Downes, *Hawksmoor* (London, 1959), p. 244.
12. Peregrine Osborne, Duke of Leeds, *A Journal of the Brest-Expedition by the Lord Marquiss of Caermarthen* (London, 1694).
13. Dated 28 December 1685, this letter was first published in John Barnard, 'Sir John Vanbrugh: Two Unpublished Letters', *Huntington Library Quarterly*, XXIX (1965–6), pp. 347–52, and again in Albert Rosenberg, 'New Light on Vanbrugh', *Philological Quarterly*, XLV (1966), pp. 603–13.
14. Downes, *Sir John Vanbrugh*, p. 238.
15. George W. Marshall (ed.), 'Le Neve's Pedigrees of the Knights', *Harleian Society*, VIII (1873), pp. 511–12 (publication of British Library MSS Harl. 5801, 5802).
16. Webb, *Letters*, pp. 4–5.
17. Charles Saumarez Smith, *The Building of Castle Howard* (London, 1990), p. 8 and n. 18.
18. Vanbrugh's account of his evidence when Talman sued Carlisle is in a letter to the Duke of Newcastle of 15 June 1703 (Whistler, *The Imagination of Vanbrugh*, pp. 35–8).
19. Saumarez Smith, *Castle Howard*, p. 33.
20. Castle Howard Archives, G2/2/1.
21. See the letters from Vanbrugh quoted below: to Carlisle, *c*. April 1700 (see note 24 below), and to Marlborough, 25 May 1716 (note 25).
22. Downes, *Hawksmoor*, pp. 234–5.
23. Whistler, *The Imagination of Vanbrugh*, pp. 227–8.
24. Webb, *Letters*, p. 6.
25. Webb, *Letters*, p. 65.
26. Webb, *Letters*, p. 56. Six days earlier he had written to Edward Southwell that 'every room in the house is like an oven' (Letters, pp. 55–6).
27. Webb, *Letters*, pp. 97–8.
28. Saumarez Smith, *Castle Howard*, p. 115.
29. John Macky, *Characters*, in Vicary Gibbs (ed.), *The Complete Peerage*, III (1913), *sub voce*.
30. Saumarez Smith, *Castle Howard*, pp. 161–8.
31. Saumarez Smith, *Castle Howard*, pp. 3–4.
32. Saumarez Smith, *Castle Howard*, pp. 151–4.
33. John Summerson, *Architecture in Britain, 1530 to 1830* (London, 1955), p. 165.

2. Estate Management and Landscape Design

1. Tom Williamson, *The Archaeology of the Landscape Park* (Oxford, 1999), pp. 46–71.
2. Chatsworth House Archives, 70.12.
3. Chatsworth House Archives, C21, 37.
4. Chatsworth House Archives, C21, 1–3. For the Cascade House design see Anthony Blunt, *Treasures from Chatsworth: The Devonshire Inheritance*, exh. cat. (Washington, DC, 1979), p. 15.
5. Chatsworth House Archives, C17.
6. Williamson, *Archaeology of the Landscape Park*, pp. 89–91.
7. E.A. Wrigley and R.S. Schofield, *The Population History of England 1541–1801* (Cambridge, 1989), pp. 208–9; M.J. Dobson, 'The Last Hiccup of the Old Regime: Population Stagnation and Decline in Late Seventeenth and Early Eighteenth-century England', *Continuity and Change*, IV (1989), pp. 395–428.

8. F.M.L. Thompson, 'The Social Distribution of
Landed Property in England since the Sixteenth
Century', *Economic History Review*, XIX (1966);
Christopher Clay, 'Landlords and Estate
Management in England', in Joan Thirsk (ed.),
*The Agrarian History of England and Wales, V, ii:
1640–1750* (Cambridge, 1985), pp. 119–250.
9. Quoted in Clay, 'Landlords and Estate
Management', p. 179.
10. Susan Neave, 'Rural Settlement Contraction in the
East Riding of Yorkshire between the Mid
Seventeenth and Mid Eighteenth Centuries',
Agricultural History Review, XLI (1993), pp. 124–36.
11. D.R. Mills, *Lord and Peasant in Nineteenth-
Century Britain* (London, 1980).
12. Neave, 'Settlement Contraction', p. 135.
13. Joan Thirsk, 'Agricultural Innovations and
Their Diffusion', in Thirsk (ed.), *Agrarian
History of England and Wales, V, ii*, pp. 533–89.
14. Tom Williamson, *Polite Landscapes: Gardens and
Society in Eighteenth-Century England* (Stroud,
1995), pp. 124–9.
15. John Evelyn, *Sylva, or a Discourse of Forest-Trees
and the Propagation of Timber in His Majesties
Dominions* (London, 1664).
16. Tom Williamson, 'Fish, Fur and Feather: Man
and Nature in the Post-Medieval Landscape', in
K. Barker and T. Darvill (eds), *Making English
Landscapes* (Bournemouth, 1997), pp. 92–117.
17. Roy Loveday and Tom Williamson, 'Rabbits or
Ritual? Artificial Warrens and the Neolithic
Long Mound Tradition', *Archaeological Journal*,
CXLV (1988), pp. 290–313.
18. Thirsk, 'Agricultural Innovations', p. 577.
19. Roger North, *The Discourse of Fish and Fish
Ponds* (London, 1713).
20. Daniel Defoe, *A Tour Through England and
Wales*, ed. G.D.H. Cole (London, 1928), I, p. 79.
21. John Worlidge, *Systema Agriculturae* (London,
1669), p. 72.
22. Moses Cook, *The Manner of Raising, Ordering
and Improving Forest Trees* (London, 1676), p. 32.
23. Quoted in Keith Thomas, *Man and the Natural
World* (London, 1983), p. 49.
24. Norfolk Record Office, Le Strange ND 22.34.
25. Williamson, *Polite Landscapes*, pp. 22–4, 46–7.
26. M. Barley, 'Rural Buildings in England', in
Thirsk (ed.), *Agrarian History of England and
Wales, V, ii*, p. 617.
27. Williamson, 'Fish, Fur and Feather', p. 94.
28. North, *Discourse*, p. 21.
29. Christopher Currie, 'Fishponds as Garden
Features, *c.* 1550–1750', *Garden History*, Journal
of the Garden History Society, XVIII/1 (1990),
pp. 22–46.
30. John Evelyn, *The Diary*, ed. E.S. De Beer
(London, 1955), p. 255.
31. Anthea Taigel and Tom Williamson, 'Some
Early Geometric Gardens in Norfolk', *Journal of
Garden History*, XI/1–2 (1991), pp. 89–91.
32. Berkshire Record Office, D/ED F 14.
33. Tom Turner, *English Garden Design: History and
Styles since 1650* (Woodbridge, 1986).
34. Norfolk Record Office, HARE 5532 223 X 5.

35. Judith Roberts, *Yorkshire Gardens: An Exhibition
of Documents in the North Yorkshire Record Office*
(York, 1993), pp. 6–7.
36. For example, the plates illustrating Goodwood,
Sussex, and Wilton, Wiltshire.
37. Gervase Jackson-Stops, *An English Arcadia,
1600–1990: Designs for Gardens and Garden
Buildings in the Care of the National Trust*
(Washington, DC, 1991), cat. 22.
38. Williamson, *Archaeology of the Landscape Park*,
pp. 132–4.
39. In the 'Epistle to Burlington' (1731); see Pope's
Poetical Works, ed. Herbert Davies (Oxford,
1966), pp. 318–20.
40. David Jacques, 'The Art and Sense of the
Scriblerus Club in England, 1715–1735', *Garden
History*, IV/1 (1976), pp. 30–55.
41. In *The Spectator*, 414 (25 June 1712); see
Donald F. Bond (ed.), *The Spectator* (Oxford,
1965), V, p. 552.
42. Stephen Switzer, *Ichnographia Rustica*, 3 vols
(London, 1718).
43. Berkshire Record Office, D/EX 258/9.
44. Switzer, *Ichnographia Rustica*, p. 317.
45. Switzer, *Ichnographia Rustica*, pp. xxx, xxxvii.
46. Williamson, *Polite Landscapes*, pp. 100–18.

3. The Formal Garden

1. For a fuller account of this phenomenon see
David Jacques, 'The Grand Manner: Changing
Style in Garden Design, 1660–1735', PhD
thesis, Courtauld Institute, University of
London, 1999.
2. Lucy Norton (ed.), *Saint-Simon at Versailles*
(London, 1980), p. 59.
3. Joseph Addison, *The Spectator*, 414 (25 June
1712), the fourth in a set of eleven essays on
'The Pleasures of the Imagination'; it is
reprinted in John Dixon Hunt and Peter Willis
(eds), *The Genius of the Place: The English
Landscape Garden, 1620–1820* (London, 1975),
pp. 141–3.
4. Stephen Switzer, *The Nobleman, Gentleman, and
Gardener's Recreation* (London 1715), pp. viii,
xii, xiii and xv.
5. Switzer, *Ichnographia Rustica* (London 1718), I,
p. xviii; Switzer, *Ichnographia Rustica*, 2nd edn
(London 1741–2), I, 'Prooemial Essay', p. 13,
and III, 'A Farther Account', p. 9.
6. Gervase Jackson-Stops, *An English Arcadia,
1600–1990: Designs for Gardens and Garden
Buildings in the Care of the National Trust*
(Washington, DC, 1991), cat. 9.
7. Jacques, 'The Grand Manner', pp. 54–6; hardly
any new broad walks were made across forecourts
after 1700, while carriage sweeps had become
increasingly common since the mid-1680s.
8. The first iron fences were seen at London's Chelsea
Hospital and at the Fountain Garden at Hampton
Court before 1690, and while they were never
numerous enough to be described as a fashion,
further examples occurred regularly until the 1720s.

9. Breast walls, such as those at Venn House, Dorset, and Dyrham, Gloucestershire, built from the early 1700s, were among the last. By contrast the differences in level were resolved at Kiveton and in Wales at Chirk Castle, Clwyd, by *glacis* slopes.

10. Early examples of forest gardens include New Park's at Richmond, Surrey, set out from 1698; Castle Howard's Ray Wood *c.* 1705; and more regular layouts, like the northern wilderness at Kensington Palace, also *c.* 1705.

11. John Harris, 'The Beginnings of Claremont: Sir John Vanbrugh's Garden at Chargate in Surrey', *Apollo*, CXXXVII (April 1993), fig. 5.

12. See the anonymous garden plan of *c.* 1705, in the Melbourne Hall archives: X Lothian, Bundle 219/1, item 18; and two views of Bulstrode in Thomas Badeslade and John Rocque, *Vitruvius Britannicus*, IV (London, 1739), pls. 40–4 (Portland's changes were made shortly before 1710).

13. See Robert Boyle, *A Free Inquiry into the Vulgarly Receiv'd Notion of Nature* (London, 1686).

14. John Evelyn, *Sylva* (London, 1664), p. 5.

15. Addison, *The Spectator* (25 June 1712).

16. This topic has been discussed extensively elsewhere, for example by Christopher Hussey, *English Gardens and Landscapes, 1700–1750* (London, 1967), pp. 28–9, and Christopher Thacker, *The Wildness Pleases* (Beckenham, 1983), ch. 2.

17. Addison, *The Spectator* (25 June 1712); most authors have seen this article in the light of the later emergence of the naturalistic English landscape garden, referring to it as the 'dawn' or the 'genesis' of the new period. However, that misunderstands Addison's purpose, which was to explore an appropriately rural style for country properties.

18. Alexander Pope, 'On Gardens', *The Guardian*, 173 (29 September 1713), reprinted in Hunt and Willis, *Genius of the Place*, pp. 204–8; figurative topiary still survived in the gardens of tradesmen, though not in the gardens of the great.

19. Hunt and Willis, *Genius of the Place*, pp. 148–50.

20. Switzer reproduced the bulk of Addison, *The Spectator* (25 June 1712) in *Recreation*, pp. 338–43.

21. Switzer, *Recreation*, pp. xxxviii–xxxix, and p. xv.

22. Batty Langley, *New Principles of Gardening* (London, 1728), title-page and p. vii.

23. Langley, *New Principles*, p. xii.

24. For this quotation, see Hunt and Willis, *Genius of the Place*, p. 189.

25. Stephen Switzer, *The Practical Kitchen Gardiner* (London, 1727), Dedication: 'if a view be taken of the writings of Cato, Varro, Collumella, Pliny and other celebrated writers of Husbandry and Gardening amongst the ancients, it will be found that those of the fruit and kitchen garden were the chief parts known and practised amongst them'.

26. The complaint is in John James's 'Dedication' to his translation (*The Theory and Practice of Gardening*, London, 1712) of A.-J. Dézallier d'Argenville's *La Théorie et la pratique du jardinage* (Paris, 1709).

27. Noted in John Dixon Hunt, *Garden and Grove: The Italian Renaissance Garden in the English Imagination, 1600–1750* (London, 1986), pp. 33 and 95.

28. Pope, 'On Gardens' (1713), in Hunt and Willis, *Genius of the Place*, p. 205; he may have been referring to Pliny the Younger's descriptions of the villas at Laurentinum and Tusculum.

29. Switzer, *Recreation*, pp. ii and xxviii.

30. Switzer, *Ichnographia Rustica* (1718), II, p. 174.

31. Switzer, *Ichnographia Rustica*, 2nd edn (1741–2), III, the section on 'A Farther Account of Rural and Extensive Gardening', the composition of which can be dated by internal evidence to *c.* 1730.

32. A.A. Cooper, 3rd Earl of Shaftesbury, 'A Letter Concerning the Art, or Science, of Design' (6 March 1712), in *Characteristicks of Men, Manners, Opinions and Times*, ed. John Baskerville (Birmingham, 1773), III, p. 398; 'Britain' rather than 'England', because of the Union in 1707.

33. James, 'Dedication' in *Theory and Practice*.

34. Switzer, *Recreation*, ch. VIII.

35. All vestiges of the forecourt were removed at Stowe before 1720 as the coach sweep was laid down in open parkland under the main steps to the house. The last forecourts to be made were at Vanbrugh's Eastbury, Seaton Delaval and Grimsthorpe, all within militaristic outworks.

36. See David Jacques, 'George London's Last Masterwork', in Katherine Myers (ed.), *The Gardens of Canons* (London, 1998), pp. 3–13.

37. See the plan of Thoresby in Campbell, *Vitruvius Britannicus*, III, pl. 81–2, a design probably proposed by Campbell *c.* 1715.

38. John Harris, *The Palladian Revival: Lord Burlington, His Villa and Garden at Chiswick*, exh. cat. (New Haven and London, 1994), p. 44ff.

39. Catherine E. Parsons, 'Horseheath Hall and its Owners', *Proceedings of the Cambridgeshire Antiquarian Society*, XLI (1948), p. 29.

40. For Hall Barn see Hussey, *English Gardens and Landscapes*, pp. 25–6 and pl. 8; for Balthasar Nebot's view (1738) of the bastioned terrace at Hartwell, see John Harris, *The Artist and the Country House* (London, 1979), no. 194a.

41. See Rigaud's oblique view (*c.* 1733) towards the greenhouse at Chiswick in Harris, *The Palladian Revival*, cat. 100.

42. Switzer, *Ichnographia Rustica*, 2nd edn (1741–2), I, 'Prooemial Essay', pp. 11–12.

43. Switzer, *Ichnographia Rustica* (1718), II, p. 163.

44. For Bramham there is an anonymous 'Map of Bramham Parke the Seat of the Rt Honble Robert Benson' (pre-1713), in the Bramham Estate archive; for Heythrop, Thomas Bainbridge's 'A Survey, Valuation and Plans of the Townships and Estates situate in the Counties of Oxford, Berkshire, Worcs & Wilts belonging to . . . the Earl of Shrewsbury' (1789) is in the Bodleian Library, MS Top Oxon d.391.

45. Philip Miller, *The Gardener's Dictionary*, 3rd edn (London, 1737), entry on 'Dwarf-Trees'.

46. For details of maps, etc., for these, see Jacques, 'The Grand Manner'.

47. Gabriel Delahaye's plan of Boughton gardens (1712) is in the Bodleian Library, Gough Drawings, a4 f. 84; these basins were subsumed within the rectangular sheet of water in 1721.

48. Shown in an anonymous engraving of the circular pool with obelisk (*c.* 1730), reproduced in Harris, 'The Beginnings of Claremont', fig. 4.

49. See the Kip and Knyff views (*c.* 1712) of Wanstead in the *Supplément du Nouveau Théâtre de la Grand Bretagne* (1728), pls. 5, 6 and 7.

50. See the painted views of Ebberston (*c.* 1745) in Harris, *Artist and the Country House*, nos. 195a–c.

51. Stephen Switzer, *An Introduction to a General System of Hydrostaticks and Hydraulicks* (London, 1729), II, p. 411 and pl. 55; Switzer's reference is to 'Down-Husband', the colloquial name for Hurstbourne Priors (to distinguish it from Hurstbourne Tarrant, 'Up-Husband'), where the cascade was built *c.* 1715. Thomas Archer had drawn up plans for a new house there, and so may have been involved with the cascade.

52. James, *Theory and Practice*, pp. 46 and 63; see also the 2nd edn (London, 1728), p. 61.

53. For Winchendon, see Harris, *Artist and the Country House*, nos. 149a–b, and Switzer, *Ichnographia Rustica* (1718), II, p. 226; for Forde see John Harris, 'The Prideaux Collection of Topographical Drawings', *Architectural History*, VII (1964), fig. 40; for Stowe see Rigaud's 'View of the Parterre from the Portico' (1734), reproduced in Peter Willis, *Charles Bridgeman and the English Landscape Garden* (London, 1977), pl. 129.

54. Horace Walpole, *The History of the Modern Taste in Gardening* (Strawberry Hill, 1785), p. 51.

55. See John Harris, 'The Artinatural Style', in Charles Hind (ed.), *The Rococo in England*, (London, 1986), p. 19.

56. Hunt and Willis, *Genius of the Place*, p. 189, quoting Castell in *Villas of the Ancients*.

57. Switzer, *Ichnographia Rustica* (1718), III, pp. 101–3 and pl. 37 opp. p. 44; he remarked of his ideas that 'any Body that has seen my Lord Carlisle's Wood at Castle-howard, will easily discern is taken from thence'.

58. Switzer, *Ichnographia Rustica* (1718), II, p. 198.

59. Switzer, *Ichnographia Rustica* (1718), III, pp. 101–3.

60. Thomas Player, 'Description of a Journey into Yorkshire' (*c.* 1712), Gloucestershire Record Office, Gloucester, D421, f. 32.

61. Lord Percival to Daniel Dering (9 August 1724), printed in Hunt and Willis, *Genius of the Place*, p. 165.

62. James, *Theory and Practice*, p. 57 and pls. 5C and 6C.

63. Switzer, *Recreation*, p. v.

64. Switzer, *Ichnographia Rustica* (1718), II, p. 136.

65. Switzer, *Ichnographia Rustica* (1718), III, p. 106.

66. See Badeslade and Rocque, *Vitruvius Britannicus*, IV (1739), pl. 84–5.

67. See the plan of Cholmondeley (*c.* 1715), in Campbell, *Vitruvius Britannicus*, III (1725), pl. 79–80; a print of Wentworth Woodhouse (*c.* 1735) attributed to John Settrington is in York Minster Library.

68. Compare James, *Theory and Practice*, pl. 8C, fig. 3, with Switzer, *Ichnographia Rustica* (1718), II, opp. p. 218, pl. 34, figs. 1 and 3.

69. Compare James, pl. 8C, fig. 1, with Switzer, *Ichnographia Rustica* (1718), II, opp. p. 194, pl. 33.

70. Bodleian Library, Gough Drawings, a4, ff. 21, 46, 57, 63 and 64, reproduced in Willis, *Charles Bridgeman*, pls 28b, 117, 81b, 61 and 46b.

71. See Harris, *The Palladian Revival*, ch. 5; in the late 1720s Burlington began introducing urns, terms, the exedra, sphinxes, ilex trees and the serpentine river.

72. James, *Theory and Practice*, p. 117 and fig. 4 in plate G referring to p. 117.

73. James Bond and Kate Tiller (eds), *Blenheim: Landscape for a Palace* (Gloucester, 1987), fig. 50.

74. Jane Roberts, *Royal Landscape: The Gardens and Parks of Windsor* (New Haven and London, 1997), p. 24.

75. Switzer, *Ichnographia Rustica*, 2nd edn (1741–2), I, 'Prooemial Essay', p. 13.

76. Moses Cook, *The Manner of Raising, Ordering, and Improving Forrest Trees* (London, 1676), pp. 70–1.

77. *Calendar of Treasury Books*, for 1702–7, p. 199.

78. See the anonymous 'Plan of the Home Park at Cirencester' and 'Plan of Oakley Great Park' in Samuel Rudder, *A New History of Gloucestershire* (Cirencester, 1779).

4. Fortified Gardens

1. Decker, cited in Laurence Whistler, *The Imagination of Vanbrugh and his Fellow Artists* (London, 1954), p. 152. Decker (1679–1749) was a noted horticulturalist; for his own garden see *'Blest Retreats': A History of Private Gardens in Richmond upon Thames*, exh. cat., intro. Ray Desmond (Richmond, 1984), pp. 51–2.

2. Whistler's own description in *The Imagination of Vanbrugh*, p. 152.

3. David Green, *Gardener to Queen Anne: Henry Wise (1653–1738) and the Formal Garden* (London, 1956), p. 102: Wise to Marlborough, 21 July 1707.

4. Geoffrey Webb (ed.), *The Letters* (London, 1928), p. 70: Vanbrugh to Sarah, Duchess of Marlborough, 30 June 1716.

5. Stephen Switzer, *Ichnographia Rustica* (London, 1718), II, p. 164. Switzer's 'Kitchen or Fruit garden' at Spye Park, Wiltshire (*c.* 1720), had bastions 'Projecting over the basin', as the caption to the plate illustrating it in Switzer's *The Practical Fruit Gardener* (1724) confirms.

6. John Gay, 'An Epistle to the Earl of Burlington' [?1715], in *Poetical Works*, ed. G.C. Faber (Oxford, 1926), p. 152.

7. James Sambrook, *James Thomson, 1700–1748: A Life* (Oxford, 1991), p. 208; a story

remembered by Mrs Piozzi, though Sambrook comments that a similar tale concerning Thomson is located, with greater probability, at Eastbury, a Vanbrugh house in Dorset.

8. For example Blenheim (in Woodstock Park), Malplaquet (at Red Rice, Upper Clatford, Hampshire) and Waterloo (Woodford Hall, Northamptonshire; Hardwick Grange, Shropshire; Spring Hill, Worcestershire). For more see Jean O'Neill, 'Battle Gardens and Plantations', *Country Life*, CLXX (17 December 1981), pp. 2166–8.

9. Whistler, *The Imagination of Vanbrugh*, pp. 229–30: Vanbrugh to the Duke of Marlborough, 22 June 1705 (this letter is not in Webb's edition).

10. Switzer, *Ichnographia Rustica*, II, p. 174.

11. Switzer, *Ichnographia Rustica*, II, p. 174.

12. Switzer, *Ichnographia Rustica*, II, p. 174.

13. Switzer, *The Practical Kitchen Gardiner* (London, 1727), p. 367.

14. For Gomme's life and works, including Tilbury, see Andrew Saunders, *Fortress Britain: Artillery Fortification in the British Isles and Ireland* (Liphook, Hants, 1989), ch. 7.

15. A useful introduction is F.J. Hebbert and G.A. Rothrock, *Soldier of France: Sébastien Le Prestre de Vauban, 1633–1707* (New York, 1989), which has an exhaustive 'Bibliographical Essay', pp. 253–69.

16. For Camaret Bay see Kerry Downes, *Sir John Vanbrugh, a Biography* (London, 1987), pp. 85–9. For Marlborough's treacherous part in it, John Childs, *The British Army of William III, 1689–1702* (Manchester, 1987), pp. 222–6.

17. Karl D. Bülbring (ed.), *The Compleat English Gentleman by Daniel Defoe* (London, 1890), pp. 230–1.

18. Switzer, *Ichnographia Rustica*, II, p. 208.

19. Jonathan Swift, 'The Battle of the Books' (1704), in *A Tale of a Tub with Other Early Works*, ed. Herbert Davis (Oxford, 1957), pp. 147–8.

20. Margaret Blundell (ed.), *Cavalier: Letters of William Blundell to his Friends, 1620–1698* (London, 1933), pp. 253–4.

21. 'The Mannour of Paston', *Ichnographia Rustica*, II, plate between pp. 112 and 113. I have not been able, unfortunately, to match Switzer's related Paston survey (his figure XII) with Paston near Coldstream, or with Paston in Norfolk, or with the most likely candidate – the Paston that now lies half-buried under the postwar new town of Peterborough.

22. Switzer, *Recreation*, p. 55.

23. Todd Longstaffe-Gowan, 'Grimsthorpe Castle', *Country Life*, CXCII (21 May 1998), p. 53.

24. This rivalry was keenly supported, and slow to abate: in January 1706, Colonel Francis Nicholson burst in on a divine raving that 'the Fortifications at Breda and Bergen op zoom the best in Europe; the latter by Cohorn, who a much better Engineer than Vaubun'; see C. Jones and G. Holmes (eds), *The London Diaries of William Nicolson, Bishop of Carlisle, 1702–18* (Oxford, 1985), p. 358.

25. For Furttenbach, see the summary account in English and notes for further reading by Dorothee Nehring, 'The Garden Designs of Joseph Furttenbach the Elder', in Monique Mosser and Georges Teyssot (eds), *The History of Garden Design* (London, 1991), pp. 160–2; for Le Nôtre, see Vincent Scully, *Architecture: The Natural and the Manmade* (New York, 1991), pp. 275–310, and Chandra Mukerji, *Territorial Ambitions and the Gardens of Versailles* (Cambridge, 1997), esp. ch. 2.

26. David Chandler, 'The Great Captain-General, 1702–1714', in *The Oxford History of the British Army*, ed. D. Chandler (Oxford, 1994), p. 89; John A. Lynn, *The Wars of Louis XIV, 1667–1714* (Harlow, 1999), p. 322.

27. A detailed account of how investments were conducted in this period is in Christopher Duffy, *Fire and Stone: The Science of Fortress Warfare, 1660–1860* (London, 1996), ch. 6.

28. Jonathan Swift, *The Journal to Stella*, ed. Harold Williams (Oxford, 1974), II, p. 397: Letter XXXIII, 23 October 1711.

29. Martha D. Pollak, *Military Architecture, Cartography and the Representation of the Early Modern European City: A Checklist of Treatises on Fortification in The Newberry Library* (Chicago, 1991), p. xxx.

30. Laurence Sterne, *The Life and Opinions of Tristram Shandy* (1759–67), ed. Melvyn and Joan New (Harmondsworth, 1997), p. 90.

31. Tobias Smollett, *The Adventures of Roderick Random* (1748), ed. Paul-Gabriel Boucé (Oxford, 1981), pp. 263–4.

32. Mark R. Wenger (ed.), *The English Travels of Sir John Percival and William Byrd II: The Percival Diary of 1701* (Columbia, Mo., 1989), Introduction, p. 7.

33. A list of Wren's fortificatory experiments is in Christopher Wren the younger, *Parentalia* (London, 1750), pp. 198–9.

34. Winde's 'Cursus Mathematicus' (British Library, King's MSS, 266–7), abandoned in 1688, includes a section on 'Military Architecture'; Aldrich's 'Elementa Architecturae', left unfinished at his death in 1710, was to have been divided equally into military and civil architecture. Information from their entries in Howard Colvin, *A Biographical Dictionary of British Architects, 1600–1840* (London, 1995).

35. See the *Sale Catalogue of Books, the Collection of the deceased William Paston, 2nd Earl of Yarmouth*, printed by Olive Payne, The Strand, London, 1734, British Library shelfmark S.C.472(1). In addition to a Coehoorn fortificatory work of 1705 (lot 376), Yarmouth's library included gardening books by Evelyn, Woolridge, Switzer, James and others.

36. For some seventeenth-century examples, see the following: Jones's library list in John Harris *et al.*, *The King's Arcadia: Inigo Jones and the Stuart Court*, exh. cat. (London, 1973), Appx III; for a reference of June 1675 to John Webb's books 'about fortification and Engines', Henry W. Robinson and Walter Adams (eds), *The*

Diary of Robert Hooke, 1672–1680 (London, 1935), p. 165; and for Pratt's library, R.T. Gunther (ed.), *The Architecture of Sir Roger Pratt* (Oxford, 1928), Appx II.

37. See 'Gibbs's Fine Art Library', in Terry Friedman, *James Gibbs* (New Haven and London, 1984), pp. 327–30 (p. 329).

38. 'A Catalogue of ye Books belonging to Mr Henry Wise of Brompton Park' in 1711 is Appendix III in Green, *Gardener to Queen Anne*, pp. 210–13. For London, see *A Catalogue of the Library of George London, Esq; late Chief Gardener to Her Majesty*, sale cat. for Exeter Exchange, London, 22–24 March 1714; British Library shelfmark S.C.301(3). London willed his most treasured item, 'my fine booke of the Surrinam Plants in Colours', to his daughter Henrietta, a botanical artist (PRO Kew, PROB 11/538, sig. 31, dated 2 December 1713). This was a hand-coloured copy of Maria Merian's *Metamorphosis Insectorum Surinamensium* (1705), presumably one of the exotic works Thoresby examined on 28 May 1712 at London's townhouse in Spring Gardens, St James's Park: J. Hunter (ed.), *The Diary of Ralph Thoresby* (London, 1830), II, p. 104.

39. See *A Catalogue of the Collection of the Pictures, Drawings, Prints & Valuable Library of Books of . . . Thomas Coke, Deceas'd*, sale cat. at Cooper's, Covent Garden, London, from 19 February 1728; British Library shelfmark C.119.h.3(7).

40. John Harris, *The Palladian Revival: Lord Burlington, His Villa and Garden at Chiswick*, exh. cat. (New Haven and London, 1994), p. 269.

41. In addition to the built works at Grimsthorpe and at Spye Park, Wiltshire, W.A. Brogden, in 'Stephen Switzer and Garden Design in Britain in the Early Eighteenth Century', PhD thesis, Edinburgh University, 1973, suggests that Switzer may have been responsible for the earthworks at Eresby, Lincolnshire (pp. 7, 165); Eslington, Northumbria (pp. 26, 212); and in Ireland at Dromoland, County Clare (p. 15).

42. Peter Willis, *Charles Bridgeman and the English Landscape Garden* (London, 1977), p. 62; for Bridgeman's plan of Westbury (not in Willis), see Krystyna Bilikowski, *Hampshire's Countryside Heritage, 5: Historic Parks and Gardens* (Hampshire County Council, 1983), ill. on p. 19.

43. E.S. Donno (ed.), *Andrew Marvell: The Complete Poems* (Harmondsworth, 1972), p. 84, stanza 36.

44. John Chamberlain (1554–1628), reporting his visit to Ware Park made in October 1606, quoted in Roy Strong, *The Renaissance Garden in England* (London, 1979), p. 123.

45. Evelyn, *The Diary*, ed. E.S. De Beer (Oxford, 1955), IV, p. 42; this form of representation originates in allegorical tourneys, for example the assault of Castle Loyal that took place in Greenwich Palace's tiltyard during Henry VIII's Christmas festivities in 1524.

46. This fort is illustrated in one of the box views in John Rocque's published *Plan of Wanstead*

(1735); for Adam Holt's possible involvement, see the Note by Fiona Cowell in *Garden History*, XXVI/2 (Winter 1998), p. 214.

47. See Annette Bagot, 'Monsieur Beaumont and Col. Grahme: The Making of a Garden, 1689–1710', *Garden History*, III/4 (Autumn 1975), pp. 66–78; Susan Bagot, *Levens Hall and Gardens*, guidebook (1989).

48. Switzer, *Ichnographia Rustica*, II, p. 164.

49. John Tracy Atkyns, 'Iter Boreale' (1732), f. 25, an unpublished travel journal now in the Yale Center for British Art, New Haven, Connecticut.

50. Castle Howard Archives, G2/1/2, f. 30; cited in Charles Saumarez Smith, *The Building of Castle Howard* (London, 1990), p. 124.

51. There is a helpful modern plan of the grounds (based on Fowler's estate map of 1727) showing this line of defences in Saumarez Smith, *Castle Howard*, pp. 118–19, who has a chapter on the gardens.

52. Webb, *Letters*, p. 142: Vanbrugh to Carlisle, 24 April 1722.

53. Webb, *Letters*, p. 152: Vanbrugh to Newcastle, 20 August 1723.

54. Webb, *Letters*, p. 173: Vanbrugh to Carlisle, 8 March 1726.

55. Webb, *Letters*, p. 106: Vanbrugh to Newcastle, 17 December 1718.

56. In a letter dated 20 August 1723 sent from Castle Howard, Vanbrugh expressed his hope to the Duke of Newcastle that, on his return south, 'I shall find the Walls at Claremont as much to my Satisfaction (and your Graces too) as those are here': Webb, *Letters*, p. 152.

57. Kerry Downes, 'The Kings Weston Book of Drawings', *Architectural History*, X (1967), cat 17, fig. 17; cat. 66, fig. 18; both drawings are annotated 'February 1717/8', i.e. 1718.

58. G.B. Clarke (ed.), *Descriptions of Lord Cobham's Gardens at Stowe, 1700–1750*, Buckingham Record Society, no. 26 (1990), p. 16.

59. The appendix to the third edition of Defoe's *Tour* (1742) includes a lengthy description of Stowe, describing the stormpoled sections as 'inclosed in a military Way, with a staked Fence'; see the reprint in Clarke, *Descriptions*, p. 82.

60. The muddled chronology in *Tristram Shandy* is notorious; for a helpful analysis see Theodore Baird, 'The Time-Scheme of "Tristram Shandy" and a Source', *Publications of the Modern Language Association of America*, LI/3 (September 1936), pp. 803–20.

61. Daniel Defoe, 'An Essay on Projects', in *The True-Born Englishman and Other Writings*, eds P.N. Furbank and W.R. Owens (Harmondsworth, 1997), p. 220.

62. Recorded by Colonel Sir Herbert Jekyll, 'Studies in Family History', a privately owned MS cited in Michael Tooley and Prudence Arnander (eds), *Gertrude Jekyll: Essays on the Life of a Working Amateur* (Witton-le-Wear, County Durham, 1995), p. 23.

63. Tooley and Arnander, *Gertrude Jekyll*, p. 29 and n. 15.

64. Gervase Jackson-Stops, 'Ribston Hall, Yorkshire – I', *Country Life*, CLIV (11 October 1973), p. 1053.

65. Stephen Porter, *Destruction in the English Civil Wars* (Stroud, 1997), p. 29.

66. For Basing and other fortified houses see Porter, *Destruction in the Civil Wars*, and Ronald Hutton and Wylie Reeves, 'Sieges and Fortifications', in John Kenyon and Jane Ohlmeyer (eds), *The Civil Wars: A Military History of England, Scotland and Ireland, 1638–1660* (Oxford, 1998), pp. 195–233.

67. Christopher Morris (ed.), *The Journeys of Celia Fiennes* (London, 1947), p. 29.

68. Victor Smith and Peter Kelsey, 'The Lines of Communication: The Civil War Defences of London', in Stephen Porter (ed.), *London and the Civil War*, (London 1996), pp. 117–48.

69. PRO, Kew, SP 29/5 74.1, cited in John Bold, *John Webb: Architectural Theory and Practice in the Seventeenth Century* (Oxford, 1989), p. 175.

70. Rosemary Weinstein, 'Southampton House and the Civil War' in *Collectanea Londiniensia*, ed. Joanna Bird *et al.* (London, 1978), pp. 332–4.

71. Weinstein, 'Southampton House', p. 344.

72. Webb, *Letters*, p. 138: Vanbrugh to Brigadier Watkins, 26 August 1721.

73. For this vanished sub-culture, see in particular George MacDonald Fraser, *The Steel Bonnets* (London, 1971), and Godfrey Watson, *The Border Reivers* (London, 1974).

74. Murray G.H. Pittock, *Jacobitism* (Basingstoke, 1998), pp. 39–40.

75. Paul Kléber Monod, *Jacobitism and the English People, 1688–1788* (Cambridge, 1989), p. 317.

76. For pro-Stuart riots and other forms of popular protest, see Monod, *Jacobitism*, chs 6 and 7. For the major armed revolts, Bruce Lenman, *The Jacobite Risings in Britain, 1689–1746* (Edinburgh, 1995).

77. What happened to Deerfield, Massachusetts, in February 1704 is salutary: see Richard I. Melvoin, *New England Outpost: War and Society in Colonial Deerfield* (New York, 1989), and John Demos, *The Unredeemed Captive* (New York, 1994).

78. See the section on 'The Officer Architect' phenomenon in Rolf Loeber's Introduction, *A Biographical Dictionary of Architects in Ireland, 1600–1720* (London, 1981), pp. 4–5.

79. Loeber, *Dictionary*, p. 61. Lord Conway's English seat was at Ragley.

80. An axonometric reconstruction of Burton House and its fortified garden is illustrated in Rolf Loeber, 'Irish Country Houses and Castles of the Late Caroline Period: An Unremembered Past Recaptured', *Quarterly Bulletin of the Irish Georgian Society*, XVI/1–2 (1973), pl. 8.

81. Cited in Loeber, 'Irish Country Houses', p. 31.

82. For Derwentwater and his part in the rising see Frances Dickinson, *The Reluctant Rebel: A Northumbrian Legacy of Jacobite Times* (Newcastle upon Tyne, 1996).

83. Cited in the Etty entry in Colvin, *Dictionary*, p. 354.

84. Leo Gooch, *The Desperate Faction? The Jacobites of North-East England, 1688–1745* (Hull, 1995), p. 160.

85. For a tracing of Adam's plan, see Tim Buxbaum, *Scottish Garden Buildings* (Edinburgh, 1989), p. 13; for the unexecuted house the garden was built for, John Gifford, *William Adam, 1689–1748* (Edinburgh, 1989), pp. 99–100.

86. This is the same Stair who, in the the 1720s, put his dragoons to work to build huge ornamental earthworks in his lakeside grounds at Castle Kennedy; see A.G.L. Hellyer, 'A Garden with a Military Origin', *Country Life*, CL (12 August 1971), pp. 384–6.

87. John Cornforth, 'Castles for a Georgian Duke', *Country Life*, CLXXXV (8 October 1992), pp. 58–61.

88. Price, *An Essay on the Picturesque* (London, 1794), Part 2, pp. 260–61.

89. For Armstrong's canal system see David Green and James Bond, 'Blenheim after Vanbrugh: The Second Phase', in James Bond and Kate Tiller (eds), *Blenheim: Landscape for a Palace*, (Gloucester, 1987), pp. 80–6.

5. *Antiquaries, Theatre and Early Medievalism*

1. For Vanbrugh's work at Blackheath see Laurence Whistler, *The Imagination of Vanbrugh and his Fellow Artists* (London, 1954), pp. 200–6; Kerry Downes, 'The Little Colony on Greenwich Hill', *Country Life*, CLIX (27 May 1976), pp. 1406–8; Downes, *Vanbrugh* (London, 1977), pp. 93–100; W.E.L. Fletcher, 'The Maze Hill Estate of Sir John Vanbrugh', *Transactions of the Greenwich & Lewisham Antiquarian Society*, VIII (1978), pp. 136–42; Neil Rhind, *Blackheath Village & Environs, 1790–1970*, II (Blackheath, 1983); Clive Aslet, *The Story of Greenwich* (London, 1999), pp. 175–85.

2. Christopher Wren the younger, *Parentalia* (London, 1750), p. 297.

3. Antony à Wood's admiration for historic buildings is discussed in B. Sprague Allen, *Tides in English Taste* (Cambridge, Mass., 1937), II, pp. 49–51.

4. Evelyn's 'Account' is discussed in Allen, *Tides in English Taste*, II, pp. 45–7. Evelyn's translation has been published in facsimile (Farnborough: Gregg Press, 1970); for the 'Account' see pp. 115–42.

5. A term first used by this author in 'Early Medievalism: "To have built in heaven high towers"': The Castle as a Theme in English Architecture before the Gothic Revival', *A Gothick Symposium*, intro. J. Mordaunt Crook (London, 1983), unpaginated.

6. Geoffrey Webb (ed.), *The Letters* (London, 1928), p. 107: Vanbrugh to the Duke of Newcastle, 25 December 1718.

7. Webb, *Letters*, p. 8: Vanbrugh to Jacob Tonson, 13 July 1703.

8. Vanbrugh's 'massive and masculine' utilitarian style, which, as Howard Colvin states in his

Biographical Dictionary of British Architects, 1600–1840 (London, 1995), p. 1006, found expression in the buildings erected by Hawksmoor for the Board of Ordnance, is apparent in the Claremont Belvedere (*c.* 1715), the Kings Weston Brewhouse (*c.* 1715), the Old Ordnance Board Room at the Royal Arsenal, Greenwich (1718–20), and the Water Tower on the Palace Green at Kensington (1722–4). For illustrations of these see Kerry Downes, *English Baroque Architecture* (London, 1966), pls. 508–17.

9.   Other notable examples of this Baroque-medieval style, overloaded with military symbolism, are William Talman's 1702–4 remodelling of the courtyard front of Drayton House, Northamptonshire, for Sir John Germain, and General John Richmond Webb's Biddesden House, Wiltshire, where in 1711 the General built a round tower on the east front to house a bell looted from Lille. For these houses see James Lees-Milne, *English Country Houses: Baroque, 1685–1715* (London, 1970), pp. 95–101 and pp. 213–18 respectively.

10.   Arthur's exhumation is discussed in Norris J. Lacy (ed.), *The Arthurian Encyclopedia* (New York, 1986), and Geoffrey Ashe, *King Arthur's Avalon: The Story of Glastonbury* (1973), pp. 180–3.

11.   For the Arthurian legend, see Christopher Dean, *Arthur of England: English Attitudes to King Arthur and the Knights of the Round Table in the Middle Ages & the Renaissance* (Toronto, 1987); Rosemary Morris, *The Character of King Arthur in Medieval Literature* (Cambridge, 1982); Lacy, *Arthurian Encyclopedia*; R.F. Brinkley, *Arthurian Legend in the Seventeenth Century* (Baltimore, 1932); Mike Godwin, *One Man's Dream: The Story of King Arthur's Great Halls, Tintagel, Cornwall, England* (Tintagel, n.d.).

12.   John Summerson, *Architecture in Britain* (Harmondsworth, 1977), p. 46.

13.   Elizabeth's tours around the country are described in John Nichols, *The Progresses and Public Processions of Queen Elizabeth*, 3 vols (London, 1823); for the Accession Day ceremonies, see R.C. McCoy, *The Rites of Knighthood: The Literature and Politics of Elizabethan Chivalry* (Berkeley, Cal., 1989); G. Kipling, *The Triumph of Honour: Burgundian Origins of the Elizabethan Renaissance* (Leiden, 1977); Roy Strong, *The English Renaissance Miniature* (London, 1983); Timothy Mowl, *Elizabethan and Jacobean Style* (London, 1993), pp. 105–10.

14.   For Smythson, see Mark Girouard, *Robert Smythson and the Elizabethan Country House* (New Haven and London, 1983).

15.   For Bolsover, see Mowl, *Elizabethan and Jacobean Style*, pp. 117–23.

16.   Allen, *Tides in English Taste*, I, p. 52.

17.   For the growth of antiquarianism, see Joan Evans, *A History of the Society of Antiquaries* (Oxford, 1956); Kevin Sharpe, *Sir Robert Cotton, 1586–1631: History and Politics in Early Modern England* (Oxford, 1979); David Douglas, *English Scholars* (London, 1939); Graham Parry, *Trophies of Time: English Antiquaries of the Seventeenth Century* (Oxford, 1995); Levi Fox (ed.), *English Historical Scholarship in the 16th & 17th Centuries* (London, 1956); J.G.A. Pocock, *The Ancient Constitution of the Feudal Law: A Study of English Historical Thought in the 17th Century* (Cambridge, 1957); Stuart Piggott, *William Stukeley: An Eighteenth-Century Antiquary* (London, 1985); Piggott, *Ancient Britons and the Antiquarian Imagination* (London, 1989).

18.   Verstegan is covered in detail in Parry, *Trophies of Time*, ch. 2.

19.   Christian's visit to England is discussed in John A. Gade, *Christian IV: King of Denmark and Norway* (London, 1927), pp. 109–14; Ethel Carleton Williams, *Anne of Denmark: Wife of James VI of Scotland, James I of England* (Harlow, 1970), pp. 109–23. See also John Nichols, *The Progresses and Magnificent Festivities of King James the First* (London, 1828), II, p. 53.

20.   Pocock, *The Ancient Constitution*, is the main authority on this aspect.

21.   For Saxon scholarship see Douglas, *English Scholars*, ch. 3; also Parry, *Trophies of Time*.

22.   For both Magnus brothers, see Kurt Johannsen, *The Renaissance of the Goths in Sixteenth-Century Sweden* (Oxford, 1991). Olaus's volume went into at least twenty editions during the next century and was translated into French, Italian, German and English.

23.   There is a tale of 'bold Sir *Bruin*' in Spenser's *Faerie Queene*, Book VI, canto iv, 17–38.

24.   For Drayton and other instances of pre-Vanbrugh medievalisms see Mowl, 'Early Medievalism: "To have built in heaven high towers"'.

25.   Webb, *Letters*, p. 14: Vanbrugh to the Earl of Manchester, 18 July 1707. The slightly later 1709 design for his own house of Chargate in Surrey, which combines regularity with a towered, battlemented profile, shows that he would soon begin to experiment with more impressive, compact plans based on Elizabethan mock castles. For his debt to these plans and profiles see Kerry Downes, *Vanbrugh* (London, 1977), pp. 48–52.

26.   John Evelyn, *The Diary*, ed. E.S. De Beer (Oxford, 1955), III, p. 560.

27.   For a history of the Order see Peter J. Begent and Hubert Chesshyre, *The Most Noble Order of the Garter, 650 Years* (London, 1999).

28.   For Sammes see Parry, *Trophies of Time*, ch. 11.

29.   The most useful discussion of this aspect of Vanbrugh's oeuvre is Frank McCormick's *Sir John Vanbrugh: The Playwright as Architect* (University Park, Penn, 1991). I am grateful to Peter Goodchild for this reference.

30.   For the *Itinerarium* see Piggott, *William Stukeley*.

31.   Christopher Morris, (ed.), *The Journeys of Celia Fiennes* (London, 1947), p. 202.

32.   Webb, *Letters*, p. 138: Vanbrugh to Brigadier Watkins, 26 August 1721.

33.   For Lumley see Downes, *Vanbrugh*, pp. 106–7 and pl. 127.

34. For a handlist of plays see Allardyce Nicoll, *A History of English Drama 1600–1900, I: Restoration Drama, 1660–1700* (Cambridge, 1995), Appendix C, pp. 386–447. For background on the period see also John Loftis *et al.* (eds), *The Revels History of Drama in English, V: 1660–1750* (London, 1976).

35. Scenery is discussed in Nicoll, *History of English Drama*, I, pp. 144–8, and in Loftis, *The Revels History*, V, pp. 83–118.

36. The Palace itself became the backdrop for Joseph Addison's later *Rosamond* of 1707. A 'Grotto', presumably Rosamond's Well, transforms into a 'Country House'; see Nicoll, *History of English Drama, II: Early Eighteenth-Century Drama*, p. 31.

37. For Vanbrugh's admission to the College of Heralds, see Downes, *Vanbrugh*, p. 34.

38. There were also two verse epics based on Arthurian themes in this last decade of the century: Sir Richard Blackmore's *Prince Arthur: An Heroick Poem: In Ten Books* (1695) and his *King Arthur: An Heroick Poem: In Twelve Books* (1697).

39. *King Arthur*, Act I, scene iii.

40. Suggested by Downes and quoted in his *Vanbrugh*, p. 54 n. 39.

41. For Vanbrugh's many bastions and moated hahas, see Downes, *Vanbrugh*, p. 72; there is a moatable haha at Seaton Delaval, and a 'fossee' was projected for Kings Weston.

42. *King Arthur*, Act V, scene ii.

43. Downes, *Vanbrugh*, p. 66.

44. For Vanbrugh's 'Reasons Offer'd for Preserving some Part of the Old Manor' (11 June 1709), see this volume, p. 191.

45. Webb, *Letters*, p. 30.

46. For the history of Woodstock Manor and Rosamond's Bower, see H.M. Colvin (ed.), *The History of the King's Works, II: The Middle Ages* (London, 1993), pp. 1009–17.

47. Webb, *Letters*, p. 74: Vanbrugh to the Duchess of Marlborough, 27 July 1716.

48. Costumes are discussed in L.B. Campbell, 'A History of Costuming on the English Stage between 1660 and 1823', *University of Wisconsin Studies*, II (Madison, 1918), pp. 187–223, and Loftis, *The Revels History*, pp. 144–8. I am grateful to Michel Baridon for alerting me to Aaron Hill's later historical research into costume; apparently Hill designed a set of 'old Saxon habits' (never made up) for his tragedy *Athelwold* of 1731.

49. For a fuller account of Shirburn, see Timothy Mowl and Brian Earnshaw, 'The Origins of 18th-Century Neo-Medievalism in a Georgian Norman Castle', *Journal of the Society of Architectural Historians*, XL/4 (December 1981), pp. 289–94.

50. Since the publication of my article in 1981 it has, however, appeared in Giles Worsley's *Classical Architecture in Britain, The Heroic Age* (New Haven and London, 1995), p. 183, ill. 214.

51. For Clearwell, see Alistair Rowan, 'Clearwell Castle', in Howard Colvin and John Harris (eds), *The Country Seat* (London, 1970), pp. 145–9.

52. Webb, *Letters*, p. 164: Vanbrugh to the Earl of Carlisle, 10 December 1724.

53. Webb, *Letters*, p. 163: Vanbrugh to the Earl of Carlisle, 21 November 1724.

54. Nomenclature explained in a letter from Hawksmoor to the Dean of Westminster, 1734–5; quoted in Kerry Downes, *Hawksmoor* (2nd edn, London 1979), pp. 256.

55. Vanbrugh's similar respect for historic buildings is revealed in his attempt to save from demolition the Holbein Gate in Whitehall: 'I find many people Surpris'd there shou'd be no other Expedient found to make way for Coaches &c, than destroying One of the Greatest Curiositys there is in London as that Gate has ever been esteem'd', in Webb, *Letters*, p. 114: Vanbrugh to the Duke of Newcastle, 6 August 1719. I am grateful to Mr N.T.C. Walker for bringing this letter to my attention.

56. For Pelham and Esher see Timothy Mowl and Brian Earnshaw, *An Insular Rococo: Architecture, Politics and Society in Ireland and England, 1710–1770* (London, 1999), pp. 88–95; Timothy Mowl, *Horace Walpole: The Great Outsider* (London, 1996), pp. 121–2.

6. Exotics and Botanical Illustration

I am especially grateful to Robert Williams for supplying me with numerous reference materials and for giving generous support that enabled me to write this essay. I would also like to thank, for their help, Douglas Chambers, Catherine Danter, Kerry Downes, John Harris, Christopher Ridgway, Marja Smolenaars, Joan K. Stemmler, Ruth Stungo, Martin Williams, and Jan Woudstra.

1. Kerry Downes, *Sir John Vanbrugh, a Biography* (London, 1987), p. 485.

2. Robert J. Allen, *The Clubs of Augustan London* (Cambridge, Mass., 1933), p. 52, quoting from Edmund Curll's *Letters, Poems, and Tales: Amorous, Satyrical, and Gallant* of 1718.

3. Geoffrey Webb (ed.), *The Letters* (London, 1928), p. 8: July 1703.

4. Webb, *Letters*, p. 7.

5. Webb, *Letters*, pp. 7, 19, 26, 30, 70, 143.

6. Webb, *Letters*, p. 35.

7. Blanche Henrey, *British Botanical and Horticultural Literature before 1800* (London, 1975), II, p. 265.

8. Quoted from *The Life of Dr Henry Compton* (1713), p. 42, in Sandra Morris, 'Legacy of a Bishop: The Trees and Shrubs of Fulham Palace Gardens Introduced 1675–1713', *Garden History*, XIX/1 (1991), p. 49.

9. Stephen Switzer, *Ichnographia Rustica* (London, 1718), I, p. 70.

10. Joseph and Nesta Ewan, *John Banister and his Natural History of Virginia 1678–1692* (Urbana, Chicago and London, 1970).

11. See here Amy R.W. Meyers and Margaret Beck Pritchard, *Empire's Nature: Mark Catesby's New World Vision* (Chapel Hill, NC, and London, 1998).

12. Morris, 'Legacy of a Bishop', list compiled with the help of Dr John H. Harvey, pp. 57–9.

13. Sandra Morris, 'Legacy of a Bishop (Part 2): The Flowers of Fulham Palace Gardens Introduced 1675–1713', *Garden History*, XXI/1 (1993), list compiled with the help of Dr John H. Harvey, pp. 20–2. *Gillenia trifoliata* is mistakenly classified in the list of trees and shrubs in Morris's first article.

14. John H. Harvey, 'The English Nursery Flora, 1677–1723', *Garden History*, XXVI/1 (1998), pp. 60–101.

15. See here George Pasti Jr, 'Consul Sherard: Amateur Botanist and Patron of Learning', PhD thesis, University of Illinois at Urbana, 1950.

16. Quoted from L. Jessop, 'The Club at the Temple Coffee House: Facts and Supposition', *Archives of Natural History*, XVI/3 (1989), p. 268.

17. David Elliston Allen, *The Naturalist in Britain: A Social History* (London, 1976), p. 10.

18. See Jessop, 'The Club', pp. 263–74. The following references are quoted from Jessop's article.

19. Quoted from Marion Tinling (ed.), *The Correspondence of the Three William Byrds of Virginia, 1684–1776* (Charlottesville, Va, 1977), I, p .72. For further reading on coffee houses, see Alison Olson, 'Coffee House Lobbying', *History Today*, XLI (January 1991), pp. 35–41; William Ukers, *All About Coffee* (New York, 1935); and Bryant Lillywhite, *London Coffee Houses* (London, 1963). There is a very useful overview of coffee houses and clubs in John Brewer, *The Pleasures of the Imagination: English Culture in the Eighteenth Century* (London, 1997), pp. 34–50.

20. Quoted from Jessop, 'The Club', p. 269.

21. Jessop, 'The Club', pp. 268–9. The following quotations are also from pp. 268–9.

22. See Douglas Chambers, '"Storys of Plants": The Assembling of Mary Capel Somerset's Botanical Collection at Badminton', *Journal of the History of Collections*, IX/1 (1997), pp. 47–58.

23. See John Harris, *The Artist and the Country House from the Fifteenth Century to the Present Day*, exh. cat. (London, 1995), pp. 26–7.

24. Ruth Duthie, 'The Planting Plans of Some Seventeenth-Century Flower Gardens', *Garden History*, XVIII/1 (1990), p. 88.

25. Chambers, 'Storys of Plants', p. 50. Sloane MS 4072, f. 202.

26. Chambers, 'Storys of Plants', p. 50. Sloane MS 4071, f. 309.

27. Chambers, 'Storys of Plants', p. 51.

28. Pasti, 'Consul Sherard', p. 97. Sloane MS 4038, f. 47: Sherard to Sloane, 10 August 1700.

29. Pasti, 'Consul Sherard', p. 97. Sloane MS 4038, f. 58: Sherard to Sloane, 31 August 1700.

30. Pasti, 'Consul Sherard', p. 98. Sloane MS 4038, f. 84, 28 October 1700.

31. Pasti, 'Consul Sherard', p. 107.

32. Pasti, 'Consul Sherard', p. 112. Sloane MS 4063, f. 54 & f. 83.

33. Pasti, 'Consul Sherard', p. 112, n. 76. Sloane MS 4075, f. 262.

34. Gloria Cottesloe and Doris Hunt, *The Duchess of Beaufort's Flowers* (Exeter, 1983). The florilegium in the muniments room at Badminton is inscribed: 'This Book was drawn by Mr Kychious (from the Life growing) at Badminton who came thither the 21st of July 1703, & staid there till the 14th of July 1705.' See Wilfrid Blunt and William T. Stearn, *The Art of Botanical Illustration* (Woodbridge, Suffolk, 1994), p. 146. Kychious also worked for Sir Hans Sloane to illustrate West Indian plants: *Catalogus Plantarum quae in Insula Jamaica* (London, 1696).

35. See Harvey, 'English Nursery Flora', p. 80. Harvey gives 1690 as the date of introduction, but elsewhere 1680.

36. See Morris, 'Legacy of a Bishop (Part 2)', p. 20.

37. See again Harvey, 'English Nursery Flora', p. 60 and n. 8, for a discussion of Henry Wise's list, which is reproduced in David Green, *Gardener to Queen Anne: Henry Wise (1653–1738) and the Formal Garden* (London, 1956), pl. 52.

38. See Mark Laird, *The Flowering of the Landscape Garden: English Pleasure Grounds 1720–1800* (Philadephia, 1999), pp. 204–11.

39. See Duthie, 'The Planting Plans', pp. 77–102 and especially p. 95 for a discussion of planting at Beaufort House and the role of florists' flowers.

40. Chambers, 'Storys of Plants', p. 47.

41. For discussion of the Danckert painting, see Harris, *Artist and the Country House from the Fifteenth Century*, exh. cat., pp. 26–7.

42. Both views are reproduced in John Harris, *The Artist and the Country House* (London, 1979), nos. 125a and 125b. See also Howard Colvin, 'Georgian Architects at Badminton', *Country Life* (4 April 1968), pp. 800–4. John Harris has suggested to me that the wilderness proposals appear to be in a 'slightly harder drawing style' that suggests Wise rather than London. He also suspects that the Smith paintings represent the actual layout in the period after 1706, possibly around 1708–10 when the old laundry was already built.

43. John Peachy (*c.* 1680–1744), later Sir John Peachey, 2nd Bt, and MP. In 1771 their granddaughter Georgiana (died 1772) married George, Lord Greville, later 2nd Earl of Warwick.

44. See Gordon D. Rowley, 'The Duchess of Beaufort's Succulent Plants', *Bradleya*, V (1987), pp. 1–16; and Jean O'Neill, 'The Stove House and the Duchess', *Country Life* (20 January 1983), pp. 142–3.

45. Kerry Downes, *Vanbrugh* (London, 1977), p. 107.

46. Switzer, *Ichnographia Rustica*, II, p. 174.

47. Quoted from Green, *Gardener to Queen Anne*, p. 107.

48. For the planting records for Blenheim, see Green, *Gardener to Queen Anne*, pp. 107–11. BL, Add MS 19592, ff. 99v–100, 19593, ff. 142v–143, 19594, f. 12 and f. 49. I am grateful to Douglas Chambers and Jan Woudstra for allowing me to consult their transcriptions of these manuscripts. For the later history of the

'military garden' at Blenheim, see David W. Booth, 'Blenheim Park on the Eve of "Mr. Brown's Improvements"', *Journal of Garden History*, XV (1995), pp. 107–10. For a discussion of Wise's plant lists (reproduced in Green, *Gardener to Queen Anne*, pl. 52), see Harvey, 'English Nursery Flora', n. 14, p. 60 and especially his n. 8. The list appears to date from after 1712, as Wise includes the exotics *Malva hispanica* (introduced 1710) and *Amaryllis belladonna* (introduced 1712).

49. Webb, *Letters*, p. 146.
50. Webb, *Letters*, p. 135.
51. Webb, *Letters*, p. 136.
52. See Joyce E. Chaplin, 'Mark Catesby, a Skeptical Newtonian in America', in Meyers and Pritchard, *Empire's Nature*, pp. 34–90 and especially p. 74.
53. Quoted from Pasti, 'Consul Sherard', p. 153.
54. Pasti, 'Consul Sherard', p. 153. Sloane MS 4067, f. 147.
55. Pasti, 'Consul Sherard', p. 193.
56. Quoted from David R. Brigham, 'Mark Catesby and the Patronage of Natural History in the First Half of the Eighteenth Centuy', in Meyers and Pritchard, *Empire's Nature*, p. 96.
57. Brigham, 'Mark Catesby and the Patronage', p. 96, Brigham's own words.
58. Quoted from Pasti, 'Consul Sherard', p. 196.
59. David Elliston Allen, 'John Martyn's Botanical Society: A Biographical Analysis of the Membership', *Proceedings of the Botanical Society of the British Isles*, VI (1967), pp. 305–24 and especially p. 308.
60. Allen, 'John Martyn's Botanical Society', p. 321.
61. For John Martyn's *Historia*, the Yorkshireman Elisha Kirkall (*c*. 1682–1742) pioneered a new method of printing several colours from a single plate. Wilfrid Blunt called it a 'half-hearted imitation' of true mezzotint. See Blunt and Stearn, *Art of Botanical Illustration*, p. 147.
62. Seven were printed by Kirkall by his new method, and fourteen etched and hand-coloured by Henry Fletcher.
63. For Mark Catesby's rôle in stimulating the consumer boom, see Mark Laird, 'From Callicarpa to Catalpa: The Impact of Mark Catesby's Plant Introductions on English Gardens of the Eighteenth Century', in Meyers and Pritchard, *Empire's Nature*, pp. 184–227. For the way John Bartram and Peter Collinson fuelled the mania for American plants, and for the later history of the shrubbery, see Laird, *The Flowering*.
64. Blunt and Stearn, *Art of Botanical Illustration*, p. 147.
65. Blunt and Stearn, *Art of Botanical Illustration*, pp. 150–1. Henry Fletcher's engravings were after paintings by the Flemish artist Pieter Casteels.
66. Henrey, *British Botanical and Horticultural Literature*, II, p. 213.
67. Henrey, *British Botanical and Horticultural Literature*, II, p. 270.
68. Castle Howard Archives, J8/1/462, 23 December 1734, cited in *Historical Manuscripts Commission*. Fifteenth Report, Appendix, Part VI (1897), p. 143.
69. See David Coombs, 'The Garden at Carlton House of Frederick, Prince of Wales, and Augusta, Princess Dowager of Wales: Bills in Their Household Accounts 1728–1772', *Garden History*, XXV/2 (1997), pp. 153–77.
70. See again Laird, *The Flowering*, especially pp. 219–24.
71. Laird, *The Flowering*, p. 169.
72. There are some interesting individual flowers, such as the 'Jacobea or Sea ragwort' (probably *Senecio elegans*, introduced 1700) or the six 'China pinks in pots' (*Dianthus chinensis*, introduced 1713), but the lists suggest much reliance on the traditional flowers available in the seventeenth century. For a discussion of the relationship of woody species to flowers in the horticultural revolution of the landscape garden, see Mark Laird, 'John Bartram's Herbaceous Plant Exports', in the forthcoming publication of proceedings from the 'Bartram 300' symposium held at Philadelphia, May 1999.
73. Charles Saumarez Smith, *The Building of Castle Howard* (London, 1990), pp. 177–84.
74. See John Dixon Hunt, 'Castle Howard Revisited', in *Gardens and the Picturesque: Studies in the History of Landscape Architecture* (Cambridge, Mass., 1992), p. 30.
75. Martin Williams has suggested to me that 'poke' was an ingredient used as an aphrodisiac, but Kerry Downes and Douglas Chambers both subscribe to an alternative reading: that a hot 'poker' was dipped into the 'cup' to turn the contents into a mulled beverage. Further doubt is cast on the first reading by the dates of introduction for the various North American plants known as 'poke'. All appear to have been introduced into England after 1720: *Veratrum viride* (1742), which is poisonous; *Nicotiana rustica* (1750), a form of tobacco; and *Phytolacca americana* (1768), whose berries early colonists used to improve cheap wine.

7. Vanbrugh's India and his Mausolea for England

My grateful thanks to Lesley Henderson for her generous help during my research into Vanbrugh's India sojourn. I am also indebted to Kerry Downes for his warm encouragement, and to Margaret Downes for her kindness in supplying me with many details concerning Vanbrugh's family and relatives.

1. That Vanbrugh had worked in India in the early 1680s as an employee of the East India Company was first explained in my article on 'Vanbrugh's Lost Years' in the *Times Literary Supplement*, 5031 (3 September 1999), pp. 13–14.
2. See Nicholas Cooper, 'Indian Architecture in England, 1780-1830', *Apollo* (August 1970), pp. 124–33; Patrick Conner, *Oriental Architecture in the West* (London, 1979), ch. 9.

3. Even so, the whimsical – Edwardian? – *chatri*-like open lantern housing the gardener's bell that is silhouetted atop one wall of Vanbrugh's kitchen-garden at Blenheim is an irritatingly provocative presence.

4. Kerry Downes, *Sir John Vanbrugh, a Biography* (London, 1987), p. 46.

5. Delboe's new appointment was confirmed by the London Court of Committees on 4 November 1675: Ethel Bruce Sainsbury, *A Calendar of the Court Minutes, etc., of the East India Company*, X: *1674–1676* (Oxford, 1935), p. 234.

6. Downes, *Sir John Vanbrugh*, p. 19; E.W. Hutchinson, *Adventurers in Siam in the Seventeenth Century* (London, 1940), p. 54.

7. Kerry Downes, *Vanbrugh* (London, 1977), p. 155 (Breton); p. 156, n. 36 (Pearce).

8. Concerning the Company's rules for its servants, see Ottewill's Introduction in Sainsbury, *Calendar of the Court Minutes, XI: 1677–1679* (1938), pp. xxi–xxiii; for the oaths, pp. 180-4.

9. British Library, London, India Office Records, Court Minutes, B/37, f. 68 (9 October) and f. 88 (8 November). The Company's Bonds and Covenants have not survived, but a unique (?late eighteenth century) index of them is in the John Rylands Library, University of Manchester, Eng. MS 153. A copy of Peter Bailey's typescript (June 1996) of this document is in the British Library's Oriental and India Library, and on p. 27 of it Vanbrugh's name appears three times – in connection with 'Surety', 'Bond to Perform Covenant' and 'Covenant and Bond'.

10. India Office Records, Court Minutes, B/37, f. 131.

11. For the Company's ships and their service dates see Jean Sutton, *Lords of the East: The East India Company and its Ships* (London, 1981), Appx 9.

12. India Office Records, E/3/90, Letter Book 7 (1682–5), f. 141.

13. The classic account of the Company's fortunes for the period 1600-1800 is John Keay, *The Honourable Company: A History of the East India Company* (London, 1993).

14. A useful tool for negotiating this labyrinthine collection is Martin Moir, *A General Guide to the India Office Records* (London, 1996).

15. For India specifically, see Meera Nanda, *European Travel Accounts During the Reigns of Shajahan and Aurangzeb* (Kurukshetra, 1994), and Kate Telscher, *India Inscribed: European and British Writing on India, 1600–1800* (Delhi, 1995).

16. Discussed in Partha Mitter, *Much Maligned Monsters: A History of European Reactions to Indian Art* (Chicago, 1992), pp. 57-9.

17. For example, the Indian boy included in Peter Lely's portrait in oils *Lady Charlotte Fitzroy*, *c.* 1672 (York City Art Gallery). Another example is the misidentified 'negro' in James Maubert's group portrait *Edward Bathurst and Family*, *c.* 1716, reproduced in Andrew Wilton, *The Swagger Portrait*, exh. cat., Tate Gallery (London, 1992), p. 104, fig. 30.

18. India Office Records, E/3/90, Letter Book 7 (1682–5), f. 141, a letter from London to Surat, 4 May 1683 carried on board the *Scipio*.

19. India Office Factory Records, G/36/91, ff. 66-7, lists the Surat staff, including Vanbrugh, in January 1684; for Vanbrugh lading the *Success* before it sailed for England on 6 January 1684, see G/36/91, f. 69.

20. For their reports see John Fryer, *A New Account of East India and Persia* (1698), in William Crooke's Hakluyt Society edition, 3 vols (London, 1909-15); John Ovington, *A Voyage to Surat in the Year 1689* (1696), in H.G. Rawlinson's edition (Oxford, 1929); and Alexander Hamilton, *A New Account of the East Indies*, 2 vols (1727), in Sir William Foster's edition, 2 vols (London, 1930).

21. Ovington, *Voyage to Surat*, p. 131.

22. Hamilton, *A New Account of the East Indies*, I, p. 96.

23. Fryer, *East India and Persia*, p. 84.

24. Ovington, *Voyage to Surat*, pp. 229-35.

25. For a summary account of the materials produced for European markets in this period, see Veronica Murphy, 'Europeans and the Textile Trade', in John Guy and Deborah Swallow (eds), *Arts of India, 1550-1900* (London, 1990), pp. 153–71.

26. Fryer, *East India and Persia*, p. 86.

27. Fryer, *East India and Persia*, p. 84.

28. India Office Factory Records, G/36/92, f. 39, 16 February 1685.

29. India Office Records, E/3/90, Letter Book 7 (1682–5), f. 493, 12 August 1685.

30. Fryer, *East India and Persia*, p. 427.

31. See John Barnard, 'Sir John Vanbrugh: Two Unpublished Letters', *Huntington Library Quarterly*, XXIX (1965-6), p. 348.

32. For an account see Howard Colvin: 'Fifty New Churches', *Architectural Review*, CVII (March 1950), pp. 189-96, 209-10. Two important recent publications of relevance are E.G.W. Bill, *The Queen Anne Churches: A Catalogue of the Papers in Lambeth Palace Library of the Commission for Building Fifty New Churches in London and Westminster, 1711–1759*, intro. H. M. Colvin (London, 1979); and M.H. Port (ed.), *The Commissions for Building Fifty New Churches: The Minute Books, 1711–17, A Calendar*, London Record Society, vol. XXIII (London, 1986).

33. This document exists in two versions, both of which are in the Bodleian Library, Oxford. One version (MS Rawl. B. 376, ff. 351r-352v) is Appx E in Downes, *Vanbrugh* (London, 1977), pp. 257-8. The other (MS Eng. Hist. C. 2. ff. 47-9) was first published by their discoverer, Howard Colvin, as 'Mr Van-Brugg's Proposals', *Architectural Review*, CVII (March 1950), pp. 209-10, where Colvin assumed that the handwriting and both sketches it includes are Hawksmoor's; it can also be found in Laurence Whistler, *The Imagination of Vanbrugh and his Fellow Artists* (London, 1954), pp. 250-52.

34. Christopher Wren the younger, *Parentalia* (London, 1750), p. 319.
35. Wren, *Parentalia*, p. 268.
36. John Evelyn, *London Revived: Consideration for its Rebuilding in 1666*, ed. E.S. De Beer (Oxford, 1938), p. 40.
37. Commissioners' Minutes for 14 November 1711, cited in Susan Lang, 'Vanbrugh's Theory and Hawksmoor's Buildings', *Journal of the Society of Architectural Historians*, XXIV/2 (May 1965), p. 128, n. 8.
38. For Hawksmoor's Bethnal Green project, see Downes, *Hawksmoor*, World of Art series (London, 1970), pp. 100-1, 106; Downes, *Hawksmoor* (London, 1979), pp. 162–3 & pl. 52a; and for a fascinating exploration of its primitivist implications, Pierre de la Ruffinière Du Prey, 'Hawksmoor's "Basilica after the Primitive Christians": Architecture and Theology', *Journal of the Society of Architectural Historians*, XLVIII/38 (March 1989), pp. 38-52.
39. Du Prey, 'Hawksmoor's "Basilica"', p. 42.
40. Julien Litten, *The English Way of Death: The Common Funeral since 1450* (London, 1991), p. 221.
41. This manner of deploying pyramids at the angles was included by Robert Castell in the engraving that reconstructs the supposed plan of Pliny's villa garden at Laurentinum in Castell's *The Villas of the Ancients Illustrated* (1728).
42. Howard Colvin, *Architecture and the After-Life* (New Haven and London, 1991), pp. 312–13. Colvin's chapter XIV, 'The Return of the Mausoleum', is an essential account of the establishment of the mausoleum in England as a fashionable building type, although here Colvin somehow fails to grasp the crucial rôle Vanbrugh played in it.
43. Colvin, *Architecture and the After-Life*, p. 309.
44. Colvin, *Architecture and the After-Life*, cites several examples, as does David Coffin, *The English Garden: Meditation and Memorial* (Princeton, NJ, 1994), ch. IV: 'Burial in the Garden'.
45. Wren's design is reproduced in Colvin, *Architecture and the After-Life*, ill. 287; in Geoffrey Beard, *The Work of Christopher Wren* (Edinburgh, 1982), ill. 95; and in Margaret Whinney, *Wren*, World of Art series (London, 1971), ill. 127. For a full account see R.A. Beddard, 'Wren's Mausoleum for Charles I', *Architectural History*, XXVII (1984).
46. See Colvin, *Architecture and the After-Life*, p. 309.
47. The design is reproduced in Downes, *Hawksmoor* (1979), pl. 10b.
48. Geoffrey Webb (ed.), *The Letters* (London, 1928), p. 147: Vanbrugh to the Earl of Carlisle, 19 June 1722, explaining the idea for a Mausoleum at Blenheim, 'I have taken the liberty, to mention . . . what your Ldship designs [wants] at Castle Howard, and has been practic'd by the most polite peoples before Priestcraft got poor Carcasses into their keeping, to make a litttle money of'.
49. Webb, *Letters*, p. 147: Vanbrugh to the Earl of Carlisle, 19 June 1722.
50. See Colvin, *Architecture and the After-Life*, ill. 140.
51. MS Rawl. B. 376, f. 352r.
52. A.F. Bellasis, *An Account of the Old Tombs in the Cemeteries of Surat* (Bombay, 1861), p. 6. A handy illustrated guidebook to the English, Dutch and Armenian cemeteries is R.N. Shelat and M.R. Bhatt, *Conservation of Built Environment: The Historic Cemeteries, Surat* (Surat, 1995), initiated by the city's Heritage Trust.
53. Details given to Streynsham Marshall in 1672, and cited in R. Barlow and Henry Yule (eds), *The Diary of William Hedges, Esq.*, 3 vols (London, 1887-9), II, p. cccvii.
54. Philip Davies, *The Penguin Guide to the Monuments of India, II: Islamic, Rajput, European* (London, 1989), p. 393.
55. William Foster, *The English Factories in India, 1634–1636*, V (Oxford, 1911), p. 87, n. 2.
56. The complete text has been transcribed and recorded in Bellasis, *Account of the Old Tombs*, p. 17.
57. See note 7 above.
58. A trawl through the indices for the seventeen volumes that make up Foster's and Sir Charles Fawcett's *English Factories in India*, which cover the period 1618-84, and those for the eleven volumes of E. B. Sainsbury's *Calendar of the Court Minutes*, covering 1635-79, reveals a scattering of Bretons, all related one suspects.
59. Sainsbury, *Calendar of the Court Minutes, VI: 1660-1663* (1922), p. 110.
60. Downes, *Sir John Vanbrugh*, p. 28.
61. Downes, *Vanbrugh*, p. 156. If these two Pearces are one and the same, then the former Surat President would be grandfather to the architect Sir Edward Lovett Pearce.
62. Sainsbury, *Calendar of the Court Minutes, V: 1655-1659* (1916), p. xii.
63. J. Grélot, *A Late Voyage to Constantinople* (London, 1683), p. 217 (translated from the French edition of 1681).
64. Ovington, *Voyage to Surat*, p. 198.
65. Ovington, *Voyage to Surat*, p. 221.
66. Hamilton, *A New Account of the East Indies*, I, p. 95.
67. Vidya Dehejia, *Indian Art* (London, 1997), p. 258.
68. Cited in Charles Saumarez Smith, *The Building of Castle Howard* (London, 1990), p. 168.
69. Cited in David Green, *Sarah, Duchess of Marlborough* (London, 1967), p. 263.
70. Ovington, *Voyage to Surat*, p. 146.
71. Hugh Meller, *London Cemeteries: An Illustrated Guide and Gazetteer*, 2nd edn (Godstone, 1985), footnote on p. 9.
72. See James Stevens Curl, *A Celebration of Death: An Introduction to Some of the Buildings, Monuments and Settings of Funerary Architecture in the Western European Tradition* (London, 1993), ch. 7.

73. For these and other examples, see Conner, *Oriental Architecture in the West*, and John Sweetman, *The Oriental Obsession: Islamic Inspiration in British and American Art and Architecture, 1500-1920* (Cambridge, 1991).

74. For a recent photograph of this intriguing portal, see Gwyn Headley and Wim Meulenkamp, *Follies, Grottoes and Garden Buildings* (London, 1999), p. 563.

75. J.C. Harle and A. Topsfield, *Indian Art in the Ashmolean* (Oxford, 1987), p. 40.

76. Barlow and Yule, *The Diary of William Hedges*, I, p. 68.

8. 'After ye Antique': Vanbrugh, Hawksmoor and Kent

I would like to thank John Harris, whose earlier ideas of the Roman civic nature of Vanbrugh's garden designs helped stimulate this essay. He, David Jacques, and the editors all made very helpful comments on the earlier draft of it, for which I am most grateful. Sir Howard Colvin very kindly transcribed for me the relevant sections of Kent's library sale catalogue in the Bodleian Library.

1. John Summerson, *Architecture in Britain*, (Harmondsworth, 1977), p. 317.

2. This paper develops ideas first touched on in my *Classical Architecture in Britain: The Heroic Age* (New Haven and London, 1995) to which readers are directed for a fuller discussion of the nature of Palladianism and neo-Classicism in early eighteenth-century Britain and the problems inherent in conventional assumptions of stylistic divisions. See, in particular, chapters 5 and 6.

3. John Harris, *The Artist and the Country House* (London, 1979), nos. 192a–e and 193. Harris's ill. 193 is identified by Harris as the stables and entrance lodges at Esher. John Rocque's plan of the gardens at Claremont of 1750 makes it clear that the buildings on the right in no. 193 are, in fact, Claremont's Home Farm.

4. Demolished, and best illustrated by a watercolour in Sir John Soane's Museum; see Geoffrey Beard, *The Work of John Vanbrugh* (London, 1986), ill. 3.

5. Victoria and Albert Museum, D124–91; see Beard, *Vanbrugh*, ill. 84.

6. Kerry Downes, *Vanbrugh* (London, 1977); Michael I. Wilson, *William Kent: Architect, Designer, Painter, Gardener, 1685–1748* (London, 1984); John Dixon Hunt, *William Kent: Landscape Garden Designer* (London, 1987), p. 143; John Harris, *William Kent 1685–1748: A Poet on Paper*, exh. cat., Sir John Soane's Museum (London, 1998), p. 30.

7. Harris, *Artist and the Country House*, p. 187, no. 193.

8. See John Martin Robinson, *Temples of Delight: Stowe Landscape Gardens* (London, 1990), p. 68.

9. Colen Campbell, *Vitruvius Britannicus*, III (London, 1725), pl. 77–8.

10. H. Colvin and M. Craig, *Architectural Drawings in the Library of Elton Hall by Sir John Vanbrugh and Sir Edward Lovett Pearce* (London, 1964), cat. 200, pl. XXXVIIa.

11. Although the site of the pavilion is marked in the version of the Rocque engraving of Claremont in Badeslade and Rocque's *Vitruvius Britannicus* of 1738, the vignette is not included. This appears in a subsequent state. See Hunt, *William Kent*, pp. 71–2.

12. *Claremont Landscape Gardens*, National Trust guidebook (1984), ill. 15.

13. Beard, *Work of John Vanbrugh*, ill. 9.

14. Hunt, *William Kent*, cats 50, 52, 53.

15. Robinson, *Temples of Delight*, p. 74.

16. Hunt, *William Kent*, cat. 34.

17. Beard, *Work of John Vanbrugh*, ill. 77.

18. Kerry Downes, *Hawksmoor* (London, 1979), pl. 56a.

19. Hunt, *William Kent*, cat. 18.

20. Hunt, *William Kent*, cat. 55.

21. Harris, *Artist and the Country House*, no. 317.

22. Hunt, *William Kent*, cat. 107.

23. Hunt, *William Kent*, cat. 62.

24. Hunt, *William Kent*, cat. 114.

25. Hunt, *William Kent*, cat. 65.

26. Edmund Spenser, *The Faerie Queene* (London, 1751), I, p. 305.

27. Hunt, *William Kent*, cat. 49.

28. Summerson, *Architecture in Britain*, pp. 338, 341–3.

29. Worsley, *Classical Architecture in Britain*, pp. 129–51.

30. Richard Hewlings, 'Chiswick House and Gardens: Appearance and Meaning', in *Lord Burlington: Architecture, Art and Life*, ed. Toby Barnard and Jane Clark (London, 1995), pp. 1–150.

31. Neither Ligorio nor Montano published in their own lifetimes, but their work circulated in manuscript and subsequently appeared in publications by others. Ligorio's 'Descrittione della superba e magnificentissima Villa Tiburtina Hadriana' was published in J.G. Graevius, *Thesaurus antiquitatem et historiarum Italiae* (Leiden, 1723), vol. VIII/4. G.B. Soria published four volumes of Montano's designs, *Architettura con diversi ornamenti cavati dal antico da Gio. Battista Montano* (Rome, 1624); *Scielta di varii tempietti antici. Con le piante et alzatte desegnati in prospettiva D.M. Gio. Batta. Montano Milanese* (Rome, 1624); *Diversi ornamenti capricciosi per deposti o altari, utilissimi a virtuosi. Novamente inventati da M. Giovanbatista Montano* (Rome, 1625); *Tabernacoli diversi, novamente inventati da M. Giovanbatista Montano* (Rome, 1628). Kent's mentor in Rome, John Talman, purchased the 'Old Rome of Pirro Ligorio in 10 sheets', Ligorio's three-dimensional reconstruction of ancient Rome (Talman letters, fols. 118, 124, cited by Hunt, *William Kent*, pp. 16, 104 n. 7). Androuet du Cerceau, *Quoniam apud veteres alio structurae genere*

32. Hunt, *William Kent*, pp. 16–7.
33. J.B. Fischer von Erlach, *Entwurf einer Historischen Architektur* (Vienna, 1721).
34. D.J. Watkin (ed.), *Sale Catalogues of Eminent Persons, IV: Architects* (London, 1972), pp. 99–105.
35. It is important to note that Kent also differed from his fellow neo-Palladians in his interest in the more heavily rusticated elements of Palladio's work and of Palladio's predecessors, particularly Giulio Romano.
36. Transcribed in Downes, *Vanbrugh*, pp. 257–8. It is, however, useful for the parallels it reveals with Colen Campbell's thinking (see Worsley, *Classical Architecture in Britain*, pp. 99–100).
37. Stephen Switzer, *Ichnographia Rustica* (London, 1718), II, p. 174.
38. Howard Colvin, 'The Grand Bridge in Blenheim Park', *Essays in English Architectural History* (New Haven and London, 1999), illus. 205–6.
39. Bernard de Montfaucon, *Antiquité Expliquée* (Paris, 1722), V, pl. 29.
40. See Robinson, *Temples of Delight*, p. 113. Although one must remember that Vanbrugh's high dome has been lowered.
41. *Les Dix Livres d'Architecture de Vitruve*, ed Claude Perrault (Paris, 1684), pl. XXXV.
42. *Les Dix Livres*, ed. Perrault, pl. IX.
43. Campbell, *Vitruvius Britannicus*, III, pls. 15, 18. John Harris in 'Diverting Labyrinths', *Country Life*, CLXXXIV (11 January 1990), pp. 62–5, raises the question of Eastbury's Antique overtones, but does not develop the Praeneste connection.
44. Rudolf Wittkower, 'Pietro da Cortona's Project for Reconstructing the Temple of Palestrina', *Studies in the Italian Baroque* (London, 1975), pp. 116–24.
45. Campbell, *Vitruvius Britannicus*, III, pl. 4.
46. Recorded in John Dixon Hunt, 'Castle Howard Revisited', *Gardens and the Picturesque: Studies in the History of Landscape Architecture* (Cambridge, Mass., 1992), pp. 27–30, 340 n. 22.
47. Geoffrey Webb, 'The Letters and Drawings of Nicholas Hawksmoor Relating to the Building of the Mausoleum at Castle Howard, 1726–1742', *Walpole Society*, XIX (1930–1); Kerry Downes, *Hawksmoor*, World of Art series (London, 1970), p. 195, ill. 175; Roger White, *Nicholas Hawksmoor and the Replanning of Oxford*, exh. cat. (London and Oxford, 1997); Worsley, *Classical Architecture in Britain*, pp. 54–63.
48. Watkin, *Sale Catalogues . . . Architects*, pp. 81–105.
49. Philip Ayres, 'Burlington's Library at Chiswick', *Studies in Bibliography*, XLV (1992), pp. 113–27.
50. Chatsworth Archives, reproduced in Hunt, *William Kent*, p. 14.
51. *A Catalogue of the library of William Kent, Esq: Late Principal Painter and Architect to his Majesty. Which will be Sold at Auction, by Mr Langford, At his House (Late Mr Cock's) in the Great Piazza, Covent-Garden. On Tuesday the 14th of February, 1748–9* (Bodleian Library, Oxford, Mus. Bibl. III 8 20). The catalogue lists 114 items, including:

Octavo
2 Nummi Britannici, – Allingham's Introduct. to Mathematicks – – 1715. (Bought by 'Fisher')
4 Ware's Palladio, *finely bound* – 1742. (Bought by 'Dr Chauncey')
6 Didoro Siculo, in Firenz. 1526 – Appian Alexandrino, in Venet. 1550. (Bought by 'B')
15 La Vita & Metamorfoseo d'Ovidio, *con fig. a Lione* 1559 – Apuleio dell'Asino – *in Firenz.* 1603
29 Pantheisticon, – *Cosmop.* 1720 (bought by 'Ld. C.')
30 Horatiana Emblemata, – Amst. 1684. (bought by 'Dr Wils'?)
33 Sermoni, Altrimenti Satire di Horatio – *in Vineg.* 1559. (Bought by 'F')

Quarto
35 Terence, Eng. & Lat. 1598.
39 Drawings of some Ruins and Colossal Statues at Thebes in Egypt, *sew'd* – 1741 (Bought by 'Dr R')
44 Le Metamorfosi di Ovidio, *con. fig. Ven* 1584. ('Browne')
48 Le Deche di T. Livio, 2 vol. Ven. 1581. ('Br')
51 Delle Imagini de gli Dei Delli Antichi di Vicenzo Cortari Reggiani – *in Pad.* 1626.
58 Discourse de la Religion des Anciens Romains – *Lyon* 1581.
63 Dicei Libri di dell Archit. M. Vitruvio, *con fig. Ven.* 1584.
75 Morris's Defence of ancient Architecture – 1728.

Folio
80 Serly's Architecture 1611.
81 Turnbull's Treatise of ancient Painting, *best Edit, with fine Cuts* – 1740 (bought by 'Dr Ch')
92 La Hypnerotomachia di Poliphilo, cioe Pregna d'Amore in Sogno – *Ven.* 1545. (Bought by 'B')
96 Hypnerotomache, ou Discourses de Poliphile *Par.* 1561 (Bought by 'B')
98 Il Romo d'Oro, Festa Teatrale Rappresenta in Vienna, *con fig.*
99 M. Vitruvii de Architectura Libri Decem. *Ven.* 1567.
105 Histoire de la Peinture Ancienne de Pline – 1735
108 Ware's four Books of Palladio's Architecture – 1738
114 L'antiquité Expliquée & Represente en Figures, par Montfaucon. 15 vol. *grand Papier* – Par. 1722.

52. Downes, *Hawksmoor* (1979), pl. 29b.
53. See Wilson, *William Kent*, ills. 67–8.
54. Bomarzo in Lazio, north of Rome, is one rare example.
55. Charles Saumarez Smith, *The Building of Castle Howard* (London, 1990), p. 149.
56. Saumarez Smith, *Castle Howard*, pp. 124–5.
57. Eileen Harris, *British Architectural Books and Writers, 1556–1785* (Cambridge, 1990), pp. 139–44.

58. Quoted in John Dixon Hunt, *Garden and Grove* (London, 1986), pp. 218.
59. Pliny, *Natural History*, Book XXXVI, IV, 23, 25, quoted by Betsy Rosasco, 'The Sculptural Decorations of the Garden of Marly: 1679–1699', *Journal of Garden History*, IV (1984), pp. 105–6.
60. *Les Dix Livres*, ed. Perrault, pl. LVI.
61. This is Hunt's assumption; see 'Castle Howard Revisited', p. 22.
62. A copy of the 1664 edition survives in the library at Castle Howard. While it does not have the 3rd Earl's pressmark, it is likely to be contemporary.
63. *Les Dix Livres*, ed. Perrault, pls. IX, LXV.
64. Rosasco, 'Sculptural Decorations', pp. 105–6.
65. Rosasco, 'Sculptural Decorations', p. 118.
66. Harris, *British Architectural Books and Writers*, p. 154 n. 25.
67. Wittkower, 'Pietro da Cortona's Project', p. 120.
68. François de Polignac *et al.*, *La Fascination de L'Antique, 1700–1770: Rome découverte, Rome inventée*, exh. cat. (Paris, 1998).
69. Stuart Piggott, *William Stukeley, An Eighteenth-century Antiquary* (London, 1985), p. 55.
70. Francis Drake, *Eboracum: The History and Antiquities of the City of York* (York, 1736), Dedication, p. 60.
71. Philip Ayres, *Classical Culture and the Idea of Rome* (Cambridge, 1997).
72. Kerry Downes, *Sir John Vanbrugh, a Biography* (London, 1987), p. 461.
73. Saumarez Smith, *Castle Howard*, p. 3.
74. Worsley, *Classical Architecture in Britain*, p. 106.
75. Horace Walpole, 'The History of the Modern Taste in Gardening', in *The Works of Horatio Walpole, Earl of Orford* (London, 1798), II, p. 538; W.S. Lewis (ed.), *Horace Walpole's Correspondence*, IX (New Haven, 1941), p. 291.

9. Stephen Switzer and Water Gardens

I wish to thank Viscountess Campden at Exton Park, Lord Neidpath at Stanway, and Mr Leo Godlewski at Shireoaks for the time they gave to me to discuss their cascades, and David Jacques and Robert Williams for their help during the preparation of this essay.

1. Roy Strong, *The Renaissance Garden in England* (London, 1979), pp. 73–112.
2. The fullest account of Switzer's career is W.A. Brogden, 'Stephen Switzer and Garden Design in Britain in the Early Eighteenth Century', PhD thesis, University of Edinburgh, 1973. See also David Jacques, *Georgian Gardens: The Reign of Nature* (London, 1983), and Douglas D.C. Chambers, *The Planters of the English Landscape Garden* (New Haven and London, 1993).
3. Less than one-third of the estates with which Switzer is associated are referred to in this essay. Many of the remainder are discussed in Brogden, 'Stephen Switzer'. It is certain that

Switzer made designs for Caversham, Berks (1718), and 'Stourton' (Stourhead), Wiltshire (1720), for example, but there is no documentary evidence for two of the Bertie properties in Lincolnshire – Belleau and Eresby – or for Culverthorpe Hall, Lincs. He was involved at several estates in Clwyd, Wales (Erddig, Leeswood and Rhual), and may also have given guidance for estates in Ireland: Breckdenstown near Dublin, Caledon, County Tyrone, and possibly Dromoland, County Clare.
4. American owners of copies of *Ichnographia Rustica* included William Byrd II, John Mercer and Thomas Jefferson; see Peter Martin, *The Pleasure Gardens of Virginia* (Princeton, NJ, 1991), p. 205 n. 19. The Earl of Stair had a copy of *Hydrostaticks*; see A.A. Tait, *The Landscape Garden in Scotland, 1735–1835* (Edinburgh, 1980), p. 17 and n. 22. English owners of *Hydrostaticks* included William Paston, 2nd Earl of Yarmouth, William Stukeley and the novelist Laurence Sterne.
5. The 'carriage' directed water parallel to Humber brook and fed a reservoir half a mile north of the house, which in turn played the fountain and watered the land: Brogden, 'Stephen Switzer', p. 177. According to Switzer, the work cost the high sum of £1,200: *Hydrostaticks*, I, p. 10.
6. His 'Report of the Present State of the Great Level of the Fens' is in Thomas Badeslade's *The History . . . of King's-Lyn* (1725).
7. Switzer, *Hydrostaticks*, II, pp. 412–13. See Brogden, 'Stephen Switzer', for Spye Park (p. 187) and Breamore (p. 204).
8. Gervase Jackson-Stops, *An English Arcadia, 1600–1900: Designs for Gardens and Garden Buildings in the Care of the National Trust* (Washington, DC, 1991) cat. 22.
9. See Howard Colvin, *A Biographical Dictionary of British Architects, 1600–1840* (London, 1995), pp. 1038–9.
10. Switzer made use of the library at Marston, the property of his employer Charles Boyle, 4th Earl of Orrery. He also researched *Hydrostaticks* while working at Breamore; see Brogden, 'Stephen Switzer', p. 15.
11. The notes supplementing Book I of *Hydrostaticks* include an advertisement for a newly patented way of making clay pipes by William Edward of Monmouth.
12. See William Barclay Parsons, *Engineers and Engineering in the Renaissance* (London, 1967) for illustrations of the types of pump in use. The sources that would assist an investigation of the use of technology in the eighteenth-century country estate include Maurice Daumas, *A History of Technology and Industry: Progress through the Ages* (London, 1980), T.K. Derry and Trevor I. Williams, *A Short History of Technology: From the Earliest Times to A.D. 1900* (Oxford, 1960), E.G. Semler (ed.), *Engineering Heritage*, 2 vols (London, 1963–6), Charles Singer *et al.*, *A History of Technology, III: From*

the Renaissance to the Industrial Revolution (Oxford, 1957). Useful journals include *Transactions of the Newcomen Society, History of Technology* and *Technology and Culture*.

13. This was probably the 17 miles of conduit known as 'Drakes Leat' (built 1589–91) that diverted water from the River Meavy to augment the supply of well-water in the town; see F.W. Robins, *The Story of the Supply of Water* (Oxford, 1946), ch. 16.

14. Switzer, *Hydrostaticks*, I, p. 274.

15. Norman Smith, *Man and Water: A History of Hydro-Technology* (London, 1977), pp. 100–1; see Stéphane Pincas, *Versailles: The History of the Gardens and their Sculpture* (London, 1996), pp. 268–74 for illustrations of the aqueducts.

16. *Hydrostaticks*, I, p. 110, Switzer condemned the cost of the construction.

17. Switzer, *Hydrostaticks*, II, pp. 296–7.

18. MS Travel Diary, Northants Record Office, Northampton, A 280, f. 26r.

19. Temple to William Pitt, 7 September 1762; cited in Leland J. Bellot, '"Wild Hares and Red Herrings": A Case Study of Estate Management in the Eighteenth-century English Countryside', *Huntington Library Quarterly*, LVI (1993), p. 17. The house was blown up in 1775. Although badly damaged by ploughing, some of Bridgeman's extensive earthworks survive; see D. R. Wilson, 'Gardens From the Air' in A.E. Brown (ed.), *Garden Archaeology*, Council for British Archaeology, Research Report no. 78 (London, 1991), pp. 29–30.

20. Sarah Markham, *John Loveday of Caversham* (Salisbury, 1984), pp. 244–5, quoted in John Dixon Hunt and Erik de Jong, 'The Anglo-Dutch Garden in the Age of William and Mary', a special issue of the *Journal of Garden History*, VIII/2–3 (1988), p. 247.

21. *Hydrostaticks*, II, p. 313.

22. *Hydrosticks*, II, pp. 314–16. It is likely that Switzer had seen the engine himself, since he remarks that he has not had time to make any 'Computations' about the amounts of water the engine could raise.

23. Switzer also commented on a scheme, possibly not executed, to link the engine to the supply of clean water from Rosamond's Well: *Hydrostaticks*, I, p. 323.

24. Howard Colvin and Alistair Rowan, 'The Grand Bridge in Blenheim Park', in (eds) John Bold and Edward Chaney, *English Architecture, Public and Private* (London, 1993), p. 161 n. 6.

25. J.H. Appleby, 'A New Perspective on John Rowley, Virtuoso Master of Mechanics and Hydraulic Engineer', *Annals of Science*, LIII/1 (January 1996), pp. 1–29. I am grateful to Cristiano Ratti for drawing this article to my attention.

26. Switzer, *Hydrostaticks*, II, p. 334.

27. Judith Roberts, 'Cusworth Park: The Making of an Eighteenth-century Designed Landscape', forthcoming in *Landscape History*.

28. For a detailed account of the grotto see Robert J.G. Savage, 'The Natural History of the Goldney Garden Grotto', *Garden History*, XVII/1 (1989).

29. Anon., 'Stourton Gardens', in *The Royal Magazine, or Gentleman's Monthly Companion* (February 1764), p. 102, lines 76–9. Henry Hoare the Elder employed Joseph Andrews to install an engine to pump water up to the villa built by Colen Campbell *c*. 1720–4. The pools in the vale were later flooded to form the lake; see Kenneth Woodbridge, 'Henry Hoare's Paradise', *Art Bulletin* (March 1965), p. 83 n. 1.

30. See, for example, William Lawson, *A New Orchard and Garden* (London, 1618) and Gervase Markham, *The English Husbandman* (London, 1613).

31. Christopher Morris (ed.), *The Journeys of Celia Fiennes* (London, 1947), p. 98.

32. Morris, *Journeys of Celia Fiennes*, p. 172.

33. Switzer refers to the site as 'Ainstone' in *Hydrostaticks*, II, p. 347. See also Strong, *Renaissance Garden*, pp. 130–33.

34. Switzer, *Hydrostaticks*, II, p. 345 and pls. 27–30; De Caus, *Les Raisons des forces mouvantes* (1615; 2nd edn, 1624).

35. Switzer refers to *Theory and Practice* and its 'ingenious Author' in his chapter on pipes and the conveyance of water: *Hydrostaticks*, I, p. 125.

36. Leonard Knyff and Jan Kip, *Britannia Illustrata* (London, 1707). For information on the editions of this work, and related publications, see John Harris, *The Artist and the Country House* (London, 1979), ch. 3.

37. John James, *The Theory and Practice of Gardening* (London, 1712), pp. 202–3.

38. Copley also built a swimming-bath in the house that could be heated. John Etty was involved in the construction of Sprotbrough Hall *c*. 1696–1700, where he had access to Copley's copy of Jean Marot's *L'Architecture Française*; see Donald Garstang (ed.), *Prospects of Town and Park* (London, 1988), p. 30.

39. James, *Theory and Practice*, p. 202.

40. See Linda Cabe Halpern, 'The Duke of Kent's Garden at Wrest Park', *Journal of Garden History*, XV (1995), pp. 149–78.

41. Vanbrugh proposed a lake at Welbeck in 1703, but it was never made. Switzer's design for Nostell Priory also includes a large, irregular lake; see Jackson-Stops, *An English Arcadia*, p. 47.

42. The description is reprinted in full in John Dixon Hunt and Peter Willis (eds), *The Genius of the Place: The English Landscape Garden, 1620–1820* (London, 1975), pp. 158–62.

43. Shireoaks Hall was built *c*. 1600, possibly by Robert Smythson, and altered *c*. 1700 and again in the nineteenth century. Sir Thomas Hewett was appointed Surveyor of the Royal Works in 1719 and was probably his own architect at Shireoaks, where he was reported to have built a 'greek Tempietto' in the gardens; see Hewett's entry in Colvin, *Dictionary*, p. 492. An elaborate, later plan of the garden is in the Sheffield City Collection: James Young, *Survey of the Manor of Shireoaks* (1790).

44. In William Taylor's painting, *A View of Stanway House* (1748), the cascade appears to feed into the end of the canal rather than the middle, but only by changing the alignment in this way was Taylor able to illustrate both features together with the house and the surrounding countryside; see John Harris, *The Artist and the Country House from the Fifteenth Century to the Present Day*, exh. cat. (London, 1995), cat. 47.

45. John Tracy's daughter Anne records an evening at Great Tew, Oxfordshire, on 18 May 1724, where she 'had the pleasure of hearing fm ye Gent. the discription of Mr. Dormers elegant way of living, his Garden Beautiful, his Cascade suprizing fine' (Anne Tracy, Diary, 1723–5, MS at Stanway House). I am grateful to Lord Neidpath for access to documents and plans relating to Stanway's cascade, currently under restoration.

46. Samuel Rudder, *New History of Gloucestershire* (Cirencester, 1779), p. 691, describes Stanway's 'good gardens, and a cascade of water seen from the vale below at a distance of several miles'.

47. See Harris, *Artist and the Country House from the Fifteenth Century*, cat. 39 for Robert Griffier's view of the house and park *c*. 1735.

48. Batty Langley, *New Principles of Gardening* (London, 1728), p. xii.

49. Switzer, *Hydrostaticks*, II, p. 405 and pl. 37. Switzer added a cascade and an extensive cross canal to Bridgeman's 'little Circular Basin', which Switzer thought was 'eclips'd by the prodigious Grandeur' of Bridgeman's amphitheatre.

50. Switzer suggested (*Hydrostaticks*, II, p. 411 and pl. 55) that Lord Lymington might have modelled his cascade at 'Down Husband' (Hurstbourne Priors, Hampshire) on that at the Villa Aldobrandini.

51. Switzer, *Hydrostaticks*, I, pp. 12–14.

52. Switzer, *Hydrostaticks*, I, p. 12.

53. Switzer, *Hydrostaticks*, II, p. 413. The design for a similar, unfinished, cascade at Breamore had to be adapted to suit local conditions, where the supply of water was more limited. Switzer says that the cascade would have been taken from a large reservoir 'collected from Engines, Rains, &c'.

54. Brogden, 'Stephen Switzer', pp. 10 and 182, has suggested that Ebberston's cascades may be by Switzer, but there is no documentary evidence to support this attribution.

55. For illustrations see Thomas Badeslade and John Rocque, *Vitruvius Brittanicus*, IV (1739), pls. 59–62; Harris, *Artist and the Country House*, no. 171.

56. *An Exact Mapp of Exton Parke Taken AD 1709* is in the Leicestershire Record Office (LRO), DE 3214 Temp. No. 603.

57. LRO, DE 3214 193/21, undated plan. The plan shows the second lake as an oblong sheet of water. A rough outline of the cascade is shown between the two lakes.

58. Switzer's working drawing for the cascade is in the Bodleian Library, Oxford, MS Gough Drawings, a4, f. 7.

10. Rethinking the Picturesque

1. Geoffrey Webb (ed.), *The Letters* (London, 1928), p. 28, an endorsement by the Duchess of Marlborough on a letter from Vanbrugh to [?Lord Godolphin], 31 May 1709.

2. For accounts of the building of Blenheim and its grounds see David Green, *Blenheim Palace* (London, 1951); Laurence Whistler, *The Imagination of Vanbrugh and his Fellow Artists* (London, 1954), ch. 2; David Green, *Gardener to Queen Anne: Henry Wise (1653–1738) and the Formal Garden* (London, 1956), pp. 96–121; Kerry Downes, *Vanbrugh* (London, 1977), pp. 57–75; James Bond and Kate Tiller (eds), *Blenheim: Landscape for a Palace* (Gloucester, 1987); Kerry Downes, *Sir John Vanbrugh, a Biography* (London, 1987), chs. 23–24; David W. Booth, 'Blenheim Park on the Eve of "Mr Brown's Improvements"', *Journal of Garden History*, XV (1995), pp. 107–25. See also Webb, *Letters*, and Henry L. Snyder (ed.), *The Marlborough-Godolphin Correspondence*, 3 vols (Oxford, 1975), and Frances Harris, *A Passion for Government: The Life of Sarah, Duchess of Marlborough* (Oxford, 1991).

3. Quoted in Green, *Blenheim Palace*, p. 92.

4. For the history of Woodstock Manor and Park see H.M. Colvin (ed.), *The History of the King's Works*, 6 vols (London, 1963–82), esp. II, pp. 1009–17; IV, ii, pp. 349–55; V, p. 37; and Bond and Tiller, *Blenheim*, chs 3–5. See also *The Victoria County History, Oxfordshire, XII: Wootton Hundred (South) Including Woodstock* (London, 1990), pp. 430–48.

5. Charles I, none the less, contemplated demolishing the Manor in order to mine saltpetre: see Kevin Sharpe, *The Personal Rule of Charles I* (London, 1992), pp. 194–5.

6. Colvin, *King's Works*, IV, pt. ii, p. 355.

7. The text of Vanbrugh's Memorandum reprinted in my Appendix is taken from Webb, *Letters*, pp. 29–30, which Webb took from the Coxe MSS transcripts then in the British Museum, access to the originals at Blenheim having been denied him. The Blenheim archives, however, have since been transferred to the British Library; the Memorandum is BL Add. MSS 61353, ff. 62–3.

8. The literature on the history of the Picturesque is extensive, but there is a valuable resumé of the subject by John Dixon Hunt in Jane Turner (ed.), *The Dictionary of Art*, (London, 1996), XXIV, pp. 740–3. This recounts the evolution of the term from its early meaning of 'as in a picture' to its later use as a term for appreciating rugged and irregular landscape. See, too, Hunt's 'Ut Pictura Poesis, Ut Pictura Hortus and the Picturesque' (1985), reprinted in his *Gardens and the Picturesque* (Cambridge, Mass., 1992), pp. 105–36. See also Christopher Hussey, *The Picturesque* (London, 1927; rpt. 1967); Nikolaus Pevsner, 'The Genesis of the Picturesque' (1944), rpt in his *Studies in Art, Architecture and Design*

(London, 1968), I, pp. 79–101; Martin Price, 'The Picturesque Moment', in F.W. Hilles and H. Bloom (eds), *From Sensibility to Romanticism* (Oxford, 1965), pp. 259–92; David Watkin, *The English Vision* (London, 1982); Malcolm Andrews, *The Search for the Picturesque* (Aldershot, 1989); and Andrew Ballantyne, 'Genealogy of the Picturesque', *British Journal of Aesthetics*, XXXII (1992), pp. 320–9. For an anthology of texts relating to the Picturesque see Malcolm Andrews (ed.), *The Picturesque: Literary Sources and Documents*, 3 vols (Mountfield, 1994), where Vanbrugh's Memorandum occupies a privileged position. For Gilpin see Carl Paul Barbier, *William Gilpin: His Drawings, Teaching, and the Theory of the Picturesque* (Oxford, 1963).

9.   Webb, *Letters*, p. 28, the same letter on which the Duchess had written her repudiation of Vanbrugh's arguments (see note 1 above).

10. For Vanbrugh and language in his dramas see Alan Roper, 'Language and Action in *The Way of The World*, *Love's Last Shift*, and *The Relapse*', *English Literary History*, XL (1973), pp. 44–69; Derek Hughes, 'Vanbrugh and Cibber: Language, Place, and Social Order in *The Relapse*', *Comparative Drama*, XXI (1987), pp. 62–83; James E. Gill, 'Character, Plot, and the Language of Love in *The Relapse*: A Re-appraisal', *Restoration*, XVI (1992), pp. 110–25.

11. Webb, *Letters*, pp. 28–9.

12. For Plot as antiquary and county historian see Michael Pafford, 'Robert Plot: A County Historian', *History Today*, XX (1970), pp. 112–17; Stan A.E. Mendyk, '*Speculum Britanniae*': *Regional Study, Antiquarianism, and Science in Britain to 1700* (Toronto, 1989), ch. 11; Graham Parry, *The Trophies of Time: English Antiquarians of the Seventeenth Century* (Oxford, 1995), pp. 300–7.

13. Plot, *The Natural History of Oxfordshire* (1705 edn), pp. 7–11. The specific mention of Chaucer's House supplies an additional layer of historical association to Woodstock.

14. Ovid, *Metamorphoses*, III, ll. 358 ff.

15. Webb, *Letters*, p. 30.

16. Green, *Blenheim Palace*, p. 170.

17. *Rosamond* first appeared in Addison's collected works of 1721 edited by his friend Thomas Tickell, where it carried a dedication to 'Her Grace the Duchess of Marlborough'. Tickell's own prefatory poem *To the Author of Rosamond*, first printed in 1707, praised 'the visionary scenes' in the drama, and contains the lines 'No farther could imagination roam/'Till Vanbrugh fram'd, and Marlbro' rais'd the dome': *Works*, 2nd edn (London, 1730), I, pp. 81–135.

18. An advertisement for the performance of George Granville's *The British Enchanters* for 22 March 1707 had also promised a scene featuring 'the intire front prospect of Blenheim Castle'; see David Cast, 'Seeing Vanbrugh and Hawksmoor', *Journal of the Society of Architectural Historians*, XLIII (1984), pp. 310–27, p. 315 n. 13; Downes, *Sir John Vanbrugh*, pp. 258, 279;

Frank McCormick, *Sir John Vanbrugh: The Playwright as Architect* (University Park, Penn., 1991), pp. 175–6. For accounts of the staging and reception of *Rosamond* see Allardyce Nicoll, *A History of English Drama, 1660–1900* (Cambridge, 1961), II, p. 228, where it is described as a 'dismal failure'.

19. McCormick, *Playwright as Architect*, p. 175; for the visit to Hanover see Downes, *Sir John Vanbrugh*, pp. 316–22.

20. Donald F. Bond (ed.), *The Spectator* (Oxford, 1965), I, pp. 453–6: no. 110 (6 July 1711). Addison alludes specifically to Locke's *An Essay on Human Understanding*, Book II, ch. XXXIII, 'Of the Association of Ideas'. For theories of the Association of Ideas in the eighteenth century see John W. Yolton, *A Locke Dictionary* (Oxford, 1993), pp. 18–23; Martin Kallich, *The Association of Ideas and Critical Theory in Eighteenth-Century England* (The Hague, 1970), especially chs 1–2. For Addison see *The Spectator*, nos. 411–21, 'The Pleasures of the Imagination', in Bond, *The Spectator*, V, pp. 535–82. See also Lee Andrew Elioseff, *The Cultural Vision of Addison's Literary Criticism* (Austin, Tx, 1963), chs 7–8; Ernest Lee Tuveson, *The Imagination as a Means of Grace: Locke and the Aesthetics of Romanticism* (Berkeley, Cal., 1960), ch. 5; William H. Youngren, 'Addison and the Birth of Eighteenth-Century Aesthetics', *Modern Philology*, LXXIX (1982), pp. 267–83.

21. Plot remarks that when projecting one's voice from Woodstock Manor 'you shall not have the least return': *Oxfordshire*, p. 10.

22. Downes, *Vanbrugh*, p. 75. Nearly twenty years before Vanbrugh's efforts to preserve Woodstock Manor, William of Orange had insisted on the preservation of the medieval castle of Oude Loo in the grounds of his new palace, Het Loo; see W. Kuyper, *Dutch Classicist Architecture* (Delft, 1980), pp. 144–7, 203. Another example of an early eighteenth-century architect interested in the relationship between buildings and their landscapes is Robert Morris, who stressed the joint importance of 'situation' and architectural character, a notion that had earlier been propounded by Roger de Piles. See David Leatherbarrow, 'Architecture and Situation: A Study of the Architectural Writings of Robert Morris', *Journal of the Society of Architectural Historians*, XLIV (1985), pp. 48–59, and John Archer, *The Literature of British Domestic Architecture, 1715–1842* (Boston, Mass., 1985), pp. 104–6.

23. Webb, *Letters*, p. 28.

24. Webb, *Letters*, pp. 215, 72, 81.

25. Webb, *Letters*, p. 72; Green, *Blenheim Palace*, ch. 9.

26. Webb, *Letters*, p. 23.

27. Webb, *Letters*, p. 66.

28. Recorded in Charles Mackay, *Extraordinary Popular Delusions* (London, 1841), pp. 598–601. Plot, while claiming that he had 'no esteem for such kind of stories', also recounted this episode – 'the History . . . of the Just Devil of Woodstock' – as reported to him by a third

party; Plot, however, declined to attribute these happenings to either human or non-human causes: *Oxfordshire*, pp. 210–14. See also *The Life and Times of Anthony Wood*, ed. Andrew Clark (Oxford, 1891), I, p. 158.

29. The fascination with ruins dates largely from the sixteenth century and the Dissolution of the Monasteries; see Margaret Aston, 'English Ruins and English History: The Dissolution and the Sense of the Past', *Journal of the Warburg and Courtauld Institutes*, XXXVI (1973), pp. 231–55. For ruins and the antiquarian background see Parry, *The Trophies of Time*; Mendyk, '*Speculum Britanniae*'; Michael Hunter, *John Aubrey and the World of Learning* (London, 1975); B. Sprague Allen, *Tides in English Taste* (Cambridge, Mass., 1937), II, ch. 14; Stuart Piggott, *Ruins in a Landscape: Essays in Antiquarianism* (Edinburgh, 1976), especially ch. 6; John Dixon Hunt, 'Picturesque Mirrors and the Ruins of the Past' (1981), rpt in his *Gardens and the Picturesque*, pp. 171–91; Watkin, *The English Vision*, ch. 3.

30. *Reliquiae Hearnianae: The Remains of Thomas Hearne*, ed. Philip Bliss (Oxford, 1857), pp. 97–8, 374–5, 395–407, 423–4.

31. *The Family Memoirs of the Rev. William Stukeley*, 3 vols, The Surtees Society, LIII, LVI, LXXX (1882–7), I, pp. 18, 32.

32. Quoted in Sprague Allen, *Tides in Taste*, II, p. 51.

33. The 'Explanation' is partially printed in Downes, *Hawksmoor*, 2nd edn (London, 1979), pp. 240–2; but the entire *Explanation of Designs for All Souls by Nicholas Hawksmoor, 17 February 1715* was printed for All Souls College as a small pamphlet by Oxford University Press in 1960.

34. Magdalen College, Oxford, MS 906 (i), quoted in Giles Worsley, 'Designs to Rouse the Dreaming Spires', *Country Life*, CXCI (27 November 1997), p. 65. For Hawksmoor and Oxford see Howard Colvin, *Unbuilt Oxford* (New Haven and London, 1983), chs. 4–5, and Roger White, *Nicholas Hawksmoor and the Replanning of Oxford*, exh. cat. (London and Oxford, 1997).

35. Downes, *Hawksmoor*, p. 242. In 1718 Vanbrugh argued for the preservation of another structure threatened with demolition, the Holbein Gateway in Whitehall, which he described as 'One of the Greatest Curiositys there is in London'; see Downes, *Vanbrugh*, p. 102, and Downes, *Sir John Vanbrugh*, p. 406.

36. For the bridge see Howard Colvin and Alistair Rowan, 'The Grand Bridge in Blenheim Park', in John Bold and Edward Chaney (eds), *English Architecture, Public and Private* (London, 1993), pp. 159–76.

37. For Holdenby see Mark Girouard, 'Elizabethan Holdenby', *Country Life*, CLXVI (18 October and 25 October 1979), pp. 1286–9, 1398–1401; *Holdenby House and Gardens*, guidebook (n.d.).

38. *The Diary of John Evelyn*, ed. William Bray (London, 1950), II, p. 104.

39. For Tillemans's sketches of Holdenby see Bruce Bailey (ed.), *Northamptonshire in the Early Eighteenth Century: The Drawings of Peter Tillemans and Others*, Northamptonshire Record Society, XXXIX (1994), pp. 97–9.

40. Daniel Defoe, *A Tour Through England and Wales*, ed. G.D.H. Cole (London, 1928), II, p. 87.

41. Parry, *The Trophies of Time*; Mendyk, '*Speculum Britanniae*'; see also David C. Douglas, *English Scholars* (London, 1939) and T.D. Kendrick, *British Antiquity* (London, 1950). See also the chronological list of publications in G.E. Fussell and V.G.B. Atwater, 'Travel and Topography in Seventeenth Century England', *Transactions of the Bibliographical Society*, XIII (1932–3), pp. 292–311; G.E. Fussell and Constance Goodman, 'Travel and Topography in Eighteenth Century England', *Transactions of the Bibliographical Society*, X (1929–30), pp. 84–103.

42. Letter to Alexander Pope, 1 May 1714, in *The Works of George Berkeley, Bishop of Cloyne*, ed. A.A. Luce and T.E. Jessop (Edinburgh, 1948–57), VIII, *Letters*, p. 83.

43. Defoe, *Tour Through England and Wales*, II, pp. 232–3.

44. See Michel Baridon, 'Ruins as a Mental Construct', *Journal of Garden History*, V (1985), pp. 84–96, esp. pp. 90–92.

45. Andrews, *Search for the Picturesque*, pp. 67–82.

46. For Stukeley see Stuart Piggott, *William Stukeley, An Eighteenth-Century Antiquary* (New York, 1985); for Tillemans see note 39 above; for Place, a tireless traveller and sketcher, see Richard Tyler, *Francis Place, 1647–1728*, exh. cat. (York, 1971). See also Henry V.S. Ogden and Margaret S. Ogden, *English Taste in Landscape in the Seventeenth Century* (Ann Arbor, 1955), chs 12–14.

47. Katherine S. Van Erde, *John Ogilby and the Taste of His Times* (Folkestone, 1976), p. 137. See also Sir Herbert George Fordham, 'John Ogilby: His *Britannia*, and the British Itineraries of the Eighteenth Century', *Transactions of the Bibliographical Society*, VI (1925–26), pp. 157–78, and Fordham, *Some Notable Surveyors and Map-Makers* (London, 1929).

48. In his recent study of Defoe, Pat Rogers suggests that in the opening years of the century 'there can hardly have been ten people alive who were closely familiar with both Cornwall and Northumberland': *The Text of Great Britain: Theme and Design in Defoe's Tour* (London, 1998), p. 56. For accounts of travel in early modern England see Joan Parkes, *Travel in England in the Seventeenth Century* (Oxford, 1925); Thomas Burke, *Travel in England* (London, 1942); Esther Moir, *The Discovery of Britain, The English Tourists, 1540–1840* (London, 1964). Apart from Defoe, other published tours of the period include Christopher Morris (ed.), *The Journeys of Celia Fiennes* (London, 1947); Sarah Markham (ed.), *John Loveday of Caversham, 1711–1789: The Life and Tours of an Eighteenth-century Observer* (Salisbury, 1984); Mark R. Wenger (ed.), *The English Travels of Sir John Percival and William Byrd II* (Columbia, Mo., 1989); James Brome,

Travels over England, Scotland and Wales
(London, 1700); John Macky, *A Journey through
England*, 2 vols (London, 1722–3). There is a
valuable list of manuscript tours and travel
diaries in county record offices in Robin Gard
(ed.), *The Observant Traveller* (London, 1989).

49. Webb, *Letters*, p. 4.

50. For Vanbrugh's driving see Downes, *Sir John
Vanbrugh*, p. 244.

51. There is an invaluable chronology of Vanbrugh's
life with mention of some of his journeys in
Downes, *Sir John Vanbrugh*, pp. xxiii–xxvii, as
well as further details of Vanbrugh's travels in
chs 28 and 30. For Vanbrugh's accounts see
Downes, *Vanbrugh*, pp. 174–241. The most up-
to-date catalogue of Vanbrugh's letters and
other documents is in Peter Beal, *Index of
Literary Manuscripts, vol. II: 1625–1700, part 2:
Lee–Wycherley* (London, 1992), under
'Vanbrugh', pp. 511–37.

52. Typical is an account of 1727: 'Came from
Malton to York. By the way had a sight of a
famous house belonging to the Earl of Carlile,
called Hinderskelf, as allso the ruins of Sheriff-
Hutton Castle'; see 'The Journal of Mr John
Hobson', *Yorkshire Diaries*, The Surtees Society,
LXV (1875), p. 269. The ruins of Sheriff
Hutton Castle, 5 miles from Castle Howard, are
visible from the Howardian Hills.

53. Downes, *Vanbrugh*, p. 124; Downes, *Sir John
Vanbrugh*, p. 486; see also R.B. Dobson and
J. Taylor (eds), *Rhymes of Robyn Hood: An
Introduction to the English Outlaw* (London,
1976; rpt Stroud, 1997), esp. pp. 23–4. Evelyn
partook of the customary drinking ritual when
passing in August 1654: *Diary*, I, p. 302. The
Revd James Brome gives a more fulsome
account: 'Being placed in the Chair we had a
cap, which they say was his, very formally put
upon our Heads, and having perform'd the
usual Ceremonies befitting so great a Solemnity,
we receiv'd the freedom of the Chair, and were
incorporated into the Society of that Renowned
Brotherhood'; quoted in Parkes, *Travel in
England*, p. 311. For Stukeley's brief comments
on the Well see *Family Memoirs*, LXXX (1887),
III, p. 373. There is also a sketch by Grimm in
the British Museum, Add. MSS 15548, f. 47.

54. No. 411 (21 June 1712), in Bond, *The Spectator*,
III, p. 537. David Cast while discussing the
importance of architectural 'effect', also notes
that the 'idea of the particular territory of the
eye was something emerging, or beginning to
emerge, in English critical discourse at the time
Vanbrugh and Hawksmoor were at work': Cast,
'Seeing Vanbrugh and Hawksmoor', p. 314.

55. Bond, *The Spectator*, III, p. 537.

56. No. 412 (23 June 1712), in Bond, *The Spectator*,
III, p. 542.

57. David Cast, describing Vanbrugh and
Hawksmoor's responses to the past and the
importance of Association, cites Hobbes's
metaphor from *Leviathan* in 'Seeing Vanbrugh
and Hawksmoor', pp. 316–17; see also Kallich, *The

Association of Ideas, and Donald F. Bond, 'The
Neo-Classical Psychology of the Imagination',
English Literary History, IV (1937), pp. 245–64.

58. This topic is covered in detail by Hunt in 'Ut
Pictura Poesis', esp. pp. 107–9.

59. Quoted in Hunt, 'Ut Pictura Poesis', p. 108.

60. William Hazlitt, 'Lectures on The Comic
Writers', in *The Complete Works of William
Hazlitt*, ed. P.P. Howe (London, 1930–4), VI,
pp. 79–84. See also Hazlitt's defence of
Vanbrugh in 'Mr Northcote's Conversations',
Works, XI, p. 268.

11. Remembering Vanbrugh

My thanks to Dr Terry Friedman and Dr Jeremy
Taylor, who read the first drafts of this essay and
made valuable comments. I am also grateful to Dr
Rosemary Llewellyn-Jones for her information
concerning buildings in Lucknow.

1.   Abel Evans, *Epitaph on Sir John Vanbrugh,
Architect of Blenheim Palace* (1726).

2.   'The History of Vanbrug's House', *c.* 1706, in
Pat Rogers (ed.), *Jonathan Swift: The Complete
Poems* (Harmondsworth, 1983), p. 91.

3.   Gervase Jackson-Stops, 'Grimsthorpe Castle',
Country Life, CLXXXI (26 November 1987),
p. 72.

4.   Joseph Gwilt, *Encyclopaedia of Architecture*, revd
Wyatt Papworth (London, 1881), I, pp. 215–17.

5.   Desmond Flower (ed.), *Voltaire's England*
(London, 1950), p. 160.

6.   Howard Colvin, *A Biographical Dictionary of
British Architects, 1600–1840* (London, 1995),
p. 492.

7.   James Bramston, *The Man of Taste* (London,
1733), p. 10.

8.   John Dodd, 'A Tour through England in the
Year 1735', British Library, Add. MSS 5957.

9.   Horace Walpole, *The Letters*, ed. Peter
Cunningham (Edinburgh, 1906), I, p. 6: letter to
George Montagu, 20 May 1736.

10. John Gwynn, *The Art of Architecture* (London,
1742, reprinted 1970), pp. 14–15, 26.

11. MS letter from James Rivers to Richard Phelps,
25 June 1765, quoted in Ken Spelman, *Catalogue
41* [sale cat.] (York, 1999), item 349, p. 93.

12. Arthur Young, *A Six Months Tour through the
North of England* (London, 1769), II, p. 61;
Young, *A Six Weeks Tour through the Southern
Counties* (London, 1768), p. 127; quoted in
David Cast, 'Seeing Vanbrugh and Hawksmoor'
Journal of the Society of Architectural Historians,
XLVIII (1984), p. 311.

13. Quoted in Kerry Downes, *Hawksmoor*, 2nd edn
(London, 1979), p. 244: letter dated 7 January
1724.

14. Giles Worsley, *Classical Architecture in Britain,
The Heroic Age* (New Haven and London), p. 93,
ills. 114–15.

15. Laurence Whistler, *The Imagination of Vanbrugh
and his Fellow Artists* (London, 1954), p. 227.

16. Walpole, *The Letters*, V, p. 403: letter to George Selwyn, 12 August 1772.

17. Horace Walpole, *Anecdotes of Painting in England . . . Collected by the late George Vertue* (London, 1862), II, pp. 638–41.

18. William Gilpin, *Observations, relative chiefly to Picturesque Beauty, made in the Year 1772, on Several Parts of England, Particularly the Mountains, and Lakes of Cumberland, and Westmoreland*, 3rd edn (London, 1792), pp. 26–9.

19. Robert and James Adam, *Works in Architecture*, I (London, 1773), p. v.

20. Sir Joshua Reynolds, *Discourses on Art*, ed. Robert R. Wark (New Haven and London, 1997), pp. 241–2.

21. Alistair Rowan, *Designs for Castles and Country Villas by R. and J. Adam* (Oxford, 1985), p. 17.

22. Rowan, *Designs for Castles*, p. 18; see David King, *The Complete Works of Robert and James Adam* (Oxford, 1991), for Culzean, pp. 165–8, ills. 232–7; for Seton, pp. 169–70, ills. 243–5.

23. Rowan, *Designs for Castles*, p. 19.

24. Geoffrey Webb (ed.), *The Letters* (London, 1928), p. 14: letter to the Earl of Manchester, 18 July 1707. For Kimbolton see James Lees-Milne, *English Country Houses: Baroque, 1685–1715* (London, 1970), pp. 102–11.

25. Gervase Jackson-Stops, *An English Arcadia, 1600–1990: Designs for Gardens and Garden Buildings in the Care of the National Trust* (Washington, DC, 1991), cat. 75.

26. Reynolds, *Discourses*, pp. 242–4.

27. Richard Payne Knight, *An Analytical Inquiry into the Principles of Taste* (London, 1805), p. 220.

28. Knight, *Inquiry*, p. 221.

29. Uvedale Price, *Essays on the Picturesque*, 3rd edn (London, 1810), II, p. 116.

30. Price, *Essays*, p. 215.

31. Price, *Essays*, p. 212.

32. Price, *Essays*, p. 217.

33. Thomas Tilestone Waterman, *The Mansions of Virginia, 1706–1776* (New York, 1945), p. 95; Mills Lane, *Architecture of the Old South: Virginia* (New York, 1989), pp. 38–41.

34. David Watkin, *Sir John Soane: Enlightenment Thought and the Royal Academy Lectures* (Cambridge, 1996), p. 618.

35. Karl Friedrich Schinkel, 'The English Journey': Journal of a Visit to France and Britain in 1826, ed. David Bindman and Gottfried Riemann (New Haven and London, 1993), p. 195.

36. Watkin, *Soane*, p. 563.

37. Watkin, *Soane*, p. 645.

38. Cited in Justin Wintle and Richard Kenin (eds), *The Dictionary of Biographical Quotations* (London and Henley, 1978), p. 753.

39. Pierre de la Ruffinière du Prey, *John Soane: The Making of an Architect* (Chicago and London, 1982), pp. 209–12.

40. See Eva Schumann-Bacia, *John Soane and the Bank of England* (London, 1991).

41. Arthur T. Bolton, 'Sir John Vanbrugh, 1664–1726', *Journal of the Royal Institute of British Architects*, 3rd series, XXXIII (1926), p. 339.

42. Derek Linstrum, *Sir Jeffry Wyatville: Architect to the King* (Oxford, 1972), pp. 122–6.

43. Derek Linstrum, 'The Waterloo Palace', *Architectural Review*, CLV/926 (1974), pp. 217–23; Linstrum, *Catalogue of the Drawings Collection of the Royal Institute of British Architects: The Wyatt Family* (Farnborough, 1974), p. 14.

44. The Marquess Curzon of Kedleston, *British Government in India* (London, 1925), I, pp. 39–74; Mark Bence-Jones, *Palaces of the Raj: Magnificence and Misery of the Lord Sahibs* (London, 1973), pp. 41–67.

45. See J.P. Losty, *Calcutta: City of Palaces* (London, 1990).

46. See Rosemary Llewellyn-Jones, *A Fatal Friendship: The Nawabs, the British, and the City of Lucknow*, 2nd edn (Oxford, 1993).

47. Jan Morris with Simon Winchester, *Stones of Empire: The Buildings of the Raj* (Oxford, 1983), p. 73.

48. Llewellyn-Jones, *A Fatal Friendship*, p. 152.

49. Neeta Das, *Indian Architecture: Problems in the Interpretation of Eighteenth- and Nineteenth-century Architecture. A Study of Dilkusha Palace, Lucknow* (Delhi, 1998), p. 38. Ouseley was a diplomat and orientalist who was engaged in commerce in India; he spoke fluent Indo-Persian, and was the Nawab's favourite riding companion.

50. Fanny Parkes, *Wanderings of a Pilgrim, in Search of the Picturesque, During Four-and-Twenty Years in the East* (London, 1850), I, p. 181; her entry is dated 23 January 1831.

51. Das, *Indian Architecture*, ill. 20. A double-scrolled pediment that has been reinstated in a recent restoration seems to have been a part of the Indianization of the group of buildings at some date between 1815 and 1857.

52. A description of Lucknow as seen from the top of the Dilkusha, cited in Das, *Indian Architecture*, p. 38.

53. James Malton, *A Collection of Designs for Rural Retreats* (London, 1803), pp. 7, 31; quoted in Cast, 'Seeing Vanbrugh and Hawksmoor', pp. 326–7.

54. Linstrum, *Sir Jeffry Wyatville*, pp. 141–62.

55. David Watkin, *The Life and Work of C.R. Cockerell* (London, 1974), p. 191.

56. Watkin, *Cockerell*, p. 57.

57. Bolton, 'Vanbrugh', p. 339.

58. Watkin, *Cockerell*, p. 115.

59. Reginald Blomfield, *A History of Renaissance Architecture in England, 1500–1800* (London, 1897), II, p. 200.

60. Blomfield, *Renaissance Architecture in England*, II, p. 197.

61. Frank McCormick, *Sir John Vanbrugh: The Playwright as Architect* (University Park, Penn., 1991), p. 94.

62. James Elmes, *Metropolitan Improvements, or, London in the Nineteenth Century* (London, 1827), p. 100.

63. Watkin, *Cockerell*, p. 138; Bruce Allsopp and Ursula Clark, *Historic Architecture of Northumberland* (Newcastle upon Tyne, 1969), p. 80.

64. Watkin, *Cockerell*, pp. 217–19.

65. Watkin, *Cockerell*, pp. 207–13.

66. Jeremy Taylor, 'Charles Fowler: Master of Markets', *Architectural Review*, CXXXV/805 (1964), pp. 174–82; Taylor, 'Charles Fowler, 1792–1867: A Centenary Memoir', *Architectural History*, XI (1968), pp. 57–73.

67. Taylor, 'Centenary Memoir', ill. 16b.

68. Taylor, 'Master of Markets', p. 174.

69. Taylor, 'Centenary Memoir', ill. 14a.

70. Taylor, 'Centenary Memoir', pp. 178–9.

71. Taylor, 'Centenary Memoir', ill. 14b.

72. Henry-Russell Hitchcock, *Early Victorian Architecture in Britain* (New Haven and London, 1954), I, p. 331; II, pl. X33. Andrew Saint, *Richard Norman Shaw* (New Haven and London, 1976), p. 8.

73. Derek Linstrum, *Towers and Colonnades: The Architecture of Cuthbert Brodrick* (Leeds, 1999), pp. 95–9, ills. 100–1.

74. Linstrum, *Towers and Colonnades*, pp. 16–42.

75. Henry-Russell Hitchcock, *Architecture: Nineteenth and Twentieth Centuries* (Harmondsworth, 1958), p. 158.

76. Linstrum, *Towers and Colonnades*, pp. 116–18.

77. Jeremy Taylor, *The Architectural Medal: England in the Nineteenth Century* (London, 1978), pp. 67–8, 212–13, pl. 5.

78. *Handbook to the Prince Consort National Memorial* (London, 1872), p. 62.

79. James Fergusson, *History of the Modern Styles of Architecture* (London, 1862), p. 283.

80. Brydon's lecture was published in *The Builder*, LVI (1889), pp. 147, 168.

81. See Alastair Service, *Edwardian Architecture: A Handbook to Building Design in Britain, 1890–1914* (London, 1977), pp. 60–73.

82. Service, *Edwardian Architecture*, p. 62.

83. See Service, *Edwardian Architecture*, ill. 178.

84. Derek Linstrum, 'Belcher's Palazzo: The Chartered Accountants' Hall', *The Alliance of Sculpture and Architecture*, ed. Terry Friedman (Leeds, 1993), pp. 1–12.

85. *The Times* (24 July 1893), p. 14.

86. Blomfield, *Renaissance Architecture in England*, II, p. 200.

87. Reginald Blomfield and F. Inigo Thomas, *The Formal Garden in England*, 3rd edn (London, 1901, reprinted 1985), p. 170.

88. Cited in Wintle and Kenin, *The Dictionary of Biographical Quotations*, p. 753.

89. A.S.G. Butler, *The Architecture of Sir Edwin Lutyens* (London, 1950), I, pp. 32–5.

90. Butler, *Lutyens*, II, pp. 28–44; see also Robert Grant Irving, *Indian Summer: Lutyens, Baker, and Imperial Delhi* (New Haven and London, 1981).

91. Watkin, *Soane*, p. 563.

92. David Green, 'The Vogue of Vanbrugh', *Country Life*, CVII (2 June 1950), pp. 1648–53.

93. Kerry Downes, 'John Vanbrugh', *The Macmillan Encyclopaedia of Architects*, ed. A.K. Placzek (New York and London, 1982), IV, p. 257.

94. 'Architectural Monographs', *John Soane* (London, and New York, 1983), folding plates V and VI; Watkin, *Cockerell*, ill. 16.

95. Reynolds, *Discourses*, p. 243.

96. Peter Willis, 'Jacques Rigaud's Drawings of Stowe in the Metropolitan Museum of Art', *Eighteenth Century Studies*, VI/1 (1972), pp. 85–98.

97. George B. Clarke (ed.), *Stowe Gardens, Buckinghamshire* [1739] (reprinted London, 1988), Introduction and note to pl. 8.

98. Gilbert West, *Stowe, The Gardens of the Right Honourable Richard, Viscount Cobham* (1732), reprinted in John Dixon Hunt and Peter Willis (eds), *The Genius of the Place: The English Landscape Garden, 1620–1820*, 2nd edn (Cambridge, Mass., and London, 1988), p. 220.

99. One of the four is reproduced in John Steegman and Dorothy Stroud, *The Artist and the Country House* (London, 1949), ill. 26, and in John Harris, *The Artist and the Country House* (London, 1979), no. 317.

100. Steegman and Stroud, *The Artist and the Country House*, p. 21.

101. Reproduced in Harris, *Artist and the Country House*, no. 381.

102. Reproduced in Eric Shanes, *Turner's England, 1810–38* (London, 1990), ill. 189.

103. Piper's *Blenheim* is in the collection of the Institute of South African Architects; his *Castle Howard* is reproduced in John Piper, *Paintings, Drawings and Theatre Designs, 1932–1954* (London, 1955), ill. 73.

104. John Piper, 'Seaton Delaval', *Buildings and Prospects* (London, 1948), pp. 87–8.

105. John Martin Robinson, *The Latest Country Houses* (London, 1984), pp. 192–6; Kelly's *Henbury Hall* is illustrated in Robinson on p. 193.

106. Peter de Figueiredo and Julian Treuherz, *Cheshire Country Houses* (Chichester, 1988), pp. 111–14, ill. 74.

107. The Hon. John Byng, *The Torrington Diaries*, ed. C.B. Andrews (London, 1934), I, p. 323.

108. Laurence Whistler, 'Vanbrugh's Smaller Houses', *Architectural Review*, CXV (1954), p. 122. The design (V&A, D111–1891) is reproduced in Whistler, *The Imagination of Vanbrugh*, ill. 96. For this proposal see *The Northern Echo* (*Darlington*) (3 December 1998), p. 3; (26 December 1998), p. 3; *The Yorkshire Post* (14 December 1998), p. 3 (main section); *The Daily Telegraph* (14 December 1998), p. 5.

109. Quoted in Christopher Ridgway, 'William Andrews Nesfield: Between Uvedale Price and Isambard Kingdom Brunel', *Journal of Garden History*, XIII/1–2 (1993), p. 85.

Bibliography

This is a select bibliography; for a more comprehensive guide to books and articles see the notes to the individual essays.

Beal, Peter, *Index of English Literary Manuscripts, vol. II: 1625–1700, part 2: Lee–Wycherley* (London, 1993), 'Sir John Vanbrugh', pp. 511–37

Beard, Geoffrey, *The Work of John Vanbrugh* (London, 1986)

Cast, David, 'Seeing Vanbrugh and Hawksmoor', *Journal of the Society of Architectural Historians*, XLIII/4 (December 1984), pp. 310–27

Chambers, Douglas D.C., *The Planters of the English Landscape Garden* (New Haven and London, 1993)

Colvin, Howard, *A Biographical Dictionary of British Architects 1600–1840*, 3rd edn (New Haven and London, 1995)

—— & Maurice Craig, *Architectural Drawings in the Library at Elton Hall by Sir John Vanbrugh* (Roxburghe Club, 1964)

——, (ed.), *The History of the King's Works*, V: *1660–1782* (London, 1976)

Cordner, Michael (ed.), *Sir John Vanbrugh: Four Comedies* (Harmondsworth, 1989)

Davis, John, *Antique Garden Ornament* (Woodbridge, 1991)

Dobrée, Bonamy & Geoffrey Webb (eds), *The Complete Works of Sir John Vanbrugh*, 4 vols (London, 1927–8); volume IV is *The Letters*, ed. G. Webb (1928)

Downes, Kerry, *English Baroque Architecture* (London, 1966)

——, 'The Kings Weston Book of Drawings', *Architectural History*, X (1967), pp. 9–88

——, *Hawksmoor* (London, 1959; revd 1979)

——, *Hawksmoor*, World of Art series (London, 1970)

——, *Vanbrugh* (London, 1977)

——, *Sir John Vanbrugh, a Biography* (London, 1987)

Green, David, *Blenheim Palace* (London, 1951)

——, *Gardener to Queen Anne: Henry Wise (1653–1738) and the Formal Garden* (London, 1956)

Harris, John, *The Artist and the Country House: A History of Country House and Garden View Painting in Britain, 1540–1870* (London, 1979; revd 1985)

——, *The Artist and the Country House from the Fifteenth Century to the Present Day*, exh. cat. (London, 1995)

Henrey, Blanche, *British Botanical and Horticultural Literature before 1800*, 3 vols (London, 1975)

Hunt, John Dixon, *Garden and Grove: The Italian Renaissance Garden in the English Imagination, 1600–1750* (London, 1986)

—— & Erik de Jong, 'The Anglo-Dutch Garden in the Age of William and Mary', *Journal of Garden History*, special double issue, VIII (1988)

Hussey, Christopher, *English Gardens & Landscapes, 1700–1750* (London, 1967)

Jacques, David & Arend Jan van der Horst, *The Gardens of William and Mary* (London, 1988)

Lees-Milne, James, *English Country Houses: Baroque, 1685–1715* (London, 1970)

McCormick, Frank, *Sir John Vanbrugh: The Playwright as Architect* (University Park, Penn., 1991)

Saumarez Smith, Charles, *The Building of Castle Howard* (London, 1990)

Tipping, H. Avray & Christopher Hussey, *English Homes, Period IV, Volume II: Sir John Vanbrugh & his School, 1699–1736* (London, 1928)

Watkin, David, *The English Vision: The Picturesque in Architecture, Landscape and Garden Design* (London, 1982)

Whistler, Laurence, *Sir John Vanbrugh: Architect and Dramatist, 1664–1726* (London, 1938)

——, *The Imagination of Vanbrugh and his Fellow Artists* (London, 1954)

Willis, Peter, *Charles Bridgeman and the English Landscape Garden* (London, 1977)

Worsley, Giles, *Classical Architecture in Britain, The Heroic Age* (London, 1995)

Index

xx